לבי ער

A Call to
MAJESTY

The Mysteries of Shofar
and Rosh Hashanah

RAV DOVBER PINSON

Published by IYYUN Publishing
232 Bergen Street
Brooklyn, NY 11217

www.iyyun.com

Iyyun Publishing books may be purchased for educational, business or saless promotional usse. For information please email: contact@iyyun.com

Editor: Reb Matisyahu Brown
Editor: Reb Eden Pearlstein
Proofreading / Editing: Reb Simcha   Finkelstein
Cover and book design: RP Design and Development

pb ISBN 978-1-7367026-2-8

Pinson, Dovber 1971-
A Call to Majesty: The Mysteries of Shofar and Rosh Hashanah
1. Judaism 2. Jewish Spirituality 3. General Spirituality

RAV DOVBER PINSON

A Call to MAJESTY

The Mysteries of Shofar
and Rosh Hashanah

IYYUN PUBLISHING

Contents

PART ONE:

The Mysteries of Rosh Hashanah

Contents

PART TWO:

The Mysteries of the Shofar

Appendix

PART ONE:

The Mysteries
of Rosh Hashanah

Opening:
CONNECTING MOMENTS

THE HIGH HOLIDAY SEASON IS WELL KNOWN AS A POWERFUL AND POTENTIALLY TRANSFORMATIVE PERIOD OF THE YEAR. Yet, often, although this time may have been transformative, it is quite difficult to pinpoint the exact moment that something actually occurred. Nevertheless, we can all acknowledge that at some point during the High Holidays there were maybe five minutes, or even just thirty seconds, when we felt connected with something very deep and real. This connection may have been one that we felt during an encounter with our own deeper self or transcendent being, with the community or another individual, with the text of the *Machzor* / prayer book or the sound of the *Shofar*, with a spiritual teaching or connecting inwardly with our ancestors and history — whatever it may have been, it positively changed our consciousness.

In these moments and periods of deep connection, we get a deeper glimpse into who we are and what our purpose on this earth is. You might receive a flash of 'who' you really are beneath all your conditioning and identification, or a glimpse of 'what' you can aspire to be. Perhaps you sensed a new horizon opening up when you asked yourself an essential and unavoidable question in the presence of the Divine.

These are 'connecting' moments, moments that help us truly focus our lives and, sometimes, even to shift the trajectory of our life completely.

Yet, even when we have such potentially transformative moments, the truth is also that "people want change to occur overnight," as the Kotzker Rebbe once quipped, "and they want to sleep that night, as well."

We are told that on Rosh Hashanah we should minimize our sleep in general, and specifically to refrain from sleep during the day — certainly we should not nap before midday. The deeper reason is that Rosh Hashanah is a time to be 'awake': to wake up to our physical, mental, emotional and spiritual responsibilities, and to our innate human potential. The work of changing our lives happens when we are awake, and it does not come passively or as instant gratification.

Rosh Hashanah is a celebration of the birthday of humanity; it is our collective and individual day of birth. The first Rosh Hashanah occurred when the Creator told the world and the angels, "I want to create human beings (Adam and Chavah / Eve)." Ever since, it is the day the Creator says of every person, 'I have such a special soul, a special person, that must exist in My world." The world may be populated with many people, yet we were each born because the Creator wants us, the world needs us, and we need each other.

On our 'birthday' (and for that matter every day, and every moment we are alive) Hashem is telling us, 'I want you. The world would feel empty without you — I desire you to be here.' Our *Avodah* / inner work on this day is therefore to fully 'be here'.

"Everything was created according to its knowledge," means that we were asked, as it were, if we wanted to be created, and we replied, "Yes" (*Rosh Hashanah*, 11a, as Rashi writes: שאלם אם חפצין להבראות ואמרו הן. Although this Rashi can be read not 'whether' they should be created, rather, 'how' to be created, as the Maharal seems to understand this Rashi. *Gur Aryeh*, Bereishis, 1:25. Rabbeinu Chananel, *Chulin*, 60a, understands this Gemara to mean that all creatures were created mature and mentally developed).

We were thus born with our own confirmation that we 'deserved' to be born; from the beginning we understood deep down that we are needed, that the world is not the same place without us. And so, on Rosh Hashanah, our collective birthday, we should reflect on these existential inquiries:

Why was I born?

Am I fulfilling my purpose?

Does the way I live my life justify my existence?

Am I fully present with my life and my potential?

It is a new year, a new beginning. We are therefore given a couple days upon which we can reflect on our lives, and experience for at least a moment or two the depths of this transformative new phase of life. Our reflections might include two elements: a) processing with the past so it does not crowd out the present, and b) focusing on the present, as a portal into a new future.

To move forward, we usually need to unload the bags that are weighing us down from our past journeys. To do this, it helps to make a compassionate but accurate self-evaluation and inventory, or spiritual accounting. This is because we need to 'own' the problems of our past before we can separate from them and then transform them into tools for growth.

'Owning our past' means looking back on the past year and noticing when we were successful and perhaps in which areas we fell short of our potential. This is a time to evaluate which traits, habits, or activities we should continue, and which ones we should release. Think about this as well in terms of your relationships — with Hashem, with yourself, with family, loved ones, co-workers, community, people in general, other species, and the earth as a whole. We have many spheres of relationship and in each one we need to honestly observe and notice the integrity or lack thereof, of what we are doing. We must ask ourselves: Where am I learning, growing, ascending, and where am I stuck, stagnant, or even descending?

The spiritual technologies of *Tefilah* / prayer, study, introspection, and self-evaluation, help us make order in our life. Such an 'ordering' process makes it possible to account for and categorize each of our 'problems' properly, so that we can clearly understand what is bothering us, and what is connecting us to joy and openness. What is lifting you and what is pulling you down? By undergoing such a soul-reckoning, you can create for yourself a new vision and program for the coming year.

Think about how your past has brought you into the present moment. Where have you been and what have you done? Envision the future. In the coming year, where do you want to be and what do you want to do, and why?

Think about how you might live more fully. Ask yourself: what do I envision for myself? Who do I see myself becoming? Where would I like to reach? What are the steps that I can take to move toward these goals? Where are my vulnerabilities and how can I be attentive to them? What are my strengths, and how can I ensure that arrogance does not creep in? Which areas in life should I invest in, and which ones are depleting my energy?

Rosh Hashanah is actually the *Rosh* / 'head' of the new year, not merely the 'first' day of the year. This means Rosh Hashanah is the 'headquarters' or 'brain' of the new year; where the template of the coming year is imprinted and projected. It is vital that we use our own *Rosh* / head on this day, to create a vision for ourselves, as the year that follows is but an articulation and unpacking of that original vision.

Shanah means year. The word *Shanah* comes from the same etymological root as the word *Shinui* / change (שנה הוא לשון שינוי. See *Zohar* 3, 277b, Ramaz, *ad loc. Shoresh Yesha*, Erech Shanah. *Avodas haKodesh*, 4:19. *Ohr haTorah*, Miketz, 338. *Likutei Sichos*, 4, p. 1323). As such, Rosh Hashanah can mean 'changing your *Rosh* / head', shifting and renewing your consciousness and way of thinking. On Rosh Hashanah we need to work on changing the way we see and think about ourselves and the people and world around us. We need to begin to see and understand things from a radically deeper perspective.

Chapter One:
WHAT ROSH HASHANAH IS:
Freedom, Responsibility & the Story of Our Birth

OUR ULTIMATE OBJECTIVE IN THIS BOOK IS TO UN-
DERSTAND THE *SHOFAR* / RAM'S HORN AND WHAT
BLOWING IT AND HEARING IT REPRESENTS, but first
we need to establish a foundational understanding of the context in which the Shofar is sounded, the day of Rosh Hashanah itself.

תקעו בחדש שופר בכסה ליום חגנו / *Tiku baChodesh Shofar baKeseh
l'Yom Chageinu* / "Blow the Shofar on the new moon, on the
full moon for our feast day" (*Tehilim*, 81:4). While *baKeseh* here
means 'new moon', it can also be translated as 'hidden'.

In this way, בכסה ליום חגנו / *baKeseh l'Yom Chageinu* can mean "at the hiddenness of the day of our holiday" (*Beitza*, 16a). In other words, we are told to blow the Shofar on the day when the moon is hidden, meaning on the first day of the month when the moon is, for the most part, unobservable. In fact, the word *baKeseh* is numerically 87, the same value as the word *Levanah* / moon (*Sefer Rokeach*, Hilchos Rosh Hashanah, 200). Rosh Hashanah therefore occurs on the day when the moon is hidden.

Moreover, not only do we, in our liturgy, 'hide' the fact that Rosh Hashanah occurs in the new moon cycle (*Tosefos*, Rosh Hashanah, 8b: פי' מתכסה שאין מזכירין מוסף של ר"ח בתפלה), Rosh Hashanah itself can be viewed as a 'hidden' Yom Tov — a mystery. We know very little about Rosh Hashanah from the Torah. The Torah only mentions that Rosh Hashanah is *Yom Teru'ah* / a day of Shofar blasts, and a day of *Zichron Teru'ah* / remembrance of the Shofar blast, but why it is a day of blowing or remembering the Shofar the Torah does not explain. This is unlike other holy days such as Pesach and Sukkos, regarding which the Torah tells us the details of why we celebrate them: our going out of Egypt or our sitting in the Clouds of Glory. By not explaining Rosh Hashanah, the Torah invites us to thoroughly explore its nature, as well as the meaning of the Shofar which is the essence of this day.

THE DAY OF TERU'AH

Rosh Hashanah and the Shofar are, as mentioned, intricately linked, "שמצות היום בשופר / for the Mitzvah of the day is Shofar" *(Mishnah, Rosh Hashanah, 3:3)*. Yet, there are two ways to think about this relationship. From one perspective, Shofar is a Mitzvah in its own right, however, the Mitzvah is to blow it specifically on Rosh Hashanah. Here there are two joined elements, much like in the Mitzvah of *Bris* / circumcision: there is a) the Mitzvah of Bris, and b) the fact that the Mitzvah needs to be performed on the eighth day of a boy's life. From a different perspective, the Mitzvah of Shofar is inseparable from Rosh Hashanah. Rosh Hashanah is not Rosh Hashanah without the Mitzvah of Shofar, and blowing the Shofar outside of Rosh Hashanah is not a Mitzvah. There are not two joined elements, rather one unit.

The latter perspective seems to be the correct way of thinking about Shofar, as the Torah itself defines Rosh Hashanah as *Yom Teru'ah* / a day of Shofar blowing: יום תרועה יהיה לכם / "A day of *Teru'ah* it shall be for you." As such, it is not that we a) blow the Shofar on b) Rosh Hashanah, due to the fact that the *Mitzvas haYom* / Mitzvah of the day is Shofar — rather, it is *Yom-Teru'ah* / 'the day *is* Shofar blowing.' There is even an opinion in *Halachah* / Jewish law, which is perhaps that of the great Polish Posek, Rav Mordechai Yaffe ("the Levush," 1530–1612), that any time a person blows the Shofar on Rosh Hashanah he is fulfilling a Mitzvah of Shofar, since '*Yom* — the entire day is — *Teru'ah.*' (At the very least, he is not violating the prohibition of 'not adding' new Mitzvos, דאטו יום תרועה פעם אחד כתיב...ביום כתיב. אבל אין בה משום בל תוסיף...תלה רחמנא: *Levush*, Orach Chayim, Siman 585. The Netziv seems to write the same, אבל אם חפץ הוא לתקוע לשום מצוה מותר לתקוע: כל היום דכל זמן שעוסק במצוה נחשב למצוה: *Ha'amek Sha'alah*, Yisro, 53. *Shu't Meishiv Davar* 1, Siman 36.)

Regarding no other *Yom Tov* / holiday does the Torah use this type of expression. The Torah does not say 'a day of remembering the going out of Egypt' with regards to Pesach, nor 'a day of *Nanu'im* / shaking the Lulav' with regards to Sukkos. But with regards to Rosh Hashanah the Torah says the 'essence of the day' is the Shofar.

Therefore, if we want to understand what Rosh Hashanah is about, we need to truly understand the Shofar — in fact, our sages explain the meaning of Rosh Hashanah based on their understanding of the Shofar. The reverse is also true. To understand the Shofar, we need to explore the meaning of Rosh Hashanah.

THE DAY OF JUDGMENT

Rosh Hashanah is called 'the Day of Judgment'; the day of accountability, the day upon which there is a personal evaluation that will impact the entire year to come (*Rosh Hashanah*, 8a). Our sages tell us (*Rosh Hashanah*, 18a) that on Rosh Hashanah all humanity passes one-by-one before Hashem, as it were, and are judged. This idea is hinted in the words we recite directly after each set of Shofar blasts: *haYom Haras Olam, haYom Ya'amid baMishpat Kol Yitzurei Olamim* / "Today is the birthday of the world, [and thus] today is established for all creatures of the worlds to be judged." Based on this, it is even theoretically possible to suggest (although it is certainly not meant to be carried out) that the nations of the world also need to blow the Shofar on Rosh Hashanah (although see *Sifra*, Emor, 11:1: בני ישראל...מקרא קדש – ואין העכו״ם מקרא קדש).

We are each judged individually on this day, yet on a deeper level, each individual needs to judge him or herself. What is meant by 'judgment' and what exactly does it mean to be 'judged'? These questions will be articulated and addressed in greater detail further on. For now, we will explore what Divine judgment inspires within us and demands from us.

The Radbaz, the esteemed 16th Century scholar Rebbe Dovid ben Zimrah, writes that on Rosh Hashanah a person has to "think about his *Cheshbon* / accounting with his Creator" (*Metzudas Dovid*, Mitzvah 111. "Which implies self-judgment. *Likutei Sichos*, 9, p. 416). The word "with" in this statement can also imply that it is a day not only when Hashem takes account of where we are in our lives, but also when we need to do so as well. 'Divine judgment' is meant to inspire human self-evaluation and evolution, and by joining together "with" our Compassionate Creator in performing it we are able to contribute to such a transformation.

QUESTIONS TO SELF

On this day of Divine Judgement we ought to ask ourselves, "Who am I? Where has my path taken me this past year? Do I own my life, or does my life own me?"

HaKadosh Baruch Hu's judgment of us on Rosh Hashanah is similar to co-partners in a joint venture, where one partner, the Ultimate Partner, is checking and auditing the books of His junior partner. HaKadosh Baruch Hu is taking a look into our heart and life to see how His investment in us is working out. We are gifted with the ability to have a face-to-face relationship with Hashem; we are not solely receiving vitality from Above, as all creatures do. In addition, we are asked to 'be like the Creator' — in consciously choosing and directing our lives. This is because we have a Divine mandate and purpose to our existence, and we need to clarify and develop it.

On Rosh Hashanah we need to contemplate whether or not we can truly answer the question of 'why' we exist. Can we 'justify' our Creator's investment in us? Each person must consider that "the world was created for me." In a sense, this means that the entire world is depending on me; am I faithfully fulfilling this profound responsibility? How and where have I been successful in honoring this bestowal? In what ways can I bring greater 'prosperity' to the ultimate Owner of this world?

We need to answer the request of our 'Senior Business Partner' to evaluate our own contributions to the growth of the 'company'. We need to take some time to ask, 'Am I living up to my true potential in the job I was given?' Of course, no one is perfect, but what steps do we need to take in order to live more meaningfully and successfully?

Is there a resounding yes to the question of 'Am I growing?' Am I prepared to fully *live* in every moment that I exist?

From Hashem's 'perspective', our lives are indeed worthy of having been created, and the proof is that Hashem created and continues to create and invest in us. Hashem already 'justifies' our existence, up until now. Proof of our worthiness is simply our presence; if our past was unjustifiable, we could not be alive in this moment. The question, however, is: from our perspective, can we justify our life moving forward? Do we share Hashem's trust in our good intentions? Can we wholeheartedly affirm that we are becoming a more and more fitting receptacle of the Divine life-force and deserve to 'live'?

Do I and my actions and level of consciousness 'deserve' to take and eat fruit from a tree, consume the meat of an animal, walk upon the ground that Hashem created, and to benefit from Hashem's 'garden' which is this world? Am I living a meaningful life to the extent that I 'deserve' to receive nourishment from so many other precious life-forms?

This is the 'judgment' of Rosh Hashanah: integrating the past, inspiring the future.

BOTH 'PARTIES' ARE JUDGED ON ROSH HASHANAH

On Rosh Hashanah both partners are judged, so to speak. We justify and affirm that we deserve to continue to exist and prosper, and say, 'Yes, I am working on my life, I am striving to be a better person, a better Jew, and even if I have not lived up to my potential until this point, I can firmly declare that now — following the month of Teshuvah in Elul — I am resolved to live my life more deeply, more honestly, more lovingly, more consciously, with more responsibility.' And Rosh Hashanah is also a day of משפט לאלקי יעקב / *Mishpat l'Elokei Yaakov* / "a judgment to the G-d of Yaakov" (*Tehilim*, 81:5). This could literally mean, "a judgment *of* the G-d of Yaakov," meaning, as the Chassidic Rebbes read it, the Creator too is being 'judged' on this day, as it were.

Our sages tell us: "When the Holy One, blessed be He, came to create Adam — on the day that would become Rosh Hashanah — the ministering angels formed themselves into groups and factions, some of them saying (not that the angels actually said this, rather, theoretically, this would be the perspective of angelic reality. Maharal, *Tiferes Yisrael*, Chapter 24), 'Let him be created,' while others urged, 'let him not be created.'… Lovingkindness said, 'Let him be created, because he will dispense acts of lovingkindness.' Truth said, 'Let him not be created, because he is full of lies.' Justice said, 'Let him be created, because he will perform acts of justice.' Peace said, 'Let him not be created, because he is full of strife.'…While the ministering angels were arguing with each other and disputing with each other, the Holy One created the first human. Hashem said to them, "Why are you arguing? Man has already been made!" (*Medrash Rabbah*, Bereishis, 8:5).

And so, every Rosh Hashanah, the day of Adam's creation, the attributes and the angels of Truth and Peace, arise and ask of the Creator, as it were, 'Is it worth it? How is this humanity that You have created working out?' (*Ohr haMeir*, Derush Rosh Hashanah). On Rosh Hashanah the Master of the Universe is on trial, so-to-speak. Truth and Peace argue: You quietly snuck away, while we were all arguing, and You created humanity without our consensus. So it now behooves you to tell us: how is that working out? Are You having the pleasure that You anticipated, or do You regret it?

It is a day when we are on trial and need to justify our existence. And a day when HaKadosh Baruch Hu, our Creator is (*Keviyachol* / 'as if') also on trial and asked to justify His creation, mankind.

The question we need to answer on Rosh Hashanah is actually the question of the angels: 'Was it worth creating humanity, or not?' What would have been better — if I, this human being, had been *Nivra* / created or *Lo Nivra* / not created?'

Amazingly, by justifying our own existence we are helping our Creator, as it were, by advocating on behalf of Hashem's act of creation, testifying in the court of angels, as it were, and proving that HaKadosh Baruch Hu was correct in creating us. By justifying our own existence, we are thus arguing on behalf of our Creator. Our own honest and positive self-judgment strengthens the vindication of Hashem's deed. Our motivational self-judgment becomes Hashem's motivational Self-judgment. Our positive verdict is HaKadosh Baruch Hu's positive verdict as well.

TO BE HUMAN IS TO TAKE RESPONSIBILITY

To be truly human is to take responsibility for oneself and

one's world. Our collective human birthday, Rosh Hashanah, was chosen as the Day of Judgment and accountability, precisely because it is the day the Creator created us (*Pesikta*, Piska 23. Ran, *Rosh Hashanah*). The implication is that the original human condition is to yearn and strive for accountability and ownership of our lives, to be the ones who guide ourselves upon the paths that we choose, and then reap the fruits of our choices.

Animals, ruled purely by instincts and circumstances, are not fully responsible or accountable for their actions in the way that humans are.* What is more, on our primordial birthday, we were charged with responsibility, not only for ourselves, but for all other creatures and Creation, as well. This is a role that can only be fulfilled when we judge and rule over ourselves as a 'partner' with the Divine Judge and Ruler of the world: "And *Elokim* (the Judge) said, "Let us (all of Creation) make man in Our image, after Our likeness...and said to them, ורדו / and you shall 'descend' (guide or gently rule) over the fish of the sea and over the fowl of the Heaven and over the animals and over all the earth and over all the creeping things that creep

---

* When the Torah says, "If a bull gores a man or woman to death, the bull is to be stoned to death" (*Shemos*, 21:28), Chazal call this a *Din* / judgment on the animal: תם שהמית והזיק דנין אותו (*Bava Kama*, 90a). This does not mean there is a judgment to punish the animal, rather, it is a punishment on the owner of the animal, for not properly watching over it. As the Rambam writes, והיות הבהמה נהרגת כשתהרוג אדם אינו לקחת דין ממנה כמו שירחיקו עלינו הצדוקים אבל הוא לקחת הדין מבעליה: *Moreh Nevuchim*, 3 40:1. The judgment is to ensure that the owner will not allow the dangerous animal to gore again.

upon the earth'" (*Bereishis*, 1:27-28). Just as Elokim is the Judge and the One responsible for all of Creation, we who are created in the Image of Elokim, and gifted with higher intelligence (Rambam, Hilchos *Yesodei haTorah*, 4:8: והדעת היתרה המצויה בנפשו של אדם היא צורת האדם השלם בדעתו. ועל צורה זו נאמר בתורה נעשה אדם בצלמנו כדמותנו) are vested with the responsibility for all of Creation, to ורדו / go down and intelligently rule over this world. We are charged to assume responsibility for all other forms of life: animal, vegetable, mineral — along with our own lives.

This impulse to embody Divine responsibility is basic and intrinsic to the human spirit; after all, our consciousness is rooted in the cosmic Day of Judgment, the day of coronating the Ruler of the Universe.

When we take responsibility for ourselves and others, we reveal our true potential. The human being is designed for noble self-mastery. When we act thoughtlessly, flouting our spiritual role, we alienate the human spirit within us and cause a downfall of all of Creation. In the times of Noach, when human responsibility was at an all-time low, even the animals became corrupt because of us: "And *Elokim* said...the earth is filled with lawlessness because of them" (*Bereishis*, 6:13). Coversly, and on a personal level, owning our actions reintegrates the 'human' with the 'being', and elevates us to our true authority, over ourselves and the world at large. Such authority can only be achieved and justified through our own commitment to transparency, humility, and responsibility

All other creatures besides humans are ruled by instinct rather than through conscious choice. They experience life and their relationship with their Creator as 'back-to-Back' — blind to the root of causality and thus responsibility and choice. When we too live 'back-to-Back' with the Creator, we are no longer a conduit of the power of Divine rulership in Creation, and we and the entire world suffer. The intrinsic urge toward accountability of those created in the Divine Image is meant to bring us back again and again into a 'face-to-face' relationship with the Divine and with all of life. We can in this way bring beneficial order and light to our lives and to the lives of all beings.

All of that being said, if we were held too strictly accountable for everything in our lives, we would eventually become so mired in our past mistakes that we would be unable to recreate ourselves anew. This is the World of *Din* / strict judgment, which is inhumane and unsustainable. However, as human beings, we do have a unique ability to move on, make radical departures from our past, and start over. Countless people throughout history have turned their lives around quite miraculously. Even as we are accountable for our past choices, we are not essentially defined by them, and part of us transcends our past and the natural order of events. Therefore, on our path of self-mastery, we must not judge ourselves too strictly or harshly; we should always balance piercing self-judgment with transcendent compassion: *Shema' Yisrael, Hashem Elokeinu...* / "Listen, you who strive to be face-to-face with the Divine, the Infinitely Compassionate One is 'our *Elokim*', our Source of holy judgment...." (*Devarim*, 6:4)

'THE FIRST MONTH' VERSUS 'THE SEVENTH MONTH'

Two great sages in the *Gemara*, Rebbe Eliezer and Rebbe Yehoshua, debate about what day 'the world was created' — referring specifically to the day that humanity was created (*Rosh Hashanah*, 11a). Rebbe Eliezer's opinion is that Creation took place on the first day of the month of Tishrei, on Rosh Hashanah. Rebbe Yehoshua, however, asserts that creation occurred on the first day of the month of Nisan. In addition, they argue over when the *Avos* / Patriarchs, Avraham, Yitzchak, and Yaakov, were born. Rebbe Eliezer says they were all born in Tishrei, and Rebbe Yehoshua says they were born in Nisan. This extends into an argument over when the ultimate Redemption will take place. Rebbe Eliezer says it will occur in Tishrei, and Rebbe Yehoshua says it will be in Nisan.

We abide by Rebbe Eliezer's opinion, and we celebrate Rosh Hashanah on the first day of Tishrei,* but what is the deeper meaning of this disagreement?

---

* Rebbe Yonasan Eybeschutz has a wonderful, novel approach to this argument, which is that both opinions affirm the physical world was created in Nisan, the first month of the year, in the *Mazal* of *T'leh* / constellation of Aries. Yet, for the first Six Days of Creation, the sun was moving through the *Mazalos* / zodiac quickly, and so on Friday it was already the sign of Scales, which is the month of Tishrei. Thus, 'man' was created in Tishrei whereas the world was created six days prior in Nisan, and there is no argument; we therefore celebrate the creation of humanity on the first day of Tishrei. Additionally, Tosefos, *Rosh Hashanah*, 27a, reconciles the opinion of Rebbe Eliezer with Rebbe Yehoshua, and teaches that the thought of creating humanity entered the Creator's mind, as it were, in the month of Tishrei, and the actual creation took place seven months later, in Nisan. As such, we celebrate, in fact, Rosh Hashanah according to both opinions. Furthermore, since "בתחלה עלה במחשבה לבראתו במדת הדין / at first the Creator intended to create it (the world) with the attribute (rule) of Din/ strict justice" (Rashi, *Bereishis*, 1:1), thus ever since, Rosh Hashanah, which is the creation of תחלה /the original creation, in the thought of the Creator, is a time of Din.

The month of Tishrei and the month of Nisan have different natural and spiritual characteristics. Even if we momentarily leave Rosh Hashanah out of the picture, the month of Tishrei contains many holy days and Mitzvos relating to *Teshuvah* / returning to the path of conscious accountability and self-mastery. The Torah calls Tishrei "the Seventh Month," alluding to the natural cycle of time. The intensive spiritual work of Tishrei is analogous to the agrarian harvest of this season. With effort, we gather to ourselves the traits and habits that will nourish us during the coming year, and we cast away those that are spoiled or harmful. The theme of Tishrei is the movement *mi-leMatah leMa'alah* / from below to Above.

The month of Nisan is the month of Pesach, and it contains many holy days and Mitzvos that commemorate Divine miracles. In fact, the adopted name Nisan is related to the Hebrew word *Nes* / miracle (Nisan, say Chazal, reflects the *Nisim* / miracles which were revealed during that month: *Pesikta Zutresa*, Bo, 12:2. *Medrash Lekach Tov*, Shemos, 12:2. In the words of Rashi, שע״י נסים נקרא ניסן / "Nisan is called *Nisan* because of the miracles": *Berachos*, 56a). The Torah calls Nisan both *Aviv* and "the First of Months." *Aviv*, meaning 'Spring', alludes to the indiscriminate renewal of life which occurs spontaneously, apart from any human effort. 'The First of Months' alludes to the 'supernatural' rebirth of the moon, along with the new Divine flow that streams into the world each Rosh Chodesh. In Nisan, Hashem descended to liberate Klal Yisrael from the degradation of Egyptian slavery and birthed them as a new nation. The theme of Nisan is the movement *mi-leMa'alah leMatah* / from Above to below.

These two possible movements, ascending and descending, are also reflected in the names of these months. The word *Tishrei* is spelled Tav-Shin-Reish-Yud. Tav, Shin and Reish are the last three letters of the Alef-Beis, in reverse order. Therefore, the letters of *Tishrei* start at the 'bottom', and ascend toward the Yud, which symbolizes Hashem. This alludes to the movement from below to Above, characterizing the month of Tishrei.

The Torah's name for Nisan is *Aviv*, spelled Alef-Beis-Yud-Beis. Here, the first two letters start at the 'top' of the Alef-Beis and move 'down' toward the Yud. This alludes to the movement from Above to below, which characterizes the month of Nisan (*Ohr haTorah*, Shemos 1, p. 261).

The names of Rebbe Eliezer and Rebbe Yehoshua also allude to these different characteristics. The Maharal (Rebbe Yehudah Loew in *Nesivos Olam*, Nesiv haTeshuvah, Ch. 8, p. 170) and the Maharsha (*Chidushei Halachos*, Hakdamah) both explain that the meaning of the name Eliezer means *E-l Ezer*, "Hashem helps." The Torah tells us in Parshas Shelach that the name Yehoshua means, "Hashem will bring you salvation." Both of their names are related to help, salvation. What is the difference between them? 'Help' implies that something is wrong and yet there is assistance. The situation may not change, but someone is there to help. 'Salvation' means that the help is so successful or profound that there is no longer any problem. Yehoshua thus represents a level that is higher than Eliezer.

It is interesting to note that the two people who led the Jewish people into the Land of Israel were also named Eliezer and Yehoshua. Yehoshua bin Nun led the Klal Yisrael across the Jordan River following the exodus from Egypt. That was a time of miracles — including the Fall of Yericho, and the day the sun stood still. Ezra, on the other hand, led the Jews back to Israel after the First Exile. They were allowed to return to Israel because King Darius gave them permission. It was a natural event (*Bnei Yissaschar*, Elul, Ma'amar 1:18). Therefore, the name Eliezer represents humanity in the condition of nature; and the name Yehoshua represents humanity in a condition of miracles.

WHO ARE WE?

In a deeper sense, the argument between Rebbe Eliezer and Rebbe Yehoshua is about the true nature of the human being. Fundamentally speaking, is our defining characteristic our ability to freely choose and take responsibility for our lives, or is it our ability to dream of a better self and brighter world? Are we rooted below in the natural world, or are we rooted above, in the realm of the miraculous? Are we built to strive towards Heaven or to escort Heaven to earth? Are we defined by our past, or by our potential future?

Rebbe Eliezer argues that it is our ability to take responsibility for our lives that makes us human beings. Rebbe Yehoshua suggests that there is *more* to a human being than that: part of us exists entirely beyond cause and effect, free from the results of our past, and inclined towards an as yet unrealized future. This is our unfettered soul.

The truth is, the two sages are not in conflict. Rather, one opinion completes the other. While Rebbe Yehoshua's main focus is freedom, he would agree that responsibility is a necessary first stage to attaining freedom. The reason that he says the human being was created in Nisan, is that the purpose of our creation is to be free, to dream and soar above our limitations. Yet, accountability grounds and supports this freedom. We are thus to take hold of and own our past in Tishrei and then 'miraculously' transcend it in Nisan. We need to own our past before we can dream about our miraculous or extraordinary future. Conversely, our 'responsibility' in Tishrei is realized and completed with our 'dreams' in Nisan.

Rebbe Eliezer is also correct, and the law follows his opinion: our emergence in the Spring, in the First Month, leads to our maturity in Autumn, in the Seventh Month. (In Halachah, for many issues, *Nisan* comes first and then *Tishrei*. Regarding Bal Te'acher, see *Rosh Hashanah*, 4b). The purpose of our lives is not just to live in a transcendent realm of miracles, rather, it is to responsibly embody spiritual freedom on earth within the realm of cause and effect.

SELF-CREATION

Later on in the tractate of Rosh Hashanah (27a), Tosefos (the classic commentary on the Gemara, from the early Ashkenazic sages of the 12th to the 15th Century) reconciles the opinion of Rebbe Eliezer with Rebbe Yehoshua, and teaches that the thought of creating humanity entered the Creator's mind, as it were, in the month of Tishrei, and the actual creation took place seven months later, in Nisan (The Arizal explains that in Tishrei the world is like a fetus in its mother's womb, and seven months later, in Nisan, the world is born. *Sha'ar haKavanos*, Rosh Hashanah, Derush 1. *Pri Eitz Chayim*, Sha'ar haShofar, 5. *Sefer haBris*, Ma'amar 2:8).

During this same debate, Rebbe Yehoshua ben Levi is quoted as teaching, "All were created according to their knowledge, and in their beauty" — 'their knowledge,' meaning their consent. Rashi, adds that before we were created, we were asked if we wanted to be created, and we replied, "Yes!" (Rashi, *Rosh Hashanah*, 11a: שאלם אם חפצין להבראות ואמרו הן).

If we combine these metaphorical teachings, an empowering message emerges. While contemplating our creation, HaKadosh Baruch Hu placed the responsibility for our lives in our own hands. We knowingly consented to life. We are thus accountable not only for how we live, but also for our very existence; not only for the content of our lives and how we process and respond to it (our knowledge and beauty), but also for the actual context of life itself (our 'yes' to existence).

Each year, through the mental, emotional and spiritual work of Tishrei, we have the opportunity to remember and reiterate our primal 'yes' to being alive. "According to their knowledge and in their beauty" alludes to the realization of our *purpose* in being alive: our 'dream', our miraculous liberation in the beautiful, spring month of Nisan.

When Rosh Hashanah approaches, may we all meditate deeply and take an accounting of our past; may we say 'yes' to life, and 'yes' to a most beautiful coming year. We need to think, together with our Creator, about our life — and with complete confidence, declare: 'Yes, I do need to exist.'

On Rosh Hashanah, may we come before the Creator and Judge of Heaven and Earth, to actively 'justify' our existence. May we honestly assert, 'I have looked seriously into the matter and I do deserve to live, and I deserve to receive all that I need. Why? It is because Hashem, *You* think I deserve to live — *You* believe in me. You gave and are giving me life. Therefore, I also believe in myself.'

May we all be blessed with a *Kasivah v'Chasimah Tovah*; to be written and inscribed for a good year — a physically healthy and prosperous year, a year of life, clarity, connectivity, growth, meaning, and realized purpose!'

Chapter Two
THE COSMIC SOUL
OF ROSH HASHANAH

Rosh Hashanah is the great renewal, not only of ourselves but of the entire universe. To understand how this is so, we need to understand what the building blocks of the universe are. Creation is not built from *Olam* / space and *Shanah* / time alone, it has another parameter. As space extends in three dimensions and time extends from the past into the future, so this third parameter extends from the inner to the outer, from the ethereal essence of being to the concrete reality that we touch and feel, from the simplicity of infinite light to the chaos of our outermost world. This third building block is *Nefesh* / the cosmic 'soul' of the universe, what we can simply call 'consciousness'.

Indeed, the entire universe may be understood as a kind of cosmic 'person', one *Adam Gadol* / vast human being. Each of us, then, is an infinitesimal micro-reproduction, called an *Olam Katan* / small world, as expressed poetically in numerous post-Talmudic texts, האדם עולם קטן, העולם אדם גדול / "Man is a small world, and the world is a big man."

This cosmic Nefesh expresses itself in space through the medium of time, since in comparison to external space, time is a more interior dimension and phenomenon. As such, whatever exists in the realm of soul exists in the realm of time, and whatever exists in time, also exists in space. In the world of soul there is a *Rosh* / head or mind from which all consciousness, of all beings, is awakened. In time, this is expressed as *Rosh Hashanah*, a point in time from which all time is renewed. In space, this is expressed as the Land of Israel, a central physical location upon which the entire world is supported.

Space, time and consciousness may seem distinct from each other, with consciousness functioning as an observer of objective space within a context of subjective time. Yet now we understand that on a more elemental level, time does not exist without space, and neither time nor space exist without an observer — since the observer effects, and essentially creates, that which is observed. This is why it would be inaccurate to speak only of the renewal of time at Rosh Hashanah without mentioning the renewal of space and consciousness.

Rosh Hashanah, the 'Head of the Year,' is not just a beginning, a starting point, as in *Techilas Hashanah*, it is a 'head'. Just as the head contains the mind and the consciousness that directs the deliberate actions of the body, so too Rosh Hashanah is that essential node in time through which passes all the dimensions of the ensuing year.

As Rosh Hashanah is the nerve center through which all time flows anew — it is also the portal through which both space and consciousness are renewed as well. By attuning ourselves to this cosmic renewal, we can restore vitality to all levels of our being, initiating a radical rejuvenation in our personal dimensions of time, space and consciousness.

THE RENEWAL OF HUMANITY

In addition to our personal renewal, Rosh Hashanah is also the day of our collective self-evaluation as it celebrates the 'head' or origin of humanity — the 'genesis' of Adam and Chavah / Eve. It is not necessarily a celebration of the creation of the world (as that was on Day One of Creation), rather it is the day Adam and Chavah (humanity) were created (Day Six), and their initiation into lives of purpose and responsibility.

Considering that Adam was the first human being, all humans can trace their genetic code back to this single ancestor. As physicality is a reflection of spiritual reality, Adam also represents *Adam Kadmon /* the primordial human being — the collective and universal soul from which all *Nefashos /* souls emanate (*Sha'ar haGilgulim*, Hakdamah 12. Ramak, *Shiur Komah*, Chapter 2. See also *Medrash Rabbah*, Shemos, 40:3. *Tanchumah*, Ki Tissa, 12. *Tanya, Igeres haKodesh*, 7). Adam is thus the embodiment of the cosmic element of Nefesh, consciousness itself. In this sense, the 'creation of Adam' did not occur just once in the past; rather it reoccurs at every moment. The 'central point' around which all these moments of renewal revolve is Rosh Hashanah, when a total renewal of strength and clarity of consciousness takes place.

A NEW BEING

Rosh Hashanah is our birthday, providing an annual opportunity to reboot and refresh. Whatever happened in your past, whoever and wherever you were, today there is a new world, a new time and a new you. On Rosh Hashanah, the Creator of All Life declares, "Today I am creating you as a בריאה חדשה / *Beriah Chadashah* / a new creation" (*Medrash Rabbah*, Vayikra, 29:12).

"With regards to all the other offerings the Torah uses the (proper) phrase, והקרבתם / 'And you shall offer....' Here (regarding the offerings on Rosh Hashanah) the Torah says, ועשיתם עלה / 'And you shall *make* a burnt offering....' (*Bamidbar*, 29:2). This is because Hashem is telling us, 'Since you came before Me on Rosh Hashanah and you have *made* yourselves established in wholeness and in peace, I consider it as if you are a בריאה חדשה / new creation'" (Yerushalmi, *Rosh Hashanah*, 4:8).

On Rosh Hashanah we are empowered to *re-make* ourselves, in a brand new image (*Olam*), a brand new narrative (*Shanah*), and a brand new lens of perception (*Nefesh*). It is the first day of our lives. Take a few moments right now to imagine that infinite potential. Sense the relieving freshness, clarity and peace of being re-made in the eternal present moment.

THE FUNCTION OF THE BEIS HAMIKDASH: THE RENEWAL WITHIN SPACE

When the *Beis haMikdash* / Temple stood in *Yerusha-layim* / Jerusalem, the center of space, all of space, time and consciousness were birthed and re-birthed there, within the eye of the world. As this was the focal point of space from which all directions flowed, there was a constant, palpable sense of newness and freshness there. For example, the *Lechem haPanim* / showbreads in the Beis haMikdash never grew stale and they always tasted perfectly fresh, even if baked a week before (*Chagigah*, 26b. Always fresh: *Tosefos, ad loc.* לענין שהיה רך ומה שאמר הפסוק חום ביום הלקחו לאו דוקא אלא דחם לא היה. The Ritva, however, writes that they were also always hot, פירוש שהיה חם בשעת סילוק ולקיחה כמו בשעת שימה. ונראה כי בשעת שימה ולקיחה היה חם הרבה עד שהיה הבל יוצא ממנו כלחם היוצא מן התנור: *Yuma*, 21a).

The Beis haMikdash was built on the site where Yaakov once slept and dreamt of a ladder to Heaven, as the Torah relates (*Bereishis*, 28:12-18). When he awoke from this dream, he exclaimed, "Surely Hashem is in this place and I knew it not!" What troubled him was that he had slept in such a holy place (Rashi, ad loc.). Sleep is "one-sixtieth of death" (*Berachos*, 57b); it is static and unconscious. A 'holy place' is bristling with life and movement, flowing with newness and awareness. Yaakov was troubled that he did not tune into the consciousness of the place of the Beis haMikdash, where 'there is no sleep' (כשהיינו שמחים שמחת בית השואבה לא ראינו שינה בעינינו: *Sukkah*, 53a. Although the attic above the Holy of Holies, the innermost chamber of the Beis haMikdash, is called the חדר המטות / "room of the beds": *Melachim* 2, 11:2, Rashi. *Medrash Rabbah*, Shir haShirim, 1:16:2. See also *Toras Menachem*, 5752:1, p. 60 — yet this represents the place of intimacy and union and even dream and imagination, but not the place of sleep itself).

Fittingly, Rosh Hashanah numerically is 861, the same value as Beis haMikdash. Today, perhaps, we aspire to consciously correct Yaakov's unconscious 'mistake', as the custom is not to sleep during the day hours of Rosh Hashanah (Rama, *Orach Chayim*, 583:2), especially not before the blowing of the Shofar (through midday: *Magen Avraham*, ad loc.). Furthermore, Rosh Hashanah, and the Shofar itself, are like cosmic alarm clocks meant to awaken humanity. Our refraining from sleep is not only a symbol of this, but is a vessel for it to manifest in the world.

Additionally, on Rosh Hashanah we also aspire to right the mistake of Adam who, as the embodiment of the collective and general soul of humanity, chose to consume the "fruit" of duality, of the Tree of Knowledge, Good and Evil. 'Tasting' and knowing life through a lens of good versus evil, me versus you, achievement versus failure, led Adam to experience a state of oldness and ultimately death. On Rosh Hashanah we strive to taste the sweet fruit of the Tree of Life, and tap into the

Divine flow of non-dual awareness, which brings a *Hischadshus* / renewal and rebirth into all aspects of our lives.

'SOLAR REALITY' INFUSED WITH 'LUNAR REALITY'

The sun does not know months, and the moon does not know years. In the solar cycle of the year there is no indication of the existence of months. In the lunar cycle of months there is no indication of the existence of seasons or years.

'Solar reality' is a world of unchanging predictability and a fixed natural order. Day in and day out, the sun is always full in the sky, whether or not clouds obstruct it or not. 'Lunar reality' is intrinsically connected with change and *Hischadshus* / renewal. The moon is constantly changing in terms of shape and radiance. The months, based on the moon cycle, are called *Chodesh*, from the word *Chidush* / new.

"The sun knows its setting" (*Tehilim*, 104:19). Say our sages, "The sun knows its setting, knows its movement, where- as the moon does not know" (*Rosh Hashanah*, 25a. Rambam, *Hilchos Kiddush haChodesh*, 17:23). The moon operates in a paradigm of 'not-knowing', as it functions in the world of surprises and novelty. "There is nothing new under the sun" (*Koheles*, 1:9), yet, as the Zohar appropriately adds, "...But the moon is new." The moon represents a perpetual 'newness' that is indeed under the sun (*Zohar* 1, p. 123b). The sun represents rigidity, linear structure and inevitability. It rises and sets in the same way each day, and it is always full, whether visible or not. The moon on the other hand, waxes and wanes, sometimes it is shining and sometimes not. Moon reality represents the potential for 'novelty', that which breaks the monotony of linear time.

Rosh Hashanah is the New Year, an expression of the yearly cycle of the sun. However, it is also the day of *Rosh Chodesh* / the beginning of the new month, the renewal of the moon (as the Gemara tells us זכרון אחד עולה לכאן ולכאן / the remembering of Rosh Hashanah includes the remembrance of Rosh Chodesh: *Eiruvin*, 40a, and this is the final ruling of the Gemara, *ibid*, 40b. וא״צ להזכיר ר״ח דקי״ל זכרון אחד עולה לכאן *Beis Yoseph*, Orach Chayim, 582:24).

While it is true that the prevailing custom is not to mention in our prayers the fact that it is a new month, and indeed this fact remains *Keseh* / hidden (*Rosh Hashanah*, 8b. Tosefos, *Eiruvin*, 40a, brings down in the name of the *Aruch*, איזה הוא חג שהחדש מתכסה בו הוי אומר זה ר״ה פי׳ שאין אומר ובראשי חדשיכם לא בתפלה ולא בזולתה. See also Tosefos, *Beitza*, 16a. Another Tosefos, ibid, does mention Rosh Chodesh on Rosh Hashanah), yet, Rosh Hashanah is nonetheless Rosh Chodesh Tishrei. Due to this, the solar New Year is intrinsically connected with the reality of the new moon.

In addition, as mentioned, Rosh Hashanah does not commemorate the creation of the natural world itself, which pertains to the solar reality, rather it commemorates the creation of Adam and Chavah (humanity). Human beings are invested with a Divine Spark and a sense of transcendence, as well as a continuously fluctuating awareness of experience. Hence, we are rooted in the more miraculous quality of the lunar reality.

Rosh Hashanah is our collective birthday. In fact, according to Rashi, when Klal Yisrael were traveling through the Desert, in their inception as a nation, every individual's birthday was also marked and counted on Rosh Hashanah (See, however, Ramban, *Shemos*, 30:12: ועוד קשה לי, כי מנין שנות האנשים אינגו למנין שנות עולם מתשרי אבל הוא מעת לעת מיום הולדו). For example, if one person was born two days before Rosh Hashanah, and another was born two days after Rosh Hashanah, upon the Rosh Hashanah one year later, they both had a 'birthday': the person born before the previous Rosh Hashanah turned two, and the person born after the previous Rosh Hashanah turned one. Even today, when we do not measure age this way, and our individual birthday is the day we are born, Rosh Hashanah is always our 'collective birthday', according to all opinions.

Essentially, Rosh Hashanah celebrates the creation of a being with free choice. The freedom to choose gives us the ability to rise above the predictable, formulaic reality of the sun, and to connect with the lunar reality of Hischadshus. Adam *haRishon* / the first human, and by extension all human beings, are by definition connected with Hischadshus and the moon.

אדם ממקום כפרתו נברא / "Adam was created from the place of his atonement" (*Medrash Rabbah*, Bereishis, 14:8). This means that his body was created out of clay taken from the location where the *Mizbeach* / Altar in the Beis haMikdash would eventually stand (Rambam, *Hilchos Beis haBechirah*, 2:2). 'Atonement' and offerings on the Altar, are expressions of *Teshuvah* / returning and 'undoing' our past mistakes. Through Teshuvah we do not allow our past to dictate our present, and this is synonymous with renewal. Humanity was created in this headquarters of 'starting afresh', this locus of infinite possibility, transcending inevitability.

In the world of predictability, where the past automatically creates the present, there is no room for Teshuvah. What was done is done. This is the world of the sun, the world of absolute cause and effect. But there is more to life than the rigid inevitability of linear time; there is the unfixed reality of the moon, in which there is always a possibility for Teshuvah, an open opportunity to create change by starting over again.

This lunar reality connects us to the constant Hischadshus and revitalization of Creation. The Creation of our world is not merely an event in the past, but an ever unfolding and continuous interruption of stasis. Every moment is a new Creation, as such, there is always a means of returning to the beginning and starting life again.

The Mizbeach is the 'essence' and the essential object of the entire Beis haMikdash (מצות עשה לעשות בית לה' מוכן להיות מקריבים בו הקרבנות: Rambam, *Hilchos Beis haBechirah,* 1:1) The Beis haMikdash, in *Makom* / Space is the essence of the renewal of life from the Source of All Life. Correspondingly, nothing gets old in the Beis haMikdash; the showbread stays fresh. The human being too, created from the earth under the Mizbeach, is deeply identified with this power of Hischadshus; it is in fact the foundation of his creation.

All Hischadshus within the realm of *Z'man* / time is rooted in Rosh Hashanah. Rosh Hashanah reveals a new Divine Light shining forth from the Creator into this world, "a light that was never yet revealed" (Based on the Pasuk in Devarim, 11:12. *Tanya*, Iggeres haKodesh 14. See also, *Derech Hashem*, 4:8, 4. Although Chazal interpret the Pasuk to refer to a judgement of physical rain, the Alter Rebbe reveals the inner quality, connected to the Kedushah of Eretz Yisrael). We human beings — who are given free choice and whose essence of being is rooted in Hischadshus — strengthen and magnify this power of Rosh Hashanah. When we tap into this new light by recreating our own lives and commitments, by, for example, accepting upon ourselves new *Hidurim* / beautifications of Mitzvos and new positive practices, we become the vessels to receive such renewed vitality in all aspects of life, individually, collectively and universally. In this way we become mediums for Hashem's light to illuminate the world

To allow the Hischadshus of Rosh Hashanah to influence our entire year, we need to sense and feel the new Divine revelation entering the world at this time, and also to tap into this infinitely renewable resource every day of the unfolding year.

LIVING WITH HISCHADSHUS

In terms of our inner *Avodah* / spiritual-mental-emotional work, Hischadshus takes on another layer of meaning. As explored, Rosh Hashanah is the renewal of our personal creation. This means we are empowered to personally re-shape ourselves and to start living again and again throughout the coming year. Self-Hischadshus is a gradual process of redis-covering our lives, and living with freshness and humility, as if we have just been born.

In self-renewal nothing is allowed to remain 'old', stale, asleep, or on autopilot. Take, for example, the act of seeing. Perhaps we have become so used to the fact that our eyes see, that we never pause for a moment to recognize the wondrous miracle of eyesight. When we were born, the first time we be-gan to see the outside world we had no capacity for reflection on our experience. However, even if sight had initially been surprising to us, at some point it became 'normal'. Indeed, for decades we may have taken the experience of sight for granted.

This is a simple, sensory example, but consider the existence of our children, family, or siblings. In all likelihood, our appre-ciation of these living miracles is also 'stale', founded on fixed assumptions and old perceptions.

And how much more so in our relationship with ourselves. We refer to an old narrative or image of ourselves when we assert, 'I cannot do this,' or 'I am not worthy of that.' Perhaps, it is true that you were not able to do something in the past, but maybe you have grown and are now capable. Just because you were able to do something in the past does not mean you cannot do so in the present. Sadly, so much of our energy is spent perpetuating our habitual shortcomings.

Similarly, a person could open the Book of Bereishis, and read, "In the beginning Hashem created the heavens and the earth..." and these words might seem something very childish to him. That is because from the time when he was five years old until now at 55, he looks at these words through the same lens. And so, what he is left with is an understanding of these words on the level of a five year old child. In fact, they actually mean much less to him now that he is older, since he has lost his childlike wonder. There is no more sense of the unfathomable mystery of the *Peshat* / simple meaning of this verse (and of any and every verse), to say nothing of the countless layers of inner meaning and transformative power within it. To him, the Torah seems to be an old book of outdated ideas, *Chas veShalom* / Heaven forbid, rather than a fresh, living stream of Divine Self-revelation.

Even more tragic, perhaps, is that the dynamic described above is also present in many people's relationship with the One who gives them life at every moment. People can walk around with a child's understanding of G-d. They accepted or forged a certain conception of what G-d is when they were a young child — maybe an old man in the sky, who, if they beg him enough, may give them candy, or if they misbehave may punish them. Sadly, some slightly more sophisticated version of this could be our own working understanding of our relationship with Hashem. No wonder so many people are not interested in exploring the world of Spirit and deepening their relationship with HaKadosh Baruch Hu.

Once, someone with a very rudimentary and reactionary understanding of Divinity approached the great Chassidic Rebbe, Rebbe Levi Yitzchak of Barditchov, and started spewing heresy at him. Reb Levi Yitzchak gently remarked, "Actually, the G-d you don't believe in, I don't believe in either!"

Hischadshus is approaching life with a sense of novelty, as if beholding everything, everyone, ourselves and our Creator, for the very first time. Without habitual lenses, everything is exciting and miraculous. Imagine right now that you are being introduced to yourself as if you are another person, for the very first time. Look at your appearance, your way of moving and speaking; then look at your talents, your capabilities, your potentials, your innate intelligence, and your wealth of experience and knowledge. Now look deeply at your sincerity, your light, your innocence, your aliveness. Here is an entirely unique person! This is clearly the creation of an Infinite Source!

Now, in the same way, imagine you are meeting your spouse, your children, or your parents, for the first time. Sense the wonder and surprise of encountering their unique light.

Imagine the awe of seeing a mountain or the sun set for the first time in your life.

Imagine it is the first time that you have ever held a Chumash or a book of Torah in your hands and are reading the Divine account of Creation. With no limited assumptions, expectations or lenses, what do these words and letters mean to you now?

Imagine you are introduced to your very own Ultimate Source for the first time. You have no preconceptions, no images, no narratives, no resistance or armoring. You are open to encounter the Ineffable and be touched by Infinity.

On Rosh Hashanah, Hashem is lovingly telling you, "Today I am creating you as a *Beriah Chadashah* / new creation" 'My child, I want you to realize that today is the first day of your life. Happy birthday!'

THE "HEAD" OF THE YEAR

As explored, the power of Hischadshus is rooted in Rosh Hashanah, the 'head', the nerve center, the innermost kernel of the entire coming year.

There is something very unique about the head, and particularly the brain or mind. In the physical realm of time and space, it takes a certain amount of time to travel a given distance. Yet, within the mind, a person can travel instantaneously to any place they want. In the blink of an eye, a person can mentally travel to the outer reaches of the planet, and beyond.

There are no set limitations to the imagination. So long as it is something conventionally possible (unlike a full sized elephant passing through the head of a needle, *Berachos*, 55b. See also *Sefer haMa'amarim*, [Rebbe Rayatz] 5700, Purim) we can easily think about it or picture it.

There is little or no *Gevul* / boundary or limitation inherent in the mind. Everything is possible, if we truly believe in it. In a certain sense, this is a *Koach Ein Sofi* / an infinite power.

Rosh Hashanah is the head, the brain, housing the 'mind' or intelligence of the coming year. During this holy day we are given the gift of entering into the 'headspace' of time, allowing us to reset the 'data source' of the year and start to live in the way we truly desire.

It is of little importance how we lived our lives up until Rosh Hashanah. After processing and owning the effects of our misaligned behaviors during the previous month of Elul, we are now blessed with the insight, "I would like to live more deeply, starting right now. Perhaps in many ways I have been semi-conscious and mindlessly reactive — but today is my birthday, the first day of my new life. I have the power to be new again and always."

Rosh Hashanah offers us this transformative gift spontaneously. We just need to be alert and awake enough to tap into the Koach of this insight, which is revealed to the world on Rosh Hashanah.

Chapter Three
AUTHORING OUR OWN STORY

WE ALL STRIVE TO BE CREATIVE, FOR WE ARE ALL BORN *B'TZELEM ELOKIM* / IN THE IMAGE OF THE ULTIMATE CREATOR. Creativity is part and parcel of our existential and spiritual nature. Our true pleasure is aroused when we work on something and create it. The human was created to exert effort, to produce. "A person would rather possess one coin earned than nine coins granted" (*Bava Metzia*, 38a). "A person would rather possess a lesser amount earned than a greater amount given" (*Sifri*, Parshas Ha'azinu). If something is given to us for free, it feels like the 'bread of shame'; there is a subtle sense of shame in 'eating' or receiving from another that which we did not earn or generate ourselves (Yerushalmi, *Arlah*, 1:3).

One reason our souls come down to this world (*Magid Meis-harim*, Bereishis, 14 Teves. *Chesed l'Avraham*, 4:4) is to become more and more like the Creator, by becoming active co-creators in developing our characters and lives — 'earning' or being the 'cause' of the goodness we experience.

Human creativity and the cosmic creative process mirror each other. To a large extent, what we observe in the 'outside' world is an image of what exists 'inside' of us. The 'objective' universe, as we see it, is tailored to our subjective projection, and we interpret the outer world based on our private, internal universe. If this process of projection and interpretation were not constant, we would not perceive our creative role in the world, and we would not be able to take responsibility for what we create. If we simply lived in a place of the outer 'effects' and not in a place of the inner 'causes' of our life, we would not be stimulated to evaluate our consciousness and behavior and do Teshuvah, return to authenticity.

A 'creator' is one who masters life, not one who is mastered *by* life. A creator is not at the mercy of his or her surroundings; their emotions and character traits are based not on coincidental circumstances, triggers or causes. Rather, a creator *is* the cause; the architect of his or her own reality and experience.

Some people must endure tragedy in order to gain empathy, and some must be surrounded by kindness in order to be open and giving. However, a creator does not need such external causes to induce his empathy or kindness. Nor does a creator allow himself to be dictated by his external surroundings and conditions. He searches deep within his own mind and heart and develops positive and 'G-dly' traits through true persistent introspection. By revealing and drawing inner truths into his thoughts, feelings and actions, he creates his own experiences. He builds his character from within.

There are those that need to be smiled at in order for them to smile; they need to be complimented to feel good about themselves, and they feel down when they are criticized. These are all examples of living from the outside-in. However, those who live from the inside-out *choose* to be compassionate, to show love or friendship regardless of what others show them. They exercise free choice in interacting positively and righteously with others, and do not wait passively for the other to initiate. They are living as the cause of their life and on account of their self-generated love and positivity. As a result of this, people around them respond in kind.

LET US CREATE A HUMAN BEING

When the Torah says in *Bereishis* (1:26), נעשה אדם / "Let Us make a human being," who is the plural "Us"? On a deep level, the "Us" is HaKadosh Baruch Hu and us human beings, together in collaboration. The Creator is saying, 'I am giving you your potential. Create yourself together with Me. Develop yourself using your inner strength and abilities. Let us together, make and fashion you and the world you experience.' We become 'our own maker' through our נעשה / "Let Us make."

Eventually, the highest level of living up to our potential and actualizing our lives, is through acceptance upon ourselves of the Creator's Torah through the process of נעשה ונשמע / "We will do ('actively *make* our lives') and we will listen ('contemplatively understand ourselves')."

Our inner world is the 'cause' of our outer world. The Creator is calling upon us to not surrender to our outer circumstances, to not just be an object, upon which things are imprinted, but rather to be a self-possessed subject, in the sense of one who does the imprinting. If we do not heed this calling, then our lives are merely at the effect of seemingly random circumstances, and we are no longer collaborating with the Creator in the creation of ourselves. When we surrender our creative ability, our Tzelem Elokim, we then begin to feel that we have no choices to make, and we are encased within the predicaments surrounding us. Our world feels separate from the "Us" of our creative process with the Creator. We sense the spoiled taste of the 'bread of shame'.

In life, we can see ourselves either as a determining factor in our experience, or as an already-determined outcome. This is our fundamental freedom, and the fundamental choice we all have to make. We can either be the cause of our life and live from the inside-out, or we can be the effect of what happens to us, and live from the outside-in. "Let *Us* create man," means that ultimately we are each responsible for the human being that we become.

Here is an example from day-to-day life: you wake up in the morning and it is rainy and gloomy outside. Do you automatically feel low energy or down? If you do, you are approaching life from the outside-in, as an effect rather than a cause of your reality. In this scenario, the weather is dictating how you feel. The same is true if you wake up in the morning and the sun is shining and you automatically think to yourself, "Today is going to be a great day!" Again, the outside world is dictating how you feel internally. But if you wake up in the morning and you declare, "Today is going to be a great day, rain or shine," you are choosing, and by extension, you are creating your day. You are choosing your experience of the world, and choosing your response to what you encounter. Your inner intent becomes an active participant in the larger context of life.

We are all gifted with a spark of the Creator, and created in the Divine image. This Divine inheritance is what gives us the drive and the ability to become co-creators of our lives. It also gives us the capacity to return to conscious choice whenever we have missed the mark and submitted to circumstances. We may not have control over what life places before us — whether it is sunny or rainy, whether another person insults us or praises us — but we always have the power to begin again and choose how we are going to process and respond to stimuli. When we return to making conscious decisions we reactivate the Divine spark, the gift of free will, and become again the cause of our life. We are, in that moment, choosing how we are going to live, no matter what may happen. Every moment of free choice that we attain builds our ability to attain it again in the future.

Rosh Hashanah is the first day, the 'head' of all the moments of the year. It is the foundation upon which the entire year is "made"; how we set ourselves up during Rosh Hashanah influences how our year will unfold. The sound of the Shofar blast centers us. It shakes us out of the dependency and infatuation with externalities, and compels us to be more real and more transparent. Ultimately, it propels us inwards, returning us home to our inner core. It brings us back to the 'head' of consciousness, which is free choice, to live responsibility and with intention.

On Rosh Hashanah we need to ensure that we are setting ourselves up to be creators, living from the place of our *Tzelem Elokim*, the inner quality of 'Creator' that exists within all of us, the spark of the Divine "Us."

PREGNANT WITH OURSELVES

As we have mentioned, Rosh Hashanah is not actually the "birthday of the world." The creation of the world itself, the First Day of Creation, occurred five days prior to Rosh Hashanah, on the 25th of Elul. Rather, Rosh Hashanah represents the Sixth Day of Creation, the birthday of humanity, of Adam and Chavah, of *us*. Yet, a simple glance at the narrative of Creation reveals something peculiar in this regard. Here is the way the Torah describes the Six Days of Creation:

Day One: Hashem creates the potential of everything, the heavens and the earth and the primordial Light.

Day Two: Hashem creates the sky and separates the upper and lower waters.

Day Three: Hashem reveals the surface of the earth from beneath the waters, collected into seas.. The earth is made to house plant life both large and small. And Hashem creates this plantlife to be self-sustaining; as plants contain their seeds within them.

Day Four: Hashem creates the celestial spheres, the sun, moon, stars, and thus the seasons, days and nights.

Day Five: Hashem creates all that lives in the water and sky, the fish, insects and all birds.

Day Six: Hashem creates the land animals, and finally, the human being.

The fact that land animals and human beings are created on the same day, suggests that man has more in common with the beasts of the wild, than a lion has in common with a bird or fish, which were created on different days.

It would seem that all the animals should have been created on Day Five, and man should have been created alone on Day Six; as Day Three is the creation of all vegetation and Day Four of all the celestial spheres. Yet, the Torah is telling us something profound. In the Rosh Hashanah Tefilos / prayers we recite, היום הרת עולם / *HaYom Haras Olam* / which literally means "Today the world is gestating," or, put another way, today the world is 'pregnant'.

Olam / world can also mean 'forever'. In this way, HaYom Haras Olam can be translated as "Today (the 'present') is perpetually pregnant." This means that on this day, as on the first day of Adam and Chavah's creation, we, i.e. "the world," are 'pregnant' with the potential to become truly human, to live b'Tzelem Elokim. Yet, the 'world' and us are only in potential, in gestation, and our birth is not inevitable; the 'birth' of becoming a true human being is up to us. We ourselves have to manifest this and birth ourselves into the coming year.

To birth ourselves as a freely-choosing human being, demands *Chochmah* / wisdom. Interestingly, Chazal refer to a midwife, one who helps the mother give birth and release the child, as a חכמה / *Chachamah* (Mishnah, *Shabbos*, 128b), and blowing the Shofar as well is also called a חכמה / *Chochmah*, a practical wisdom (*Rosh Hashanah*, 29b). For it is through the act of blowing the Shofar, that we birth ourselves and a beautiful new year of blessings into this world.

We need to actively harness our higher intellect in order to birth ourselves anew. For without such wisdom we are, in many respects, mere animals of the field. If we surrender to our selfish or base instincts, and behave like animals who do not have intellect or free choice, we will, sadly, resemble such animals.

Indeed the human dimension of a 'human being' is not a given, rather it is something that needs to be accessed, earned and self-created.

What we therefore celebrate on Rosh Hashanah is our 'pregnancy', the fact that we 'carry' the potential within us to rise above our animal self and become a true human being. Yet, we need to nurture this innate ability in order to birth ourselves in the light of the Divine Image. This is the call of the Shofar: "Wake up to your potential! You have so much possibility. You can live on such a high level. You carry a Divine soul within you. Choose it, carry it, nurture it, and birth it into the world, for 'today is the birth of your world, your humanity.'"

Chapter Four
TWO DAYS OF ROSH HASHANAH:
Spiritual Judgment & Physical Judgment

BEFORE WE DELVE INTO THE MEANING OF THE TWO DAYS OF ROSH HASHANAH, WHAT THEY EMBODY AND REPRESENT, A FEW BASIC QUESTIONS NEED TO BE ANSWERED. The Torah simply says, "On the first day of the seventh month, a day of (blowing the) *Teru'ah* (Shofar) shall be to you." It appears as a 'one day' Yom Tov in the Torah, yet we find in the times of the later Prophets, and even in the Land of Israel, that Rosh Hashanah was celebrated for two days (*Nechemyah*, 8:2-13. Says Rashi, ad loc., וביום השני של ראש השנה. Rashi, *Beitzah*, 6a). Why this change, and why two days?

In fact, in the Torah, all holidays are defined as one day; there is one day of Shavuos just as there is one day of Yom Kippur. However, outside of *Eretz Yisrael* / Israel, all Yamim Tovim besides Yom Kippur are celebrated for two days (יש מחמירים לעשות שני ימים יום כפורים ויש לזה התרה ואין לנהוג בחומרא זו משום דיש לחוש שיבא לידי סכנה: Rama, *Orach Chayim*, 624:5. רבא הוה רגיל דהוה יתיב בתעניתא תרי יומי *Rosh Hashanah*, 21a. Says Rabbeinu Chananel, ומלתא יתירתא עבד ולא חובה הוא עליו).

Why are holy days celebrated for two days in the diaspora, whereas in Israel for only one day? And why is Rosh Hashanah then celebrated for two days even in Israel?

First let us understand why there are two days of Yom Tov in the Diaspora.

In Torah law, "the first day of the seventh month" is the day of Rosh Hashanah. Months, of course, follow the lunar cycle, and in the times of the Beis haMikdash, the beginning of the new monthly cycle was established when two witnesses came to the High Court and testified that they had seen the new moon.

A lunar cycle is 28 days, however, because of its interaction with the solar cycle within our vantage point, it usually takes approximately 29.5 days for the new moon to be revealed to the eye. Since the moon is only visible after 29 days, and even then it might not be immediately seen, months can have either 29 or 30 days.

If, on the 30th day of a month, two witnesses came forward and properly testified that they saw the new moon, then the High Court would declare *Mekudash Mekudash* / "sanctified, sanctified," and that day would become Rosh Chodesh, the first day of the new month. As a result, the previous month would be retroactively defined as a 29-day month. If no witnesses came forward on the 30th day of the month, (or came later in the afternoon), then the High Court would establish the following day as the first day of the new month, and the previous month would have had 30 days.

After the High Court had established the new month, only those close enough to Yerushalayim would know when the new month had begun. This is because messengers would be sent out to notify Klal Yisrael of the day when Rosh Chodesh had occurred. In those times, there were no reliable means of communication other than traveling by foot or by animal, and for those who lived further than a 15 day route from Yerushalayim, the timing of the 15th day would be uncertain. The Yom Tov of Pesach, for example, *must* begin on the 15th day of Nisan. Since the distant communities could not have been informed that the previous month had been only 29 days, the day that they might assume to be the 15th, based on their own observations of the moon, could in fact be the 14th.

Our Sages ruled that such a community should celebrate Pesach on *both* days: on the day they assumed to be the 15th, and on the day they assumed to be the 16th of the month, but might in fact have really been the 15th. Since one of the two days would be the actual 15th day of the month, the actual day of Pesach, the distant communities would fulfill the Mitzvos of Pesach on the correct day. As for the inevitable outcome of celebrating one of the two days of Pesach on the wrong day, a *Safek* / doubt regarding a *Mitzvah d'Oraysa* / Torah-based Mitzvah should be approached with stringency; it is better to celebrate Yom Tov on the wrong day than to not celebrate it on the right day.

This is the historical and Halachic reason that holidays are observed for two days in locations outside of the Land of Israel, where it would have taken longer than 15 days for messengers to arrive. Today, despite the numerous advances in calendrical science, we continue this practice since it was the universal custom of our ancestors.[*]

---

[*] According to the Rambam, כל מקום שהיו השלוחין מגיעין היו עושין את המועדות יום טוב אחד ככתוב בתורה / "Every place that the messengers would reach, they would make the festivals, one day Yom Tov — as is written in the Torah": *Kiddush haChodesh*, 3:11. In other words, a new city that was built in Israel would need to keep two days of Yom Tov, as no messengers had ever been sent there... או שהיא עיר שנתחדשה במדבר ארץ ישראל או מקום ששכנו בו ישראל עתה. עושין שני ימים כמנהג רב העולם / "Or if it is a newly formed city in the Midbar of the Land of Israel, or a place that Jews inhabit (only) now, they make two days like the custom of the majority of the world": *Kiddush haChodesh*, 5:12. Since אין עשיית יום טוב אחד תלויה בקריבת המקום. כיצד, אם יהיה מקום בינו ובין ירושלים מהלך חמשה ימים או פחות שבודאי אפשר שיגיעו להן שלוחין, אין אומרין שאנשי מקום זה עושין יום טוב אחד, שמי יאמר לנו שהיו השלוחים יוצאין למקום זה, שמא לא היו השלוחים יוצאין למקום זה מפני שלא היו שם ישראל / "The observance of one day of the other festivals does not depend upon the proximity of a location to Jerusalem. For example, a locality at a distance of five days' journey or less from Jerusalem could certainly have been reached by the messengers in time; yet it cannot be said that the residents of this place should observe only one day. As who will tell us that the messengers went out to this place? Possibly no messengers were ever sent out to this

Rosh Hashanah, however, poses an additional set of issues since Rosh Hashanah is also the *first* day of the new month of Tishrei, as opposed to the 15th day in the middle of the month, when the other major festivals begin. When the 30th day of the previous month of Elul arrived, no one in a distant community could know for certain if witnesses had shown up at the Sanhedrin having seen the new moon, making that day into Rosh Hashanah, the first day of the month of Tishrei. Neither could they know if no witnesses were showing up, making that day the 30th of Elul and the next day Rosh Hashanah (Although Elul, since the times of Ezra, is fixed as a 29-day month: *Rosh Hashanah*, 19b).

---

place because there were no Jews there" *Ibid*, 5:9. (And what the Rambam writes ובני ארץ ישראל בזמן הזה עושין יום אחד כמנהגן שמעולם לא עשו שני ימים / "But the residents of Eretz Yisrael at our time should continue to keep only one day, according to their [ancient] custom, for they never observed two days" Ibid, 5:6, this refers to the parts of Eretz Yisrael that were settled and the messengers would come. *Shu't Sheilas Ya'avetz*, Siman, 168). Yet, most Rishonim and the Geonim hold that today the distinction between celebrating a one-day and a two-day Yom Tov is the difference between Eretz Yisrael and the Diaspora; in Eretz Yisrael there is only one day, and in the Diaspora there are two, this is the opinion made popular by the Ritva, ואי אמאי נהוג כ"ע למעבד בא"י כל המועדות יום א' לבד מר"ה ובני חוץ לארץ עושין אותן כולם שני ימים: *Ritva*, Rosh Hashanah, 18a. *Ritva*, Sukkah, 43a. See also, *Shu't Eretz HaTzvi*, Siman, 41. הקב"ה ציוה את משה עבדו והוא אמר לישראל, כי בארץ יהיה להם יום אחד, ובחו"ל שני ימים, וכן היה מעולם / "HaKadosh Baruch Hu commanded Moshe, who told it over to Klal Yisrael, that in the Land they will have a one-day Yom Tov, and in the Diaspora they will have two days, and that is the way it was established": Rav Saadia Gaon, quoted in *Shu't Mishpetei Uziel*, 3, Orach Chayim, 47. *Otzar haGeonim*, (4) Beitza, Teshuvos. In other words, this distinction already existed from the time of Moshe. See also Rashi, who apparently makes the same distinction, albeit, according to Rashi it is an injunction of Chazal — חכמים קבעום לחובה על בני גולה לעשותם שני ימים טובים לדורות: *Beitza*, 4b.

On Rosh Hashanah, there were specific offerings and songs of the Levi'im / Levites that needed to be offered and sung in the Beis haMikdash, yet the witnesses could arrive at the Sanhedrin until the end of the 30th day of Elul. Suppose the witnesses showed up a few minutes before the end of the 30th day; that would mean that it had been Rosh Hashanah and yet, inappropriately, the offerings and songs of a regular weekday had already been performed. Because of this problem, our sages and the prophets of the Beis haMikdash period established that on the 30th of Elul, just in case witnesses would end up coming, we would not do any mundane activities and the day was sanctified. They furthermore established that the witness could not arrive after the afternoon Minchah offering to testify that it was already Rosh Hashanah. In case they did come after that late hour (since theoretically, if their testimony was accepted, that day would have been [the *only* day of] Rosh Hashanah), both the present day and the next would be sanctified as holy — the present day with no work and the following day with the proper offerings and songs for Rosh Hashanah (*Beitzah*, 5a. Rashi, ad loc. *Yerushalmi, Eiruvin,* 3:9).

In this way, even during the times of the Beis haMikdash, and even in Israel and Yerushalayim and in the Beis haMikdash itself, Rosh Hashanah was at times celebrated for two days.* This two-day celebration is referred to as *Yoma Arichta /*

---

* The only puzzling issue is why then is the first day of Rosh Hashanah the 1st of Tishrei and not the 30th of Elul? The simple answer could be the following. Originally, when Rosh Chodesh was established through testimony, and when witnesses arrived too late on the 30th of Elul, after the Minchah service, indeed the two days of Rosh Hashanah were the 30th of Elul and

one long day. The entire 48 hours of Rosh Hashanah is considered a single extended day.

The concept of one long day of 48 hours is also related to the fact that the 'first Rosh Hashanah' was also 'one long day' with 48 hours. The day upon which Adam and Chavah were created was Friday the 30th of Elul. This Friday was 24 hours long, yet according to tradition, on that evening there was no darkness: "the night was illuminated as the day," and it only became dark on Saturday night (*Medrash Shocher Tov*, Tehilim, 92). As such, the two days of Friday and Shabbos were "one long day" (*Yearos D'vash*, 1, Derush 11. Chida, *P'nei Dovid*, Bereishis, 19).

Today, even as the new months are based on precise calculation and we have a set calendar, we continue the tradition of our ancestors as a reminder of the time when we established

---

the first of Tishrei. However, today we use a set calendar and Elul is always a 29 day month (and in fact Elul has been a 29 day month for thousands of years: *Rosh Hashanah*, 19b), thus we celebrate the two days of Rosh Hashanah on the first and second of the month of Tishrei. Alternatively, when the months were sanctified by witnesses and no witnesses showed up on the 30th of the month, that day remained the 30th of the previous month and the next day was the first day of the new month. On Rosh Hashanah, however, (as above,) there was a decree not to accept witnesses after a certain hour on the 30th day, and so, potentially the 30th could have been the first of the month, thus it is considered as the first of the month, and the second day of Rosh Hashanah the second day of the month. Indeed, Rashi maintains that when no witnesses show up early on the first potential day for Rosh Hashanah and the second day was sanctified as Rosh Chodesh (Rosh Hashanah), still, we count the days of the month from the first day. Rashi, *Menachos*, 100b. See also Tosefos Shantz, *Pesachim*, 47a.

the new months the way the Torah tells us to — with witness-es. As such, we all celebrate Rosh Hashanah for two days, and these 48 hours are considered as one long day.

Interestingly, since our calendar is based upon calculation, we now know for certain that the first day of Rosh Hashanah is the first day of the new month and the second day of Rosh Hashanah is the second day of the new month. Therefore, the first day of Rosh Hashanah is clearly a Torah-based obligation, whereas the second day, one might assume, is a Rabbinical enactment. On the other hand, in the times of the Beis haMik-dash, if witnesses did not appear on the first day which could potentially be celebrated as Rosh Hashanah, then the *first* day would be retroactively revealed as the Rabbinical obligation (as it was really the 30th day of the previous month), and the second day would have been the Torah obligation, as it was the actual first day of the new month.

DEEPER REASONS FOR THE TWO-DAY HOLIDAY

Everything has both an outer and an inner reason, a body and a soul, a vessel and a light. The above discussion was the 'body' or the 'outer' reason for why we observe two days of Rosh Hashanah, in both Israel and the diaspora, even though we know for certain when the first day of the month is. How-ever, there is also a deeper reason why this is the case.

In general, the inner reason that we celebrate holidays for two days, rather than one, outside of Eretz Yisrael is that the *Ohr* / light of the Yom Tov that is revealed within 'exile' can only be revealed in two distinct and separate stages, as the very definition of exile means separation and alienation. The first day illuminates our spiritual experience of Yom Tov, and the second day illuminates our physical experience. In the language of the holy Arizal, "On 'day one' there is an elevation of the internal, the level of souls (*Neshamos*), and on 'day two' the external is also elevated (*Olamos*)" (*Sha'ar haKavanos*, Inyan Rosh Hashanah, Derush Beis). In a world of exile and separation, the physical and the spiritual, the external and the internal, are separated from each other, and therefore, two days are required for full assimilation of the light of the Yom Tov.[*]

For this reason, the 'judgment' of Rosh Hashanah as well is divided into two; on 'day one' of Rosh Hashanah there is a judgment on *Neshamos* / souls, the inner aspect of reality, and on day two there is a judgment on the *Olam* / world, the

---

[*] In *Derech Mitzvosecha* (Hosafos, 198a), the Tzemach Tzedek writes: ענין יו"ט שני של גליות, שבא"י עושי' יו"ט ראשון ואחרון של פסח וסוכות ויו"ט של עצרת הכל יום א' ובח"ל עושים שני ימים, ויובן עפמ"ש בס' אור נערב להרמ"ק ז"ל שח"ל להיותו גשמי אינו יכול לקבל ההארה ביום א' כמו שמקבלת א"י אלא מתחלקת לשני ימים כו', ופי' כי כל יו"ט הוא המשכת והתגלות קדושה עליונה מלמעלה מהזמן בבחי' זמן (כמ"ש במ"א ע"פ מארז"ל ישראל אינהו דקדשינהו לזמני' משא"כ שבת הוא למעלה מהזמן כי הוא בחי' עליו' העולמו' ולכן אינו משתנה לפי המקום וח"ל וא"י שוים בו) ולכן עושי' אותו היום יו"ט: והנה בא"י שהיא ארץ אשר ה' דורש אותה שקרובה לאלקות ומזוככת במעלה ומדרגה אזי יכולים לקבל ביום א' אות' ההארה המאירה ומתגלה, משא"כ בח"ל אין הארה זו מתיישבת ביום א' ולא יכולים להכילה כלל ביום א' מצד ריחוק מעלת ח"ל מאלקות ולכן עושי' ב' ימים שבמשך ב' ימים יכולה היא שתתקבל כמו שבא"י ביום א' כו. Similarly, the Alter Rebbe teaches: ועד"ז יש לפרש בענין יו"ט שביו"ט ראשון מקבלים כנס"י מבחי' ה' עילאה וביו"ט שני מבחי' ה' תתאה. ...אפ"ל שזהו ענין יו"ט שני כו' ואפשר שהן הן ג"כ ב' בחי' אספקלריא הנ"ל. ועפ"ז י"ל שזהו מ"ש הרמ"ק בספר אור נערב שבח"ל אינם יכולים לקבל ההארה ביום אחד כמו שמקבלים בא"י אלא צ"ל יום שני כו Likutei *Torah*, Derushim Shemini Atzeres, 92c. The kernel of this idea is rooted in a Torah by the Ramak, in *Ohr Ne'erav*, as quoted. Interestingly enough, as the Rebbe pointed out, in the known editions of Ohr Ne'erav this Torah is not found. The Rebbe, *HaMelech b'M'Sibaso* 1, p. 163.

outer reality, the body (*Ya'aros D'vash*, 2, Derush 1 and Derush 10, *Bnei Yissaschar*, Tishrei, 2:2. *Avodas Yisrael*, Derush Rosh Hashanah sheChal b'Shabbos). In the language of the holy Arizal, "On 'day one' there is an elevation of the internal, the level of souls, and on 'day two' the external is also elevated" (*Sha'ar haKavanos*, Inyan Rosh Hashanah, Derush 2).

Appropriately, on the first day of Rosh Hashanah we pray for matters of the soul, and on the second day, for matters of the body (*Chidushei haRim*, Rosh Hashanah, 253). On the first day, we focus on co-creating our spiritual, mental and emotional wellbeing, and on the second day of Rosh Hashanah, we focus our attention on co-creating our physical life; livelihood, health, and so forth.

Before our collective physical and spiritual exile from the Holy Land, when we were more unified within ourselves, with each other, with the world, and with Hashem — we were able to receive the *Ohr* / light of Yom Tov on all levels at once. As there was yet no artificial separation imposed between body and soul, we were able to elevate ourselves in both the internal and the external dimensions simultaneously, all in one day.

Although the lights of Shabbos and Yom Tov are beyond space and time, they are expressed in every single place on the globe according to its particular time zone. Indeed it can be Yom Tov in one area of the world and in another time zone Yom Tov has already concluded (Alter Rebbe, *Shulchan Aruch*, Orach Chayim, (second version) 1:8. *Teshuvas haRadbaz*, 1, Siman 76). Moreover, the Ohr of Yom Tov is revealed according to the particular vessels of each place. In a place of exile, first the Ohr is revealed in the spiritual vessels of the people of that area, on day one, and then in the vessels of their physical experience, on day two. In other words, the light of Yom Tov is relative; one's positionality in space and time affects their ability to access and receive the Divine influx as it enters the world.

Rosh Hashanah is when we are judged on how well we are living up to our personal mandate, our purpose, our *Tikkun /* soul articulation. Since on Rosh Hashanah we commemorate our emergence as human beings, distinct from the creation of the world as a whole, it is appropriate for us to ask, "How well am I performing my role as a human being?" It is a time to judge ourselves and ask, "Who am I? Do I own my life, or does my life own me?"

Our comprehensive evaluation on Rosh Hashanah includes the Divine allocation of all spiritual progress we will attain in the coming year, as well as all physical abundance that we will receive. As mentioned, Rosh Hashanah is the "head" of the year, not just a beginning. Just as the brain controls all that occurs in the body, so too Rosh Hashanah is the essential node through which the entirety of the coming year first flows. Everything physical and spiritual that you will receive or experience in the coming year is drawn into potential on Rosh Hashanah. During the course of the year the blessings we received on Rosh Hashanah will be unpacked and revealed.

With regards to the blowing of the Shofar on Rosh Hashanah, the verse in *Tehilim* (81:4-5) says, "Blow the Shofar...because it is a חק לישראל / *Chok l'Yisrael* / a decree for Israel and a משפט לאלקי יעקב / *Mishpat l'Elokei Yaakov* / a judgment for the G-d of Yaakov." This reveals two dimensions of judgment on Rosh Hashanah: "Chok l'Yisrael" and "Mishpat l'Elokei Yaakov." The *Chok* / decree is a judgment for our physicality in the coming year (in general *Chok* refers to physical sustenance, הטריפני לחם חקי: *Mishlei*, 30:8. *Beitzah*, 16a). The *Mishpat* / judgment is for the *Elokus* / G-dliness of Yaakov, meaning, what level and type of spirituality will we, the children of Yaakov, attain during the coming year (*Likutei Torah*, Derushei Rosh Hashanah, 54d -55a. See *Likutei Sichos*, 19, p. 292 and the sources quoted. First the blessings are revealed on a spiritual plane, and then a physical plane: *Sichos Kodesh*, Rosh Hashanah, Tav-Shin-Yud-Gimel).

In general, the *Shefa* / flow of blessing originates in the spiritual realm and comes down into the physical realm, so that is the sequence of its appearance here as well; the first day is a judgment on the spiritual blessings of the coming year and the second day is a judgment on the physical blessings.

Essentially, this means that the judgment of Rosh Hashanah is not over after the first day. This is aligned with the opinion that we should say *leShanah Tovah Tikasev* / "for a good year you shall be written," even on the second night of Rosh Hashanah (*Taz*, Orach Chayim, 582:9:4. Although he writes that we should do so for a different reason. Most authorities write that we should not say this blessing on the second night — and not even on the first day, after the third hour of the day. *Levush, Magen Avraham, Mishnah Berurah*, ad loc.).

We ought to offer others this blessing on both nights, as the first night we are wishing them spiritual success, and the second night we are wishing them physical and material success.

Day one, says the Arizal, corresponds to the inner *Rosh* / head of all the Sefiros, which is the Sefirah of *Keser* / crown, the deepest transcendental will and desire for Creation. Day two corresponds to the Rosh of the Sefiros that is *within* the Ten Sefiros, which is the Sefirah of *Chochmah* / wisdom revealed within Creation. Therefore, our movement through the 'Ten Days of Teshuvah', which begins with Rosh Hashanah and ends with Yom Kippur, is a movement from Keser to the tenth Sefirah, *Malchus* / kingship. This Malchus then becomes the Keser of the subsequent structure, which is the entire coming year.

Of course, the ultimate work of Yisrael, our work, is to ensure that there is no separation between the realms of souls and worlds, spirit and body. Even though we live in exile, in a place-time-consciousness of separation, we aspire for *Yichud* / unity. To illustrate this, the numerical value of the word *Yisrael* is 541, which is also the value of the word *Olam* / world (146) plus *Neshamah* / soul (395); 146+395=541, as we live to reveal the underlying unity between the 'outer' world and the 'inner' soul. *Yisrael*, as well, equals "light and darkness," *Ohr* / light is 207, and *v'Choshech* / 'and darkness' is 344; 207+344=541, alluding to the even deeper work of forging a unity between the apparent darkness and confusion in life, and the inner world of light, meaning and purpose.

SPIRITUAL & PHYSICAL
AS THE INTERIOR & EXTERIOR

On a more subtle level, there are many instances when it is difficult to differentiate between physical and spiritual. Our physicality can be deeply spiritual, for example, when making a living is done as part of our spiritual path, or in order to give Tzedakah or help people in other ways.

The language the Arizal uses is that there is a judgment of the פנימי / *Penimi* / internal or 'spiritual' dimension on the first day of Rosh Hashanah, and there is a judgment of the חיצוני / *Chitzoni* / external or 'physical' dimension on the second day.

Our *Penimi* / internal reality is largely determined by our mindset, emotions and spiritual clarity; how we think and feel about life. But how you think and feel is actually going to manifest in your *Chitzoni* / external world. Even though on the first day of Rosh Hashanah there is a download for our internal, subjective world, how we are going to think and feel in the coming year, and on the second day there is a download of how we are going to act and experience the external and objective world, these inner and outer dimensions are not really all that separate.

Parnasah / finances, for example, are not material only; they are a direct manifestation of how our Penimiyus is being expressed in our worldly experience. In this subtler understanding of the relationship between physicality and spirituality they are in truth one seamless reality. Indeed, Rosh Hashanah is understood as one seamless process as well; one long day, not two compartmentalized days, a single continuous download of blessings for the coming year.*

---

* Although on some level, all judgments on Rosh Hashanah — even the more spiritual, mental, and internal forms, are mostly related to our physical well-being: *Hagahos Maimoniyos*, Hilchos Teshuvah 3, in the name of the Ramban. Ramban, *Sha'ar Gemul*. although see *Tosefos* on *Rosh Hashanah*, 16b. Tishrei is connected with Adam whereas Nisan is connected with Klal Yisrael. In Tishrei, the world is pregnant, Haras Olam, only to be birthed in Nisan: *Pri Eitz Chayim*, Sha'ar haShofar, 5. See also, *Elye Rabbah*, Orach Chayim, 592: 6. ולעניות דעתי לתרץ על פי מה שהקשה תוס' בראש השנה דף כ"ז על ר' אלעזר הקליר ומסקי דבתשרי עלה במחשבה לבראות ולא נברא העולם עד ניסן אם כן שפיר נקט הריון שהוא על מחשבה אבל לידה נקרא מעשה. See also, *Ben Yehoya-dah*, Rosh Hashanah, 10b. Winter is a time of pregnancy, when the world is more concealed, for this metaphysical reason there is less flourishing of vegetation and less sunlight. Spring is the birth of the world. In Tishrei, the Chitzoni worlds were actually created. This is the first month of the solar year, the sun being connected with the 'revealed', the external world, whereas in Nisan, the Penimi world of souls was created: *Sha'ar haKavanos*, Derush 1, Rosh Hashanah. Nisan is the first month of the year, the beginning of the lunar year. The moon represents the hidden, the mystery, the internal world. In other words, the 'birth of Klal Yisrael' is in Nisan, as Chazal tell us: "the going out of Egypt was like a fetus being removed from her mother's belly." The solar year flows from Tishrei to Nisan, following the 'evolutionary' order of Creation: first the Chitzoni of the world was created and only on the Sixth Day were Adam and Chavah created, beings with Neshamos, and only then was Shabbos (*vaYi-Nafash* / Nefesh) brought into the world. Even within the creation of Adam, first his body was created and only later did Hashem blow into his nostrils a breath of life: *Sanhedrin*, 38b. What this means is that with regards to the *Penimiyus* of the world, the perspective of the soul, Tishrei is only the pregnancy and Nisan is the real birth. But with regards to the Chitzoniyus of the world, Tishrei is the 'birth' of the world, and Nisan is a further maturation. All opinions agree that Sarah was *Nifkad* / Divinely 'remembered' on Rosh Hashanah (*Rosh Hashanah*, 11a), when she became pregnant with Yitzchak, the first person to be 'born Jewish'. While Avraham *entered into* the covenant — in a sense born as a body and only later manifesting a spiritual soul, as all of Creation — Yitzchak was born into the covenant, born with a Neshamah, and

LEAH & ROCHEL: THOUGHT & SPEECH

The Arizal also speaks of the two days of Rosh Hashanah in relation to Leah and Rochel (the wives of Yaakov), who represent the inner 'world of thought' and the outer 'world of speech', respectively. "The eyes of Leah were tender..." (*Bereishis*, 29:17). The word for "tender," as translated by the Targum, means אינ / 'beautiful'. Leah was "beautiful" in her spiritual Penimiyus; her 'eyes' or inner world was beautiful. By contrast, the Torah describes Rochel as being beautiful on the outside as well: she was "beautiful in appearance and in shape," she had an external beauty.

All *Zivugim* / matches and all relationships that will be formed in the coming year are drawn down on Rosh Hashanah. In general, there are two types of traditional matches, either the male goes out and finds the female, or the female comes to the male (*Medrash Rabbah*, Bereishis, 63:3). Yaakov, the male, went to find Rochel, whereas Rivkah, the female, went to encounter Yitzchak, as the Medrash above writes (*Ohr haTorah*, Bereishis, 864).

If, when a relationship began, the female went and found the male, then we know that the 'judgment' predicting that they would meet had transpired on the first day of Rosh

---

he was born in Nisan, the month of the birth of Klal Yisrael. The Din on Tishrei is primarily with regards to the external reality, the physical world whereas the judgment on Nisan is primarily with regards to the Penimiyus of the world.

Hashanah. This is the paradigm of Leah / spirituality / Penimiyus, as Leah is the one who went to Yaakov.

If the male goes out and finds the female, that means the match was made on the second day of Rosh Hashanah. This is the paradigm of Rochel / physicality / Chitzoniyus, as Yaakov went and found Rochel (*Bnei Yissaschar*, Tishrei Ma'amar 2:15).

Everything begins in the Penimiyus and evolves into the Chitzoniyus; things are first conceived in the inner spiritual realm and then they become manifest in the outer physical realm. On a personal level, this means that our ideas begin in the mind as 'dreams', and then they may move into the practical realm. In this way, the initial opening of our creative process that occurs in our spiritual, mental and emotional faculties is the most difficult stage. Once there is such an opening on the Penimi level, the transition to the physical level is much more smooth. For example, in the context of relationships, a person first needs to dream, imagine, desire and think about a relationship with another; indeed this is actually the hard part — to inwardly make room in their life for that special other they so desire. But once this inner space is created, they will find and attract that person much more easily. In fact, they may even be able to recognize that other person, if the person was already present in their sphere of life. This is another reason why the Arizal teaches that day one of Rosh Hashanah is a time of *Din Kasheh* / harsh judgment, and day two is a time of *Dina Rafiah* / light judgment. The harsher, more complicated judgement is in the realm of spirit and mindset, yet, once there is already an opening with a positive judgment on day one, the lighter judgment flows more effortlessly and moves into the world of matter, the physical world.

DAY 1 OF ROSH HASHANAH	DAY 2 OF ROSH HASHANAH
Rosh 'beyond' all Sefiros: *Keser*	Rosh 'within' the 10 Sefiros: *Chochmah*
Neshamos / Soul / Spirituality	*Olamos* / World / Physicality
Penimiyus / Inner Reality	*Chitzoniyus* / Outer Reality
Leah (*'initiates' relationship with Yaakov*)	Rochel (*Yaakov 'initiates' relationship with her*)
World of Thought	World of Speech
Din Kasheh / harsh judgment	*Dina Rafiah* / light judgment
Cerebral, Intellectual	Practical
Breath within the Shofar	The Actual Shofar

FIRST DAY BREATH, SECOND DAY SHOFAR

Over all, the Mitzvos that are performed through speech, such as telling the story of going out of Egypt on the night of Pesach, affect the inner, spiritual, Penimiyus layer of the world. Mitzvos that we feel, such as loving Hashem, are also in this category. The Mitzvos that require physical actions affect the physical reality, the Chitzoniyus of the world (see *Eitz Chayim*, Sha'ar 40, chap. 3).

Shofar is a unique Mitzvah in that it is an action — we must perform a physical activity with a physical horn (Rashash, *Nahar Shalom*, 38b), and yet it also utilizes 'breath', which is similar to the world of speech but even more inward than speech. Accordingly, Shofar is associated with the service that is *P'nim* / inside the Beis haMikdash (כיון דלזכרון הוא כבפנים דמי: *Rosh Hashanah*, 26a), although it is a physical activity. Shofar thus has a dual nature: it is a Mitzvah of Chitzoniyus and Penimiyus dimensions, requiring both a physical and spiritual act.

Day one of Rosh Hashanah is more connected with the Penimiyus, linked with the first 'breath' of the year. This is the Penimiyus level of the Shofar blowing. The second day of Rosh Hashanah is more connected with the Chitzoniyus level of the Shofar blowing.

The above can help us understand a perplexing issue: when Rosh Hashanah falls on Shabbos we do not blow the Shofar. (The only place the Shofar was blown on Shabbos was in the Beis haMikdash or in a place with an established Beis Din.) The Gemara gives the reason for this (the fear that maybe someone will carry the Shofar in a public domain, see Chapter 12), but it is still puzzling, given that the whole idea of Rosh Hashanah, and the Mitzvah of the day, is Shofar.

Today it is impossible for the second day of Rosh Hashanah to fall out on Shabbos; our calendar dictates that only the first day of Rosh Hashanah can ever be on Shabbos (Tur, *Orach Chayim*, 428). This means that on the day of

'Chitzoniyus' we *always* actually blow the physical Shofar. And only on the first day of Rosh Hashanah, which is the day of Penimiyus, do we not always blow the Shofar physically, as on Shabbos we 'blow' the Shofar on a purely Penimi, meditative level. Therefore, on Shabbos, which is the Penimiyus of the Chitzoni, mundane work week, and on the first day of Rosh Hashanah which is the Penimiyus of the two days, we conceptually 'blow Shofar' on a level of Penimiyus. Regarding the latter, the Rashash writes (*Nahar Shalom*, 38a) that on Shabbos Rosh Hashanah we should contemplate the *Kavanah* / intentions of the Shofar, i.e. the Penimiyus, even though we do not actually blow it on the level of Chitzoniyus. In this way, when Shabbos is the first day of Rosh Hashanah we do 'blow the Shofar', just on a Penimiyus level of Kavanah and desire.

However, in the Beis haMikdash, where the spiritual and the physical were unified and there was no exile and separation, the Chitzoniyus was not separated from the Penimiyus, and we did indeed blow the Shofar even on Shabbos. There, in the Beis haMikdash, thoughts (Penimiyus) were synonymous with actions (Chitzoniyus). For example, in the laws of *Pigul* / invalid sacrifices, if a Cohen did not have proper intentions when offering sacrifices, his thoughts would render the physical offering invalid. In the Beis haMikdash, the Penimiyus and the Chitzoniyus were not considered different; thus we blew the Shofar on the level of Chitzoniyus even on Shabbos, a day of Penimiyus. This was the significance of the Beis haMikdash, it was where the two seemingly variant dimensions of reality and experience were revealed as one.

SERIOUS JOY

Rosh Hashanah is a serious time. We do not recite Hallel, as the Gemara tells us, because it is such a 'serious' time, a time of judgment. "Is it possible," say our sages, "that the King is sitting on the seat of judgment and the books of life and death are open, and we are singing songs?" (*Erchin*, 10b: אפשר מלך יושב על כסא הדין וספרי חיים וספרי מתים פתוחין לפניו וישראל אומרים שירה). However, it is also important to understand that 'serious' does not mean gloomy or downcast; to the contrary, when we are serious enough to realize that Hashem is the Master of our life and that we are in the guiding Hands of HaKadosh Baruch Hu, it brings tremendous inner joy and a profound lightness of being. Joy comes from knowing that "There is a master of this home," that there is order, progress, purpose, and that life is not a chaotic stream of random accidents or aimless and unintentional events. Awakening to this fact brings immeasurable joy and perpetual bliss.

In fact, whenever HaKadosh Baruch Hu 'judges' the world there is joy and the world becomes happier, as order is restored and reestablished. This is the joy in judgment itself. Dovid haMelech expresses this frequently throughout *Tehilim*, for example in Chapter 96: "The heavens will rejoice and the earth will exult; the sea and its fullness will roar. The field and everything in it will jubilate; then all the forest trees will sing praises before Hashem, for He has come, for He has come to judge the earth; He will judge the inhabited world justly and the peoples with His faith." This is the joy of Divine judgement, as everything in the world is re-calibrating and returning to its natural alignment; this process, though difficult and painful at times, brings about a blossoming of profound delight and spiritual pleasure.

When we in fact rejoice that we are to be judged with Divine faithfulness, we open ourselves up to the very purpose of judgment. And when we show that we are ready and open to be accurately judged, this itself creates a *Mituk* / sweetening of Din and all judgments (*Ya'aros D'vash* 1, Derush 6). This, too, increases our joy, and our joy in turn creates an even more favorable judgment.

'BLOW THE SHOFAR WITH PASSION AS IF FOR THE FIRST TIME'

תקעו בחדש שופר / *Tiku baChodesh Shofar* / "Blow, on the new month, the Shofar" (*Tehilim*, 81:4). The Baal Shem Tov raises a question, 'Isn't this statement grammatically incorrect'? The verse should have said תקעו שופר בחדש / *Tiku Shofar baChodesh* / blow the Shofar on the new month, not *Tiku baChodesh Shofar*. Why this peculiar wording? The Baal Shem Tov answers: It means that we always need to blow the Shofar with a sense of '*Chodesh*' or *Chidush* / newness — with joyful excitement as if we are doing it for the first time. If we do not, as the verse continues, there will be *Mishpat l'Elokei Yaakov* / "judgment of the G-d of Yaakov;" there will be judgments against us, 'Yaakov'. We need to ensure that we perform the Shofar blowing — the first Mitzvah of the new year, the foundation for all Mitzvos throughout the entire year — with *Chayus /* aliveness and with passion. This will empower us to approach all our Mitzvos and all of life, with a sense of novelty, wonder and excitement (*Toldos Yaakov Yoseph,* Parshas Tzav. *Keser Shem Tov,* Siman 119. The Levush, seemingly addressing the same peculiar wording in the verse writes, תוקעין ג״כ כל החודש שיעשו טוב. וסמך לדבר תקעו בחדש שופר, משמע שיתקעו חדש שלם: *Orach Chayim,* 581).

Since day two is the day on which we always blow the Shofar, the Baal Shem Tov's lesson most strongly applies to the second day of Rosh Hashanah. We have to blow the Shofar with aliveness, newness and joy, as if it is the first time, even when the first day of Rosh Hashanah was not Shabbos, and we already blew the Shofar. What's more, since the 'physicality' of the second day is the outward expression of the inner 'spirituality' of the first day, in reality it *is* like blowing the Shofar for the first time, on that particular level of our being and of reality.

SECOND DAY / MANIFEST / ACTUALITY

If we can enter the second day of Rosh Hashanah without it seeming old or routine, if we can maintain the same enthusiasm as the first day, it means that we are manifesting 'externally' the positive judgment of the first day. This will also bring us merit for a favorable judgment for the 'external' reality, dispensed on the second day. The positive enthusiasm and renewed joy that we bring to the second day is thus both a sign of and a cause for favorable judgment.

Newness automatically brings excitement and passion. We are all inspired by new projects, fresh ideas, and in this context, the first day of Yom Tov, but this inspiration and excitement comes from 'outside' us. The real *Chidush* / novelty is on the 'second' day, when the Yom Tov and the Shofar are seemingly already routine. If we can become inspired about the day's holiness and the awesome power of the Mitzvah of Shofar on the second day, and not just take them for granted, then we will know that the 'child', the new year, the new 'us', will not only be real 'in utero' — inwardly, as a spiritual, mental and emotional state (first day) — but it will be born and expressed in an outward, 'practical' reality as well. Cultivating enthusiasm on the second day of Rosh Hashanah demonstrates that what needs to be born this coming year, all the blessings we need to receive in our lives, will not only remain a reality in 'pregnant' potential. These blessings will not remain confined to the spiritual and mental realms, but will be born in real time.

When Rebbe Leibel Eiger came home for the first time after becoming a Chassid of Rebbe Mendel of Kotzk, his father asked him, "What did you learn in Kotzk?" "Three things I learned," replied Reb Leibel, "and these are: that a man is a man and an angel is an angel; that if a man wants it enough he can become higher than an angel; and that 'G-d created the beginning' (*Bereishis Bara Elokim*) — but only the beginning; after that it is man who must create the endings." We all start strong, we all get inspired by the events of 'day one', but we cannot honestly take credit for them, because it is Hashem

Who creates beginnings. New beginnings are Divine gifts of motivation and inspiration. But our responsibility is how we create the continuations and the 'endings'; how we show up on day two, and beyond.

Our perseverance on the second day of Rosh Hashanah ensures that the blessings and newness of the coming year do not merely remain concealed in Penimiyus, but are manifest in Chitzoniyus.

לא־תירא לביתה משלג כי כל־ביתה לבש שנים / "She is not worried for her household because of snow, for her whole household is dressed in crimson" (*Mishlei*, 31:21). Inwardly this verse means that, we are not worried about the 'snow', the coldness, the lack of enthusiasm and passion in our *Avodas Hashem* / service of Hashem, because our homes, our space, is covered with שנים / 'two' (see Rashi, ad loc. *Medrash Rabbah*, Mishlei, 31:4. כי כל ביתה לבש שנים, שנים, שבת ומילה. *Tanchuma*, Chayei Sarah, 4); in other words, we have mastered the art of seconds and the reality and requirements of 'day two', we have learned how to self-generate excitement when it is the second (or third or fourth, etc.) time around.

CONFUSE THE SATAN

'Why do we blow the Shofar?' ask our sages, 'Because the Torah told us to blow it. But why, then, do we blow it more than once; why should we proceed to blow a second set, the *Tekias Me'umad*, after we have blown the first set? The reason for this second set, conclude the sages, is לערבב השטן /

l'Arbev haSatan / "to confuse the Satan" (*Rosh Hashanah*, 16a-16b. See *Meiri*, ad loc.; *Ravyah*, Rosh Hashanah, Siman, 529; *Baal haItur*, Shofar, p. 101a). What does this mean? Tosefos (ad loc.) brings down in the name of the Aruch (Rav Nasan ben Yechiel of Rome, c. 1035–1106), that the Satan, the negative / obstructive quality of the universe, 'thinks' that the second blowing of the Shofar is the sound of the coming of Moshiach. But what does this mean?

There are many alternative ways to understand this idea of "confusing of the Satan." In our context it means doing something a second time after the inspiration has faded, yet still doing it with intentionality, passion, and alacrity. If we can pick ourselves up when we are not moved and blow the Shofar again, if we can show up on the second day of Rosh Hashanah when there is no *Bereishis*, no excitement externally generated by the newness of the moment, and self-generate a sense of renewal from within — then we can plow through all obstacles, we can 'confuse the Satan' and truly break all the negativity of the world and usher in Moshiach, a time of pure positivity and holiness. It is truly up to us.

Our second day blowing of the Shofar corresponds to a state of exile, in which there is no externally imposed excitement. This is where the real work is required. If we can preserve our *Hisorerus* / awakening within the paradigm of 'the second day', then we can ensure that the blessings we received on the first day do not remain on a Penimiyus level, but are actually birthed into the world in a tangible form.

The second day is akin to the final blow of the 100 blows; the first 99 blasts represent the cries of a mother who is about to give birth, crying as she is trying to push the baby out, the 100th cry is the one that gets the baby out and into the world. There are 100 cries a mother cries out during childbirth (*Medrash Rabbah*, Vayikra, 27:7). The first 99 cries are pre-birth and with the hundredth cry the child comes out of the womb, and the mother knows she is going to live (*Tanchumah*, Tazriah, 4. *Meshech Chochmah*, Emor). Hashem created the 'beginnings' of the baby and created the miraculous process of development within the womb, yet it is the mother's one hundredth cry at the 'end' of the process that moves the child from a potential within her *P'nimiyus* into an actuality in the Chitzoniyus of the world, a living, breathing child.

This is the power of the 'second' day; to bring all of HaKadosh Baruch Hu's blessings for health, wealth, and happiness down into our lives, and to ensure that they manifest positively in the world. In the birth of the new year, we are thus mother, midwife, and child.

Chapter 5
YOM HADIN: THE TIME OF JUDGMENT & THINKING POSITIVELY

T HE TORAH CALLS THE DAY OF ROSH HASHANAH *YOM TERU'AH* / A DAY OF TERU'AH. *Teru'ah* comes from the root word *Reu'ah* / to tremble, to be in awe (as in *Tero'em b'Shevet Barzel* / תרועם בשבט ברזל — *Tehilim*, 2:9. Ritva, *Rosh Hashanah*, 33b). The Torah does not call Sukkos '*Yom Sukkos*', nor Pesach '*Yom Pesach*', but with regards to Rosh Hashanah the Torah uses the term *Yom Teru'ah*, a day of trembling in judgment. It is not a day in which we sit in a Sukkah or eat Matzah, rather, the entire day is Teru'ah. Rosh Hashanah *is* Teru'ah.

Practically speaking, as one of the three types of Shofar sound, *Teru'ah* refers to the broken-patterned Shofar blast, which arouses trembling or even dread.

TIME OF APPREHENSION & FEAR

On a seasonal level, Teru'ah is connected with the ensuing rainy season in Israel, making it a time of Tefilah /prayer and trembling over the viability of the future (*Ta'anis*, 2b). In preparations for the first rains of the season, fields are sown in Israel during the month of Tishrei. Throughout the fall and winter the crops slowly grow and finally bear fruit and blossom with the onset of spring in Nisan. Then, coming full circle, one harvests their fields and fruits and enjoys them until the middle of Tishrei (*Pesachim*, 36b. Rashi, *Devarim*, 26:11), initiating a new cycle of planting and prayer.

Tefilah and blowing a Teru'ah are deeply linked and, in past centuries, these were commonly performed together in times of need. In fact, blowing a trumpet (or perhaps Shofar, see *Mishnah Berurah* below) is considered by some to be part and parcel of the act of *Davening* / praying. There are two modes of Davening: one with articulated speech and one with the visceral cry of a Teru'ah. In the words of the Rambam, מצות עשה מן התורה לזעק ולהריע ...על כל צרה שתבוא על' הצבור / "It is a positive commandment from the Torah to cry out and sound Teru'ah... for all troubles that come upon the community" (Rambam, *Hilchos Ta'anis*, 1:1. The Magen Avraham wanders why this is no longer practiced — ותמה אני למה אין אנו נוהגין לתקוע בעת צרה הלא מדאורייתא מצוה לתקוע בלא תענית ויש מאחרונים שתירצו שמדאורייתא מצוה זו נוהג רק בא"י ... ויש. *Orach Chayim*, 576.

שכתבו דאפשר דאף בא״י דוקא כשהיה תחת רשותינו ואפשר עוד דדוקא כשהגזרה הוא
על רוב ישראל: Mishnah Berurah, 576:1).

As winter is approaching, feelings of anxiety and Ra'u'ah about the unpredictable coming year are natural sensations and emotions that arise. Today, we live buffered from nature, with heated homes, lit streets, advanced desalinization and irrigation systems. We are no longer so sensitive to the concerns of impending winter. However, we still do feel the effects of colder weather and the loss of sunlight, and these aspects still make a visceral impression upon our psyche. If spring is marked by a tangible lightness and joy, the fall can certainly arouse a more serious, somber response. Similarly, those who are returning to school in the fall sometimes experience a sense of foreboding or a subtle trembling of anxiety or excitement.

DAYS OF AWE IN THE PALPABLE PRESENCE
OF THE HOLY 'OTHER'

Our sages call Rosh Hashanah *Yom haDin* / the Day of Judgment, and the High Holidays *Yamim Noraim* / Days of Awe (The term Yamim Noraim / ימים נוראים seems to have been used for hundreds of years. The Ra'avyah speaks about ימים נוראים. *Ra'avyah*, Berachos, Siman 39: 1). But to fully understand what the latter phrase refers to, we have to delve into what "awe" means, and what it means to 'stand in awe.'

Many assume that awe is 'fear', as this is the Time of Judgment, so we should be in 'awe' or fear of what our judgment will be. Fearing a negative judgment is spiritually shallow and based on mere egoic anxieties. Why, then, did some great Tzadikim speak of being paralyzed, not being able to move a muscle in Davening on the Days of Awe? It was certainly not from fear of having a 'bad' year, as they would have been ready to give up their entire lives for HaKadosh Baruch Hu, and their deepest pleasure was to serve Hashem under any conditions, whether 'good' or 'bad'. Insofar as a difficult year did not phase them, what then was and is the 'fear' or awe being referred to in this context?

Forty days before Yom Kippur is the first day of Elul, the beginning of the Days of Awe, when the 'winds of Elul' begin to blow and awe is palpable. Forty is a powerful number that reminds us of both repentance and revelation. Moshe was up on the mountain for 40 days to receive the first set of *Luchos* / tablets, as well as the second set. During the 40 days of the Yamim Noraim, we strive to receive the revelation that results from true repentance and authentically 'turning around' to face our lives and to face Hashem.

But what does all this have to do with awe? 'Awe', in this context, refers to the moment when you stop being defined by or contained within your limited self, and you enter into a state of being that is much larger and more expansive. Let's say, for example, you chance upon a magnificent sunset and your eyes become entranced by such indescribable beauty, that you become immobilized in a natural state of awe, standing motionless and speechless. In that moment, before you attempt to conceptualize or understand why you are feeling awestruck, before your rational brain tries to make sense of and grasp the experience, you are completely lost in the majesty of the sunset. The Yamim Noraim induce this type of awe, and more. It is a time when we become lost in a reality that is much bigger than our personal self. And after this experience of losing ourselves in awe, we are later able to find ourselves in a recreated, reimagined, healthier and more wholesome sense of self. This is the process and goal of the forty days of awe, from the first of Elul through Yom Kippur.

The ultimate experience of awe, self-negation and self-transcendence is to be touched by Infinity, and to sense the palpable Presence of HaKadosh Baruch Hu, the holy 'Other'. When we are *Lifnei Hashem* / in front of our Creator, we feel real 'awe' (*Toldos Aharon*, Re'eh). This is the deeper sensation of *Yirah* / awe that we experience during these days: "Everyone feels this *Pachad* / urgency and trembling, during these days" (*Yosher Divrei Emes*, 52). It is the experiential practice of *Shivisi Hashem* / placing yourself before Hashem, literally and viscerally.

Imagine the awe you would experience if you were to stand in front of an all-powerful king, in all his glory, and in whose hand was life or death. Your senses would become sharp, your mind and attention would become clear, your entire self, your Gestalt, would become centered, utterly present, alive and focused. Admittedly, this metaphor is hard to understand for modern man, as we have not experienced royalty in this sense. The modern mind struggles with simple Yirah, reverence for another, and sadly even respect. Nevertheless, we can try to imagine living one thousand years ago, when absolute monarchy was the way of rule. Just for a moment, picture yourself living in a small, impoverished town, and one day you are granted an audience with the resplendent king, the absolute ruler, in whose hands is your life, death, and livelihood. Try to feel the awe, the trepidation, the hyper-vigilance, and the instinctive urge to honor him.

This is a mere *Mashal* / metaphor of what it means to stand in the Presence of the King of Kings, the Infinite Power of the Creator of all life. If you truly sense this *Kirvas Hashem* / proximity to the Infinite, everything suddenly changes; you are overwhelmed yet electrified, focused and ready to serve. Your limitations drop away, your self-oriented narrative is silenced, your ego falls away, and you cannot even move from your own initiative, as you are absorbed in the existential embrace of the Unmoved Mover.

A DAY OF JUDGMENT

Rosh Hashanah is called *Yom haDin* / the Day of Judgment, as there is a general judgment and apportioning of all our physical needs and spiritual attainments for the coming year.

Additionally, Rosh Hashanah is called the *Rosh* / head of the year, not the *Techilas* / beginning of the year. Just as the head or brain controls all that transpires in the body, so too Rosh Hashanah is that essential node through which all the vitality of an entire year travels. Everything physical and spiritual that you will receive in the coming year is drawn into potential on

Rosh Hashanah. During the course of the year the blessings we receive on Rosh Hashanah will be unpacked and revealed.

Just as there is a judgment on Rosh Hashanah, there is a judgment every day and even more specifically every moment (*Rosh Hashanah*, 17a). Hence, we also *Daven* / pray to receive blessings of health, wealth, wisdom and life every day. The difference is that on Rosh Hashanah the judgment and the blessings for the entire year are created on a spiritual, ethereal plane. Every day and every moment after that, through our prayers, we have the ability to draw those blessings from that ethereal plane into our lives and our world (see, Rebbe Rashab, *Kuntres Umaayon*).

ROSH HASHANAH IS A TIME OF ELOKIM, JUDGMENT & JOY

In the beginning of the Book of Iyov / Job, it says, "One day the sons of Hashem came to stand before Elokim, and Satan came among them" (1:6). Which day is this?" asks Rashi, "It is Rosh Hashanah." This is the day we "stand before Elokim."

Elokim is the Divine Name of Judgment. Elokim is defined as the Mighty Ruler and Sovereign of the Heavens and the earth (Tur, *Orach Chayim*, 5). *Elokim* means 'ruler' (*Medrash Rabbah*, *Shemos*, 3), 'king' (Even Ezra, *Bereishis*, 1:1), 'judge' (*Kuzari*, 4:1), and 'master' (Rashi, *Bereishis*, 6:2). All of these meanings allude to the idea of *Din* / judgment, law, order, nature, and the creation of strict definitions.

In numerical value *Elokim* is 86. Ten times *Elokim* is 860. The word רש / *Rosh* (the word for 'poor', *Rosh* without the letter Aleph) in numerical value is 500. The word השנה / *Hashanah* is 360*. Thus, *Rosh Hashanah* / 'poor' year is 860, corresponding to *Elokim* and Din.

If the letter Aleph is added to the word *Rosh* / ראש, instead of meaning 'poor', lacking, needy and stuck, it means 'head' — fullness, giving, and openness (Note, *Yuma*, 76b. זכה נעשה ראש, לא זכה נעשה רש). The numerical value of ראש השנה is 861. Aleph is 1, signifying the Divine Oneness, the Source of all Life and blessing. The Aleph, when added to "poor," transforms the depths of Din into openness, expansiveness, and limitless potential.**

Besides being a day of *Ra'u'ah* / trembling, as in *Yom Teru'ah* / a day of Teru'ah (*Bamidbar*, 29:1), Rosh Hashanah is also a joyous day and a Yom Tov (and indeed Teru'ah can also mean crying from joy: Chasam Sofer, *Toras Moshe*, Derush 27th Elul. היטיבו נגן בתרועה: *Tehilim*, 33:3). This is intimated by the Torah's other term for Rosh Hashanah, *Zichron Teru'ah* / Remembrance of a Teru'ah (*Vayikra*, 23:24). To "remember the Teru'ah" means to remember the Shofar of the past and of the future. In the past, we were lovingly given the Torah with the sounds of the Teru'ah. In the future, we will be redeemed with the sound of the Great Shofar. As such, within the Torah itself, both aspects of Rosh

---

* Aleph/1, Lamed/30, Hei/5, Yud/10, Mem/40 = 86. Reish/200, Shin/300, Hei/5, Shin/300, Nun/50, Hei/5 = 360.

** The Name אדנ-י / *Ado-noi*, without the Aleph, is also the letters of *Din* (דין / Dalet, Yud, Nun). Adding the Aleph 'sweetens the Din' and completes the name.

Hashanah are revealed: the awe and the joy, the awe of Rosh Hashanah, and the joy of remembering Hashem's love for us in the past, the present, and the promised future.

In the language of the Mishnah, Rosh Hashanah is called *Yom Tov shel Rosh Hashanah* / the Good Day of Rosh Hashanah (*Rosh Hashanah*, 4:1). We do not find this type of expression in the Mishnah with regard to any other Yom Tov of the year; for example, we do not find there the expression *Yom Tov shel Yom Kippur* or *Yom Tov shel Pesach*.

This is to teach us that although it is a 'day of judgment', Rosh Hashanah is also a 'good day', literally a *Yom Tov*. As the prophet proclaims regarding Rosh Hashanah, "לכו / Go eat fatty foods and drink sweet drinks" (*Nechemyah*, 8:10). The Shulchan Aruch explains, "It is a Mitzvah to eat, drink, and be joyful on Rosh Hashanah" (*Orach Chayim*, 593. There is a Mitzvah for Simchah on Rosh Hashanah, *Shu't Sha'agas Aryeh*, 102). This suggests that Rosh Hashanah is not only a day to experience 'spiritual joy' (note, *Magen Avraham*, 597:1), but also physical joy, with food and drink. Of course, we are not to take physical joy to an 'excess', as the Rambam writes, but we are to experience it nonetheless: "On the days of Rosh Hashanah and Yom Kippur we do not recite Hallel since these are days of Teshuvah, awe and dread, not days of *excessive* joy" (Rambam, *Hilchos Chanukah*, 3:6).

There is no mourning or weeping from sorrow on Yom Tov (Rambam, *Hilchos Avel*, 10:8), and this includes Rosh Hashanah as well (*Ibid*, 10:3). A Yom Tov is by definition a day of joy (*Tosefos*,

Moed Katan, 23b), and thus even Rosh Hashanah is a day of joy — just not "excessive joy."

LEAVE YOUR PERCEPTION & EXPERIENCE JOY

One question, however, arises within this dialectic. Why does the prophet say לכו / *Lechu* / "go" and eat, why not simply 'Eat fatty foods?' Where were the people he was speaking to coming from, and where did they need to "go"?

The answer is, they needed to "go" out of their limited and limiting perception of what they thought Rosh Hashanah is: a sad or frightening day, a day of harsh Din, judgment. It is a very serious day, but not a sad day. People confuse the two, they think that seriousness is synonymous with sadness and anxiety, but you can be very serious and yet very happy. The people needed (and we also need) a *Shinui Rosh* / a change of mindset regarding what Rosh Hashanah actually is, and thus what life is on the deepest level.

Chapter 8 in Nechemyah opens with the following words: "All the people came together as one in the square before the Water Gate. They told Ezra, the teacher of the Law, to bring out the Book of the Law of Moshe, which Hashem had commanded for Israel. So on the first day of the seventh month, Ezra the priest brought the Law before the assembly, which was made up of men and women and all who were able to understand" (8:1-2). While Ezra was reading the Mitzvos and laws of the Torah to the people, they began to weep, to which he responded (*Nechemyah*, 8:9): "'This day is holy to

Hashem, your G-d. Do not mourn or weep.' For all the people had been weeping as they heard the words of the *Torah* / Law."

The people were weeping and mourning because they "heard the words of the Law," understood the discrepancy between their behavior and the Torah's guidance, and began to express Teshuvah. However, the fact that this day was Rosh Hashanah also suggests they assumed that the way to enter the 'awe and trembling' of Rosh Hashanah was with weeping and mourning. And so, the prophet Ezra needed to tell them: "This day is holy to Hashem, your G-d. Do *not* mourn or weep. Go, eat fatty foods and drink sweet drinks and send portions to whoever has nothing prepared, for the day is holy to Hashem. And do not be sad, for the *joy* of Hashem is your strength" (8:10).

Rosh Hashanah is a very serious time. It is our collective and personal birthday and a time of introspection and self-judgment; a time to justify, in the presence of the Master of the Universe, our continuous creation and existence. This self-accounting is necessary in order to choose a life of responsibility; to "hear the words of the Law." Moreover, the wellbeing of the entire world is placed within our responsibility. This may weigh heavily upon the heart, but it does not and should not cause depression or anxiety.

Tov / good, also connotes *Ratzon* / will and desire (See Mishnah *Sanhedrin*, 52a: פותח את פיו בצבת שלא בטובתו), so *Yom Tov* also means a 'day of our *Ratzon*'. We desire and will our continued existence on this day, and it is a day upon which we 'justify' Hashem's will and desire to create us, and 'judge' that it was worth it. Through our Tefilos and presence on Rosh Hashanah we 'prove' that recreating us is a good investment, and we show that we desire what HaKadosh Baruch Hu desires for us.

THREE BOOKS: ALIGNING OUR BOOK WITH THE CREATOR'S BOOK

"Three books are opened on Rosh Hashanah: the book of the *Rashayim* / wicked, the book of the *Tzadikim* / righteous, and the book of the *Beinonim* / intermediate people. Tzadikim are immediately written and inscribed in the book of the righteous, for 'life'. Rashayim are immediately written and inscribed for 'death'. The fate of the Beinonim sits on the scales from Rosh Hashanah until Yom Kippur, and if they are worthy they receive life, if not, they are inscribed for death."[*]

---

[*] *Rosh Hashanah*, 16b. זכו נכתבין לחיים לא זכו נכתבין למיתה / זכו נכתבין לחיים לא זכו נכתבין למיתה / if they are worthy they receive life, if not, they are inscribed for death. In other words, when there is a balanced scale, even doing a little more Mitzvos tips the scale. The Rambam, however, writes "The *Beinoni* / intermediate person's verdict remains tentative until Yom Kippur. If he *repents*, his [verdict] is sealed for 'life'. If not, his [verdict] is sealed for 'death'": *Hilchos Teshuvah*, 3:3. According to the Rambam, (based on the *Yerushalmi* / Jerusalem Talmud's version of "the three books" אם עשו תשובה נכתבין עם הצדיקים ואם לאו נכתבין עם הרשעים. Rosh Hashanah, 1:3. (7a)), if the intermediate person does not do Teshuvah for his negative actions, he is deemed to 'death', whereas, in the above quoted version, since he is an intermediate, there is no reason to do Teshuvah, just if 'they are worthy,' meaning, if the intermediate person does even *one* more Mitzvah, he gains life — although Teshuvah is always preferable. It seems clear that according to the Rambam, simply adding Mitzvos during this time period, without doing Teshuvah, is not helpful to tip the scale. Either because the weighing of the scales has already been done, and is only done once on Rosh Hashanah, and afterwards all we can do is Teshuvah. *Emek Beracha*, Erech Teshuvah. Or because the sin of not doing Teshuvah during this most auspicious time period for Teshuvah outweighs any performance of Mitzvos. *Kochvei Ohr*, Siman 5.

One question is, as the Ran (Rabbeinu Nisim of Gerona [1320–1380], ad loc.) asks: "Is it true that every Tzadik has life and lives, while every Rasha has death and dies?" This statement seems to contradict reality. In fact, as Tosefos (ad loc.) writes, it is often the opposite, and often the Tzadikim suffer mightily in this world (*Kedushin*, 40b).

Another question: what are these three books — and why are these inscriptions written in "books"?

First it must be clear that "life" and "death" are not to be understood literally (*Tosefos*, ad loc. *Ben Yehoyadah*, ad loc. Zohar 3, Gra, Zohar Bamidbar, *Likutim*, 31:2. It can also mean protection from 'accidental' death; Maharal, *Rosh Hashanah*, ad loc. The Ramban also writes (*Sha'ar haG'mul*) that part of physical death is physical hardship while alive, and all goodness in life is called 'life'). The meaning of "life" in this context is the fullness of life, also called the life of *Olam haBa* / the future world.* Life, in general according to the sages, means to live with meaning, hope, spirituality, purpose, intention, connection and passion; being truly alive. 'Death' is then living without meaning, purpose, inner peace, or hope, becoming more despondent and disconnected. A perfect Tzadik is truly

---

* From the Rambam it seems that he is of the opinion that on Rosh Hashanah we are judged for literal life and death: *Hilchos Teshuvah*, 3:3. This is because he writes about the judgment on Rosh Hashanah as a continuation of the prior Halachah, *Hilchos Teshuvah*, 3:2, in which the terms are that a wicked person "dies right away." On the other hand, the *Lechem Mishnah*, ad loc., says, 'dying right away' (or 'living') means at the time of a person's death he would immediately experience spiritual 'life or death', i.e. Olam haBa or not.

alive and awake, while the wicked are 'dead' even during their lives.

On Rosh Hashanah we are judged regarding what kind of life we are going to live in the coming year. Will it be a life of 'aliveness', productivity, growth, and connection, or will it be a life of 'death', fruitlessness, stagnation and disconnection?

And what are these "books" that are opened on Rosh Hashanah? The *Sefer Yetzirah* begins with these words, "With 32 mysterious paths of wisdom... (Hashem) created the universe, by means of three elements: בספר / *b'Sefer,* וספר / *v'Sefar,* וספור / *v'Sipur* / "with a 'book' (quality, space), and a 'numbering' (quantity, time), and a 'story' (communication or consciousness)." The first two words, ספר / *Sefer* / book and ספר / *Sefar* / numbering, have the same letters, and according to other readings the first two words are both translated as 'book'. (Indeed, neither space and time, nor quality and quantity, can be completely divorced from one another.)

According to this reading, the world was founded on three principles: 1) the book of the Author of Creation, 2) the book of Creation, which is our story, and 3) the 'story' — the 'book' of dialogue. These are the books that are opened on Rosh Hashanah: the Book of the Creator, the Book of Creation, and the Book of Co-Creative expression.

Furthermore, there are three types of books of Creation: those of the *Reshayim* / wicked, those of the *Tzadikim* /

righteous, and those of the *Beinonim* / intermediate people. (In the beginning of *Sifra d'Tzniusa* the Gra writes that the three books that are opened on Rosh Hashanah — the book of the righteous, the book of the wicked and the book intermediates — are the three "books" that Sefer Yetzirah mentions: Gra, *Sefer Yetzirah*, 1:4.)

Often, how an author expresses himself through his book is not the same as how the reader reads the book. For the most part, the author is separate or 'dead' from the experience of the reader, and the reader is the one who 'resurrects' the text as he reads it. In this way there are two books, so-to-speak; the author's *Sefer* and the reader's *Sefer*. *Sipur*, the third 'book', is the intermediary place of the 'story', where the author and reader conceptually meet.

Sadly, many times, what is written in the Book of the Creator, our destiny, our perfect self, is not the way it is 'read' in the Book of Creation. Sometimes, these two books say different things, much like, on a mundane level, when the author is 'dead' and the reader basically creates his own book, through his own interpretation and imagination.

סּפור / *Sipur*, the place of the 'story', in which the author and reader meet and the actual "Book" is co-created, is where Hashem's version of the book of our life and our version of our book of life converge.

סּפּור / *Sippur* is the place where HaKadosh Baruch Hu is dialoguing with us, the 'reader', in our search for meaning and connection. This perfect dialogue is the 'space' where we hear our Divine calling, our purpose, and thus it is where the two books, the Divine Author's book and our book, the reader's book, are aligned as one book, telling one consistent story. This is where the intention of the Author is exactly aligned with our intention. Through our collaboration with Hashem, the book of Creation — our 'story', the way we live — can align with the book of the Creator, Hashem's 'story' of us and our potential. This communication or alignment between human consciousness and Divine Consciousness is the work and state of a Tzadik.

Verbal, *Panim-el-Panim* / face-to-face communication is the *Avodah* / work of Rosh Hashanah. We have the power to speak to Hashem in Tefilah and to listen to Hashem's *Kol* / voice through the revelation of Torah. And through these two movements of dialogue, the third dimension, the *Sipur*, the story, becomes aligned with the Author's book, and then book one and book two are unified; HaKadosh Baruch Hu's book and our book are thus one.

A person in his state of perfection is how he exists in the world of *Adam Kadmon* / the primordial being. This is his highest potential; how he could live his earthly life in the highest, deepest way. The Book of the Author is the 'Book of Life', the book of our perfect life in Hashem's eyes. This is the way our lives are envisioned, as it were, in HaKadosh Baruch Hu's perception; the book in which we are living up to our fullness and maximum potential. This is Book One.

Book Two is the Book of Creation, how we are actually living in the world.

For the Tzadik, Book One and Book Two are one and the same; how he could live and how he actually lives are one. A Tzadik is a creation who is a direct reflection of the desire of the Creator, the Author. He writes himself into the "Book of Life," of oneness with the Source of Life.

For the Rasha there is an inconsistency between the Author's objective and how he lives his life. He reads another story; he actively changes the story based on his own subjective prejudices. For him, Book Two is separate from Book One, and he writes himself into the 'book of death', the world of death and separation (see *Derashos Maran haBeis Yoseph*, Avos, 3:1).

The intermediate person is neither a Tzadik nor a Rasha. The book of the Beinoni is the book most related to the element of the *Sippur* / communication, where one listens to both voices, the objective voice of the Creator and the subjective voice of the Yetzer. This realm of struggle between one's inner authentic voice and the external voice of the Snake is the place of free choice.

Yom Kippur, and in fact the whole period between Rosh Hashanah and Yom Kippur, is a propitious time to choose life, to listen to the inner voice, "to hear the words of the Law" and align ourselves more and more with the higher and more perfect Book of the Creator. It is a time to communicate verbally with the Author through prayer, and to correct our 'edition' of Book Two.

This time period, the nine days from Rosh Hashanah through Erev Yom Kippur, is a time of self-excavation, evaluation, and inner work. In nine days there are 216 hours (9 x 24 = 216), which is the numerical value of the word *Gevurah* (Gimel/3, Beis/2, Vav/6, Reish/200, Hei/5 = 216) — the idea of constriction and *Din* / judgment. These nine days are days full of the beneficial constriction of self-judgment, and then comes Yom Kippur, the day of expansive forgiveness and Divine compassion.

These are the days to deeply 'read' ourselves, to 'judge' and ensure that our Book of Creation, our story, is aligned and harmonized with Book One, the Creator's story. Through *Sipur*, we can retell any parts of our story by living our lives in harmony with the Book of the Creator.

OUR BOOK RECORDS ALL OF LIFE & IS OPENED ON ROSH HASHANAH

The second book, the Book of Creation, is the same book the Mishnah speaks about in *Avos* (2:1): "Know that all your actions are written in the Book" (Gra, *Zohar* 3, ibid). What is "the Book"? This, teaches the Mekubalim, is a person's surrounding 'air', or aura (*Zohar* 1, p. 191a; 3, p. 43a. *Pardes Rimonim*, Sha'ar 31:4).

Essentially, everything a person does, thinks or feels has multi-layered and multi-dimensional effects. A mental manifestation, a projected image, is fashioned and emanated in one's aura through every thought, word, action or omission of action. All of a person's attributes are thus projected into their surroundings.

Our personal book that is opened on Rosh Hashanah is our aura, 'inscribed' with everything we have thought, spoken and done. This book becomes 'open' or revealed on Rosh Hashanah.

Our story, the Book Two that we are writing every day and moment to moment is 'read aloud' and evaluated on Rosh Hashanah. That is, our book, our mind, our aura, is opened, and is lined up against Book One, with our potential higher self, our Creator's vision of us.

The book that is opened on Rosh Hashanah, teaches the Magid of Mezritch (See *Avodas Yisrael*, Nitzavim and Avos, 5:2), is the 'thoughts' of a person — a representation of their 'mind' and 'heart'. The book is thus composed of the contents of our 'mind' and 'heart'.

This is perhaps similar to the idea of the aura in relation to the general judgment of our lives after we pass on. Rebbe Menachem Azaryah De Fano writes that the universal book recording all human actions is a sapphire-colored ether that surrounds the human being (*Asarah Ma'amaros*, Ma'amar Chikur Din, 2:12. *Ma'amar haNefesh*, 2:10), and this is where every thought, word, action, experience, encounter and sensation is recorded and eventually revealed after the body passes away. Upon dying, our entire life, in every minute detail, becomes revealed.

In any case, on Rosh Hashanah the book that is open is our own mind, and the Creator looks at our thoughts. In the words of the Magid (see ibid, *Avodas Yisrael*), "'Written for Life in the Book' means engraved within the thoughts of man. Because the non-righteous, when they remember their misdeeds, perhaps they tremble and are afraid, but they have no self- control and do not have the inner ability to change their ways and do Teshuvah, and so they are right away written in the Book of Death (as their lives are 'dead' with no meaning, higher purpose and mission).... The Tzadikim, however, even though they too may tremble from the awe and fear of Divine Judgment, they are filled with trust and certainty in Hashem's salvation and kindness and they strengthen themselves to return to Hashem, and they are thus written right away into the Book of Life. And upon their thoughts there is a writing for the good."

In other words, HaKadosh Baruch Hu looks at the state of our thoughts during these moments of Rosh Hashanah, and based on them we are 'judged' or evaluated regarding what may need to happen in our lives in order for us to grow closer to Hashem.

Throughout this process we are not meant to become sad or morbid, but to keep a positive, hopeful, even joyful mindset.*

---

* Even Yom Kippur, which for the 'average' man is the time of his/her final judgment, one is not to be sad. So much so that the sages changed the location of the 'red thread' so as not to cause people to be sad on Yom Kippur. תנו רבנן: בראשונה היו קושרין לשון של זהורית על פתח האולם מבחוץ, הלבין – היו שמחין, לא הלבין – היו עצבין ומתביישין. התקינו שיהיו קושרין על פתח אולם מבפנים / "The Sages taught: At first they would tie red strip to the opening of the Entrance Hall on the outside. If the strip turned white they would rejoice.

Despite our past, we can grow and we can live deeper and higher; so long as there is life there is possibility. We need to think about our lives, hope for Hashem's salvation, and then draw down from the Ein Sof life, hope and more Divine kindness.

Our mindset on Rosh Hashanah affects the entire year, as Rosh Hashanah is the seed of the year from which everything emerges.

OUR THOUGHTS ON ROSH HASHANAH CREATE OUR YEAR

As we have seen, on Rosh Hashanah we ourselves are actually "writing" with our thoughts in the "books" that are opened. Thus, the purity and positivity of our thoughts as recorded therein — where our minds are during these 48 hours — is what will steer our experience of the coming year. And so it is of utmost importance to focus on positive thoughts about ourselves on Rosh Hashanah, and to sense that we will be judged favorably.

When the book of our life is opened for judgment, the page that is opened to, as it were, is the current state of our thoughts; in this case, our thoughts during Rosh Hashanah.

If it did not turn white they would be sad and ashamed. When the Sages saw that people were sad and distressed on Yom Kippur, they established that they should tie it to the opening of the Entrance Hall on the inside." *Yuma,* 67a.

It is the way of the world, says the Medrash (quoted in Tur, *Orach Chayim*, Chap. 581. *Medrash Rabbah*, Vayikra, Parsha 29), for most people to feel uncertainty and humility when they stand to be judged, as they do not know the ultimate verdict. They may show up in court dressed in black (mourning colors), unkempt, with uncut nails and looking a little downtrodden and frail. Yet Klal Yisrael acts differently. Before Rosh Hashanah we take haircuts, which is a celebrative act. We dress in white garments, white being the color of the garments of the Tzadikim in Gan Eden (*Nidah*, 20a). We come to Shul in our finest attire, we eat, drink and rejoice, לפי שיודעין שהקב״ה יעשה להם נס / "knowing that HaKadosh Baruch Hu will perform a miracle for them," and surely the Creator will find favor with us and annul all negative decrees.

Rosh Hashanah is, as mentioned, a time that we celebrate our birthday, which is generally a time of introspection and self-reflection, but also a time when our Mazal is most pronounced and strong and hence a time of miracles.*

---

* The day of a person's birthday is the day when his/her Mazal is most manifest. This is the reason Amalek chose warriors to go to battle on the day of their birthday. *Yerushalmi, Rosh Hashanah* 3:8. *Karban Eida* ad loc. The *Chida* writes that this is true of the Jewish people as well — although *Ein Mazal L'Yisrael* / there is no Mazal for Klal Yisrael — and there are sources for this idea based on Sod. *Chomas Anach, Iyov*, 3. See also Rebbe Tzadok, *Divrei Chalomos*, 20. Rebbe Yonasan Eibeshitz, *Ya'aros Devash*, 1:17. Because a person has "strong *Mazal*" on one's birthday, he/she should take upon themselves new spiritual endeavors on this day; deciding to work on overcoming certain negative traits, or developing certain positive traits for instance (see *Arvei Nachal*, Shemini). Additionally, one's birthday is also a propitious time to introspect (the Rebbe, *Hayom Yom*, 11th of Nisan). Our birthday is also a time where we can experience real miracles, as a person's

Thinking about Rosh Hashanah in this context, as a day of strong Mazal and miracles, allows us to enter Rosh Hashanah with a sense of spiritual confidence, knowing that HaKodash Baruch Hu will perform miracles for us (יודעין שהקב״ה יעשה להם נס); coupled with this knowing is a corresponding sense of profound unknowing, and hence the seriousness surrounding the magnitude of the day.

This is the mindset of Rosh Hashanah.

Fittingly, the letters that make up the words *Rosh Hashanah* can be rearranged to spell *Shinui haRosh* / a change of head. On Rosh Hashanah we have to change our mindset, press the reset button on our life and begin anew, with a new level of consciousness. On Rosh Hashanah, the world itself is experiencing a new beginning: it is a new moon, a new season and a new year. We can optimize our benefit from this state of new beginning when we infuse it with a positive and holy outlook, thereby achieving a Shinui Rosh.

Coming out of the hard spiritual work that we have done in Elul, we can now move into Rosh Hashanah with a clean,

---

Mazal is stronger, and thus a time to celebrate, the *Ben Ish Chai, Ben Yo-hoyada*, Berachos, 28a. ולכך הצליח לעשות לו נס זה, דידוע שיום הלידה יהיה המזל של האדם חזק בו ומוצלח, על כן נוהגים שכל אדם יעשה יום הלידה יום טוב לעצמו / this is the reason why a miracle occurred (to Rebbe Elazar ben Azarya), as it is known that on the day of a birthday the Mazal of a person is strong and successful, and for this reason, the custom is for people to celebrate their birthday as a good day.

or at least cleaner, slate. In fact, throughout the Rosh Hashanah liturgy there is no mention of sin or negative actions (*Magen Avraham*, Siman 584). According to the Arizal, we should not
mention any sin on Rosh Hashanah (*Sha'ar haKavanos*, Hakdamah,
Derushei Rosh Hashanah), and not even eat foods that could, ever
so slightly, remind us of sin (The Maharil speaks about not eating nuts
on Rosh Hashanah: See also *Shulchan Aruch*, Orach Chayim 583:2, Rama.
Besides causing extra saliva and phlegm, making it harder to sing and *Daven*,
'nuts' and 'sin' have the same numerical value. Although in simple Gematriya
they are not the 'exact' same value, yet, since they hint to sin, we refrain: אגוז
בגימטריא חט). However, this clean slate, this level of clarity and
certainty, comes through the hard *Avodah* / spiritual work that
has been done during the month of Elul, as in the month of
Elul we toiled in Teshuvah to amend our ways of being, thinking, feeling and reacting. Now when Rosh Hashanah arrives,
we enter it with an authentic sense of joy and powerful awe.

Rosh Hashanah thus completes our realignment, cuts away
all traces of negativity, and focuses our life moving forward.

HACHNA'AH / SUBMISSION
THEN HAVDALAH / SEPARATION

In Elul we 'accept' our wrong-doing and take full responsibility for our actions; '*I* spilled the milk', not 'the *milk* spilled.'
This is the stage of *Hachna'ah* / acceptance or submission. This
total acceptance of responsibility for what we have done is the
first step of Teshuvah. Elul is the *Achris haShanah* / end of year,
and the word *Achris* is related to *Achrayus* / responsibility. In

Elul we 'inhale' the entire past year, and assume full responsibility for our actions and mindset.

Then we are prepared for the stage of *Havdalah* / separation. This is inspired by the sound of the Shofar. While the Shofar orients us to the spiritual task at hand, it also pushes away all distracting 'static'; much like when a person claps their hands or hears a sudden noise, their entire focus is on that noise to the exclusion of all other thoughts or noises. Have you ever been walking down the street distracted by an onrush of thoughts, your mind bumping around from one thought to another in rapid succession, and then there is a sudden loud noise and your entire mind becomes fixated for the moment on that sound. In this way, the sound of the Shofar focuses and sharpens our mind, allowing us to cut ourselves free from lingering and scattered thoughts.

This is the idea of the sound of the *Teru'ah* (again, the Torah says Rosh Hashanah should be "a day of Teru'ah"), as *Teru'ah* comes from the word *Ra'ah* (Reish Ayin Ayin), to weaken, smash or damage: *Tero'em b'Shevet Barzel* / "You will *smash* them with an iron rod" (Tehilim, 2:9. Ritva, *Rosh Hashanah*, 33b). This relates to the second stage of our spiritual work on Rosh Hashanah. That is, focusing on the good and simply cutting away all the negative. We smash all negativity in our lives with the Shofar blast, and thus do not mention or even allude to sin on Rosh Hashanah.

This is also why, on Rosh Hashanah, we perform *Tashlich* / walking to a body of water with fish and symbolically 'casting away' our sins (The Maharil, *Minhagim*. Hilchos Rosh Hashanah, 9. Quoted later by the Rama, *Orach Chayim*, 583:2. Note, Rashi, *Shabbos*, 81b). We call this practice *Tashlich* based on the verse in Michah (7:19) "...and 'cast' (*Tashlich*) into the depths of the sea all of their sins." Inwardly, this practice triggers a psychological and spiritual 'throwing away' of, and 'separation' from, our negative thoughts, emotions, words and even actions. On Rosh Hashanah we recognize that there is 'what we did' or did not do, and there is 'who we are.' We may have sinned and perpetuated negativity during the past year, but on Rosh Hashanah we stand in front of HaKadosh Baruch Hu and 'cast' away all negativity and sin, courageously declaring, "I may have done such and such, but that is *not* who I am." We therefore practice a *Havdalah* / separation between ourselves and what we may have done.

Whereas in Elul we claim complete responsibility for our thoughts, words and actions — on Rosh Hashanah we smash and cast away all negative or unholy urges and behaviors and become decisively aligned with positivity. This opens the way for a great *Hamtakah* / sweetening of our lives on Yom Kippur, as we will explore further on.

REMEMBER US FOR LIFE

It is repeated in the name of the Magid of Mezritch that when we ask the Master of the Universe in our Davening to "remember us for life," we do so because *we* remember ourselves for a life of "life," a life of purpose, mission, holiness, depth and authenticity.

This means, when you think positively about yourself and about others, this itself is an activation of "remember us for life" because everything is dependent on your thoughts, and your thoughts are the 'book' that is opened on Rosh Hashanah.

If one has no love and unity with others, G-d forbid, then there is no unity within oneself, and thus one suffers from lack of self-esteem and cannot think well about himself or others. Then, the opposite of 'life' and goodness is what is remembered.

On Rosh Hashanah we need to have a total shift of mind, to begin looking at ourselves as a vessel for blessings. So long as we cling to our old perceptions of self and world, we are closed and stuck in them and nothing can change. We need to let the past go, like the trees let go of their leaves during this season. After *Hachna'ah* / submission to the reality of what we have done, we therefore need to practice *Havdalah* / separating who we truly are from our past actions in order to become a vessel to receive Hashem's blessings for the coming year.

In such a state of Havdalah we are empty of the old, and ready for the new. In the words of our sages "A year that begins "poor" will end up being "rich" at the end" (*Rosh Hashanah*, 16b). *Rash* / poor is the state of feeling like an empty vessel. "Rich" is the state of being filled with new blessings and aliveness.

Once we have let go and emptied ourselves, we are able to see ourselves as an open vessel. At such a precipice, we should certainly appreciate the tremendous amount of work we have accomplished to get us to this point, including our preparations during Elul. Now we can just be open to receive. As you stand before Hashem on Rosh Hashanah, picture yourself as a perfect and holy vessel, ready to absorb all the blessings that you can contain. Open up to the Source of all Life and humbly acknowledge that you are in the hands of HaKadosh Baruch Hu at all times.

The 'book of yourself' — your 'aura', your 'mind' — is now open. Allow your inner Tzadik to become more present, and be blessed to receive "life," and be written and inscribed into the Book of Life. In the root of our *Neshamah* / soul we are all Tzadikim, and on Rosh Hashanah we reveal this inner Tzadik by casting away all negativity, and Davening that this holier, more wholesome self emerges more fully and consistently. During these days there is a custom, according to the Rama, to wish another "לשנה טובה תכתב / l'Shana Tova / for a good year, may you be written (in the book of Life)." Upon this, the Magen Avraham adds "ותחתם / and inscribed" (Orach Chayim, 582:9). As explored earlier, only Tzadikim are immediately written and inscribed in the book of life. Therefore, on Rosh Hashanah, according to the Magen Avraham, we need to thus think of ourselves and others as Tzadikim (וכן נכון שיחזיקו לצדיק שנחתם לאלתר לחיים). By making this shift and connecting or reconnecting with our inner Tzadik, we are blessed for a year of increased "life," thereby becoming a conduit of meaning, purpose, spirituality, tranquility, hope, growth and positive movement.

What is the difference between a Tzadik and a Rasha? It is not simply the way they act, although that is obviously highly significant. On a more subtle level, the basis of their difference is their mindset. Broadly speaking, there are two types of people: those who are full of hope and optimism, and those who lack hope and optimism. Someone who expresses the belief that what has been done is done and nothing can or will ever change, is in that moment a *Rasha* / 'conduit of negativity'. The Torah says, "Distant from the Rasha is salvation" (*Tehilim,* 119:155). Such a person has distanced himself from salvation in that moment of pessimism. By contrast, someone who expresses hope, even when there have been or are negative occurrences happening, is in that moment a *Tzadik* / 'conduit of righteousness'. With reference to the Tzadik, the Torah says, "My salvation is soon to come" (*Yeshayahu,* 56:1). This person recognizes the always-present opportunity to redirect his life, grow, and bring salvation near.

In this way, when our sages affirm that a Tzadik is blessed with life, it is because his mind, his inner reality is filled with hope, with life and with dynamism, especially on Rosh Hashanah. When our sages teach that a Rasha is inscribed for death, this means that, because he continues to cling to and affirm thinking that is characterized by a lack of possibility beyond what currently is, he will continue to experience an absence of hope and a void of value and deeper purpose.

On Rosh Hashanah we need to choose to be the Tzadik we essentially already are. This is who we are when we are born, and it is who we are in our timeless, primordial state, we just need to firmly align ourselves with this dimension of ourselves in the current moment. In doing so, we will draw down the blessing of life, inner peace and success on all levels, for ourselves, for all of Klal Yisrael and for the entire world.

ROSH HASHANAH: OUR BIRTHDAY, THE DAY WE ARE 'PERFECT'

Rosh Hashanah is the day of the birth of Adam and Chavah — and thus the collective birth of all humanity. As they were born, Adam and Chavah emerged in a perfect state, as "the handy-work of Hashem Himself."

Rosh Hashanah is a Yom Tov that 'predates' Matan Torah, as it were. It has been revealed as a special day since the beginning of Creation, the day of the creation of human beings. In fact, as it predates even the *Cheit* / misaligned act of eating from the Tree of Knowledge, it is rooted in the Tree of Life, Gan Eden, the place of perfection, the way Adam and Chavah existed prior to their (and our) descent.

We, too, all human beings, are born 'perfect', in an Edenic state, just like Adam and Chavah on the day of their creation and prior to eating from the Tree of Knowledge.

To commemorate this birthday we blow the Shofar, which is a primordial sound, prior to language, prior to the paradigm of the 'Tree of Knowledge of Separation', prior to duality and imperfection.

In our primordial state, as the cosmic *Adam Kadmon /
Primordial Being*, the truth that "Your nation are all Tzadik-
im" eternally reverberates (*Yeshayahu*, 60: 21. Furthermore, Klal Yisrael
as a whole, the Tzibur, is eternal and always perfect: R. Simchah Zisel of
Kelm, *Chochmah uMusar*, 85. There is no death of the collective: אין צבור מתים.
Horiyos, 6b. And צבור קיימא / the collective always stands: *Tosefos*, Meilah,
9b. Indeed, there is no *Galus /* exile, dispersion of the *Tzibur /* collective:
Maharal, *Netzach Yisrael*, 10).

This is the state we come from, and are born into. This is
how we always exist in the timeless Book One of the Creator.
And on Rosh Hashanah we have the ability to start anew, and
to once again lay claim to who we truly are. Perfect righteousness and illumination is our birthright.

When we begin again, we can reach out to Hashem from
our inner point of perfection, no matter how we may have lived
in the past. Rosh Hashanah is a total renewal of existence,
and we are thus recast as if we are a newborn, without any
conditioning, limited (and limiting) narratives, or self-images.
Our continuing *Avodah /* contemplative work then carries this
awareness of indestructible purity achieved on Rosh Hashanah
into the rest of our lives. We must resolve and work to activate
and appreciate this primordial level of our soul on a day to day
basis. In this way, we can make everyday the first day of the rest
of our lives.

REJOICING WITH AWE

The Medrash (quoted in *Tur Orach Chayim*, Chap. 581. *Medrash*

Rabbah Vayikra, Parsha 29) teaches us that on Rosh Hashanah we should dress in white, and come to pray in white garments, with our hair trimmed and our body clean and fresh. The Rashal, Rebbe Shlomo Luria (1510–1573), who was one of the great *Poskim* / decisors of Jewish Law and teachers of his time, asks a question on this Medrash (see Bach, *Orach Chayim*, 581): 'Why do we dress in white and not in colorful clothes? If the idea of dressing up is to demonstrate our confidence in judgment, why dress in white?'

Black clothes show that we are afraid, yet colorful clothes could indicate that we are not even aware that we are being judged, expressing a degree of callousness and indifference (אין כאן הוכח שבטוח בו ית' כי שמא אינו מפחד מיום הדין כלל ואינו חש). White clothes, however, represent the fact that we know that we are being judged, and we are in awe of this moment, but we are also confident and have trust in Hashem that our judgment will be for the good.'

Yom haDin arouses awe, seriousness, perhaps even dread (See Shmuel 1, 28:15. *Medrash Rabbah*, Emor, 26). But coupled with this raw and intense realism must be a sense of love, joy,*

---

* In fact, many Geonim were of the opinion that in the text of our Tefilah and Kiddush we should refer to Rosh Hashanah and Yom Kippur as days of joy. Here is what the Tur writes, אבל רב שר שלום כתב אומר בב' ישיבות בר"ה וביה"כ בין בתפלה בין בקדושה מועדים לשמחה חגים וזמנים לששון את יום הזכרון הזה שהרי כתיב אלה מועדי ה' בריש ענינא ובסוף ענינא וידבר משה את מועדי ה' וקאי אכל ענינא אפסח עצרת ר"ה ויה"כ סוכה ושמיני עצרת כולהו איתקוש להדדי לקרותו מועדי ה' מקראי קודש וכ"כ רב פלטוי גאון זצ"ל ותתן לנו ה' אלהינו באהבה מועדים לשמחה חגים וזמנים לששון את יום הזכרון הזה וכ"כ רב שמואל בן חפני מנהג ב' ישיבות לאומרו: Tur, *Orach Chayim*, 582.

confidence, and "*Gilu beR'adah /* rejoicing with trembling" (*Tehilim*, 2:11). In the words of the Medrash: יראתי מתוך שמחתי ושמחתי מתוך יראתי / "Within my joy I am in awe, and within my awe I am in joy" (*Tana d'Vei Eliyahu Rabbah*, 3).

In fact, our perfect and resolute *Bitachon /* trust that we will be judged favorably and granted a year of life and goodness is sourced in our deep sense of awe regarding the majesty and responsibility of this awesome day. In the words of the Taz, ואע"ג שאנו בטוחים שנצא זכאים בדין מ"מ צ"ל ירא וחרד מאימת הדין ועי"כ נזכה לזכות / "Although we have full Bitachon that we will be meritorious in judgment, yet, we ought to (and if we simply meditate on this day, we will be) in a state of dread and awe from the awesomeness of judgement, and through this, we will merit good judgment" (Taz, *Orach Chayim*, 584:1. Quoted also in *Mishnah Berurah*, ibid, 1).

The joy and trust we are meant to experience on Rosh Hashanah are not in contradiction to the tremendous sense of awe one experiences, knowing that they are standing in front of the Master of the Universe, being judged, and are expected to justify the *why* of our existence. Nor do joy and trust contradict the awe of recognizing who you could be and courageously stepping into your true potential. These deep emotions rise up simultaneously. And in truth, the awe demands of us that we strive to live deeper and higher, more mindfully and seriously. It keeps us in check and stimulates even more Bitachon in ourselves and a joyful confidence that we 'deserve' a positive judgment and will thus merit a sweet and good year.

In other words, the *Yirah* / awe and awesomeness of being in the Presence of the King (as distinct from a crippling anxiety and nervousness, which will be explored later), forces us to strongly focus or refocus on our mission and purpose. This Yirah brings a person to a state of deeper clarity, of knowing what his purpose of being is, why he has been created, and how he can live in alignment with that truth and thereby justify his existence. In this way, the Yirah itself ensures a more positive judgment, which in turn elicits immense joy, and these are the two emotions that naturally rise up together on Rosh Hashanah, almost on their own.

FEELING OTHERS' PAIN & LOWLINESS

On Rosh Hashanah, in the midst of this unique type of joy, we do not sing *Hallel* / passages of praise. "Said the angels on high to the Holy One, 'Why doesn't Klal Yisrael recite before You Hallel?' 'Is it possible,' responds the Holy One, 'and does it make any sense, that on a day when the King sits on the seat of judgment, when the books of life and death are open, they should sing songs?'" (*Rosh Hashanah*, 32b)

This is puzzling; if we are dressing in white, and we are joyfully confident in our judgment for life, why not sing Hallel? (As the Taz quoted above, [*Orach Chayim*, 584:1] asks). This can be understood with another teaching from the Gemara (*Sanhedrin*, 39b). At the Splitting of the Sea, the angels wished to sing praises to Hashem when the Egyptians were about to be destroyed by the walls of water collapsing back on them. Hashem rebuked the angels saying, "My handiwork (the

Egyptian army) is drowning in the sea, and you would utter song before Me?" On hearing this rebuke, the angels stopped singing (This is also a reason we don't say Full Hallel on Pesach. Taz, *Orach Chayim*, 490:3).

What this means is that we are not to make ourselves fully joyful when someone else, in the same predicament as ourselves, is perishing or suffering — even if he has brought it upon himself with his own commitment to negativity. For example, we may be sitting in Shul on Rosh Hashanah, our mindset completely positive and holy, G-d willing, securing for ourselves and family a happy, healthy, prosperous year. Sitting next to us, there may be someone who is still tied to the past, still stuck in the pull of the negative actions of the 'last' year, and thus not being remembered "for life." Perhaps, just as a matter of sympathy, it makes sense to refrain from singing Hallel during such an existentially fraught and psychologically precarious time.

HEALING SISRA'S MOTHER

Our custom is to blow a total of 100 blasts of the Shofar on each day of Rosh Hashanah. We "cry" the 100 sounds of the Shofar, writes the *Aruch* (כנגד מאה פעיות דפעיא אימיה דסיסרא. Tosefos, *Rosh Hashanah*, 33b), which parallel the 100 sobs of Sisra's mother when she was anxiously waiting to hear what happened to her son in battle, as we will explore later on.

On a deeper level, this is not just a parallel, but our Shofar sounds are actually bringing a *Tikkun* / rectification and healing to the cries of Sisra's mother. On Rosh Hashanah our cries, our yearnings, our dreams, are not only for ourselves, but for all the people we love, the people around us, and for the entire world. All human beings are judged on Rosh Hashanah, therefore our cries to Hashem are for the benefit of all.

In fact, the sound of the Great Shofar that will be blown at the time of the ultimate Redemption is a composite of all the cries, from all the sufferings and exiles throughout history; it is the sound of all the yearnings to wake up from our spiritual slumbers and to be brought back home from our exile.

On Rosh Hashanah, we are, as one human family, crying out for all of Hashem's creation to have a year of blessings; indeed this should be the year of the complete redemption of all creation, with the coming of Moshiach.

Everything happens by Divine orchestration, and so we always need to ask, what is the message for me in what is happening around me? How am I related to it? We should never say, "It simply happened." Nothing simply happens. There is always something for us to learn from or strive for.

Sisera was an archenemy of the ancient people of Israel, and in fact, he was killed running away from battle, a battle he was waging against the Jewish people. On our part, as the historical victors, we need to think deeply: perhaps the reason an enemy waged war against us in the first place was because of a spiritual misalignment within ourselves. As the Rambam writes, "This practice is one of the paths of Teshuvah: when a difficulty arises, and the people cry out (to Hashem)…everyone will realize that (the difficulty) occurred because of their negative conduct… Conversely, should the people fail to cry out (to Hashem) and sound the trumpets, and instead say, 'What has happened to us is merely a natural phenomenon and this difficulty is merely a chance occurrence' — this is a cruel conception of things, which causes them to remain attached to their negative deeds, and thus that time of distress will lead to further distress [rather than being a cause for growth and learning]" (*Hilchos Ta'anis*, 1:2-3).

We always need to reflect back on ourselves in any situation, albeit, not G-d forbid to excuse or justify any perpetration of negativity and brutality by others, as that is rooted in their own negative free-choice, but to never miss an opportunity to refine ourselves. With such radical self-reflection in mind, the cause of Sisera's death can be seen, in some sense, as our responsibility; if we had been living in our original state of perfection and inner harmony, there would have been no war (*Degel Machaneh Ephrayim*, end of Balak), and without the war, there would be no death in battle. Perhaps his death would have occurred anyway, but in a way which would not have made his mother cry in such a tormented way. As such, we can view her cries as a direct result of our own misalignments.

On Rosh Hashanah (see *Seridei Aish*, LeP'rakim, p. 510-513), we are creating a Tikkun for the tears that we caused a mother, albeit a mother of an arch enemy of our people — yet a mother nonetheless, who loved her son and desperately wanted him to live. With this profound empathy for a parent's love, we send a message to HaKadosh Baruch Hu: 'The love of a mother is Your love, Hashem, and the pain of a mother is Your pain, so-to-speak. May we never 'hurt' You again! Please accept the cries of our Shofar-blowing as honoring Your love within Sisera's mother's cries. May this rectify the fact that we were in any way a cause of those bitter cries. For You too yearn that we, Your children, should live — despite the fact that we too have acted like an 'enemy' (Chas v'Shalom), through our destructive misalignments. Your power to help us is limitless, and therefore we have confidence that You will give us a good year of life and blessings.'

Indeed, Hashem answers and believes in us; the proof is that we are alive. And we are entrusted to use our life in order to create a Tikkun for all the personal and collective suffering in the world, now and for all time.

A JUDGMENT OF SPIRITUAL GREATNESS

Rosh Hashanah is a judgment of our spiritual greatness and responsibility. Imagine waking up one day and having the entire world at your feet, asking you to guide them, to make their life more meaningful, more filled with love, spirituality and Torah wisdom.

This indeed is what occurred on the first Rosh Hashanah, and continues to reoccur on a metaphysical level, every year. When Adam came to consciousness, he stood up, says the Medrash (*Pirkei d'Rebbe Eliezer*, 1), and began to look and ponder what is above and below. When he had gazed upon all the various creatures that had been created, he declared, "O Compassionate One, how manifold are Your works!" As he stood there, he was illuminated with the Divine image and all the creatures saw and were in awe, thinking he was their Creator. They came to prostrate themselves before him. But Adam said to them, "Come, let us, you and I, proclaim as sovereign over us the One who has created us." Adam did so first, and all the creatures followed him.

On Rosh Hashanah we are like Adam haRishon, a perfect 'Tzadik.' There is thus no mention of our negative past or sins in the day's liturgy, and where we do mention these past mistakes during Tashlich we cast them into the river. We are the perfect agents of the King. It is therefore our responsibility to coronate the King and reveal HaKadosh Baruch Hu's Presence in this world.

We are reborn on Rosh Hashanah like Adam and Chavah on the day of their creation. On this day we embody our pure essence, the way we exist in Adam Kadmon, who, essentially, we really are.

On Rosh Hashanah we are able to become evermore conscious of this birthright and lay claim to it. Then our lives will be truly harmonized with the Book of the Creator, and we will be written and inscribed for a year of life and blessings.

A KAVANAH FOR OUR MINDSET
ON ROSH HASHANAH

I am new; today is a new beginning.

I am remembered for life and deserving of blessings.

I am gifted with the unbelievable power

To coronate Hashem as the Master of the Universe.

This spiritual greatness is my birthright and responsibility —

To bring the Torah's light,
values and inner guidance to all Creation.

PART TWO:

Mysteries of the Shofar

Chapter One

THE 'REASONS' FOR THE SHOFAR

Let us review the basic sources and understandings of why we blow the Shofar on Rosh Hashanah.

THE SOURCE IN THE TORAH FOR SHOFAR

IN THE TORAH, REFERRING TO ROSH HASHANAH, IT SAYS, "A DAY OF *TERU'AH* IT SHALL BE TO YOU" (*BAMIDBAR*, 29:1). *Teru'ah* refers to one of the three sounds made by the Shofar. And since the Torah uses the word *Teru'ah* three times with regards to Shofar (*Vayikra*, 25:9 and 23:24; *Bamidbar*, 29:1), we know that we need to blow a Teru'ah sound three times during the day. And since every Teru'ah sound should be preceded by a Tekiah sound and followed by a Tekiah, we need to blow nine sounds: three sets of *Tekiah–Teru'ah–Tekiah* (*Rosh Hashanah*, 34a).

THIRTY SOUNDS

Today, when we recite the blessing on the Shofar, we immediately follow it with thirty sounds. How does the number of sounds grow from nine to thirty?

A *Tekiah* is an elongated, piercing blast. There are slightly different customs of how the Tekiah sound is to be blown: as one continuous *Kol Pashut* / simple sound with no ups or downs (as the custom of the Maharil Diskin and Brisk, *She'eilas Shelomo*, 2, Siman 55), as one long blast ending with a slide or glissando into a higher tone, or as one blast that continuously moves from a lower to a higher sound, getting continually stronger and stronger (as was the custom of the Ramchal and his students, and later the Jews of Amsterdam). Either way, a Tekiah is a single blast, with one breath.

What then is the sound of a Teru'ah? From the very beginning there were varying opinions and customs regarding how to blow a Teru'ah. Some understood *Teru'ah* to mean a blast broken into three smaller sounds, what we call today *Shevarim* / broken sounds, calling to mind groans of grief. Another view was that Teru'ah is a series of many rapid staccato or 'shattered' sounds, which are like sobbing or whimpering; and this is what we call a *Teru'ah* today. This is because *Teru'ah* comes from the word *Re'uah* / shaky. Yet another view was that a Teru'ah is both of the above sounds fused together: first three broken sounds and then a series of staccato sounds. This is again like someone crying: first there are a couple deep groans and then a quick succession of sobs.

To include and integrate all of these opinions, in a universally significant continuum, we blow the nine blasts with a Shevarim inserted between each pair of Tekios, then we blow nine blasts including a Teru'ah inserted between each pair of Tekios. Finally, we blow a set of 12 sounds with a Shevarim-Teru'ah between each pair of Tekios — making 30 total (9+9+12=30).

To review, here is a chart of the three basic sounds, and the order in which we blow them before the Musaf services of Rosh Hashanah.

PATTERN	GRAPHIC NOTATION	TRANSLITERATION
Tekiah	———————	tuuuuuuuuu
Shevarim	——— ——— ———·	tu–uu–tu, tu–uu–tu, tu–uu–tu
Teru'ah	– – – – – – – – –	tu–tu–tu–tu–tu–tu–tu–tu–tu

Tekiah — Shevarim — Tekiah

Tekiah — Shevarim — Tekiah

Tekiah — Shevarim — Tekiah

Tekiah — Teru'ah — Tekiah

Tekiah — Teru'ah — Tekiah

Tekiah — Teru'ah — Tekiah

Tekiah — Shevarim-Teru'ah — Tekiah

Tekiah — Shevarim-Teru'ah — Tekiah

Tekiah — Shevarim-Teru'ah — Tekiah

It is important to keep in mind that the issue was never actually in doubt; it was never not known how to blow the Shofar. For if so, it would mean there had been a break in the tradition, resulting in a time when they did not blow the Shofar, but this is not the case. The way Rav Hai Gaon explains this phenomenon (*Otzar haGeonim*, Siman, 117. Also cited by the Rosh, *Rosh Hashanah*, 4:10, and the Ran on the Rif, *Rosh Hashanah*, 10a, Although see the Chasam Sofer, *Toras Moshe*, Rosh Hashanah, 906-907) is that from the very beginning of our history there were two or three ways to blow the Shofar.* And it remained this way for centuries, with each community blowing it their way, because that was their *Mesorah* / tradition (On the other hand, according to the Rambam and the Smag, *Esin*, 42, it was a real *Safek* / doubt in *Din* / the law that came about through exile. *Hilchos Shofar*, 3:2: תרועה זו האמורה בתורה נסתפק לנו בה ספק לפי ארך השנים ורב הגלות ואין אנו יודעין היאך היא. See *Beis Yoseph* and *Bach*, Orach Chayim, 590). Different communities blew their own type of Teru'ah, and perhaps throughout the generations sometimes people blew one way and then in the next generation people blew another way, as the Ritva, Rebbe Yom Tov Asevilli (Seville, 1260s–1320s), explains (Ritva on *Rosh Hashanah*, 34a).

---

* This is similar to the different order of the Parshiyos in the Tefilin of Rashi and the Tefilin of Rabbeinu Tam. In *Shu't Min haShamayim* / "Responsa from Heaven," Teshuvah 3 (by one of the Baalei Tosefos), it records that he asked Heaven which opinion is correct, Rashi or Rabbeinu Tam? And he was answered, *Eilu v'Eilu...* / "These and these are the words of the living G-d. Just as there is a debate below, so there is a debate Above." See also *Shibolei haLeket*, Inyan Tefilin, 192. Fascinatingly, in the Qumran caves, various different types of sets of Tefilin were found.

Later, the rabbis, in particular Rav Avuah, desired to establish 'one way' to blow the Shofar, so all Jews could share the same custom. In the academy of Caesarea, Rav Avuah established the use of all three sounds, to include both customs for the Teru'ah (three short blasts and staccato blasts). He therefore established the custom to blow three times Tekiah / Shevarim / Teru'ah / Tekiah, three times Tekiah-Shevarim-Tekiah, and three times Tekiah / Teru'ah / Tekiah (*Rosh Hashanah*, 34a. Rabbeinu Chananel, ad loc.).

Unifying the custom in this way was especially relevant after the destruction of the Second Beis haMikdash. As the Jewish people would eventually live all over the globe, dispersed to the four corners of the world and no longer predominantly concentrated in Israel or the Middle East — to unify them as a people, a single practice was established and adopted by all. This has been the universal practice ever since.

THE 'REASON BEYOND REASON' FOR THE SHOFAR

The Torah does not offer a 'reason' to blow the Shofar; it only says, "It shall be a day of Teru'ah..." As such, the 'reason' we blow the Shofar is simply because the Torah tells us to blow it. There is a tradition that before the blowing of the Shofar, the holy Baal Shem Tov would pronounce in Yiddish, איהר און איך און גאט / "You, Me and G-d."* He would repeat this

* Further on in the present text, the three sounds of the Shofar will be connected with Avraham/*Chesed*/Kindness, Yitzchak/*Gevurah*/Strength and Yaakov/*Tiferes*/Mercy. Interestingly, the Baal Shem Tov's Kavanah alludes to this fact. The word איהר / "you" in numerical value is 216, the same as the word *Gevurah*. איך / "me" is numerically 31, the same as the Name *E-l*,

statement a few times, and then signal for the blower of the Shofar to start blowing (Rebbe Tzvi Hirsh of Smotrich, *Kesem Paz*, p. 17a). This is a simple yet profound *Kavanah* / intention before blowing the Shofar; bringing to mind the acute awareness of *Nochach Pnei Hashem* / Standing in the Presence of HaKadosh Baruch Hu.

And truly, notwithstanding all of the technical Kavanos, this is the perfect Kavanah for blowing the Shofar — to simply be aware that we are standing in the Living Presence of HaKadosh Baruch Hu and that we are performing Hashem's will as stated, "It shall be a day of Teru'ah..." In the language of our sages, the 'reason' why we blow the Shofar is רחמנא אמר תקעו / *Rach'manah Amar Tiku* / "The Merciful One said to blow it" (*Rosh Hashanah*, 16a), and so we do.

Indeed, as the great Chassidic Rebbe, Reb Elimelech of Lizensk teaches, the deepest Kavanah a person can have while blowing or hearing the Shofar is that they are fulfilling Hashem's will by doing the Mitzvah — nothing more.* This is because on the deepest level, since Mitzvos are rooted in the absolute simplicity of Hashem's Unity, there are ultimately no 'reasons' for Mitzvos. Any reason other than the fact that it

---

which is the Name of Hashem connected with Chesed. And גאש is numerically 13, corresponding to the Thirteen Attributes of 'Mercy' (Tiferes).

* A later Chassidic Rebbe, a student of Reb Elimelech, the Maor vaShemesh (*Rimzei*, Rosh Hashanah), would also could teach that the Kavanah of blowing the Shofar simply because Hashem has told us to blow is greatly cherished in Heaven and the highest Kavanah possible.

is Hashem's will suggests something outside itself, as if when you do one thing you will cause another thing, making the Mitzvah merely a means to an end. In the reality of Divine Oneness, there is no separation between Hashem's will and Hashem, and thus there are no 'reasons' for Mitzvos at all, they simply are. Furthermore, a reason cannot be the original cause of any Mitzvah, as the world is preceded by Hashem's Torah and in fact is created through Hashem's Torah, not the other way around. Having a 'reason' for a Mitzvah, such as 'to refine man' for instance, would suggest that the world precedes the Torah, and that the refinement of man in the world stimulates a 'need' for the Mitzvah to be commanded in the Torah.

Such a Kavanah is deceptively simple. For, it is, on the surface, not sophisticated intellectually, however it is mentally very deep. The challenge in achieving and maintaining this Kavanah is therefore not in its ideational conception, but in its meditative continuation. The mind, by nature, is restless and wants to grasp at finer and finer threads of discourse, until they dissolve into nothing. A Kavanah, such as the one the Baal Shem Tov suggests, short-circuits the mind's tendency to mindlessly chase its own brilliant tail in the search for unnecessary complexity. To hold onto a single, simple Kavanah that connects us straight to the source of the Mitzvos, Hashem Himself, sidesteps the whole wormhole of thought, leading us straight through the gates of the heart into the garden of our soul. This is a ritual application of the profound maxim that, 'the *Sod* / secret is the *Peshat* / simple meaning.'

FLOWING INTO THE WORLD OF REASON

Our sages tell us that, a) blowing the Shofar is "a *Chochmah /* skill, and not a work" (*Rosh Hashanah*, 29b), and, b) "the beginning of Chochmah is the awe of Hashem" (*Tehilim*, 111:10). Therefore, the "beginning" or fundamental requirement for the *Toke'a /* blower of the Shofar is to be aware that he is doing a Mitzvah and thus fulfilling the awesome will of Hashem. Yet, "the beginning of Chochmah," suggests that there are other elements and dimensions of the Shofar blowing that may be developed.

"Sound the Shofar on the New Moon, on the appointed time for the day of our festival. For it is a statute (*Chok*) for Israel, the judgment (*Mishpat*) of the G-d of Yaakov" (*Tehilim*, 80:4-5). The term *Chok* generally refers to a Mitzvah that is beyond reason, and *Mishpat* refers to a rational Mitzvah. This Pasuk suggests that the Shofar is both a Chok and a Mishpat; it has both aspects (*Chidushei haGriz* [in the back of the *Beis haLevi*], 203. *Reshimos haTalmidim*, HaGriz, *Tehilim*, 81:4). Shofar is *both* 'beyond reason' and 'within reason', and we should blow the Shofar having both of these intentions in mind; it is simply the will of Hashem, and it also has incredibly deep and profound 'reasons' behind it.

As the Rambam writes, any Mitzvah for which you can find a reason, תֵּן לוֹ טַעַם / *Ten Lo Ta'am /* "give it a reason" (*Hilchos Temurah*, 4:14). This terse statement implies that we should not assume that the reason we ascribe to any given Mitzvah is 'the' reason for its performance, rather to "give it a reason" means to make the Mitzvah relevant to you. Ponder it, explain it, and understand the rationale for its practice in your own life. Hashem wants us to decipher the Mitzvos according to the unique ways we think, feel and appreciate. In every generation HaKadosh Baruch Hu is 'talking' to us through the interface of the world as it is in that moment, including the current realms and discourses of science, worldly wisdom, technology and so forth. Therefore, the Mitzvos also need to be understood in relevant and even 'contemporary' terms, they need to fit securely into our lives and even our personalities.

As the great French scholar, the Meiri, Rabbeinu Menachem (1249–1306) writes (Hakdamah), עת לעשות לה׳ הפרו תורתך / Eis La'asos laHashem Heferu Torasecha / It is a time to act for Hashem; Your law is being violated" (Tehilim, 119:126). The Meiri reads the verse this way: if someone says that they do this or that Mitzvah simply because it is an Eis La'asos la-Hashem, i.e., 'I am blowing the Shofar simply because "it is the time to act for Hashem" and blow the Shofar,' he is הפרו תורתך / Heferu Torah'secha / he is subtly "violating" the Torah. He is not truly observing the Torah's inner depths.

Dovid haMelech says in Tehilim (89:15), אשרי העם יודעי תרועה / Ashrei ha-Am Yod'ei Teru'ah / "Fortunate are those who know Teru'ah," who contemplate and connect to its deeper power. It is in a sense not enough to merely blow the Shofar; we need to "know" it, to intimately understand, examine, and elaborate the inner meanings of its symbolism.

The renowned Mekubal, Rebbe Shalom Sharabi, 'the Ra-shash', writes (*Nahar Shalom*, p. 39a. Also quoted in the *Pele Yo'etz*), "The main point of the Shofar is the Teshuvah that comes along with the sound. Because if we simply blow without intention or inner movement, it is merely like playing an instrument." The call of the Shofar is not just a sound coming from a ram's horn; when we apply intention, focus, commitment, and meditation, it becomes the sound of Teshuvah, beckoning us home to the place of our soul. Later, the dynamics of Teshuvah will be explored in greater detail.

A great student of the Rashba, the Spanish 14th Century Rabbi, Rebbe Yeshohua Ibn Shuiv, writes in his homilies that the meaning of the verse ארור הגבר אשר יבטח באדם / "Cursed is the person who trusts in man" (*Yirmiyahu*, 17:5), means cursed is the person who puts his faith in others who have pondered and explored the meaning of the Mitzvos, but does not care to understand them himself and perform them with his own understanding (*Derashos al haTorah uMoadei haShanah*, Tzav, p. 207). We have to personally understand the Mitzvos and not rely on the fact that others have understood them. We must understand their relevance in our own lives.

In the coming pages we will explore a plethora of profound intentions for the Shofar in some detail; each one of us must aspire to understand and integrate these intentions in the most personal and relevant way.

THE 'REASONS' FOR THE SHOFAR

Whenever our sages offer a 'reason' for blowing the Shofar, they also reveal a practical Kavanah. The Yerushalmi (*Ta'anis*, 2:1) records, "Rebbe Yaakov explained, why do we blow animal horns (on a fast day)? It is as if to say, 'Treat us as if we were squealing like animals.'" Such a primal sound, like the cry of an animal, evokes a raw, visceral sense of existential urgency, a desperate being seeking its endangered survival. Acknowledging the precariousness of our all-too-certain lives while blowing the Shofar, establishes an emotional resonance that intensifies the other specific Kavanos.

In general, there are two primary 'purposes' to blowing the Shofar. According to the Rasag, Rav Saadia Gaon (9th–10th Century Baghdad), the purpose is to coronate Hashem as King (and this is one of the ten reasons brought down by Rav Dovid Avudaraham in the name of the Rasag. See also Ritva, *Rosh Hashanah*, 16a. *Malachim* 1, 1:39). The purpose offered by the Rambam, however, is to awaken us from our spiritual slumber. These two purposes represent the two basic objectives of the Shofar. The 'coronation of the King' invokes an arousal from Above, awakening Hashem's Mercy and Compassion upon His Creation. 'To 'awaken us from spiritual slumber' stimulates an arousal from below, encouraging those who hear the call of the Shofar to more deeply desire a connection with the King.

TEN 'REASONS' FOR THE SHOFAR

Before we delve more deeply into the two seemingly contrasting ideas above, it is worth mentioning the ten reasons for the Shofar recorded by Rav Dovid Avudaraham (14th Century Spain) in the name of the Rasag:

1) Trumpets are blown at the coronation of a new king. On Rosh Hashanah we are 'crowning' HaKadosh Baruch Hu as the King of the Universe, and so we blow the Shofar.

2) The Shofar is a call to Teshuvah. A king may proclaim a period in which amends can be made prior to the enactment of a decree. The Shofar sound proclaims, 'Whoever wishes to do Teshuvah, now is the time.'

3) The Shofar reminds us of Mount Sinai, when the sound of a Shofar was heard (*Shemos*, 19:19). This stimulates us to reaccept upon ourselves the revelation of the Torah.

4) The sound of the Shofar reminds us of the words of our Prophets, whose words are compared to the sounds of the Shofar (*Yechezkel*, 33:3).

5) The sound of the Shofar awakens within us a yearning for the Beis haMikdash, which was destroyed amid the sound of enemy trumpets.

6) The Shofar reminds us of the binding of Yitzchak, whose

place on the altar was taken by a ram (thus we use a ram's horn for the Shofar). On Rosh Hashanah we celebrate the birth of the new year and as such the death of the old year. When we blow the ram's horn we identify with Yitzchak who was saved from death, and reborn; we thus invoke his merit on our behalf as we stand in precarious judgment (*Rosh Hashanah*, 16b. אותו האיל שנברא בין השמשות לא יצא ממנו דבר לבטלה קרניו של איל, של שמאל שתקע בו בהר סיני שנ' ויהי במשוך בקרן היובל, ושל ימין שהיא גדולה משל שמאל שהוא עתיד לתקוע בה לעתיד לבא: *Pirkei DeRebbe Eliezer*, 31:13).

7) The sounds of the Shofar instill in us the awe of the Creator.

8) The sounds of the Shofar remind us that Rosh Hashanah is a time of Divine Judgment.

9) The sounds of the Shofar awaken within us a yearning to return from exile to the Holy Land, since the ingathering of the exiles will be accompanied with the sound of the Shofar Gadol / Great Shofar (Tikkunei Zohar, Tikkun 21).

10) The sounds of the Shofar strengthen our faith in the resurrection of the dead, when the sound of the Great Shofar will be heard, as Yeshayah proclaims (18:3). This is the sound of the 'end of time', meaning the time of Redemption.

CREATION (PAST), REVELATION (PRESENT), REDEMPTION (FUTURE)

Shofar is the sound of the 'exhale' that births the world. 'Coronating the King', too, is connected with Creation, the 'beginning of time'. The Shofar of the Redemption and Resurrection relates to the 'end of time'. The Shofar of the Revelation at Mount Sinai resounds in between these two, in the present moment. Thus the Shofar embraces and unifies past, present, and future. It is the sound of beginnings and endings, starting anew, ending the old, and being present with HaKadosh Baruch Hu in the infinite now.

The Shofar unites...	Creation, Coronation	the past; all beginnings	...in the 'eternal now' of Hashem's Presence.
	Revelation	the present	
	Redemption, Resurrection	the future; all endings	

Bereishis is the first word in the Torah. As the first *Ma'amar* / utterance of the Ten Utterances of Creation, it is the original, primordial sound-vibration-pattern that gives rise to physical matter. The Ten Divine Utterances are the ten primary sounds or vibrations that generate Creation, yet, the root of the ten is the first, all-inclusive utterance, through which the primary matter of all of Creation was created. As such, the sound of the word *Bereishis* is the primordial meta-root of all Creation. In the teaching of the (Tikkunei) Zohar, the letters of the word *Bereishis* can be rearranged to spell the words *Bara Tayish* /

created a goat or ram. Both a goat's horn and a ram's horn can be used as a Shofar, even though the preference, as our sages tell us, is that of a ram. In this way, the Shofar sings the song of *Bereishis*; the sound of the Shofar is the original and most primal sound of Creation.

The eternal moment includes past, present and future as one. As such, the past exists deeply in the present. Nothing of the Creation of the world is actually ever in the 'past', as every moment of existence is completely new. This is especially important to keep in mind on Rosh Hashanah, the renewal of Creation. Similarly, this is true of the future. Although Redemption is not yet present, at least not to all of Creation, we all have the ability to tap into the redeemed future, as it too exists in the present moment.

Our Shofar blowing, in a sense, exists between the Revelation of the present and the Redemption of the future. Through the sound of the Shofar we are drawing upon the power of renewal (Creation), aligning ourselves with the Divine Will (Revelation), and ushering in the awareness of a perfected world (Redemption). As we anticipate the future, we are empowered by the past in the vibrations of the present moment.

Our custom is to blow the Shofar from the *Bimah* / lectern, immediately following the Torah reading in the same location (ונוהגין לתקוע על הבימה במקום שקורין: *Orach Chayim*, 585, Rama). Perhaps the reason is because we first want to draw from the Shofar of Revelation (Note, *haGahos haGra*, ad loc., from the Rokeach. The Rokeach,

Hilchos Rosh Hashanah, 201, writes that we blow the Shofar after Kerias ha-Torah, not right away in the morning, so that we can fill ourselves up with more Mitzvos before we blow. The *Kaf haChayim*, 585:8,1, offers a few other reasons). By filling ourselves first with the power of Revelation, we are liberated from all negativity, and prepared to be open to the Sound of the Great Shofar of Redemption.

THE CORONATION OF THE KING, THE HUMILITY OF HUMANITY

As mentioned, the 'main' reason provided by the Rasag for blowing the Shofar is the idea of coronation. This is consistent with the simple reading of the sages who say "Pronounce before Me (verses of) Kingship, so that you shall crown Me King over you... How? With the (blowing of the) Shofar" (*Rosh Hashanah* 16a, as the Rashba and Ritva, *ad loc.*, explain. We pronounce the verses of Kingship and as we do so, we coronate Hashem as King of the World, through the blowing of the Shofar. Alternatively, "with the Shofar" can mean 'with the verses of Shofar'. *Sefer HaPardes l'Rashi*, Hilchos Rosh Hashanah [Ehrenreich edition], pp. 217-218. See also *Likutei Sichos*, 34, pp.180-181). Interestingly, there is an older Ashkenazi custom to mold the top of the actual Shofar to resemble a crown, as the sound of the Shofar is the medium through which we crown HaKadosh Baruch Hu as our King.

Blowing the Shofar is of course related to the coronation of earthly kings as well. We are thus ritually performing the principle of "as Above so below," and therefore, "The kingship below mirrors the Kingship Above" (*Berachos*, 58a). Just as the coronation of kings below involved blowing Shofars, so does the coronation of HaKadosh Baruch Hu, Above (Rashba and the Ritva on *Rosh Hashanah*, 16a. Rabbeinu Bachya, *Kad Kemach*, Rosh Hashanah). We find in *Tanach* / scripture, that during the coronation of a new king the Shofar was blown and then the people would exclaim, "Long live the king!" With regard to Shlomo haMelech / King Solomon, the verse says, "And Tzadok the Priest took the horn of oil...and anointed Shlomo, and they blew the Shofar, and all the people said, "Long live King Shlomo!" (*Melachim* 1, 1:39). Later on, with King Yeihu, the verse says, "And they hastened...and they sounded the Shofar and said, "Yeihu has become king!" (*Melachim* 2, 9:13).

The Rambam, however, writes that the sound of the Shofar 'mainly' serves as a wakeup call for Teshuvah. The piercing sound arouses us from our spiritual slumber. In his own words: "Although the sounding of the Shofar on Rosh Hashanah is a Torah decree (without a given reason), there is an allusion in it as well. It tells us, 'Be roused, sleepers, from your sleep, and slumberers, wake up from your slumber; search your deeds and return in Teshuvah'" (*Hilchos Teshuvah*, 3:4. Note, the Rambam does not offer this reason in the laws of Shofar, but rather in the laws of Teshuvah, perhaps suggesting, that the deeper reason for Shofar is beyond 'reason' altogether, and thus, he does not offer any reason for Shofar in the laws of Shofar).

Parenthetically, this argument regarding the 'reason' for why we blow the Shofar can also be linked to another argument among the early Rishonim and Geonim: what is the ultimate objective, and thus the blessing to be recited when blowing the Shofar: *Lishmo'a* / to 'hear' the sound of the Shofar, or *Lis-ko'a* / to 'blow' the Shofar? (לשמוע קול שופר or לתקוע בשופר. Rav Hai, Rav Amram rule לשמוע; Rav Yehudai and Rav Achai rule לתקוע). If the sound of the Shofar is the coronation of the King, then, the act of 'blowing' is primary. If the act of blowing the Shofar is meant to arouse our sentiments of Teshuvah, then 'hearing' the sounds of the Shofar is the point.

WAKING UP

When considering the Rambam's reason for blowing the Shofar, i.e., to arouse us from our spiritual slumber, one would be well served to ask: what does it mean to be spiritually asleep and then to become awakened? Lets say, for example, a person is put to sleep prior to an operation in which they remove a sick limb. The pain and awareness of the loss of the limb does not surface while the person is asleep, rather, the very moment he awakens and becomes alert is precisely the point at which the pain and sense of loss kicks in. Similarly, when a person is going through life semi-consciously, even if he is indeed 'removed' from the Source of all Life and disconnected from his deeper self, he does not recognize his spiritual estrangement. Since he is spiritually, mentally and emotionally asleep, he remains carefree and worriless. He is not wracked with any sense of anxiety or 'spiritual pain' that would compel him to do something to untangle himself from his inescapable alienation. It is only once he is aroused from his slumber and awakened to the depths of life that he realizes something is terribly amiss, and only then does a strong desire to transform become tangibly felt.

We therefore must first 'wake up' before we are able to realize that our true desire is to do Teshuvah. The Shofar is a spiritual alarm clock, awakening us to become fully conscious and mindful. In that moment, we are palpably alive, but in the same breath we also realize what a loss it is to live without meaning and higher purpose.*

Sadly, many people do go through life in a semi-conscious state. The distinction between what is real and what is fantasy, between what they truly want and what society has influenced them to desire, between being in touch with the soul and con-

---

* This reasoning is consistent with the statement in the Gemara that the Shofar reminds us of the sound of weeping. *Rosh Hashanah*, 33b. It appears that, according to the Rambam, the sound of the Shofar awakens the person to want to do Teshuvah. Yet, the Zohar seems to suggest the opposite, that first comes Teshuvah and then the sound of the Shofar, albeit, also a sound connected with Teshuvah: *Zohar* 3, 99b. Perhaps the Zohar is connected with how the Tur establishes the blowing of the Shofar in Elul. The Tur writes, "We have learned in *Pirkei d'Rebbe Eliezer* that on Rosh Chodesh Elul Hashem told Moshe, 'Ascend to Me on the mountain,' for then he went to receive the second Luchos. And they then blew a Shofar in the camp, so everyone should know that Moshe went up the mountain, so that they should not make the same mistake and end up serving idols (since the first time Moshe ascended, they miscalculated his return date and when he did not arrive on the mistaken date, they created the Golden Calf to replace him.) Therefore, our sages instituted that we blow Shofar on Rosh Chodesh Elul every year. And the entire month the sound warns us to do Teshuvah, as the verse says, "Could the Shofar be blown in the city and the nation not tremble? And also to confuse the Satan": Tur, *Orach Chayim*, 581. In other words, there is a blowing of Rosh Chodesh, as a reminder of the Shofar that was blown in the Desert, and there is a blowing of the entire month of Elul, which is connected with Teshuvah (and confuses Satan). The Rosh Chodesh blowing was to ensure that they do not 'sin' again. They have already done Teshuvah and are just ensuring that they do not fall again. And the blowing throughout the month is therefore to awaken one to Teshuvah.

trolled by the ego, is devastatingly blurred. Even more sadly, some people walk around in a complete spiritual slumber, unattached and unconnected to their deepest selves, living in a world of false dreams and superficial illusions, a world where satisfaction is never attainable, and alienation reigns supreme. And then one day, it is possible that something dramatic or tragic occurs which jolts them out of their stupor, and suddenly they wake up. In other words, they receive a proverbial 'slap in the face' and suddenly realize that their life up until this point was a lie, an illusion, a shell with no substance. The Shofar is a gentle, albeit piercing sound that, when listened to properly, rouses us from our own spiritual stupor, on whatever level we are holding. It is the sudden sound that wakes us up and shows us that we have been 'asleep' all this time. We become alert and ready to live. This is the power of the Shofar upon our psyche, jolting us out of our ignorance and waking us up to our purpose, our mission, our reason for being.

"Could the Shofar be blown in the city," thunders the prophet, "and the nation not tremble?" (*Amos*, 3:6). The 'trembling' that the Shofar arouses during Elul (see Tur, Beis Yoseph, *Orach Chayim*, 581) and on Rosh Hashanah is not merely the dread of judgment or punishment, rather, something much more existential and profound. The Shofar wakes us up and causes us to tremble at the thought: perhaps we have been sleeping all this time. Perhaps we are just passing through life and have never been aware and awake to our higher purpose. Perhaps we are only alive, as harsh as it may sound, because 'we have not been killed in an accident.' We are like robots walking through life. And so, when we hear the Shofar, this great fear and trembling sets in. We awaken to the real value and opportunity of being alive.

When Torah speaks about Yom Kippur, the culmination of Rosh Hashanah, it says, "For any person אשר לא־תענה / 'who will not be afflicted' on that very day, shall be cut off...." (*Vayikra*, 23:29) Says the Chasam Sofer, it could also be read as follows: "Any person who does not *feel* afflicted or moved on that very day (should know that he is already) cut off" from the Source of All Life. If on Yom Kippur you are not moved to yearning or tears, if you don't tremble at the ways you have been asleep in your life, this may mean that you are living as if you were separated from the Source of all Life, and that therefore you are currently in a state of *Kares* / cut off, Chas v'Shalom.

If the sounds of the Shofar on Rosh Hashanah and the days of Teshuvah leading into Yom Kippur have not already aroused and awakened you, and you are still not feeling anything, know in this moment that you are, regrettably, 'cut off'; you are so far removed and disconnected from anything holy and real that even the jolting sounds of the Shofar do not awaken you and have 'fallen on deaf ears'. But of course, one should not despair, as this bitter awareness itself, when taken to heart, has the power to penetrate one's cynical defenses and compel them to Teshuvah. The very fact that you feel uncomfortable about not being awakened, and that you consciously recognize this insensitivity, will itself ever-so-slightly crack open your heart and stimulate a subtle movement of Teshuvah.

THE CALCULATIVE BEINONI

As discussed earlier, a *Beinoni* / intermediate person is someone on the fence, neither a Tzadik nor a Rasha, having "half of his deeds good, and half of his deeds negative." The fate of the *Beinoni* rests on the scales from Rosh Hashanah until Yom Kippur; "if they are *worthy* they receive life, if not, they are written to death" (*Rosh Hashanah*, 16b). It comes to reason that if he is 'worthy', meaning during the time period from Rosh Hashanah until and including Yom Kippur he does at least one more worthy act, then his scale tips to positivity, and he is considered a *Tzadik b'Din* / a righteous person in a legal sense.

That is the way the *Bavli* / Babylonian Talmud records this teaching. The Rambam (based on the *Yerushalmi* / Jerusalem Talmud's version) writes: "The Beinoni's verdict remains tentative until Yom Kippur. If he *repents*, his [verdict] is sealed for life. If not, his [verdict] is sealed for death" (*Hilchos Teshuvah*, 3:3). In other words, according to the Rambam, if the intermediate person does not do Teshuvah he is inscribed for 'death'. The question is, why does he need Teshuvah? According to the *Bavli*, and the simple meaning of *Beinoni*, the difference is purely quantitative: if the Beinoni does even one more Mitzvah than sin during this period, he gains life. Why then does the Rambam's version use 'Teshuvah' as a rubric of "worthiness"? And what is so special about Teshuvah?

There are, perhaps, two types of Beinonim: the existential Beinoni and the calculative Beinoni. The existential Beinoni is one whose life is a constant struggle. For him, some days are better than others. Sometimes his higher self wins the struggle and he is swayed to do good, holy, noble things. And sadly, sometimes even within the same day, he is too weak to fight and he gives in to his lower, base desires. His life is perpetually full of ups and downs and he is in an existential state of being 'in the middle'. For this type of Beinoni, to become considered more "worthy" all he needs to do during this time period is perform more Mitzvos, and he will be sealed for life.

A 'calculative Beinoni' is a person who is always making sure that he is doing the right thing, but in a calculated way. If he spends extra time praying in the morning, then he figures, 'Now I can afford to rush through *Mincha* / afternoon prayers.' If he already gave his daily twenty dollars to Tzedakah, then if someone else stretches out their hand, he says, 'Sorry, I don't have any. Come back tomorrow.' If he has learned Torah for a few hours, he gets up and says, 'That's enough, now I need a few hours break.' Everything is with a *Cheshbon* / quantification. Yes, he is a Beinoni *b'Din* / in judgment, but if, at least during the period of Rosh Hashanah through Yom Kippur, he does not take a spiritual plunge and go beyond his calculated minimum expenditures on Mitzvos, do actual Teshuvah and change his ways, this is a sign that his scales are tipping sharply toward negativity.

Regardless, no matter where you stand on the ladder of spiritual development, it is fitting to allow yourself to be moved and inspired during the days between Rosh Hashanah and Yom Kippur, and to use that motivation to reach beyond your current level of spiritual commitment. Your life is acutely hanging in the balance (as it always really is) and you should aspire to cry out for deeper connection, and express your sincere willingness to grow. To do Teshuva is to wake up to the reality of your life and to strive to do better. In fact, a person's calculative or inconsistent way of living is a clear indicator that you have an urgent need for Teshuvah.

"One who does not cry during this time period," says the Arizal, "his soul is not complete." In other words, if you are not shaken by the reality of your life during this entire period of focused introspection there is an incompleteness or emptiness within you. On some fundamental level you are living your life robotically, uninspired and unconnected. If you are not growing around Rosh Hashanah time, you are stagnating; if you are not in an accelerating process of waking up, you are decelerating. If you are not getting in touch with your deepest self, you are cutting yourself off from your soul, from others and from the Source of all Life.

The sound of the Shofar is your wake up call. If you don't get up with your alarm, it means you are too tired to live. You are so deeply asleep that even when a new day is knocking at your door, you remain asleep and unaware. However, if the Shofar did not jolt you out of your spiritual complacency, do not despair, allow the disappointment to break open your heart so you can truly hear and heed the wake up call of the Shofar.

Allow yourself to hear the alarm of the Shofar with a sense of trembling and awe: 'How am I living my life?' Allow the magnitude of existence to come into focus. Allow the pain of your habitual resistance to permeate you until you can only break down and let out a cry of yearning, and sincere longing for connection.

Even if nothing is happening, no inner movement, inspiration, desire or yearning, then simply stop everything and recognize that you are in a deep mental, emotional and spiritual slumber. Recognize that the Shofar is meant to arouse you to at least *desire* to feel your spiritual stagnation, to 'want to want' to have a relationship with *Elokim Chayim* / the living Presence of Hashem. This recognition is, in itself, a miniature form of Teshuvah. If you do not even make space in yourself for this minimal acknowledgment, if you do not even 'want to want' to wake up in your life, the Rambam writes that you are in effect 'cutting yourself off' from life at an existential level.

The word *Teru'ah*, used to describe the sound of the Shofar, comes from the word *Reu'a* / broken, as we find in the Prophets: "Could the Shofar be blown in the city, and the nation not tremble?" This refers to the fact that the Shofar was sounded to alert the public of an ensuing battle. The sound thus inspired fear, 'breaking' people's humdrum state of mind, and alerting them to the immediate urgency of their situation. This could be one reason that the Rambam says the Shofar awakens Teshuvah. The sound stimulates a healthy survival instinct, rallies the troops of positivity and even pierces the ego, causing the inner adversary to tremble and break down.

'CORONATION' AND 'AROUSING FROM SLEEP': TWO ASPECTS OF TAKING RESPONSIBILITY

These two basic reasons for blowing the Shofar, coronation and arousal, seem like polar opposites. One stresses our tremendous value and self-worth: we are honored above all creatures to coronate HaKadosh Baruch Hu as King and Master of the Universe. The other stresses our lowliness and distance, that we are spiritually asleep and need to wake up. Yet these modes of confidence and humility are actually two sides of one coin. They are two aspects of 'accepting responsibility for our life', which is the theme of Rosh Hashanah. Both lead to the realization of our 'partnership' with the Creator. And in our partnership with Hashem there are two complementary aspects of our responsibility: owning up to our behaviors and their consequences, and acknowledging Hashem's ultimate power in our life.

Taking responsibility for our life allows us to affirm that we deserve to be recreated this year. Elul is the period of *Yetziras haVelad* / formation of the fetus. We are being formed, through our Teshuvah, into a new being. Then we are ready to be born as a completely formed fetus on the Eve of Rosh Hashanah. At that point we are authentically prepared to say, 'Hashem You are the King, and I am ready to enter the world and accept my royal mission.'

On Rosh Hashanah, our collective birthday, we assume total responsibility for our lives and recognize that our lives truly matter. Yet, for genuine responsibility to flourish we need to establish a positive, healthy foundation for our life. For example, it is easier for a child who was loved unconditionally to assume responsibility when they grow older. Elul is thus a time when "the King is in the field," available and accessible for us to approach Him. During this spiritually formative period, the King shows each one of us a pleasant and joyous countenance (as the famous parable of the Alter Rebbe suggests), and openly reveals His Thirteen Attributes of Divine Mercy. Elul is the unconditional, supportive foundation of our relationship with Hashem, and from the fields of Elul we can follow the King into His palace as a loyal servant, and assume full responsibility for ourselves and our world.

Rosh Hashanah is a time when we take upon ourselves, once again, with vigor and dedication, this awesome responsibility of being fully human, completely dedicated to our Divine mission and purpose. It is a time when we once again confirm that Hashem is Melech, and we are entrusted with making sure that we, and the world at large, recognize and live this truth.

From this perspective, the main idea of Rosh Hashanah really is *Malchus* / kingship.

As the Mekubalim write, the inner, hidden letters of the three letters of the Hebrew word *Din** equal 496, which is the numerical value of the word *Malchus* (*Asarah Ma'amaros*, Ma'amar Ma'yan Ganim). This hints to the idea that the main idea of Mal-

---

* Dalet/4, Lamed/30, and Tav/400. Yud/10, Vav/6, Dalet/4. Nun/50, Vav/6, Nun/50, minus the Dalet/4, Yud/10, Nun/50 = 496.

chus, that Hashem is King, is that there is absolute *Din* / rule, and on the Day of Din everything is judged and returned to its allotted place and purpose within the Divine Kingdom.

This means that the purpose of Creation is for everything to do exactly what it was created to do. With human beings this fulfillment of purpose comes about through our free choice, when we consciously recognize and take responsibility for our role and purpose in creation. *Din* / judgment and the revealing of Malchus bring us into existential alignment with our Divine mandate and objective.

Although this is one process, the Rasag's reason for the Shofar focuses more on Hashem's role, i.e., that Hashem should be King, the Rambam, however, focuses more on our human role, i.e., waking up and taking charge of our higher mission.

BETWEEN A KING AND A RULER

There is a fundamental difference between a *Melech* / king and a *Moshel* / ruler (as both the Alter Rebbe and the Gra explain: *Likutei Torah*, Derushim l'Rosh Hashanah, 56b. *Pirush haGra*, Tehilim, 22:29). In principle, "There is no king without subjects" (*Rabbeinu Bachya*, Bereishis, 38:30. *Kad Kemech*, Rosh Hashanah 2. *Emek haMelech*, Sha'ar Sha'ashuai SaMelech, 1. *Tanya*, Sha'ar haYichud v'haEmunah, 7), meaning that a king only rules with the consent of his people; when they coronate him and willfully accept upon themselves his kingship. Such coronation actually invests him with the power to be king. A *Moshel* / ruler, by contrast, is a sovereign who rules by force, without or against the will of the people, in other words — dictator. Hashem wants to be our Melech not our Moshel.

Rosh Hashanah celebrates the creation of the first human being on the Sixth Day of Creation. Before this event, before human consciousness existed, there was no creature capable of having an intellectual awareness of the Creator. Humanity was — and remains — unique in its ability to ponder and acknowledge a Higher Power. The quest for transcendence, spirituality and deeper meaning is indigenous to humans. Before Adam and Chavah, there was nothing in Creation that could have a *Panim-el-Panim* / face-to-face relationship with the Divine.

On the day they were created, Adam and Chavah were empowered to gather all the animals and present to them their Creator. Until then, the Creator was without a cognizant and willing 'kingdom' of subjects. The Creator only 'became a King' when Adam and Chavah facilitated such recognition of Hashem as the Sovereign of all.

Before Rosh Hashanah, Hashem was merely the Creator and ruler of the world, a Moshel; on Rosh Hashanah, HaKadosh Baruch Hu became, and becomes, the benevolent King of the world, the Melech.

FREE CHOICE

Shofar is the only Mitzvah in the Torah connected with the act of 'blowing', or breath. There are many Mitzvos that are performed with speech, even more with action, but only one Mitzvah through breath alone. Blowing is a fundamental reminder of what it means to be human. As it says in the Torah, "Hashem blew into the nostrils of Adam a 'breath of life', and he became a living being," the first creature with intellectual consciousness and free choice. Adam therefore became a full human being only after Hashem blew into his nostrils a breath of life, a soul. With this new faculty of soul (and thus free choice), Adam had the ability to either stray from the path of his inner existence, or to make Hashem his King. As soon as Hashem had blown into the 'Shofar' of Adam's body, the process of His coronation had begun. With this 'blowing' Hashem began to assume the role of Melech, not just Moshel, of the world.

If Hashem wanted to be only a Moshel, Hashem could have imposed rulership on the world without creating a being with free choice. In fact, even today, Hashem is a Moshel to all other forms of life, besides the human being. Everything in creation besides the human being operates in a deterministic manner — the way it was created is the way it is and always will be. A lion does not 'choose' to roar or hunt or be a carnivore. Human beings, however, have the most God-like of powers: the power to choose and *create* their own reality. Only humans can be such 'creators' of their lives. And therefore, only humans, who possess this creative quality, can crown their Creator as their Melech.

Only creatures into whom Hashem has blown His Own breath have free-choice and hence the ability and responsibility to blow the Shofar. Therefore, by blowing the Shofar we demonstrate the essential purpose of our humanity: to consciously coronate HaKadosh Baruch Hu as the Beloved Sovereign of the Universe.

SUBJECTS OF THE KING: CLOSE AND DISTANT

On a deeper level, human beings must combine two apparently opposing dimensions of self to make the coronation of Hashem as Melech possible. These opposing elements are comparable to the two essential requirements for an earthly king to assume kingship, which is a mirror image of the Supernal Kingship. First, the king and his subjects must be related and of the same kind of being — for instance, a human being cannot be a king over animals. Although he can rule over them as a Moshel, he cannot be elected, crowned or accepted by them as their sovereign. Second, the king and his subjects cannot be related too closely. For example, a father cannot truly be a king over his children if he desires the closeness of being a parent. These two vital elements of a king-subject relationship can thus be characterized as closeness and distance.

So it is with human beings and their Creator. We are both children and servants of HaKadosh Baruch Hu. It is thus written, "Israel is My son, My firstborn," and also, "To Me, Israel is My servant." Our souls are inextricably intertwined with the essence of the Infinite, and we are an integral part of the All. We are like our Creator's children, and made in our Creator's image. But we are also physical entities with material bodies, and, as such, are separate and seemingly independent from the Source of All Life, rendering us servants.

Since our souls are 'Godly', we have the 'closeness' and status necessary to anoint Hashem as King. And because we exist in bodies, we also have the perceptual and existential distance to relate to our Creator as an awesome King.

HaKadosh Baruch Hu desired to create a being that labors under the illusion of separateness and yet submits willingly to the Creator. It is not sufficient for some or most of humanity to come to this awareness, if there is even one individual who does not recognize this truth, then the purpose of Creation is not complete. Therefore, each of us is singularly important; as the Gemara teaches (*Sanhedrin*, 37a), "For me, the world was created." This is true for each and every individual. Moreover, beyond our unique being, everything we do, every single action we take or fail to take, can and does have cosmic effects, tipping the scale in either direction of merit or its opposite.

ACCEPTING HASHEM AS ABSOLUTE KING

Hashem wants us to want Him. And it is specifically through the blowing of the Shofar and all the spiritual work we do on Rosh Hashanah, and of course throughout the entire year, that we are able to emphatically express our acceptance of HaKadosh Baruch Hu as our absolute master.

To accept Hashem as our King means to recognize that there is only One master in our lives, to the exclusion of anyone or anything else. This precludes all excuses or circumstantial claims that such and such a force or person made us do something against the will of the King. We can no longer complain that our life would be different if this or that had happened to me, if only I had the dream job, the perfect relationship, or a different upbringing. As a subject of the King alone, we do not blame anything or anyone, for the only truth is the will of Hashem. Hashem is the One and Only.

In the Rosh Hashanah Davening, at the end of Malchiyos, we recite the verse, *Shema Yisrael Hashem Elokeinu Hashem Echad* / "Hear Israel, Hashem is our G-d, Hashem is One" (*Devarim*, 6:4. *Rosh Hashanah*, 32b). It is important to realize that this verse is personally addressed to you. Suppose your name is Simcha. Think: *Shema* Simcha, *Hashem Elokecha, Hashem Echad* / 'Listen, Simcha, Hashem is *your* Divinity! Hashem is your Only One.' The Shema is not only addressed to *Klal Yisrael* / the collective of Yisrael, Hashem is speaking to you directly as well. Then contemplate deeply: 'What does this mean in my personal life? What are the practical implications of Hashem being my *Elokim*, my only source of power? That Hashem is the only Master of my life. What does it mean for me that Hashem is the One Existence, that Hashem is truly All That Is?'

On a more inward, personal level of *Avodah* / self-refinement, the masters of Mussar teach, "If you want to coronate Hashem as your King, go and crown your *Seichel* / mind over yourself" (*Sifsei Chayim*, Moadim 1, p. 154). Make sure that your higher mind, that which understands the will of Hashem, is in control of your body (*Chochmah uMusar* 2, 139). In other words, in order to accept Hashem as our King, we must also be a king or master over ourselves. Our center of higher consciousness must guide our heart, our center of desire and yearning.

Melech / King has three letters, Mem, Lamed, Ches, which stand for *Moach* / mind, *Lev* / Heart and *Kaved* / Liver, in this order. Our internal governance should move from our higher mind, to our emotional heart and finally to our liver, which, according to the sages, is the seat of our actions. If we really want Hashem to be the Melech of our lives, not just conceptually; if we want to deeply know and have faith that Hashem is the only true cause of everything, and to tangibly let this influence our Midos and behaviors, then we need to make sure that our higher mind controls our heart. We cannot claim Hashem to be our King if we are simply puppets dangling on the strings of our unconscious emotional attachments, or living in constant reactivity to the world around us.

Furthermore, by being a Melech, a king, a master over our own lives, we are actually allowing for the ultimate revelation that Hashem is Melech. For we can not meaningfully grant a power to another that we cannot wield ourselves. What is more, the Mishnah (*Chagigah*, 11b) talks about someone trying to grasp ideas that are beyond his capacity, and comments that such a person לא חס על כבוד קונו / "has no concern for the *Kavod* / honor and glory of his Maker." What is the connection between the Kavod of Hashem and a person misusing his intellectual capabilities? Regarding this Mishnah, the Rambam writes (*Pirush haMishnayos*, 2:1), כל שלא חס על כבוד קונו רוצה בו מי שלא יחום ויחמול על שכלו כי השכל הוא כבוד השם / "One who has no concern for the Kavod of his Creator — this means a person who is not careful with his intellect (meaning, he is delving into areas that cannot, by their very nature, be understood), for *a person's intellectual capacity is the Kavod of his Creator.*" The Rambam, as a 'rationalist' philosopher, sees honoring the boundaries of reason and knowability as an absolute necessity. What is 'ours' is ours and what is Hashem's is Hashem's.

By extension, when we *are* living fully with what is 'ours' — focusing on the knowledge, potential and talents that have been given to us, and not squandering them — we are revealing the Kavod Hashem in this world. Just as a painting reflects the painter, and a car reflects its maker, when we, human beings, 'fire on all cylinders', and actualize our potential fully, living as a Melech, a master over ourselves as our Creator intended, we reflect positively on our Creator. Indeed, it is through our very lives, lived to their fullest, that we bring *Kavod Hashem* / the honor of Hashem into the world. We thus reveal the Creator's intention through our every action. We are, as explained, thereby 'justifying Hashem' for creating us, by giving glory to His Name and electing Him as King.

LIVING AS A UNIFIED EXISTENCE

Nothing simply 'happens' to us. Everything is really one unified Divine *Malchus* / Kingdom. With this as your perspective, you can no longer mindlessly 'react' to challenges in life; to the contrary, you accept the fact that everything is from Hashem, you feel this deeply, and then you mindfully respond.

Part of true *Kabbalas Ol*, accepting upon oneself that Hashem is Melech, the sole master of the world, is truly accepting that Hashem is *Echad*, and all there is.

We conclude the section of Malchiyos in Rosh Hashanah Davening with the declaration, *Shema Yisrael... Hashem Echad*. In the words of Rashi (*ibid*), this sentence means, "Hashem, who is now '*our* G-d', will be (declared) in the future "the one G-d"; meaning that eventually everyone in the world will, of their own volition, choose to embrace HaKadosh Baruch Hu as the One and Only Reality.

"On that day Hashem will be One...." (*Zecharyah*, 14:9) Say our sages, 'Is not Hashem's Name already *One*, today?' Rav Acha ben Chanina says, 'This world is different from the World to Come. In this world, upon good news, a person says, "Blessed (are You) Who is Good and Gives Goodness," whereas on bad news one says, "Blessed (are You) the True (just) Judge." Whereas in the World to Come, a person will say the same blessing on all that occurs , "...Who is Good and Gives Good'" (*Pesachim*, 50a. Rashi writes שאין שם בשורה רעה / because there will not be any bad news, see however, *Tzlach*, ad loc.).

What does this mean experientially? In the way of "this world" we can reach a level in which we recognize that

Hashem is actually the sole 'root cause' of everything that is going on in my life. And so, when good or pleasant things occur, I bless Hashem, '...Who is good and is giving me goodness'. And when difficult things occur, I bless Hashem as '...a just Judge'; I trust that there is a good reason for every occurrence, even if I do not comprehend it.

Using these two different blessings is the way of "this world." It is a high level of Emunah, to be sure, yet it is still within the paradigm of duality; it is *Hashem Elokeinu*, but not yet *Hashem Echad*. We are still saying that 'good things' and 'bad things' happen to me, yet I trust that HaKadosh Baruch Hu has reasons for all of them. As such, you do not yet see that what is occurring to you is *part* of you, rather you still see it as something occurring *to* you — from the outside — yet you accept it as the will of the Creator.

Thus, for 'good news' in your life you say, 'This is *Tov* / good,' as you recognize that the occurrence is 'completing' you. For instance, during the Bar Kochva revolt, when after much time elapsed they were finally able to bury those killed in the devastating massacre of Beitar, the bodies were miraculously preserved. The sages reacted in wonder by exclaiming the blessing later inserted in the *Birchas haMazon* / the blessing after eating a meal, "...Who is Good and Gives Goodness" (*Berachos*, 48b. *Ta'anis*, 31a). When an unburied body returns to the earth, it is a 'completion', as earth returns back to earth. "Goodness" is defined as the completion of an object (In the language of the Rogatchover "טוב היינו דאין צריך שום תיקון / Tov means something that does not need a Tikkun" *Tzafnas Paneach*, Torah, Vaeschanan, on the Pasuk, ובתים מלאים כל־טוב. See Yerushalmi, *Shevi'is*, 6:1). "Hashem saw it was *Tov /* Good," when an act of Creation was complete.

At this point in history, not many people have the capacity to see negativity, hardships and difficulties as 'completing' them or even being part of them; rather such struggles and obstacles seem like foreign invaders or merciless daggers thrown at them in attack. There will come a time, however, when Hashem's plan will become revealed and HaKadosh Baruch Hu will be revealed to all as the Melech and the Only One. Then all will recognize that everything that has happened and is currently happening to them is but an extension of themselves, expressing the Oneness, the completeness of reality.

Practically, this perception of ultimate Unity allows you to realize that nothing is happening *to* you, rather it is *part of you*. For example, a person who has a healthy body image and a holistic sense of self does not usually have a sense that 'I *have* legs. I *have* a brain.' Rather, they sense, 'My legs and brain are expressions of me.' Living a deeper life, with an awareness of Olam Haba in the present, means that we extend this perception to everything in our lives, and realize that everything is nothing other than an expression of Echad. Things do not actually happen *to* us, rather they are expressions *of* us.

This is a higher way of living with and embracing the understanding that Hashem Echad, revealing the deeper *Achdus /* unity even within the smallest details of our lives.

HASHEM MELECH: THREE LEVELS

In summary, the three fundamental principles that form the foundation of the recognition that *Hashem Melech* / Hashem is King are: a) I am ceasing from blaming anyone or anything for the state of my life, and I recognize that everything is only an expression of HaKadosh Baruch Hu. b) Furthermore, everything I experience is an expression of myself. Not only did Hashem want these things to happen to me, but from the perspective of Echad, everything is an expression of the One, including myself. And with this recognition, c) I am hereby accepting responsibility and taking control over my life and ensuring that my 'mind', my higher consciousness, controls my heart.

The Maggid of Mezritch teaches, "A person should contemplate the fact that the inner Divine World of Speech (Yetzirah) is speaking through you, and if it were not for the World of Speech speaking through you, you would not be able to speak…. It is the same with thoughts. Without the influence of the World of Thought (Beriah) you would not have any thoughts. This is like the Shofar: what you blow into the Shofar is the exact sound that comes out of it, and if you stop blowing there is no sound. The same is true with the Divine Life Force, if not (Heaven forbid) for this force, one would not be able to think or speak" (*Likutei Amarim*, 146).

When we realize that it is HaKadosh Baruch Hu who is 'blowing' our life into and through us, we realize that we are "like the Shofar." And when we in turn blow our breath through the Shofar on Rosh Hashanah, we are returning that original breath from whence it came, back to the source of All Life. This is how we, as creations, are able to coronate the Creator as King.

That is why we celebrate the day that human beings were created, rather than the day the world at large was created. We are celebrating the opportunity to crown Hashem as the revealed Master of the World, so we can have a *Panim-el-Panim* / face-to-face relationship with the Only One. This very ability, unique to the human being made in the Divine's Image, was and is Hashem's birthday present to us.

To fully realize Hashem's Kingship, we need to understand the true definition of a king, which is, ultimately, to be a servant of the people. Everything a true king does is meant to benefit the lives of his people, not himself. "The king is לב כל קהל ישראל / the heart of the people" (Rambam, *Hilchos Melachim*, 3:6). Ultimately, Hashem wants us to want Him so that He can be our Melech, and not just our Moshel. Our freewill is what makes this "revolution" possible. For once the King is chosen and crowned, the channels are open for us to petition Him for our needs, and for the King in turn to lovingly bestow upon us all manner of benefits and blessings.

These are but some of the awesome implications of coronating HaKadosh Baruch Hu as King on Rosh Hashanah, viscerally evoked and announced on Rosh Hashanah through the piercing sounds of the Shofar.

Chapter Two

SOUNDS OF JOY &
SOUNDS OF WEEPING

WITH ALL OF THIS IN MIND, HOW THEN SHOULD WE APPROACH THE MITZVAH OF BLOWING OR HEARING THE SHOFAR? Perhaps tears of Teshuvah, longing, or yearning for closeness and connection would be the most appropriate and natural. Or maybe our tears should be withheld, as it is more fitting to express unbounded joy when coronating the Creator as King? Or perhaps one should approach this act meditatively, contemplating the symbolism of the Shofar and its sounds and deeper intentions? Or should one simply do the Mitzvah with utter simplicity, just because it is a Mitzvah?

In other words: Should the Shofar be blown with *Ahavah* / love, or *Yirah* / awe?* Of course every Mitzvah needs both of these emotions, but what feeling should we cultivate more actively while blowing the Shofar?

Every Mitzvah requires joy, as we learn, "Serve Hashem with joy" (*Tehilim*, 100:2). Even the very serious Mitzvos of Teshuvah and Yom Kippur demand joy. This helps explain why the day before Yom Kippur is a day of joyful feasting. We must rejoice in the Mitzvos of the Day of Atonement, of Yom Kippur, but since we cannot eat or drink on Yom Kippur itself, we have to celebrate the day of Yom Kippur with a feast on the previous day.

Indeed, joy is crucial to our *Avodah* / spiritual service, even when the Mitzvah is focused on regretting our past and doing Teshuvah.

Regarding the blowing of the Shofar, the Gra writes that one should perhaps withstand the urge to cry and aspire not to cry, but rather to blow it with *Simchah* / joy. Also, he maintains that, in general, we should not cry during the Rosh Hashanah period, as it is a *Yom Tov* / a day of pure goodness and positivity (*Ma'aseh Rav*, Rosh Hashanah).

---

* Although in general, throughout the year, we need two wings, Ahavah and Yirah, yet it is generally understood that in our day-to-day life we need more Ahavah than Yirah. On Rosh Hashanah, however, we need more Yirah than Ahavah: *Toldos Yaakov Yoseph*, Kedoshim. *Baal Shem Tov al ha-Torah*, Hisorerus l'Teshuvah, 37.

Similarly, when the Second Beis haMikdash had just been built, Ezra tells us that many who had seen the First Beis ha-Mikdash wept, while ורבים בתרועה בשמחה להרים קול / "Many others shouted joyously *b'Teru'ah* / at the top of their voice" (Ezra, 3:12. Rashi says, ibid., those who shouted with Simchah were those who had never seen the First Beis haMikdash and they rejoiced over their going out of exile.) Clearly, we see in this verse that the word *Teru'ah* can also mean a shout of overwhelming love and joy. In fact, the word *Teru'ah* can be related to the word *Re'ah* / beloved, so it is naturally an expression of joy and love. Indeed, even a Shevarim could resonate as cries of awesome joy and love: *Ah! Ah! Aha!*

Yet, this interpretation seems to contradict the teachings of the holy Arizal, who writes that if someone does not cry on these days, "his soul is not complete" (*Sha'ar haKavanos*, Inyan Rosh Hashanah, Derush Aleph). Moreover, the Arizal himself would cry profusely during the Davening of Rosh Hashanah (*Ba'er Heitev*, Orach Chayim, 584:3).* As such, the practice of Chassidim is to focus one's attention on the organic urge to cry during the Shofar blowing, and many Tzadikim would weep bitter tears during the Shofar blowing and in general on Rosh Hashanah, consistent with the teachings of the Arizal.

---

* And these tears were not tears of joy or tears of being overwhelmed in ecstasy, as we find by Rebbe Akiva. *Sichos Kodesh* 1, (Tav/Shin/Chof/Ches), p. 7. Although, see, *Likutei Torah*, Ki Tetze, 36c. ע״ד שאמרו על ר' עקיבא כשאמר שיר השירים זלגו עיניו דמעות שהבכיה הלזו היא מחמת דביקות הנפש בשרשה למעלה... ועל ענין בכיה זו איתא בשם האריז״ל שכל מי שאינו בוכה בר״ה וייוה״כ אין נשמתו שלימה.

Perhaps this apparent disagreement seems to go back to the two main reasons given for why we blow the Shofar: to coronate the King, according to the Rasag, and to 'awaken' us from spiritual slumber in order to do Teshuvah, according to the Rambam. The Gra follows the reasoning of the Rasag, hence the joy of triumphant blasts. The Arizal, and the Mekubalim and Chassidim whose paths flow from his teachings, focus on more mystical explorations that are closer to the Rambam's view, and therefore lean more in the direction of bitter tears.

THE WORK OF TESHUVAH

Parenthetically, let us keep in mind that to awaken to Teshuvah we need to do the actual work of Teshuvah. It is not enough to simply listen to the sound of the Shofar, nor even to cry with awe or regret, as the Shofar is being sounded. The soul-stirring sound of the Shofar may open us up to begin Teshuvah or to deepen the Teshuvah that we have embarked upon, but it is not the end of the journey. Regarding this, the following story was told by the Dubna Maggid, Rav Yaakov Krantz.

There was once a simple villager who observed that when there was a fire in the village, people would call loudly and then all the villagers would run to fetch buckets of water and attempt to douse the flames. Sometimes their strenuous efforts were effective, but often not. One day he went to the big city and happened to see a fire breaking out in a building. Suddenly, he heard a loud siren and leapt up to find a bucket and some water. The city dwellers laughed and told him that the alarm sirens were calling the fire department and trucks with professional firemen would put out the fire. Indeed, within minutes, firemen arrived and completely extinguished the fire.

Amazed and overjoyed at this new technology, the next day the villager went to the market and bought several fire alarm sirens. When he returned to the village, he set up the alarms around town, and instructed everyone: "O villagers, this is how it's done now! Next time there is a fire, do not worry about fetching water, just sound these sirens, and firemen will come immediately with huge trucks full of water! I promise you, the fire will be completely extinguished in no time!"

Needless to say, within two weeks, the village had burned to the ground.

To truly accomplish Teshuvah, to effectively put out our fires of negativity and make lasting spiritual progress, we ultimately have to rely on our own 'fire department', our own decisive action. Tools like the Shofar are meant to arouse within us a *Hirhur* / inner stirring of Teshuvah, but not to replace the inner work of Teshuvah itself.

A TOOL FOR SHATTERING NEGATIVITY

The Mekubalim, including the Zohar, the Arizal, and others, look at the shape of the Shofar, listen to the sounds of the Shofar, and analyze the word *Shofar* itself, to reveal and expound its spiritual meanings and effects. Every aspect of a

Mitzvah (as all of life) is loaded with meaning, and every detail, no matter how big or how small, is there to teach us something.

All the phenomena connected with the Shofar, its shape, how we hold it, the sounds that come out of it, what the word means, and so forth, demonstrate that the Shofar is connected to the work and concept of 'breaking through Kelipah' — dismantling all confinement, concealment and negativity. These revelations are aligned with the thought of the Rambam: The Shofar is meant to inspire Teshuvah, humility and awakening from slumber.

Accordingly, the word *Teru'ah* itself is related to the term 'breaking open', as it says, "You shall break them (*Tero'aim*) with a rod of iron; you shall dash them in pieces like a potter's vessel" (*Tehilim*, 2:9. Ritva, *Rosh Hashanah*, 33b). The shattering blast of the Teru'ah sound breaks all negativity and blockages, like an iron rod shattering pottery.

BEYOND OPPOSITES

On a deeper level, it can be said that the apparent argument between the Rasag, who says the Shofar coronates the King, and the Rambam, who maintains that the Shofar is meant to awaken Teshuvah, is not a definitive disagreement. Perhaps the Rasag is speaking primarily about the sound of the *Tekiah* / blast sound, and the Rambam is speaking about the *Teru'ah* / wailing sound. In fact, this is clearly alluded to in the Chinuch, who follows the Rambam, and describes the reason for blowing the Shofar specifically in terms of the Teru'ah:

"Because man is composed of matter he cannot be awakened to non-material issues except through an external factor which awakens him. This is like men who are engaged in battle who yell and even scream in order to be aroused for the battle. Similarly, on the day of Rosh Hashanah, which is the day appointed from earliest times for the judgment of all beings... everyone must awaken his nature in order to ask for mercy for his sins from the Master of Mercy... the sound of the Shofar awakens the heart, *and certainly the sound of the Teru'ah*, meaning, the broken sound" (*Chinuch*, Mitzvah 405).

Rav Yoseph Gikatalia (1248–c. 1305), the great Mekubal known as Rebbe Yoseph Ba'al haNisim / Rabbi Yoseph the Miracle Worker, writes in his book *Ginas Egoz*, that the word *Teru'ah* (תרועה) is related to the word *Te'Urah* (תעורה) which means 'to awaken' (*Ginas Egoz*, 48a). Seen in this light, the Teru'ah sound is understood as awakening us. However, Rav Yoseph further explains that the Tekiah sound is related to the word *Tekuah* / steadfast and resolute, a sound expressing power and dominance.

In other words, the broken Teru'ah sound is connected with awakening to Teshuvah, and the powerful blast of the Tekiah is associated with power and confirmation, related to the confirmation and coronation of a powerful king.

In the Torah, the sound of the Tekiah is clearly connected with joy and empowerment: "On the day of your joy and your holidays...ותקעתם /*U-skatem* / you shall sound the Teki-ah" (*Bamidbar*, 10:10). This blast of triumph is clearly related to the concept of coronation, as distinct from the Teru'ah sound which is a sound of humble crying, like a person yearning to turn and be closer to HaKadosh Baruch Hu.

In general, as the Radbaz writes (*Metzudas Dovid*, Mitzvah 112), the Tekiah is a sound of *Rachamim* / compassion, whereas the sound of the Teru'ah is the sound of *Din* / judgment.

UNITY & SEPARATION

As noted previously, the literal meaning of Teru'ah is 'break-ing', from the word *Re'u'a* / broken. This suggests a feeling of distance and separation. Tekiah comes from the word *Teka*, and in the language of the sages, this word can mean 'physical intimacy' (נפל מן הגג ונתקע: *Yevamos*, 54a). This suggests a coming together, an intimate closeness. In other words (*Sefer haKanah*, Sod Tekias Shofar), Tekiah alludes to unity, and Teru'ah alludes to separation (according to *Derush* / a homiletic interpretation, this is the in-ner meaning of the Mishnah that says, כל מקום שיש תקיעה אין הבדלה / "Every place there is Tekiah [sounds of the Shofar that initiate the day], there is no Havdalah [ceremony and declaration of separation]": *Chullin*, 26b). Tekiah is merciful kindness and Teru'ah is harsh judgment.

According to the *Zohar* (3, 99b), the Tekiah blast is connected with Avraham and Chesed — resonating the qualities of unity, confidence and love. The Teru'ah, on the other hand, is con-nected with Yitzchak and Gevurah — echoing feelings of bro-kenness and separation. Shevarim, the three medium sounds, is connected with the third patriarch, Yaakov and Tiferes. Tiferes is a balance of Chesed and Gevurah, which surrounds us in compassion. As the Shevarim sound is 'broken' it has some of the Gevurah of Teru'ah, and yet it is composed of three shorter 'Teki'os', and thus it contains Chesed as well. According to the Shaloh, the element of Chesed within Shevarim is connected with Yaakov, and its Gevurah element is connected with Dovid haMelech (Shaloh, *Siddur*).

Rasag: "Coronation"	View of the Gra	Tekiah: *one long blast*	Avraham	Chesed: *unity*
Rambam: "Teshuvah"	View of the Arizal	Teru'ah: *several short sounds*	Yitzchak	Gevurah: *separation*
Unity of Views	Inclusive View of Chasidus	Shevarim: *three medium sounds*	Yaakov	Tiferes: *including unity and separation*

Today, perhaps an effective compilation of Kavanos we can use while listening to the Shofar is the following: When the Tekiah sound is blasted, meditate on the Kavanah of the Rasag (Chesed, joy and coronation). When the Teru'ah sound is blown, meditate on the Kavanah of the Rambam (Gevurah, tears, Teshuvah). When the Shevarim are blown, join those two emotions in 'joyful Teshuvah', moving one to tears of awe in coronating the King.

TEKIAH BEFORE AND AFTER EACH TERU'AH

According to Rebbe Yehudah (*Sukkah*, 53b) the three separate blasts of Tekiah, Teru'ah and Tekiah in a single series all comprise one Mitzvah. This means that while the Torah tells us to blow the Teru'ah sound on Rosh Hashanah, every Teru'ah must necessarily include a Tekiah before and after it. The 'main' Mitzvah is the Teru'ah, but it needs to be sandwiched between two Teki'os (*Shu't Galya Masechtah*, Orach Chayim, 3. This would be true even according to the *Chachamim* / sages [*Sukkah*, ibid], who hold that they are separate Mitzvos).

For our humility and self-judgement to be healthy and productive, rather than leading us toward dejection and resignation, we need to cushion the bitter quality of Teru'ah with the exultant quality of Tekiah. The Teru'ah has a humbling effect and the Tekiah instills confidence, thus before and after every Teru'ah there needs to be a Tekiah. First there is a blast of empowerment, lifting you up to the exalted level of being able to coronate Hashem as the Master of the Universe. Then come cries of humility, which allow you to see your existential lowliness and brokenness clearly. Who are you to crown the awesome Creator? This is the feeling of Teshuvah. However, to prevent you from becoming despondent from such penetrating reflection and intense humility, there comes another Tekiah sound to lift you up again to the highest level.

The Tekiah that comes before the Teru'ah is in truth very different from the Tekiah that comes after the Teru'ah. The

Mishnah (*Rosh Hashanah,* 33b) teaches, "If one blows a prolonged (Tekiah) to make it equal to two (Tekios), it only counts as one." This is commenting on the fact that after the Teru'ah there is a Tekiah, as mentioned, and then the next set of sounds begins with yet another Tekiah. What if one were to blow a very long Tekiah after the Teru'ah, having in mind that it should also count as the first Tekiah of the next set of sounds? Says the Mishnah, it does not work and he needs to blow another Tekiah to begin the next set. What does this mean inwardly? The Tekiah that lifts a person up *before* he realizes his brokenness and humility, and the Tekiah that lifts him up and restores his confidence *after* he has realized his humility, are not 'the same sound'.

The confidence that comes before humility is still naive. It is like a healthy child whose parents shower him or her with positivity: 'You are so amazing, so smart, so capable!' The child walks around with a good dose of healthy self-confidence. But then, one day, another child pokes fun at him, or an unskilled teacher crushes their confidence, and they come home broken and humiliated.

Now the parents need another type of Tekiah to lift their child back up. They have to explain to them that despite what people might say, he really is highly capable. Or they may need to explain to the child that there are different types of intelligence, one person is good at math, another has strong writing skills, and that he is simply more endowed with another type of intelligence. If the child fails his test because of a lack of study, the parent may need to encourage him not to give up, and to support him in building better study habits and so on.

The same is true with adults. Sometimes we may feel like we are on top of the world — expansive, empowered, capable, focused, confident in our soul mission. This is the Tekiah 'before' brokenness. And then, sometimes we may fall into constriction, confusion, or depression. Many people can manically fluctuate between expanded states and self-inflicted harmful patterns of behavior, or get stuck in an old emotional rut. Feeling the effects of a fall and honestly acknowledging one's distance from their potential is like the broken, weeping sound of the Teru'ah. In this state, such a person needs to be uplifted and instilled with a deeper, more thoughtful confidence, a sense of hope that is not so easily destroyed. This post-Teru'ah type of Tekiah is more mature and may require a different Kavanah.

In general, as we have said, Tekiah expresses a joyful state of closeness to HaKadosh Baruch Hu. There is a sense of spiritual closeness that one may feel prior to 'sinning' or falling, but there can be a much more nuanced sense of spiritual intimacy after getting up again.

Within the process of Teshuvah there emerges a Teru'ah from one who has fallen or feels crushed, and who is crying out to reconnect and to rise out of their spiritual malaise. And then there resounds a Tekiah of resilience, of getting back up again, resolving to recreate and empower oneself, and of believing deeply in oneself despite everything that has happened. This second Tekiah is the acknowledgment and activation of the Tzadik deep within, our essential being.

From a slightly different perspective, the first Tekiah is not naive confidence but an important first step in our process of Teshuvah on Rosh Hashanah or any time. We should begin the Teshuvah process with a Tekiah, with an affirmation and awareness of our ever-pure essential nature, which is our potential to live as a Tzadik. Only then should we turn our focus to the many ways in which we are broken, fragmented and scattered like a Teru'ah sound. Then we must arise in our consciousness and conclude with a Tekiah of confidence and resolve to truly live like a Tzadik.

BREAKING AND REBUILDING

On an inward level, the Tekiah can also be viewed as the blast of a hammer that breaks the stone covering the heart, allowing us to open up to change. After the Tekiah, the stone is broken into chunks with the Shevarim. Then with the rapid blows of the hammer, the Teru'ah sound breaks the chunks into smaller pieces until they are but dust.

This is the process of taking a seemingly unmanageable load of *Yeshus* / heavy, egoic 'somethingness', breaking it down through intense self-evaluation, and then turning into dust, into *Ayin* / selfless 'no-thingness'. Yet, we do not end there; we conclude the series with another Tekiah blast, reconstituting the dust into cement to shape a new Yesh, a new self, a new reality for the coming year.

Simply put, we must break down our resistance to change, and learn from it. The strength of that resistance can be repurposed to build strong, righteous and upright character traits.

FROM WHOLENESS TO BROKENNESS, & BACK TO WHOLENESS

We all begin life whole and perfect, unbroken: "Elokim made man *Yashar* / upright or straight" (*Koheles*, 7:29). Later in life, although the 'details' of our life may seem to have become fragmented and totally unrelated to each other — we can override our confusion and see reality as one seamless whole. This integral perspective reveals all aspects of our life to have been but details of a larger, all-inclusive blessing. Then, from that redemptive and holistic perspective, we can get up in an instant and offer a Tekiah of complete confidence and *Sheleimus* / wholeness.

Our lives are often a story of fragile wholeness, traumatic *Shevirah* / breaking, and finally conscious *Tikkun* / repair. We may begin our adult life like a Tekiah, confident in who we are and in what our gifts and skills are, full of energy and an overarching sense of a singular purpose and direction. As we mature, however, we may get so immersed in the minute and seemingly unrelated details of life — the day to day struggles of earning a living, juggling relationships, raising children, maintaining our health and tending to any number of obligations — that our life may feel like a disjunctive series of fragmented Shevarim. We may have lost sight of the wholeness and unifying coherence of our youth, and we may have wept many times. We may even feel smashed into little pieces like the broken sounds of the Teru'ah. And yet, by the end of our life, if we have achieved a degree of *Yishuv ha'Da'as* / settled mind, we can look back and recognize that all the details, all the ups and downs, the twists and turns, the ins and outs, were actually all part of a greater 'single overarching theme' of our life. We thus conclude with another blast of Tekiah, expressing a triumphant awareness of how all the details were ultimately interrelated and connected. This is a much more profound Tekiah and sense of confidence than the first. It is the cry of faith one has earned with their very life.

THE WAY OF BROKENNESS

As the Shaloh HaKadosh teaches (Meseches Rosh Hashanah, p. 163), the Tekiah, a *Yashar* / 'straight' or unbroken sound, represents the 'upright' person, meaning one who is still as wholesome as he was the day he was born. This rare individual perhaps never veered from the 'straight and narrow' path of righteousness, not even once.

The broken sounds of the Shevarim and Teru'ah, on the other hand, represent the Baal Teshuvah, someone who has veered to some extent from his inner alignment — perhaps even repeatedly — and now desires to return to wholeness. In his self-alienation, his anguish and brokenness, he breaks into sobs of yearning.

"And Hashem created man Yashar, but they sought many inventions (alternatives)" (*Koheles*, 7:29). Sometimes we take a left turn, and our trajectory becomes a little crooked or warped. Our internal compass becomes misaligned or off track; we are no longer as upright as we once thought we would or should be. However, we always have the potential to straighten ourselves out, to find our 'true north', to become Yashar again. We can and will all become whole again, if we so desire.

When you listen to the Shofar you can contemplate the panorama of your spiritual life and let the sounds stimulate a deeper Teshuvah process. Experience the sound of the Tekiah as a vibration of your *Yashar* / straight or upright self. Imagine the state of purity and wholeness you had on the day you were born, or when you found yourself living most authentically, in total alignment with your ideals.

Hear and feel the Shevarim sound as an echo of your inner brokenness, your out-of-balance state which naturally results from existential misalignment. As you realize how connected you once were, and how fragmented you now are, open to the distress and regret welling up inside as a subtle cry. Then hear the Teru'ah sound as the beginning of Teshuvah, your broken-heartedness becoming staccato sobs of yearning to reconnect, resolving to re-shape your life and return to wholeness.

Then let the final Tekiah of triumphant joy wash over you, straightening out your life and returning you to wholeness. Imagine the relief of feeling totally forgiven and blessed. This is the sound of complete Teshuvah.

THE MACROCOSM

The meditative suggestions above can be contemplated on a cosmic scale as well. The sound of the Tekiah expresses the utterly simple, timeless Unity that exists prior to the Tzimtzum of Divine Self-concealment. The deepest part of our soul resonates with this complete wholeness prior to any possibility of separation or brokenness.

Teru'ah tells a tale of the post-Tzimtzum reality — of seemingly separate objects and moments and beings, the place of alienation and exile.

The final Tekiah is the wholeness that comes after the brokenness, the *Yichud* / unification after the *Pirud* / separation, the Final Redemption after all exiles. This is the higher level of Yichud, which transcends and includes all binaries — eternity and time, unity and multiplicity, light and darkness, doubt and certainty, and soul and body.

Our work in this world is to take all the fragmented, broken parts of reality, and bring them to a state of Yichud, wholeness and Redemption. This is the story of the sounds of the Shofar.

SITTING VS. STANDING BLASTS

The initial blowing after the recitation of the Shofar blessings is called the *Tekios Meyushav* / sitting blasts, even though today we stand during this Shofar blowing. There are additional rounds of Shofar blowing during the private *Amidah* / standing prayer and in the repetition of the Amidah, and these are called *Tekios Me'umad* / standing blasts.* Later on, the 'sitting' and 'standing' sets of Shofar blowing will be explored in greater detail; for now, this is an introduction to these ideas.

It could be argued that the main focus of the Tekios Meyushav is to get rid of negativity, to break open the ego or the rock of the heart, and to arouse a humble Teshuvah, whereas the focus of the Tekios Me'umad is the act of coronation (This is aligned with the Chasam Sofer who writes that the Tekios Me'umad are connected with a posture of joy. *D'rashos*, Rosh Hashanah).

Before we sound the Tekios Meyushav, we recite selected verses from Tehilim that prepare us for the sound of the Shofar. Expressing the major theme of the Meyushav set, we recite, "From a place of constriction I call upon Hashem; answer me from a place of expansion" (*Tehilim*, 118:4), and we actively contemplate our constriction and distance from HaKadosh Baruch Hu. After declaring this verse, we recite six additional verses. The acrostic, formed from the first letters of these verses, spells the phrase קרע שטן / *Kra Satan* / 'rip apart the Satan.' This cry to rip asunder the Satan, the force of 'spiritual impediment', reflects a crying out of someone yearning to come closer, some-

---

* *Tosefos*, Rosh Hashanah, 33b, in the name of the Aruch. The Rambam, *Hilchos Shofar*, 3:7, however, rules that only during the repetition is there Shofar blowing. See also, *Shiltei HaGiborim*, on the Rif, 6b. The Magen Avraham writes יש מקומות שנוהגים לתקוע כשמתפללין בלחש ואין לנהוג כן לכתחלה. *Orach Chayim*, 592:1. Yet, the Minhag Chabad and all those who follow the teachings of the Arizal is to blow, as the opinion of the Aruch and Tosefos, see *Kaf HaChayim*, ibid.

one longing to break through the Kelipah of separation, and attain some measure of unity and alignment with his deepest self, with others and ultimately with HaKodsh Baruch Hu.

Later, just prior to blowing the Tekios Me'umad during the Amidah, we recite verses that begin with לא הביט און ביעקב / Lo Hibit Avon b'Yaakov / "Do not see any fault in Yaakov." The name Yaakov is related to the word *Eikev* / heel. This verse therefore suggests that now we need not struggle with any impediment or obstruction within our 'heel', our lower self, for the negativity of the 'Satan' has already been neutralized, and thus, there are no faults even in the place of the 'heel'. In this state of Divine closeness and alignment, we joyfully recite verses pronouncing Hashem as King, verses affirming Hashem's remembrance of His love for us, and verses describing how Hashem was revealed to us on Mount Sinai. Some verses even speak of the Great Shofar that will announce the coming Redemption. The essence of these Shofar soundings is a triumphant declaration of acceptance: מלוך על כל העולם כולו / *M'loch al Col haOlam Kulo* / "Reign over the entire world!"

The overall unfolding of the day of Rosh Hashanah is that first the Tekios Meyushav blow away all negativity and empty the vessel of our perception and existential reality. Then the Tekios Me'umad fill that fertile void with a breath of new life and *Shefa* / Divine flow of abundance, ushering in a new year of blessings.

NINETY = MELECH:
TOTAL NUMBER OF SOUNDS

The full set of Shofar sounds consist of 30 individual blasts, as explained earlier:

1) Tekiah — 2) Shevarim — 3) Tekiah

4) Tekiah — 5) Shevarim — 6) Tekiah

7) Tekiah — 8) Shevarim — 9) Tekiah

10) Tekiah — 11) Teru'ah — 12) Tekiah

13) Tekiah — 14) Teru'ah — 15) Tekiah

16) Tekiah — 17) Teru'ah — 18) Tekiah

19) Tekiah — 20-21) Shevarim-Teru'ah — 22) Tekiah

23) Tekiah — 24-25) Shevarim-Teru'ah — 26) Tekiah

27) Tekiah — 28-29) Shevarim-Teru'ah — 30) Tekiah

This set of 30 sounds are blown three times: once for the Tekios Meyushav, once for the Tekios Me'umad during the silent Amidah, and another set of Tekios Me'umad during the repetition of the Amidah — totaling 90 sounds.

Ninety is the numerical value of the word *Melech* / King. In this way, all of the Shofar sounds are ultimately connected with the coronation of the King of the Universe, and all the sounds stimulate joy in the realization that we are entrusted to fulfill this awesome mission of revealing HaKadosh Baruch Hu's sovereignty in the world.

In every set of 30 sounds, there are 18 Tekiah sounds, one before and one after each mini-set. Eighteen is the numerical value of the word *Chai* / life, as today, on Rosh Hashanah, we are given new life, for a new year, through our act of blowing the Shofar below and stimulating a Divine 'blow' or exhale to come into the world from Above.

There are six Shevarim sounds in a set of 30, and each of the Shevarim consists of three 'notes' (3x6=18), again equaling 18, the number representing 'life'.

There are 6 Teru'ah sounds in a set of 30. Each Teru'ah consists of (at least) nine staccato notes or 'beats' (9x6=54). Adding up all of the above (18+18+54) we arrive again at 90, representing the word Melech.

As such, not only are there 90 total sounds (in the three sets of 30), but in each set of 30 there are 90 individual 'beats' — suggesting the fact that Hashem is *Melech haM'lachim* / King over all other apparent rulers. This affirms our recognition that we submit to no power other than Hashem, the omnipotent King of Kings.

270 'BEATS' — NULLIFYING THE RA / NEGATIVITY OF IDOL WORSHIP, REVEALING NAKEDNESS & SPILLING BLOOD

The sound of a Teru'ah is nine beats. Similarly, the prescribed length of both the Shevarim and the Tekiah is also nine beats (see *Tosefos*, Rosh Hashanah, 33b). If every sound has the length of 9 beats, there are a total of 270 'beats' in the set of 30 sounds: 30 sounds x 9 = 270. 270 is the numerical value of the word רע / *Ra* / evil (Reish/200, Ayin/70). As such, a full set of Shofar blasts breaks the Kelipah of evil decrees and negativity. As there are three sets of 270 'beats', each set is directed at breaking a specific form of *Ra*.

The Arizal teaches (*Sha'ar haKavanos*, Rosh Hashanah, Derush 9) that in the first set of 30 blasts, the Tekios Meyushav, one should meditate on ridding oneself and the world of the Ra of *Avodah Zarah* / Idol Worship. In the second set of 30, which are blown during the private and silent Amidah, one should meditate on ridding oneself and the world of the Ra of *Gilui Arayos* / illicit relations, including, adultery, and any other self-ish distortion of physical intimacy or pleasure. In the third set of 30, which are blown during the repetition of the Amidah, one should meditate upon ridding oneself and the world of the Ra of *Shefichas Damim* / murder and all forms of violence. Parenthetically, the 10 sounds blown after Musaf break the Ra of *Lashon haRa* / negative speech.

This contemplation on the three sets of Shofar blowing is related to the fact that by eating from the *Eitz haDa'as* / Tree of Knowledge, Adam and Chavah transgressed those three cardinal sins (*Zohar* 3, p. 111b). In this sense, the Shofar shatters the bonds of death introduced by consuming the fruit of du-ality, realigning us with the *Eitz Chayim* / the Tree of Life. In addition, Adam accepted Lashon haRa from the snake (*Bereishis Rabah*, 5:9), which corresponds to the 10 sounds that are blown after Musaf.

Although the transgression of Adam and Chavah in the Garden seems to be rooted in their simple disobeying of Hashem's command not to eat from the Tree of Knowledge, on a deeper level, their act violated all three cardinal sins. Initially, Hashem had told Adam and Chavah that they could eat "from all the trees in the Garden." But then, stipulated that from among one particular tree they must not eat. So, when Adam and Chavah 'separated' one particular fruit from among all the fruits in the Garden ("all" being the paradigm of the Tree of Life), on a profound level, they were in effect separating a 'something' from the 'Everything'. This very act is the root of *Avodah Zarah* / idolatry, separating and eventually worshiping a 'something' distinct from Hashem, the 'Everything'. On an inward level, the ego is, or at least can be, an inner 'idol', constantly vying for our devotion; it is, psychologically speaking, the 'part' that confuses itself for the 'whole'.

Once they entered a world of dualistic 'separation', a state of separation within their own selves arose, as well as a dissociative dichotomy between their minds and bodies. This state prompted them to become shamefully aware of their nakedness, and this was the root of all forms of Gilui Arayos, which literally translates as "revealing nakedness." Bodily dissociation and shame together drive the unhealthy indulgence of cravings and other futile methods of trying to overcome our inner emptiness through purely physical means. Man's wholesome, innate desire to create life is the principal casualty of Gilui Arayos.

Adam and Chavah became mortal, and began a gradual process of decay once they ate from the Tree of Knowledge. This descent into the world of death and dying is the meta-root of Shefichas Damim, beginning with the 'spilling of their own blood'. This then became the 'death instinct' in man, the unconscious tendency toward self-destruction, aggression, and externally directed violence toward others.

The beginning of the Tikkun of the *Cheit Eitz haDa'as* / sin of eating from the Tree of Knowledge, as the Zohar explains, comes about through the *Avos* / our root ancestors. Avraham rectifies Avodah Zarah by declaring to the masses the Unity of Hashem. Yitzchak — by submitting to and surviving the Akeidah — rectifies the idea of Shefichas Damim. By working seven extra years with diligence and honesty for Rochel, Yaakov rectifies Gilui Arayos. (Moshe — through whose throat the Divine Presence spoke — rectifies Lashon haRa: *Megaleh Amukos*, Vayetze.) In this way, the intention of the Shofar is to create a *Tikkun* / rectification and healing for our eating from the Tree of Knowledge, a Tikkun of the entire notion of separation, and hence a reconnection to the Tree of Life, and Unity.* This we achieve by taking our life-breath, the breath of life that was blown into us by Hashem, which is our Neshamah, and blowing out a seamless sound of Unity. This idea will be explored more deeply further on.

All Ra, separation, negativity and sin is removed from the

* The Medrash, in *Pirkei d'Rebbe Eliezer*, 32, relates the cries of Sarah to the sounds of the Shofar. Sarah was the *Gilgul* / reincarnation of Chavah and her life was instrumental in creating a Tikkun for the sin of Chavah. Arizal, *Sefer haLikutim*, Shoftim, 15.

world, and goodness and Divine compassion fills the void, through the pure sound of the Shofar.

As a result, עלה אלקים בתרועה ה' בקול שופר / *Ala Elokim biTeru'ah, Hashem b'Kol Shofar* / "Elokim is elevated with the Teru'ah, Hashem with the sound of the Shofar" (*Tehilim*, 47:6). Inwardly, this means that when the Shofar is blown, the *Sheim Elokim* / the 'name' or reality of Divine contraction and judgment is elevated to a more expansive level, dissolving all spiritual opposition to simple unity. When the Name Elokim is elevated, the *Sheim Havayah* / the Name 'Hashem', the reality of Divine Compassion (Tiferes is associated with the Name of Hashem) and expansive kindness is drawn down to us and our world.

In the words of the Zohar and the Medrash, "The Shofar below awakens the Shofar above and the Holy One, blessed be He, rises from His Throne of Judgment (and duality) and sits upon His Throne of Compassion (and unity)" (*Zohar*, Parshas Emor).

TEARS OF JOY & UNITY

In general, the practice of Chassidus is aligned with the Arizal's perspective on the nature of the Shofar blowing: it expresses tears and cries coming from a place of constriction, and reaching out to a place of expansion.*

---

* There is a Ma'amar of the Alter Rebbe in the Siddur (*Siddur Im Dach*, p. 488) which begins, "To understand the idea of blowing the Shofar ..." (according to the Kavanos of the Baal Shem Tov), and yet, as the Rebbe asks, where are the Kavanos of the Baal Shem Tov for Blowing of the Shofar to

On the other hand, we find a teaching from the Baal Shem Tov which refocuses the literal meaning of the Arizal's words: "The day of Rosh Hashanah is a time of joy...and the Arizal teaches regarding the need to cry that...the crying is a form of rejoicing in that we have arrived at this day, and in acknowledgment of the awesomeness of this day" (*Keser Shem Tov*, 2:22b. *Baal Shem Tov al haTorah*, R'H-Y'K, 29). In fact, the Sha'agas Aryeh writes that there is a Mitzvah of *Simchah* / joy on Rosh Hashanah (*Shu't Sha'agas Aryeh*, 102). And as the Shulchan Aruch rules, "There is a Mitzvah to eat, drink, and be joyful on Rosh Hashanah" (*Orach Chayim*, 593). This indicates not only a 'spiritual' joy; we also need to experience physical joy.

On the deepest level of interpretation, there is only *Yichud* / unity; there is no division, alienation or fragmentation which would motivate crying. Tears, in this view, can only express the command to *v'Gilu biR'adah* / "rejoice with trembling" (Trisker Maggid, *Magen Avraham*, Ki Savo). Tears of Teshuvah can be understood in this context as being loaded with the joy of hav-

---

be found? There are known Kavanos of the Baal Shem Tov for the Mikvah printed in *Pri haAretz*, and also explored by the Alter Rebbe in the *Siddur*, but where exactly are the Kavavos of the Baal Shem for blowing the Shofar located (*Sichos Seudas Rosh Hashanah* 1, Chaf Gimel)? It must be that these Kavanos are to be found within the Ma'amar itself, which explores the nature of simple sound and crying, and the Chassidic explanation of the teachings of the Arizal about sweetening judgment; these points are understood as providing the foundation for the Kavanah of the Baal Shem Tov for blowing the Shofar. *Sichos, Seudas Rosh Hashanah* 2, Tav-Shin-Chaf-Aleph.

ing arrived at this opportunity to do Teshuvah and experience of *Deveikus* / oneness. Even tears of constriction can be filled with the joy that HaKadosh Baruch Hu is at that moment answering us with expansion: *HaMelech Ya'aneinu beYom Kor'einu* / "The King will answer us on the day (at the moment) we call!"

The path of joy — characterized by a tangible sense of confidence, empowerment, expansiveness, closeness, and connection — and the path of tears — characterized by feelings of longing, distance, yearning, and constriction — are both true and valid. In true Yichud, these seeming opposites can even be expressed and experienced simultaneously. In this way, the Shofar can be understood as an instrument of unification, bringing together all of our many emotions and intentions into a simple unity of sound and revelatory reverberation.

Chapter Three

THE SHAPE, THE WORD, THE SOUND, & THE NUMERICAL VALUES OF THE SHOFAR

S O MUCH OF HOW WE FEEL ABOUT OURSELVES AND ABOUT LIFE IN GENERAL, AND SO MUCH OF OUR EMO-TIONAL AND MENTAL STATES, DEPENDS ON OUR PHYS-ICAL ACTIONS AND WELL-BEING. We are, in essence, a unified, inter-connected bio-psychic feedback loop, with the mind affecting the body, and the body, in turn, influencing the mind.

Furthermore, every point within this psycho-physical system is directly linked with our deepest spiritual reality, our soul. The ethereal soul and the material body are ultimately part of one integral organism. For this reason, there is symbolism, meaning and import in everything that we do. The physical actions that we perform open us up to specific feelings and ways of thinking, and they can also shift our spiritual state. How we act externally alters our internal reality, and vice versa. All of this is especially true about our actions at the beginning of the year, the 'headquarters of time', as we are given a 'clean slate' and are invited to inscribe on it the content and quality of our reality for the coming year.

"Now that you have said an omen is significant," says Abaya, "a person should habituate himself to eat at the beginning of the year *Kara* / gourds, *Rubya* / fenugreek (a type of herb), *Karti* / leeks , *Silka* / beets, and *Tamrei* / dates" (*Kerisus*, 6a. In another version, it says a person should "look at them" — יהא רגיל למיחזי בריש שתא: *Horayos*, 12a. See *Beis Yoseph*, on the Tur, *Orach Chayim*, 583. Thus, if one cannot eat them, he should endeavor to at least look at them: *Kaf haChayim*, *Orach Chayim*, 583:6. He should "place them on the table." Meiri, *Horayos*, ibid).

The symbolism of these particular foods is either that they ripen quickly, and as such eating them represents our confidence in increased merit and fruitfulness in the coming year, or they are sweet tasting and eating them represents our confidence in HaKadosh Baruch Hu's willingness to sweeten any judgments hanging over us, the community, or the world in the year to come.

Other sources write that the significance of these species of food is in their names. For example, the word *Rubya* is related to the Hebrew word *Rov* / abundance or increase, as in, "May our merits increase." The word *Karti* is related to the Hebrew word *Kares* / cut off; hence when eating *Karti* we should pray that all our external and internal enemies will be 'cut off'.

If these customs can help us shift our coming year, how much more so is this true of the Shofar, the only positive physical Mitzvah from the Torah that we have today to perform on Rosh Hashanah. To truly get into the heart of the meaning of the Shofar we need to explore the nature of the Shofar, its physical shape, the sound it produces, and even what the word *Shofar* means. As Abaye said, "An omen is significant..."; every detail of an object contributes to its spiritual power.

In the words of the Arizal (*Pri Eitz Chayim,* Sha'ar haShofar, 1), "(To know) the secret of the Shofar we need to know who the blower is, in which it is blown, what the (form of the) Shofar is, and what is its sound."

To truly understand the spiritual and symbolic import of the Shofar, we must first and foremost look at its physical dimensions and characteristics.

SHAPE: BENT

Our sages debate whether the shape of the Shofar should be *Kafuf* / curved, or *Pashut* / straight (*Rosh Hashanah,* 26b). On a deeper level, this is a debate about whether the Shofar is meant to express a 'bent' or broken heart, or a 'straight' or pure heart (as explored earlier regarding the Tekiah and Teru'ah sounds). In the end, says the Gemara, we should blow a curved Shofar. (According to the Rambam the Mitzvah *requires* a curved Shofar, and this is our practice.) Indeed, most ram's horns are naturally curved.

On the most simple level, a curved or 'bent' Shofar symbolizes a broken heart, and a willingness to bend our personal, egoic will to the Will of the Creator.

SHAPE: NARROW TO WIDE

Another aspect of the shape of the Shofar is that the end where the mouth is placed is narrow, and from there the horn widens incrementally until it is much wider on the end where the sound emanates.

There is profound symbolism in this shape and structure. Fundamentally, the Shofar stimulates a movement from 'constriction to expansiveness'. As the Arizal teaches, we should direct our attention to the actual, physical Shofar, as it is narrow below and wide above, expressing the secret of the verse, "From a narrow place I call out to You, and You answer me with expansiveness" (*Tehilim*, 118:4).

In this way, the Shofar guides us subtly along two complementary paths — bending in humility, and confidently moving out of our spiritual narrowness and contraction into a more expansive place.

Interestingly enough, the *Ashkenazi* / German Jewish custom is to use tools to flatten the circumference of the Shofar, while simultaneously maintaining the curve of its length. Besides the aesthetic value of the flat shape, and that it is easier to store and to hide in times of religious persecution, the Shofar in this flattened form has more of a *Pashut* quality in terms of its circumference. In this way, it includes the spiritual quality of a 'straight', pure heart, along with the quality of a 'bent', broken or humbled heart.

THE SIZE OF THE SHOFAR

וכמה שיעור תקיעה פירש רשב״ג כדי שיאחזנו בידו ויראה לכאן ולכאן / "And (regarding the length of the Shofar), what measurement is sufficient in order to sound a (proper) blast? Rabban Shimon ben Gamliel explained, 'Enough so that when one holds it in his hand, it can be seen (protruding) on one side (of his hand) and on the other side'" (*Rosh Hashanah*, 27b).

There are three parts of a Shofar: 1) the middle which is grasped by one's right hand, 2) the part that protrudes to the right of the hand grasping it, and 3) the part that protrudes to the left of the hand grasping it. Rebbe Levi Yitzchak Schneerson, the illustrious Mekubal and father of the Rebbe, writes (*Likutim v'Igros*, p. 355) that the phrase from the Gemara, above, ויראה לכאן ולכאן / "it can be seen on this side and that," numerically equals 430, which is exactly the numerical value of Avraham (248) and Yaakov (182). As such, the two protruding sides correspond to Avraham and Yaakov.

The middle of the Shofar that we hold (or the body of the Shofar as a whole) corresponds to Yitzchak and Gevurah:

"Why does one sound a blast with a Shofar made from a ram's horn on Rosh Hashanah? Says the Holy One, Blessed be He, 'Sound a blast before Me with a Shofar made from a ram's horn, so that I will remember for you the binding of Yitzchak, son of Avraham, in whose place a ram was sacrificed, and I will ascribe it to you as if you had bound yourselves before Me'" (*Rosh Hashanah*, 16a).

As we blow Shofar, the inspiration originates from the pure breath of Avraham / Chesed, the vibration then travels and twists through the realm of Yitzchak / Gevurah, and finally the sound emanates out of the mouth of Yaakov / Tiferes. In other words, the physical design of the Shofar moves us from a place of Gevurah and constriction into an expansive place of Tiferes and compassion. This pattern parallels the three primary sounds blown with the Shofar, which correspond to Avraham, Yitzchak and Yaakov, as explored earlier.

SOUND

The sound of the Shofar is like a human cry or wail. The Arizal teaches that whoever does not cry during the period from Rosh Hashanah to Yom Kippur, "his soul is not complete." The Arizal also teaches that when you spontaneously weep during the two days of Rosh Hashanah, or even when a subtle sensation of tears wells up in you at any point, know that this is the moment of your judgment (*Sha'ar haKavanos*, Inyan Rosh Hashanah). Needless to say, this is a most auspicious moment to be judged; when we are inwardly open, moved, and vibrating with awe, or yearning for Teshuvah.

Physiologically, crying releases tensions and blockages that have been held in the body, allowing certain areas to relax and expand in relief. In the act of blowing the Shofar, the sound 'moves' from a narrow space, and the tiny, tense aperture of the contracted lips, to a wider place where it has become a powerful sound. The sound itself is an enactment of our soul moving *Min haMetzar* / from the contraction of our being, *laMerchavyah* / to Divine expansion and openness: מן המצר קראתי קה ענני במרחב קה / "In contraction I cried to Hashem; Hashem answered me with expansive relief!" (*Tehilim*, 118:5).

SHAPE: HOLLOW

The horn of the Shofar needs to be hollowed out before it can be blown. To receive blessings we too need to be a hollow, open vessel, like a Shofar that gradually opens more and more until it resonates powerfully. The emptier the vessel, the more Light it can channel.

Before the Shofar is filled with sound it is empty and silent. As mentioned, the Maggid says this is how we need to see ourselves as well; we are empty, we cannot do anything, not even utter a word or think a thought, without HaKadosh Baruch Hu breathing life into us and filling us with Divine vibration and vitality.

Our body and mind, our emotions and spiritual path, are 'shaped' like the Shofar; hollow and bent, receptive and resonant.

The coming year itself is also like a hollow vessel; in its emptiness it is also full of potential. When we perform the Mitzvah of filling the hollow Shofar with breath, the coming year too is filled with holiness and connectivity.

TYPE OF SHOFAR: RAM'S HORN

All horns are Kosher to blow the Shofar — besides that of a bull (*Rosh Hashanah*, 26a). However, the optimal horn to use for the Shofar is that of a ram, a male sheep (in fact, according to the Rambam all other Shofars are not Kosher: *Hilchos Shofar*, 1:1). Sheep, in general, are gentle animals, and the cry of a sheep, which is called 'bleating', naturally awakens compassion in the listener (*Siddur Im Dach*, Rosh Hashanah, 470). Perhaps this has to do with the fact that their bleating sounds similar to the cries of a young child. In any case, it is associated, symbolically and viscerally, with the awakening of compassion.

Kabbalisticaly as well, sheep embody the attribute of *Tiferes* / 'beautiful' compassion. When we blow the Shofar and draw a cry through its narrow aperture, we are also drawing Light through the twisted realm of Divine constriction, out of the tunnel of transformation and into our experience. When we create the sound of a bleating sheep, we are also arousing the Compassion of the Supernal Shepherd, who immediately turns to gather us into the safety of the flock, lifting us up, holding us, and speaking words of affection and blessing to our hearts.

Sheep are considered meek, gentle, and pure animals. They do not portray aggressive behavior as do bulls and other animals. Using a ram's horn to blow the Shofar reminds us of our own inner gentleness, and our real selves, which are always perfectly pure. By projecting our breath through the gentle, pure conduit of the Shofar, we reveal and convey our soul into the world, pure and simple.

A horn is a simple and natural object, not manufactured or molded by human hands and ingenuity. Today, on Rosh Hashanah, we wish to reveal that deeper 'me', that un-manufactured innocence, that dimension of spirit that is untouched by our human manipulation and intervention.

THE MEANING OF THE WORD SHOFAR

The word *Shofar* is related to the word *Shipur* / beautify, as in the charge to *Shapru Ma'aseichem* / "beautify your actions" (בחדש הזה שפרו מעשיכם: *Medrash Rabbah*, Vayikra, 29:6). As the Shofar is a call to action, arousing us from our spiritual slumber in order to deeply recognize that we are all beautiful children of HaKadosh Baruch Hu, entrusted with actively coronating the Creator as the infinitely majestic Master of the Universe. The call of the Shofar is therefore a call to live beautiful lives.

Shofar comes from the word *Shefoferes* / tube or sheath (Ran, Rashba, *Rosh Hashanah*, 26a. *Sha'ar haKavanos*, Inyan Rosh Hashanah, Derush Zayin. *Zohar* 3, 231b), implying that the Shofar is also a spiritual *Kaneh* / pipe through which we draw down Eternal Light from Above.

For the body to survive it needs 'wind' (oxygen) and food. There are two pipes connecting the head and the body, the windpipe and the food-pipe, the trachea and the esophagus. We 'damaged' the food-pipe by *eating* from the Tree of Knowledge, but the windpipe, which is not used for eating or drinking, is still in complete connection with the higher world (Olam haBa: *Zohar* 3, p. 232a. Shaloh, *Sha'ar haOsyos*, Os Kuf, Kedushas haAchilah, 232), and thus it is precisely through breath and blowing that we can draw down new *Chayus* / life into the world.* This Chayus and *Mochin* / consciousness is rooted in the Tree of Life, the paradigm of Unity and Perfection.

When we blow our breath into the hollow tube of the Shofar, into the 'empty space', we are mimicking the act of Creation, in which the Creator breathed or spoke the world into existence. This renewed creation occurs every moment, as well as once a year on Rosh Hashanah morning, as a cosmic renewal of Creation.

Having explored the semantic definition of the word *Shofar*, we will now decode even deeper meanings using its root letters and numerical values.

ACRONYM OF THE WORD SHOFAR

The four letters of the word Shofar form an acronym for (אין) שטן ואין פגע רע / *Satan, V'ein Pega Ra* / "There is a 'Satan', but there is no negative effect" (Taz, *Orach Chayim*, 585. Note, Tur, *ad loc.*

---

* *Chayus* is called *Mochin* / intellect by the Arizal, and Kaneh is also connected with Mochin. See *Berachos*, 56b, "One who sees a Kaneh in his dream merits wisdom," and, "One who sees many Kanos should anticipate higher understanding."

The letter Vav in *V'ein* is graphically the same letter as the Vav-Cholam, the "o" in *Shofar*).

This means that although 'Satanic' negativity can exist on Rosh Hashanah, unlike on Yom Kippur when it does exist at all (*Yuma*, 20a), this quality is mitigated since we "confuse the Satan" by the means of the Shofar. Essentially, the Shofar neutralizes the possibility of our being harmed by this 'adversary', and it therefore has "no negative effect." It is a day "on which we become free from the Angel of Death" (*Pesikta Rabasi*, Parsha 40), which is another name for the Satan (*Bava Basra*, 16a). All of our enemies, both external and internal, and their poisonous barbs, are neutralized.

The Vav of the word Shofar is used to spell the word *V'ein* / "and there is no" in the quote above. However, as the Chasam Sofer points out, the letter Vav can also stand for *V'Yesh* / there *is* — meaning, *V'yesh Pega Ra* / and there *is* a negative effect. So, on what basis do we assert that the Vav indicates *no* negative effect?

In truth, whether our reality will be characterized as *V'yesh* or *V'ein* depends on us. On Rosh Hashanah there remains the *possibility* of Satan or negativity to take hold, and it rests on our shoulders, our work, mindset and 'beautiful actions', to ensure that it does not. Rosh Hashanah is a celebration of humanity, it is a day marked to celebrate beings with free choice, as such, we must choose to assume responsibility and create the reality we want to inhabit.

The letter Vav implies connection, since it grammatically functions as the word 'and' when it is added to the beginning of a word. Also, as a word in itself, Vav means 'a hook', a connector or unifier. The Vav in the word Shofar alludes to the unifying factor between negativity and positivity. Numerically, Vav is 6, alluding to the Sixth Day of Creation, the birthday and origin of humanity and human responsibility. Ultimately, we are the Vav that can choose to connect to a good, sweet year, or hook into the opposite, Heaven forbid.

NUMERICAL VALUE OF THE WORD SHOFAR

The word Shofar itself, as a tube or pipe, implies constriction, and the blowing of the Shofar symbolizes a 'blowing open' of all constriction. Shofar is spelled Shin, Vav, Pei, Reish (שופר). Numerically, the total value of Shofar is 586 (Shin/300, Vav/6, Pei/80 , Reish/200). This is also the numerical value of the word *Tokef* / strong or harsh (Tav/400, Kuf/100, Vav/6, Pei/80 = 586). This expresses the fact that the Shofar breaks through all the harshness, and all the Din, in us and in the world (*Sha'ar haKavanos*, Iyan Rosh Hashanah, Derush Zayin). By Divine Providence, 586 is also the *Siman* / chapter in *Shulchan Aruch*, The Code of Law, that speaks of the laws of Shofar.

As explored, the Shofar is an expression and symbol of Din, but by blowing a breath of life through the Shofar, the Din is sweetened. The *Kol* / sound and the *Hevel* / breath that produce the blast are connected with the Supernal Breath, which enlivens and expands our world and reality. Also as the human windpipe was not damaged in the eating from the Tree of Knowledge, it is a fitting instrument to draw down *Rachamim* / compassion, new *Chayus* / life force, and *Mochin* / intelligence into our lives.

SHOFAR AND THE NAME ELOKIM

The word שופר / Shofar is composed of four letters: Shin/300, Pei/80 and Vav/6 (=86), and finally Reish/200. These three numbers, 300, 86, and 200 are, as will be explored, intricately connected with the Name *Elokim*, representing judgment and constriction. Blowing through the constriction of the Shofar thus implies elevating and sweetening all *Dinim* / judgments and constrictions, and releasing them into openness and compassion.

The definition of the Name Elokim* is "the Mighty Ruler and Sovereign of the Heavens and the Earth, the Master of All Natural Forces, the Force of Forces." *E'l* means 'power', and *Heim* means 'those'. *Elokim* is thus the Power and Ruler over all 'those' other forces (Ramban, *Bereishis*, 1:1).

As frequently mentioned, the Name Elokim is connected with *Din* / strict judgment, that Divine Power which sets limitations, laws, boundaries and apparent constrictions. This can be seen in the laws of nature themselves, which are full of fixed definitions, functions and quantifiable dimensions. Fire

---

* The Name Elokim is written here the way it would be pronounced in everyday conversation, when the letter Hei as in 'H' is replaced with the Kuf as in 'K' — *Elokim* in the place of *Elo-him*. However, in Tefilah and recital of the Torah, it should be pronounced with its proper letters, i.e. *Elo-him*.

is hot and if you touch it, you will get burned. The sun comes out during the day. If you throw something up in the air it will eventually come down. This is the level of the universe governed by strict judgment, which emerges from the Name Elokim.

"In the beginning Elokim created the Heavens and the earth." Heaven and earth, up and down, plurality and polarity, are created through the Name Elokim. That is why *Elokim* is 'plural' as opposed to *Elokah*, the singular form.

The Shofar is a representation of the Name Elokim. The numerical value of the letters that spell the Name Elokim is 86 (Aleph/1, Lamed/30, Hei/5, Yud/10, Mem/40 = 86). When counting the 'full value' of each of these same 5 letters, the total is 300:

The word *Aleph* is spelled Aleph/1, Lamed/30, Pei/80 = 111.

The word *Lamed* is spelled Lamed/30, Mem/40, Dalet/4 = 74.

The word *Hei* is spelled Hei/5, Yud/10 = 15.

The word *Yud* is spelled Yud/10, Vav/6, Dalet/4 = 20.

The word *Mem* is spelled Mem/40, Mem/40 = 80.

111 + 74 + 15 + 20 + 80 = 300.

The numeric value of these five letters, when cumulatively counted, is 200:

Aleph = 1.

Aleph, Lamed = 31.

Aleph, Lamed, Hei = 36.

Aleph, Lamed, Hei, Yud = 46.

Aleph, Lamed, Hei, Yud, Mem = 86.

1 + 31 + 36 + 46 + 86 = 200.

These numbers signify the inner dimension of the word Shofar in all its numerical values. Shin (300) is the 'full value' of the five letters of the Name Elokim, Pei-Vav (86) is the simple value of the Name Elokim, and Reish (200) is the five letters of the Name Elokim when cumulatively counted.

Rosh Hashanah is a time of Elokim, of Dinim, of judgment. In the beginning of the Book of Iyov / Job, the Torah says, "One day the sons of Hashem came to stand before Elokim and Satan came among them" (*Iyov*, 1:6). "Which day is this?" asks Rashi, "it is Rosh Hashanah." This day is a time to "come stand before Elokim."

Elokim is also encoded within the phrase Rosh Hashanah. Ten times Elokim (86) = 860 (10x86=860). Phonetically, Rosh can be spelled Reish-Shin. Without a letter Aleph, Rosh actually means 'poor', whereas Rosh with an Aleph means 'head'. In any case, this phonetic spelling has a numerical value of 500 (Reish/200, Shin/300). Hashanah is 360 (Hei/5, Shin/300, Nun/50, Hei/5 = 360). And 500+360=860, which is ten times Elokim.

If the letter Aleph (1) is added to the above spelling of רש / *Rosh* / poor, it becomes ראש / *Rosh* / 'head'. The numerical value becomes 861, which is the value of ten times Elokim, plus 1 for the *Kolel* / the word itself. Aleph signifies Hashem, the 'One' and Only. When added to the word 'poor' — which conceptually relates to the constriction of the world of plurality — the Oneness of Aleph transforms the depths of Din (ten times Elokim) into *Rachamim* / compassion. When we add Hashem's unifying Presence into our lives, our 'poverty' is sweetened and we experience a new 'head', a new beginning.

In the same general category as Elokim is the Name אד'נ'י / Ado-noi. The inner difference is, this Name actually contains the letters of the word דין / *Din* (Dalet, Yud, Nun), plus an א / Aleph which makes it into a sweetened Name, representing sweetened Din.

The four letters in the Name אדנ'י / Ado-noi correspond to the sweetening and healing process that takes place from the day after Tisha b'Av until Sukkos. The Nun (50) of Ado-noi corresponds to the 50 days from the Tenth of Av until Rosh Hashanah. The Yud (10) corresponds to the 10 days from and including Rosh Hashanah until and including Yom Kippur. The Dalet (4) symbolizes the four days between Yom Kippur and Sukkos, and the Aleph (1) symbolizes the first day of Sukkos (*Avodas Yisrael*, Devarim).

NEUTRALIZING THE 280 KELIPOS

The word Shofar is spelled Shin-Vav-Pei-Reish. As such, the word can be split into two, Shin-Vav, which spells the word *Shav*, and Pei-Reish which spell the word *Par*.

Pei (80) and Reish (200) together have a numerical value of

280. The number 280 is also the sum of the values of *MaN-TzePaCh* / the five 'final letters' in the Hebrew alphabet. These are the five letters of the Hebrew alphabet that change shape when they appear at the end of a word (MaN-Tze-PaCh: Mem/40, Nun/50, Tzadik/90, Pei/80 and Chaf/20 = 280). Because these shapes appear only at the ends of words, the five MaN-Tze-PaCh letters are considered 'limiting' letters; they end or restrain words. If they were not there to establish the ends of individual words, all the letters on a page would be read as one long word. Thus they represent the five Gevuros, Dinim, the five basic forces of constriction and concealment in the universe.

These five letters are connected with the five letters of Elokim (Aleph, Lamed, Hei, Yud, Mem), as well as the five senses. Appropriately, although they are the portals through which we connect to the world outside of us, the senses function as instruments of division and separation. When we look at one object, we eliminate the vast majority of our scope of vision; when we listen to one sound we restrain ourselves from listening to other sounds. In this way, our brain functions more as a filter than a sponge.

These two letters Pei and Reish, appear in the roots of many words, such as *Pru'ah* / to reveal, or *L'pharek* / to break apart. *Par* is therefore considered a force of breaking apart, of dividing and damaging; it is a force of Din and Kelipah.

As mentioned, Shin and Vav together spell the word *Shav* / equal. In this way, the word *Shofar* (Shav-Par) can be understood to represent an equalizing or neutralizing of the extreme *Gevuros* / restrictions born from the MaN-Tze-PaCh.

The word *Shav* in numerical value is 306 (Shin/300, Vav/6 = 306), which is the same as the word *D'vash* / honey. *Sho-far* or *Shav-Par* thus means 'the Din of *Par* becomes sweetened.' This is why we dip apples in honey on Rosh Hashanah; the power of honey is that it transforms everything that is dipped into it into pure sweetness (see, *Ma'amarei Admur HaZaken*, Ketzarim, D'vash, p. 454. Even if the non- kosher legs of the bee are mixed with the honey, the honey is permitted to be eaten, as everything submerged in honey becomes permitted as the honey. *Rabbeinu Yonah*, Rosh, Berachos, 43). So the *Shav* (306) of the Shofar is the *D'vash* (306) that sweetens all the *Par* (280) and Dinim, thereby neutralizing any potential negativity decreed in the year ahead.

NEUTRALIZING THE 320 KELIPOS

Associated with the Shofar is the hand that holds it. The word יד / *Yad* / hand has a value of 14 (Yud/10, Dalet/4 = 14). A hand has 14 parts; the four fingers each have three bones (12), while the thumb has two. When we add the value of *Yad* (14) to the first two letters of Shofar (*Shav*/306), the sum is 320.* In Hebrew, the number 320 is Shin-Chaf, spelling *Sheich*.

---

*The reason the *hand* is 'included' in the overall numerical value of Shofar (although technically we do not need to hold the Shofar in our hand to blow it: Tosefos, *Rosh Hashanah*, 34a) is because we find in Chazal that the measurement of a small Kosher Shofar is one that a person can hold in his hand and can be seen on both sides of the hand. So we see that the hand is especially connected with the Shofar: *Rosh Hashanah*, 27b.

Just as the Shofar breaks the Kelipah of *Par* / 280, and the Dinim of ManTzPach, the Shofar also breaks and sweetens (Shav / *D'vash* / honey) the Kelipah of *Sheich* (320).*

Par (280) and Sheich (320) are also the 280 Divine sparks and the 320 Divine sparks, the two major categories of sparks that are camouflaged within Kelipah. Together, these numbers equal 600. If we add 5 for their meta-root, the Five Gevuros (Chesed of Gevurah, Gevurah of Gevurah, Tiferes of Gevurah, Netzach of Gevurah, Hod of Gevurah), the sum is 605. On Rosh Hashanah we recite, היום הרת עולם / *HaYom Haras Olam* / "Today is the gestation of the world." The word הרת / *Haras* has a value of 605. *HaYom Haras Olam* can therefore mean, 'Today is a day of Din (605) for the world.' *Olam* / world also means *Helem* / hidden; 'Today is a day to address the 600 Divine sparks that were "hidden" in the Kelipos of Din (5)." Practically speaking, this all alludes to the fact that Rosh Hashanah is a day upon which we need to neutralize and *Mamtik* / sweeten the Dinim through our blowing of the Shofar.

One antidote to the Kelipah of Sheich (320) is the presence in this world of אברהם / Avraham. Avraham (248) is the

---

* In *Sha'ar haKavanos* (Inyan Rosh Hashanah, Derush Zayin), Rebbe Chayim Vital explains that the 320 Kelipos are the feminine aspect of Kelipah and the 280 are the masculine aspect of Kelipah. Yet, in other places in *Kisvei Ari* it says the opposite, that the 320 Dinim are the masculine, from the level of Chochmah, and the 280 Dinim from the feminine, from the level of Binah: *Eitz Chayim*, Sha'ar Te'n'ta, p, 23b. Indeed, there are aspects of the masculine in the feminine and the feminine in the masculine.

embodiment of the quality of *Chesed* / giving, kindness. חסד / Chesed in numerical value is 72; 248 + 72 = 320 (*Sheich*). At certain points in his life, Avraham's kindness was slightly imbalanced (however we understand this), therefore Avraham needed to bring Yitzchak, who embodied the opposite quality of Gevurah, into the world. יצחק / Yitzchak has a value of 208. He, however, was at times out of balance in his Gevurah, and therefore he required an additional dose of Chesed (72), bringing his sum equal to *Par*, 208 (208 + 72 = 280). (The Akeida is the *binding* of Yitzchak (Gevurah) to Avraham (Chesed), and Avraham (Chesed) to Yitzchak (Gevurah), thus we read the Akeida story on Rosh Hashanah.) The sum of Avraham and Yitzchak in their balanced state is 600 (320 + 280 = 600), which equals and counteracts the combination of Sheich and Par.

One more element, however, is needed for complete balance and rectification. Fully sweetening Din requires *Ahavah* / love. אהבה / *Ahavah* is numerically 13. When added together, 600+13=613. This means that, in addition to balancing our Chesed and Gevurah, we need to perform the 613 Mitzvos to draw down Hashem's love and desire for Creation, and His will to continue to create and sustain the world, and us, with love. This is the whole-system formula, the balanced equation, that neutralizes the Dinim of *Sheich* and *Par*.

The word אחד *Echad* / one is also numerically 13. Kelipah is the consciousness of separation, divisiveness, and restriction. *Kedushah* / holiness is wholesome balance, unity, and inter-connection. Through the Mitzvos we reveal Unity within the world of apparent separation. By revealing Hashem's oneness, we neutralize the 280 and 320 Kelipos, and sweeten all of Creation.

WHAT ARE THE 320 KELIPOS?

In the beginning of Creation there is a 'concealment' of Hashem's Oneness, as such, the word *Olam* / world comes from the root word *Helem* / concealment. In the first chapter of Bereishis, which expands upon the Days of Creation, only the Name Elokim is employed. Elokim, as explained, is the Source of Din, which is the source of physical life and the "laws of nature."

The Name Elokim is mentioned 32 times in the beginning of the Creation narrative. Since every realm or level of Creation contains ten dimensions or Sefiros, we can multiply 32/Elokim by 10/Sefiros, which produces 320. Consequently, there are 320 levels of Kelipah rooted in Din.

In numerical value, the word Din is 64 (Dalet/4, Yud/10, Nun/50 = 64). As mentioned, there are five Gevuros or Dinim corresponding to the five 'final' letters (MaN-Tze-PaCh), and these are: Din of Chesed, Din of Din, Din of Tiferes, Din of Netzach, and Din of Hod. Five times Din (64) is 320 (5x64=320).

"A person does not commit a negative act unless a *Ruach Sh'tus* or 'spirit of folly' enters him" (*Sotah*, 3a). Foolishness, which is the opposite of being truly mindful, is the root of all negative and harmful actions. *Sh'tus* is an act of foolishness; a *Shoteh* is a fool. Rebbe Pinchas of Koritz teaches that the numerical value of שוטה / *Shoteh* is 320. The Bnei Yissaschar adds that the Hebrew word for 'fool' is נער / *Na'ar*, and *Na'ar* is also 320.

As is becoming clear, the word Shofar embodies and alludes to the root of all forms of constriction, limitation and judgment, and blowing the Shofar breaks all boundaries and sweetens all judgments. What begins as a constriction widens and culminates as an expansion. In the words of our sages, "Every year that is poor at its beginning becomes wealthy in the end" (*Rosh Hashanah*, 16b). On Rosh Hashanah, when we feel ourselves 'poor', meaning, as Rashi explains, when we feel the constriction, pain, hardship, and Din of our world of Helem, we cry out through the bellowing of the Shofar, and thereby draw down abundant physical and spiritual blessings for ourselves and for the whole world.

Additionally, the numbers 60 and 600 are intricately connected with the Shofar. The word Shofar (Shin/300, Pei/80, Vav/6, Reish/200) equals 586. With the Yad (Yud/10, Dalet/4, and the 14 parts of the hand), the hand that holds the Shofar when it is blown, the total number is 600.

The constriction of the Shofar alludes to the Name Elokim, and the expansion alludes to the Name Havayah. Ten times Elokim (Aleph/1, Lamed/30, Hei/5, Yud/10, Mem/40 = 86) is 860. Ten times Havayah (called also Hashem, the four letter name, the Yud/10, Hei/5, Vav/6, Hei/5 = 26) is 260. The difference between Elokim (860) and Havayah (260) is 600. This demonstrates that when we blow the Shofar we break all the 'differences' between the Gevurah of Elokim and the Chesed of Havayah.

The difference in number between Elokim itself (86) and Havayah itself (26) is 60. The first time in the year that we blow Shofar is the beginning of Elul, the last time in the High Holiday cycle that we blow the Shofar is on Yom Kippur,* during the month of Tishrei; the full two months together add up to 60 days. Blowing the Shofar during the days of Elul and Tishrei breaks all Din and allows for the revealing and drawing down of an influx of Chesed from on High.**

---

* The blast of the Shofar at the end of Yom Kippur is to announce that Yom Kippur is over and we should go celebrate, with a festive meal, as Tosefos writes: *Shabbos*, 114b: מה שתוקעים במוצאי יוה"כ אינו אלא להודיע שהוא לילה. The Smag writes the same: Siman, 69.

** The Shofar is also connected with the Name of Hashem spelled out to equal 63, also referred to as the Name *Sag* / 63 — which is Binah, the root of all Din. Yud, Vav, Dalet = 20. Hei, Yud = 15. Vav, Aleph, Vav. Hei, Yud = 15. In total is Sag / 63. The 'filled letters' of Sag, i.e. the Vav/6 and Dalet/4 (of Yud), the Yud/10 (of Hei), the Vav/6 and Aleph/1 (of Vav), and the Yud/10 (of Hei) = 37. Sag is connected with the word *Hevel*/breath, which numerically is 37. We blow the Shofar with our *Hevel* / breath. 63+37=100, the 100 sounds of the Shofar *Pri Eitz Chayim*, Sha'ar haShofar, 1. According to Chasidus (see Rebbe Aaron of Zitomer, a student of the Berditchever, *Toldas Aharon*, Parshas Bamidbar), the name Sag is connected with the word *Nasog* / pushed aside. As the Shofar pushes aside all Kelipah and negativity. *Sag* is rooted in the world of Binah, and with Sag we Mamtik the Dinim at their source; as "All sweetening of Judgments (Din) is only through their Source." Through the blowing of the Shofar, which is rooted in Binah, we are drawing out (blowing outwards) the lights of Zeir Anpin and Malchus

The Shofar is our primal instrument to mitigate and sweeten all judgments, to dissolve or release all constrictions, to return and reintegrate all exiled parts of ourselves. In its soul-stirring resonance, may we hear resounding echoes of the triumphant blast of the Great Shofar of Redemption, calling us all back home to the land where we belong.

---

that rose up to Binah, and we are drawing them downward, now, into a rectified configuration.

Chapter Four

BEING IN THE NOW WITH NO FEAR
VS. BEING IN THE FUTURE WITH FEAR

WHAT IS THE ESSENCE OF THE SOUND OF THE SHOFAR? Among the commentators there is an extensive debate regarding what the sound of the Shofar represents, as explored earlier. Is it a sound of joy and coronation, or is it an existential alarm clock, bidding us to wake up now before it's too late?

In the Torah itself, we find that the sound of the Shofar is a battle cry, as the verses describe regarding Yehoshua at the border of Yericho: "And seven priests shall bear before the Ark seven trumpets of ram's horns: and the seventh day they shall circle the city seven times, and the priests shall blow the seven trumpets. And it shall come to pass, that when they make a long blast with the ram's horn (a Shofar), and when they hear the sound of the trumpet, all the people shall shout with a great shout; and the walls of the city shall fall down flat" (*Yehoshua*, 6:4).

Similarly, "Moshe sent them on the campaign, one thousand from each tribe…with the sacred utensils and the trumpets for sounding in their possession" (*Bamidbar*, 31:6. See also *Bamidbar*, 10:9).

The Torah also describes the blowing of trumpet horns as a means to gather the people: "Make yourself two silver trumpets; make them of hammered work; you shall use them to summon the congregation" (*Bamidbar*, 10:2). Additionally, the blast of a horn is also a signal that movement is about to ensue: "…and to announce the departure of the camps" (ibid). It is also the sound marking the end of a period of time, as in, "When the sound of the Yovel (Shofar) is blown they are allowed to ascend the mountain" (*Shemos*, 19:13).

The Shofar also serves as a sound of warning, as in: "When he sees the sword come upon the Land, he should blow the trumpet, and warn the people" (*Yirmiyahu*, 33:3); as well as an announcement of freedom, as after a Shofar is blown the slaves go free in the fiftieth year: "In the seventh month, on the tenth of the month, on the Day of Atonement, you shall sound the Shofar throughout your land. And you shall sanctify the fiftieth year (Yovel), and proclaim freedom (for all slaves) through-out the Land for all its inhabitants…" (*Vayikra*, 25:9-10). Finally, the Shofar is the sound of Redemption — the sound of the Great Shofar that will be blown to usher in the Messianic era.

A CRY OF UNCERTAINTY

All of these allusions and ideas notwithstanding, on Rosh Hashanah we derive the specific quality of and type of sound we aim to produce from the cries of the mother of Sisrah, when her son was engaged in battle with Klal Yisrael (*Rosh Hashanah*, 33b). We read in *Sefer Shoftim / The Book of Judges*, that when Sisrah went into battle and he was late in returning home, "The mother of Sisrah peered through the window and cried through the lattice: 'Why is his chariot so long in com-ing? Why do the hoofbeats of his chariots tarry'" (*Shoftim*, 5:28)?!

What type of sound was this cry? Sisra's mother was not crying because he had died, as she did not yet know that he had died, although she may have suspected that. Rather she was crying because he had not yet returned from battle, and he was late.

Her cry was a cry of uncertainty and apprehension, plagued by the worst nightmare that maybe something terrible hap-pened, yet at the same time it was also a cry of hope. This is like the worry of a mother when her child is late returning home from school; her worst nightmares are intertwined with her hopes that everything is just fine. This cry, therefore, is not of pain, nor of joy, nor of mourning, but rather of *uncertainty*.

Peering through the window she cried and thought, 'Has my son been killed, captured, tortured? Was he victorious in battle and late only because he is celebrating his victory?'

This ambivalent, unsteady emotion is clearly related to the general uncertainty of us all on Rosh Hashanah, the day of judgment and trembling, as explored earlier. When we sound the Shofar it expresses our uncertainty regarding our judgment and how our year will unfold.

Uncertainty creates the worst kind of suffering, producing intense psychological pain and discomfort. This is because when you imagine the worst possible scenario, your body and mind react as if you have, in actuality, lost control of your most basic physical and emotional security. The cry of Sisra's mother, and of the Shofar on Rosh Hashanah is one of worry, and worry is always about the future.

In particular, worry stimulates and amplifies the fear of having little or no control. The mind responds by projecting itself into an imaginary future with some kind of solution to the threat, and this provides the mind with a semblance of security. The trick is, the mind itself created the problem in the first place, by worrying, and thus the mind seeks to regain its stability by heroically solving its own self-induced crisis.

Yet, there is also a positive type of fear. If a person has no healthy fear of water, for instance, they may drown; if they have no fear of fire they may get burned. There is a motivating 'anxiety' that rouses us from complacency and propels us to take action or make the necessary moves in life. In Hebrew there are two words indicating this healthy form of fear: *Pachad* and *Yirah*.

PACHAD IS IN THE NOW, YIRAH IS IN THE FUTURE

When a lion is roaring right in front of you, the experience is of *Pachad*. The Hebrew word *Pachad* comes from the words *Poh Chad* / here is sharp, i.e. here is a clear and present danger — a sharp knife, waters too dangerous for swimming, or a trail unsafe for walking.

The purpose of Pachad is to alert you to act immediately. It forces you to actively change course or protect yourself right now, in the present. Pachad stimulates the fight or flight response. The energetic force of such a visceral reaction creates a corresponding spiritual awakening that is helpful to initiate the process of Teshuvah.

Yirah is similar to the word for 'seeing'. The worldly level of Yirah is, in fact, fearfully 'seeing' or looking into the future, an imaginary world which you cannot do anything about. The mind may become gripped by thoughts such as, 'What will happen if I lose my job?' 'How will I continue if so-and-so passes on?' Since you do not actually know what the future will bring, there is no reasonable action in the present that will secure your protection. For example, one may spend great efforts and resources on creating job security for the future by going back to school and getting a new degree, but one's field can change overnight with the introduction of some new technology, leaving much of one's learning irrelevant. This kind of security will always remain elusive and just out of our grasp.

PACHAD IS CONNECTED WITH ELOKIM — YIRAH IS CONNECTED WITH HASHEM

In the Torah, in general, the term Pachad is connected with the Name Elokim, as in *Ein Pachad Elokim l'Neged Einav* / "There is no fear of Elokim before his eyes" (*Tehilim*, 36:2).

Yirah is generally called *Yiras Hashem* / awe of the Infinite One; the phrase *Yirah Elokim* also appears in Torah (*Bereishis*, 22:12), but it is more often called *Yiras Hashem*, or in the language of Chazal, *Yiras Shamayim* / fear of Heaven (a reference to the Divine).

Elokim is connected with *Teva* / nature; as *Elokim* and *haTeva* / 'the natural world' both numerically equal 86. This is why the story of Creation in the Torah only mentions the Name Elokim, "In the beginning Elokim created…" The creation and maintenance of this physical, natural world is therefore considered the provenance of Elokim. Philosophically, the concept of 'Nature' refers to the physical, empirical and observable, and hence the immediate reality. In terms of fear, Pachad Elokim refers to actual and immediate danger, such as the snarling lion in front of you.

Hashem, on the other hand, is the Infinite, and infinity is 'forever', connected with future or unseen potential, that which is perpetually beyond us. *Shamayim* also means 'Above', distant, (םש / there), Transcendent, beyond. *Yiras Hashem* means to be in awe of the Everything beyond us, the Unrevealed Transcendence, the mysterious and forever Hidden One.

Whereas worldly Yirah is comprised of negative, anxious, self-defeating thoughts about the future (the proverbial 'what if', that produces only nerve-wracking stress); higher Yiras Hashem is liberating and expansive, inducing a state of tangible wonder.

Often, a movement from lower Yirah to higher Yirah comes about through an experience of the immediacy of Pachad. For instance, imagine a person obsessing about his future, living with constant anxiety of what will be and obsessively conjuring up the worst nightmare scenarios of what could go wrong. Then, all of a sudden, he trips and begins to fall down the steps (G-d forbid). At this point Pachad takes over; his obsessions about a theoretical future disappear and all he can focus on is this moment of falling. Once the immediate Pachad eclipses the lower Yirah , he now becomes open to the higher Yirah, the infinite expanse of everlasting awe. Sitting at the bottom of the steps, he realizes he very well could have been mortally injured, but instead he was saved from Above in a remarkable way. He trembles and cries and eventually relaxes in appreciation.

Extended anxiety and fear stiffens the body, tightens and constricts the limbs and organs, and even interrupts the natural flow of blood. This is the devastating effect of lower Yirah, apprehension and anxiety (In the words of Chazal fear is צמית: *Sotah*, 20. *Nidda*, 71a). Sudden, immediate fear (Pachad) does the opposite; it relaxes and loosens the body (*ibid*), and in fact one can lose control over certain movements of the body in such circumstances. Pachad catapults a person out of his or her rigidity, stuckness and stiffness. It is a forced loosening of Din, and it opens the person up to move from the lower, crippling Yirah of apprehension and uncertainty about an unknowable future, into an expansive, free-flowing, awe-inspiring state of higher Yirah.

There are two movements in the blowing of the Shofar. First, the blower takes a deep inhale (which, as will be explained later, is the higher Hei) and then they blow into the Shofar, which is the exhale (the final letter Hei). On a subtle level, the inhale is the 'potential', which means the "future" (Yirah). The exhale, the actual blowing of the Shofar, is the idea of Pachad, the awareness of clear and present danger, as it were, arousing in the listener a call for immediate action, namely Teshuvah. In this way, the lower Yirah, a vague directionless anxiety about an undefined future, is transformed into a Pachad Elokim, a clear sense of immediate judgment, responsibility and urgency in relationship to the Creator.

עלה אלקים בתרועה ה' בקול שופר / "*Elokim* is elevated with the Teru'ah; *Hashem* with the sound of the Shofar" (*Tehilim*, 47:6). The Name Elokim is connected with the Teru'ah, and the Name Hashem with the *Kol Shofar*, meaning, the Tekiah.

And it is through the sound of the Kol Shofar, the Tekiah, that there is a transformation from the judgment of Elokim to the compassion of Hashem.

Our first step in this Avodah is to elevate our worldly Yirah to Yiras Elokim or Pachad. This shift occurs through the broken sound of the Teru'ah. Then this Yiras Elokim can be elevated to Yiras Hashem, with the Tekiah.

We might enter Rosh Hashanah with a more worldly level of Yirah: 'What is the new year going to bring?' Perhaps on account of our habituated lack of mindful presence, we are gripped with anxiety about our judgment and the unknown future. In this case we are like Sisra's mother, overwhelmed with worry mingled with vague hope of what will be.

Perhaps nervous anxiety and uncertainty are the most likely and natural sensations to overwhelm us as we enter Rosh Hashanah. Yet, ideally, we need to try and move from this lower Yirah (anxiety about the future) up to Pachad (fear in the immediate present) and eventually to higher Yirah (awe of the infinite unknown).

Arguably, it is human nature to worry, to feel like Sisra's mother felt, especially as we are entering a new year and a moment of judgment. Yet, coupled with *Bitachon* / trust and confidence, reflected in how we dress and celebrate on Rosh Hashanah, we should allow the sounds of the Shofar to move us from lower Yirah into Pachad and then into higher Yirah. We need to allow the Teru'ah to enter into our worldly fears and raise them up to the level of Pachad Elokim. And even before this Teru'ah, we need to allow the first Tekiah blast to give us a burst of confidence and strength.

Specifically, this first blast of the Tekiah stimulates a visceral feeling of Pachad and forces us to focus on the present, canceling out and overriding all thoughts of the future and removing all worldly Yirah. Without such self-centered anxiety in the picture, Pachad can even feel joyful and relieving, as it energizes us to act in the moment.

The Torah calls the day of Rosh Hashanah "a day of Teru'ah." As we have explored, *Teru'ah* comes from the root word *Re'u'ah* / trembling, to be in awe. The sound of the Teru'ah is meant to stimulate feelings of Re'u'ah. The root of the word Re'u'ah is *Ra* / shaky, unstable. *Ra'u'ah* in the language of the Gemara means something that is shaky, uncertain. Imagine the broken sound of the Teru'ah; it is like a person gasping for air, in a panic. We need this sound to stimulate and reveal the worldly fear that we hold just beneath the surface of our personality. Only when it is uncovered can we consciously address it.

The Mishnah teaches, "If a בריא / *Bari* / healthy clay vessel is plastered... (but if it is a) vessel that is רעוע / Ra'u'ah (then it has a different law)" (*Kelim*, 3:5). This suggests that *Ra'u'ah* is the opposite of 'healthy', something that is shaky in the sense of sickly or broken. Seasonally, this shakiness is connected with the onset of fall and winter. Instinctually, people ask, certainly people who live more connected to the earth and in an agricultural society, 'Will I have enough food and fuel to sustain me through the winter?' The Torah reveals a further spiritual reason for this anxiety that is deeper than psycho-seasonal instincts: people feel afraid and uncertain during this period because it is a time of Divine Judgment, a time that will determine their future success.

As mentioned previously, the word *Shofar* in numerical value is 586. This is the same value as the word *Tokef* / strong, or harsh (Tav/400, Kuf/100, Vav/6, Pei/80 = 586). In contrast to the Teru'ah, the Tekiah blast is especially strong, expressing bold certainty and unwavering confidence.

"אם־יתקע שופר ועם לא יחרדו / *Im Yitaka Shofar* / If a Tekiah is blown in the city, will people not *Charadu* / tremble?" (*Amos*, 3:6). The root of חרדו / *Charadu* is חד / *Chad* / sharp, like the word פחד / *Pachad*. The sound of the Tekiah does not suggest 'shaky' (lower) Yirah, but rather Pachad, sharply motivating us to act decisively and with confidence in the moment.

Lower Yirah is connected with the Teru'ah. Pachad is connected with the Tekiah. The idea is to enfold one's worldly Yirah in the immediacy of Pachad, so that we can energize and elevate ourselves into higher Yirah. From this place we can live a life of wonder, and radical amazement, rather than constant unfounded anxiety.

100 CRIES

As already explained, we blow 100 blasts of the Shofar on Rosh Hashanah, and one of the inner reasons for this number is that a woman who is giving birth symbolically cries 100 cries. The first 99 cries are for the pain of labor and the process of birth; cries of agony and sometimes of worry that the baby or the mother herself may not survive this experience. This is similar to Sisra's mother's cry of uncertainty and fear of the future, which is almost always worse than reality itself.

At last, there is the one-hundredth cry that pushes the baby out of the womb, this is a cry of release and joy, a triumphant bellow of realization from the mother that she will indeed live and that she has now successfully given birth to a beautiful child (Medrash, *Vayikra Rabbah*, 27:7. *Tanchumah*, Tazriah, 4. *Meshech Chochmah*, Emor). This final cry can wipe away all the pain and uncertainty of the first 99 cries, and the mother is left marveling at the wonder of her new born baby. Following the struggle of birth, the mother will often become tender, loving and peaceful, as if the agony and trauma of labor has completely evaporated, and all she is left with is with the miracle of new life.

On Rosh Hashanah when we blow the Shofar 100 times, our first 99 cries may be cries of trembling, like the Teru'ah. Our final cry, however — the *Tekiah Gedolah* / the Great Tekiah, at the end of the service — is a triumphant cry of joy and an expression of our conviction and certainty that our prayers have been answered, and that we will live and be inscribed in the Book of Life and blessings.

YOM KIPPUR AS THE FINAL DAY OF YOUR LIFE

Yom Kippur is perhaps the most existentially challenging day of the year. It is a day when we are invited and given strength to penetrate our very essence and ask ourselves; 'Who am I?' By 'deleting' all of the externals of our life, all our contingent attributes, and everything that is not technically necessary to our existence, food, drink, possessions and power, we are able to deeply reflect and consider: what (or who) is left when everything has been stripped away? On Yom Kippur we must imagine that it is the last day of our lives. In these final moments, what would we hold onto and what would we let go of? What is fundamental to your identity? What is essential to your existence?

At the end of this day-long meditation, as Yom Kippur comes to a close, we blow the Shofar one last time and declare, "Next year in Yerushalayim!" After the entire process of Rosh Hashanah and Yom Kippur, we conclude with the consciousness that: in the coming year everything will be good, as it always already is, right now. The new year begins at this very moment, the eternal 'now'.

NEXT YEAR IN YERUSHALAYIM

Malki-Tzedek (who was Shem, the son of Noach) first named the city of which he was king, "Shalem." Following this, Avraham then named the city, and more specifically the place of the Akeidah, "*Hashem Yireh* / the Infinite will see" (*Bereishis*, 22:14). "Said the Holy One, blessed be He, 'If I call the place

'Yireh' like Avraham did, the righteous Shem will complain. However, if I refer to it as 'Shalem', the righteous Avraham will complain. Rather, I will call it 'Yeru-shalayim', and that name will combine the ways it was called by both of them: *Yirah-Shalem*'" (*Medrash Rabbah*, Bereishis, 56:10).

One meaning of *Yirah-Shalem* is 'Complete Yirah'. This indicates the transformation and completion of Yirah — from negative, lower Yirah, a fear of life itself, to *Yiras Hashem* / awe of the Transcendent Source of Life.

We have a choice: we can live in fear and apprehension over the unknowable future, plagued by uncertainty and racked with anxiety, or we can live in awe and surrender to HaKadosh Baruch Hu's plan, and live in wonder from moment to moment.

Shalem also means *Shalom* / peace and wholeness. Therefore, at the pinnacle and conclusion of Yom Kippur we sound the Shofar and proclaim that this coming year will be lived 'in *Yirah Shalem*.' This means that our lower Yirah, our egoic fears and anxieties, will become holistically elevated, allowing us to reside in the *Shalom* / peace of Yiras Hashem.

This final Shofar blast was also the signal of the beginning of the Yovel year at which point the slaves or indentured servants would go completely free and return home, and the ownership of a piece of land would revert to its original owner. For us today, this blast signals our 'freedom' from servitude to our limited image of what should or should not be, and ultimately, "freedom from sin" (הוא סימן חירות...חירות מעבירות הגופות: *Levush*, Orach Chayim, 623:5). With this blast, our apprehension about our future disappears, and the chains of fear can fall away forever.

May we merit to experience the literal meaning of the words, "Next year in Yerushalayim," the words we proclaim following the blast of the Shofar at the end of Yom Kippur,* with the revealing of Moshiach and the building of the Beis haMikdash speedily, in our days.

---

* Note that the word Shofar in numerical value is 586, the same value as the word ירושלם, which is ירושלים without the Yud, one of the ways *Yerushalayim* is written in Tanach, for example — ויהי כשמע אדני־צדק מלך ירושלם: *Yehoshua,* 10:1.

Chapter Five

BEYOND LANGUAGE & DUALITY: CONNECTING TO THE TREE OF LIFE

BEYOND WORDS

WHEN WE SPEAK ABOUT SOMETHING THAT IS HIGHLY RELEVANT TO US PERSONALLY, OUR WORDS FLOW FORTH EFFORTLESSLY AND ARE CHARGED WITH PASSION AND VIGOR. When we are deeply inspired and wish to express our feelings in words, our words seem more poetic, gracefully revealing that which has so enlivened us.

On the other hand, there are things in life that shake us to the core, so much so that our minds are unable to truly grasp what is even occurring, we become dumbfounded and are 'at a loss for words'. This often transpires when we experience something that overwhelms our capacity to intellectually conceptualize, such as a devastating tragedy. There are no words that can describe or contain certain overwhelming feelings, and often, the only natural outlet left to us is either sighing or sobbing.

Rosh Hashanah is, of course, not a day of tragedy or melancholy, in fact it is a celebration of our collective birthday and thus a time to celebrate, yet a simple meditation on the awesomeness of this majestic day, the day of our judgment and justification, the day of our crowning Hashem as the Master of the Universe, causes us to quake and tremble. Words fail the awesomeness of the moment. We can only shudder in the face of the Tangible Immanence of the Real and collapse with the guttural cry of the Shofar.

Shofar gives voice to a primal sound, a cry that is lodged deeper than human language, a visceral sound emanating from the primordial "animalistic" part of self. Our prayers, yearnings, longings and hopes are channeled through the Shofar, through the 'voice of the animal'. This is not a crass, vulgar, or animalistic voice, rather it is a raw, primal expression that comes from the 'gut', a nonverbal place where the human mind can neither fathom nor feign. The Shofar can also be likened to the sound of a small child calling out to his or her parent. It is an existential expression older than language itself. In the awe of Rosh Hashanah, we are at a loss for words and all we can manage to do is pick up an animal horn and blow a raw sound, a wordless prayer.

This dimension of Tefilah is alluded to in the parable attributed to the holy Baal Shem Tov:

There once was a king's child who was sent away to study. After a while, far from home, the child forgot that he was in fact a son of the king. After many years in this state, he spontaneously experienced a strong desire to reconnect with his parents. He dredged up early memories, asked people many questions, poured over maps, and finally determined the area where his family must have been located. A royal palace!

Following a long and winding path of return, he found his way home. But having been so far away for so many years, the guards did not believe that he was the son of the king — in fact, he did not even speak the language of the kingdom. The son was distraught. All he could do was stand outside of the king's court and cry aloud in hope that the king would recognize his once familiar voice.

This pure guttural sound of a lost child is the sound of *Teshuvah* / return. Through such a cry, a unification is made, loved ones are reunited and healing occurs. The simple sound of the Shofar inspires us to do Teshuvah, to reclaim our inherent connection to that palace of integral wholeness within.

BEYOND THE WORLD OF DUALITY

This primordial wail is in fact the *Tikkun* / rectification of humanity's consumption of the *Eitz haDa'as* / Tree of Knowledge, the fallen perspective of duality and dichotomy that led us so far from our royal home. It is through this wordless prayer, the pure sound of the Shofar, that we are able to put the fruit back onto the Tree of Knowledge and come home to the deeper truth of Infinite Unity rooted in the Tree of Life.

A Shofar has to be *Shaleim* / whole and not broken. A Shofar that was split and glued back together is not Kosher (*Mishnah Rosh Hashanah*, 27a). This is because the sound of the Shofar is connected with the perfect, whole 'sound' of reality before the cosmic *Sheviras haKeilim* / breaking of the vessels, as well as the innocent wholeness that existed before the *Cheit* / mistake of the Eitz haDa'as. For this reason, the instrument itself must be beyond brokenness. What is more, the sound of the unbroken Shofar comes from the inner essence of a person that is 'pure' and whole and always perfect, and transcendent of any sense of brokenness.

Shofar takes us back to the Garden of Eden, to the inner reality of the Tree of Life. The history of Rosh Hashanah itself pre-dates the Cheit Eitz haDa'as; Adam's birthday was the first Rosh Hashanah, and he and Chavah only ate from the Tree of Knowledge some hours later. Rosh Hashanah is therefore rooted in the Tree of Life, in Gan Eden, the 'place' of perfection and unity, prior to any sin or separation. The sounds of the Shofar that we blow today awaken the power of the original Rosh Hashanah, and propel us deeper along an inner journey of elevating consciousness back to the paradigm of life, wholeness, peace, and blessing.

SOUND VERSUS WORDS

Indeed, cosmically speaking, all sounds and vibrations emanate from a place of Unity and infinite silence, beyond the *Tzimtzum* / the contraction of the Infinite Light of Hashem. As such, all language, being the configuration and manipulation of unified sound, is expressed through a filter of finitude, definition and division — the post Tzimtzum world of *G'vul* / finite boundaries. Sound is 'oneness', Language is 'twoness'.

In order to create words we take an undifferentiated sound, which rises up from the belly and lungs, and channel it into our mouth. Once in our mouth the sound is 'shaped' to create distinct articulations of sound, which are woven together to become speech. These distinct articulations are created by the Five Gevuros, the 'five restrictions' embodied in the mouth: 1) the throat which creates guttural sounds, 2) the palate which creates palatal sounds, 3) the tongue which creates lingual sounds, 4) the teeth which create dental sounds, and 5) the lips which create labial sounds. Each of these different areas has a unique vibrational and spiritual quality borne of its particular 'constriction' or restraint and the way it characteristically gives shape to undifferentiated sound.

Therefore, whenever we utter a word we first emit a pure undifferentiated sound, a singular *Kol* / voice. For this simple, unified sound to become speech, it must be modified and manipulated through the constrictions of the throat, palate, tongue, teeth and lips, as above. Through this processing, what comes out of the mouth is a string of precisely defined sounds which are sequenced in a way that forms a word of *Dibbur /* speech.

Kol is connected with the world of Unity and rooted in silence, whereas Dibbur is connected with the world of duality. מן השמים השמיעך את קלו / "From Heaven you heard His *Kol"* (*Devarim*, 4:36). Kol is thus associated with Heaven and Dibbur is associated with earth, the finite, physical world (*Pirush haGra*, Shir haShirim, 2:6. *Ohr haTorah*, Devarim 4, p. 1934. *Besha'ah Shehikdimu* 5672, p. 497).

Kol, which is 'one', also corresponds to *Sheim Havayah /* the Name Hashem (Yud-Hei-Vav-Hei), the Infinite Transcendent Name of Hashem. Dibbur, which is composed of distinctions and separations in sound, corresponds to *Sheim Elokim*, the Divine manifest in the world of plurality. *Bereishis Bara Elokim /* "In the beginning, Elokim created...." Elokim creates the world of duality via 'speech', the Ten Utterances.

Whereas language is obviously created through separation and division, the truth is, any kind of 'expression' is based on a dynamic of separation as well. When we are unified with an experience, we cannot express it in any way. In deep trauma, for example, a person cannot even think about his pain, much less put it into words, or express it in tears. Only once there is some distance and detachment from the initial event, only then might one begin to cry, or begin to speak about it or express it artistically.

How can one speak of the pure, undifferentiated, ineffable experience of awe and total eclipse of selfhood? How can we outwardly express something that is so inwardly felt? Only by blowing the Shofar. The simple, guttural wail of the Shofar allows us to connect to, and begin to express, the awe that is transcendent of all language and expression.

Our sages confirm that all Shofars are Kosher, besides those made of the horn of a bull (*Rosh Hashanah*, 26a). One of the reasons for this ruling is that the horns of bulls have many internal layers, and blowing one creates multiple sounds, not the single sound of a 'unified' horn. On a deeper level, this means that bull horns represent the world of *Pirud* / separation, and our intention in blowing the Shofar is to connect to *Yichud* / unification (*Tola'as Yaakov*, Sod haShofar). The primal sound of the Shofar is a pre-verbal expression, one that is lodged in the Tree of Life, the root of unity. Quite simply, it is breath made audible.

When Adam and Chavah ate from the Tree of Knowledge, their conscious spiritual constitution and revealed connection to the Tree of Life was damaged, yet their *Neshimah* / breath and *Neshamah* / soul remained unscathed and pure. Our breath too always remains pure, sourced, as it is, in the Supernal Breath, the Divine animating life-force of Creation.

For the body to survive it needs oxygen and food. There are two tubes connecting the head and the body: the trachea and the esophagus — the wind-pipe and the food-pipe, respectively. We human beings damaged our food pipes by eating from the Tree of Knowledge, but the wind-pipe, which does not experience eating and drinking, is still attached to the higher, deeper worlds (*Zohar* 3, p. 232a. Shaloh, *Sha'ar haOsyos*, Os Kuf, Kedushas Achilah). Since our connection with the Supernal Breath of Life was never severed or tampered with, our breath is always a portal into the world of the Tree of Life. When we use our breath to blow the Shofar we draw down blessings and compassion from the Source of Life into our bodies and minds and into the entire world.

This is the power of the primordial sound of the Shofar, the sound of Unity, beyond language, expressing the ineffable simplicity of the Essence of the Creator.

Chapter Six
SHOFAR AS THE 'BIRTH CANAL' OF THE NEW YEAR

O N ROSH HASHANAH, THE BIRTHDAY OF HUMAN CON-SCIOUSNESS, WE CELEBRATE AND REENACT THIS BIRTH, SO WE CAN ENTER THE NEW YEAR WITH FRESHNESS AND ALIVENESS.

A CRY OF BIRTH

Alluding to the birthing of human consciousness, the Shofar physically resembles a birth canal. The mouthpiece of the Shofar — where the breath enters — is narrow and constricted. The body of the Shofar then twists and turns as it gradually opens. This is the dark canal of transformation through which the breath travels on its way to being born as sound.

The sound of the Shofar is thus like the first cry of a new-born baby, a new human being. In our Rosh Hashanah liturgy we recite many times the phrase *HaYom Haras Olam* / 'Today is the pregnancy of the world,' but *Haras* can also mean 'birthday' (הרה גבר :*Iyov*, 3:2) — as in, 'Today is the birthday of the world' (Avudaraham, *Malchiyos*, p, 273. See also Tzemach Tzedek, *Yahel Ohr*, Tehilim, 20:9). The world, on this day, is similar to a woman sitting on a birthing bed or chair, about to give birth (*Sefer Rokeach*, Hilchos Rosh Hashanah, 201). As such, we need to blow (at least) nine Tekios, and there are nine blessings in the Musaf prayer (*Eiruvin*, 40a-b), which both correspond to the nine months of pregnancy (*Sefer Rokeach*, ibid.). Additionally, the sound of the Shofar is like the voice of the mother during labor and at the exultant moment of birth after nine months of pregnancy (*Yahel Ohr*, ibid).

THE CRY OF LIFE

Traditionally, a baby who emerges out of her mother's womb without crying is gently slapped in order to stimulate crying. Crying is a sign of life, an opening of the breath.

Aliveness is characterized by *Tenuah* / movement, sound, vibration. The opposite of aliveness, death, is defined by silence and stillness. The Angel of Death is called *Dumah* / silence. People who have passed on are called *Yordei Dumah* / those who have descended into silence (*Tehilim*, 115:17). Even a mourner, one who experiences the presence of death, heaves "a sigh in silence" (האנק דום :*Yechezkel*, 24:17. *Moed Katan*, 15a).

As the New Year is about to begin we need to cry out, to show that we are alive, moving, aspiring, and growing. On this day of *Hischadshus* / renewal and reset, we are moving from the death of the old to the birth of the new, and thus we give a loud cry, like a newborn babe.

Shofar has four Hebrew letters: Shin, Vav, Pei, Reish (שופר). The letters that come before each of these are Reish (before Shin), Hei (before Vav), Ayin (before Pei), and Kuf (before Reish), spelling the word עקרה / *Akarah*, the Torah word for 'barren' (*Bris Kehunas Olam*, Ma'amar "Ailo Shel Yitzchak," 45). This means the power of the Shofar is to blow into us new 'fertility' or potential for new life, healing any prior 'barrenness' or stuckness. Indeed, on Rosh Hashanah, many Torah figures whom the Torah described as *Akara* / barren conceived children. בר"ה נפקדה שרה רחל וחנה / "On Rosh Hashanah, Sarah, Rochel and Chanah were remembered (and conceived sons)" (*Rosh Hashanah*, 11a). Inwardly, through the cry of the Shofar (connected with a word associated with birth: *Sotah*, 11b) we too give birth to the next phase of our very own lives.

Rosh Hashanah is both a day that gives us life and a day for us to come to *Chayim* / life. Numerically, *Chayim* is 68. The great Tzadik Rebbe Eliezer of Worms (c. 1176–1238) writes that in Parshas Pinchas where the Torah describes the laws of Rosh Hashanah, "life" is written 68 times (*Sefer Rokeach*, Hilchos Rosh Hashanah, 200). On Rosh Hashanah we are remembered for life, and we in fact become alive.

A MOTHER'S CRY AT BIRTH

The cry of the Shofar gives voice to the tension and contraction before the release of the child from the birth canal. The cry of a mother when her baby is lingering within the birth canal is the deepest, most raw cry in the world. She feels an overwhelming need to push the child out, and yet it is tremendously painful for the child to come out. This cry helps her break through this immense tension of pushing the child out. It allows her to overcome all the *Dinim* / constrictions and limitations in herself. After 99 cries of tension, fear, trembling, and labor, she finally emits a 'Tekiah Gedolah' of release and euphoria. A seemingly impossible task has been achieved. A new life has been brought into the world.

The joy that comes with the delivery of a new life wipes away all the previous cries of pain and uncertainty. The joy and euphoria that follows the release and birth of the baby is a joy of overcoming the seemingly impossible, and with it is also expressed the joy that comes with the realization that she will live, and that she has just given birth to a beautiful child.

Our consciousness on Rosh Hashanah may be similar to a woman about to give birth. Initially we may be fearful of the Day of Judgment, what will be? How will I be judged? Do I deserve life? Can I birth myself anew in this coming year? Fear, awe and apprehension may be the dominant emotions. But ultimately, coupled with this sense of awe is our joy and confidence that HaKadosh Baruch Hu will shower us with blessings for life and goodness, that we will be successful in birthing and revealing our deepest, physical/mental/emotional and spiritual potentials in this world.

THE CRY OF RELEASE FROM SLAVERY & CONSTRICTION

In the Book of Shemos the Torah mentions a woman by the name of Shifra. The words *ShoFaR* and *ShiFRa* share the same root letters, revealing a close conceptual connection between the two (*Pri Eitz Chayim*, Sha'ar haShofar, 3. When Moshe cries in the basket [*Shemos*, 2:6] it is the sound of the Shofar, as Moshe is born from Shifra/Yocheved: *Imros Tehoros,* Reb Baruch of Mezhibuz). Shifra was a revolutionary midwife for Klal Yisrael during the time of the birth of Moshe in Egypt. Her name means 'to make beautiful', as she would beautify (משפרת) the newborn infants (*Sotah*, 11b). Her job was to help bring new life into this world, in the face of defeat and despair, and to make sure that the babies were healthy and receiving proper care. She caressed and massaged the newborn babies, which beautified them and made them strong.

Yetzias Mitzrayim / the Going out of Egypt was the 'birth' of Klal Yisrael. As the Medrash says, Klal Yisrael was like a fetus who was being pulled out of the belly. This birth required the *Tzimtzumim* / contractions of their pain and the hardship of the ten plagues, the various Dinim, for example, the *Dam* / blood, and finally the breaking of the waters. At last, when safety had been reached, and the birth process complete, there was a cry of triumph and a song of celebration — the song we sang after the Splitting of the Sea.

Every creative project, every new business venture, requires a process of Dinim and Tzimtzumim before it can be born. The sense of tribulation allows for new levels of productivity and success, much like a seed must decompose before germinating and sprouting new life. This is the natural order.

Even intellectually, before an idea can be clarified, solidified and developed, many times there is a phase of Dinim, perhaps an experience of doubt and uncertainty. To put a new idea into action, a person questions himself, 'Can I really do this?' This too is a state of contraction similar to a woman in labor, when her baby is 'crowning' or lingering at the opening of the canal, and she is questioning whether she has the strength to push the baby out.

Blowing the Shofar, as explored previously, is about breaking the Dinim, pushing through the Name *Elokim* / a Divine name that represents constrictions, limitations and narrowness (the numerical value of Shin/300 and Pei-Vav/86 and Reish/200 are all connected with the Name Elokim, as discussed).

Between conception and birth intense Dinim take hold; a resistance to leave the womb, the water breaking, blood, tears, pressure, cries, and the excruciating pain the mother must go through. Then, suddenly comes the final push and cry, and a child is born. The same dynamic holds true for all of our beautiful ambitions for what we want to bring into this world. We may plan to learn more Torah, to commit to a healthy diet, to make time for composing music, or painting, to develop more concentration in Tefilah, more patience with our family, or more mindful presence in life, and so forth. We are all pregnant with inspirations and resolutions. The challenge comes when the Dinim arise between conception and birth, when doubt or resistance sets in: 'Who am I fooling? I can't do this. This is not for me....' This internal narrative, this holding yourself back, is *Kelipah* / shells that trap life-force and create stagnation.

Despair is the overarching theme of Din and Kelipah. *Yei'ush* / giving up, asserting, 'It's not possible to manifest my inspiration. There is nothing I can do; this is fate, no one can change this.' There is a subtle wail of despair in such statements.

When the embodiment of Kelipah, 'Satan', gleefully goes to inform Sarah about the Akeidah, he says, "Have you not heard what has happened? Your husband has taken your son Yitzchak and slain him and offered him up as a burnt offering upon the altar. And the child, Yitzchak, was crying and howling because he was not able to save himself" (*Pirkei d'Rebbe Eliezer*, 32).

Satan presents the cries and howls of Yitzchak as expressions of despair, as if Yitzchak had been trying unsuccessfully to free himself. However, in reality, Yitzchak had been completely at peace, and the theoretical 'slaughter' never happened. Satan represents the lie of despair.

Tears of deep *Yei'ush* / despair are tears of *Tumah* / stagnancy, closure or blockage of possibility, which is impurity, and a kind of spiritual 'death'. They construe life as tragic. Cries of tragedy promote the idea that we can aspire and try to work against fate, but in the end, fate always wins. Tragedy says, life is predictable and inevitable and there is really no room for you to change fate.

This is the voice of Tumah, of Kelipah. We should never listen to or become ensnared by such a negative voice, whether it is internally or externally generated. There is always hope and possibility, especially on Rosh Hashanah, the time of ultimate *Hischadshus* / self-renewal. Indeed, there is also a *Nekudah* / point of Hischadshus within each moment of life, the 'Rosh Hashanah' within every instant that allows for re-birth at any time.

Our sages continue the above narrative: when Sarah heard this news, she immediately cried three times corresponding to the three Tekios, and then howled three times corresponding to the Teru'os, and then her soul fled and she passed away.

Here, in the place of the 'cries and howls' of Yitzchak, which, according to Satan, expressed his despair and death, the great Tzadekes Sarah cries 'three Tekios' and 'three Teru'os', the sounds of the Shofar. It could be said these are sounds of bitter yearning. It could also be said that they are sounds of Transcendence. She passes away, as the Koznitzer Maggid teaches, in holiness and purity (*Avodas Yisrael*, Chayei Sarah). In complete opposition to the tragic narrative of Satan, she actually experiences Divine ecstasy as she cries out and her soul transcends her body.

In our practice today, by proactively blowing the Shofar on Rosh Hashanah, we are pushing out the 'baby' and giving birth to our new self and new year. The Shofar shatters all the Dinim and resistance to new life. The word Shofar has the same letters as שורף / *Soref* / burns, as the Shofar burns away all negativity and despondency, breaks all Kelipos, and pushes out the 'baby' of holy and productive accomplishment.

With the cry of the Shofar we realize that we cannot go backwards, we cannot spiritually, emotionally, physically or intellectually regress. We cannot push the baby back into the womb and forget about giving birth. A mother knows there is no going back, even if the thought arises repeatedly. The urgency of the Shofar sound is like the final 100th cry of childbirth, when the mother screams because there is no other option; the baby must come out *now*.

When we blow the Shofar all the doubts, uncertainties, and Dinim are broken asunder; there is a total *Kara Satan* / ripping open of all Kelipos and concealments, giving birth to a new year, and a new you.

The Shofar is the birth canal of the new year. We push and blow with urgency and our prayers and cries echo and reverberate until they reach the cosmic womb, the "mother and father" of Creation, as it were. According to the Arizal, the Shofar creates a *Zivug* / coupling between *Aba* / father [Chochmah] and

Ima / mother [Binah], and a new *Shefah* / flow is given to Ze'ir Anpin [the masculine Divine attributes], so that it can unify with and impregnate Malchus [the feminine Divine attribute]. Finally, Malchus gives birth to a sweet new year.

With the blast of the Shofar the Divine Presence shifts modalities from harsh judgment and Dinim to Divine compassion and Shefa. In the words of the Zohar, "The Shofar below awakens the Shofar Above, and the Holy One, blessed be He, rises from His Throne of Judgment and sits upon His Throne of Compassion" (See also *Medrash Tehilim*, 47). We are then held within the Divine Embrace like a baby in the arms of Shifra, the *Shofar* of *Shipur* / beautification (*Sha'ar haKavanos*, Inyan Rosh Hashanah, Derush Zayin). Through our Shofar blowing we draw down a beautiful new year, full of blessings and positive potential.*

---

* The above is primarily based on the opinions that maintain that the *Ikar* / main aspect of the Mitzvah of Shofar is the act of blowing, rather than hearing. There is a debate among the Geonim and early Rishonim if the (Ikar) Mitzvah is to 'blow' the Shofar (Rav Achai Gaon, *She'iltos Rav Achai Gaon*, 171. Rav Yehudai Gaon. Semag, Mitzvah 42. Rabbeinu Tam, *Rosh Hashanah*. Rosh, Chapter 4:10. *Yire'eim*, Siman 117), or if the Mitzvah is to 'hear' the Shofar, which is the opinion of Rav Hai Gaon, Rav Amram Gaon, Rav Saadia Gaon, and the Rambam (*Hilchos Shofar*, 1:1-3. *Ibid*, 2:1). The Shulchan Aruch rules that it is the Ikar to hear the Shofar (*Orach Chayim*, 585:2, as the ruling of the Tur, *ibid*, 585). If the Mitzvah is to 'hear' the sound of the Shofar, then the reason offered by the Rambam — to awaken a desire for Teshuvah in the listener — is most applicable. Indeed, the Ritva writes this clearly (Ritva on *Rosh Hashanah*, 34a): "Since the main Mitzvah of Shofar is to awaken one to Teshuvah, and this awakening occurs through listening, thus, *hearing* the Shofar is the Mitzvah." If the Mitzvah, however, is in the blowing itself, then the 'objective' is the *blowing* and what the blowing symbolizes, as in blowing a new year into manifestation.

Chapter Seven

SHOFAR:
Initiating the Cosmic Exhale
& the Four Stages of Creation

REATION IS NOT A PAST EVENT, RATHER IT IS CON-
TINUOUS AND THE DIVINE LIFE FORCE ENTERS AND
EXITS CREATION CONTINUOUSLY. *Chayus* / Divine
vitality flows into the world in the form of מטי ולא מטי / *Mati
veLo Mati* / reaching and not reaching. This means that Chayus reaches the world to create, sustain, and nourish, and then
immediately retracts, then it enters again, and so on, in a rapid
flickering or back and forth movement.

The physical world, the vessel of life, cannot maintain its appearance as a separate entity if there is too great an influx of Divine Chayus; it would simply be overwhelmed and cease to exist independently if the Chayus did not retract. On the other hand, the Divine flow cannot tolerate being entrapped within form or vessels for too long. For this reason, the Divine flow enters and then immediately returns Above. This pattern of Chayus entering and exiting, filling and retreating, is similar to the idea of breathing. HaKadosh Baruch Hu is (*Kaviyachol* / as if) breathing out, filling Creation with Chayus, and then breathing in, gathering the world back inward (*Ohr haEmes*, Imrei Tzadikim, p 4. See also *Pri haAretz*, Parshas Bo).

Every living thing breathes, whether plant, animal or human. We receive life force and existence, and then release it back into the universe. 'Respiration' pervades the entire cosmos, and even the seasons of the year 'breathe'. In the summer and autumn the earth 'exhales', or expresses itself. In the depth of winter there is an 'inhale' and the fleeting moment of 'retention'. In the spring new life and 'inspiration' are filling the 'lungs' of nature before bursting forth again in summer.

Nature below mirrors the Divine process Above; the microcosm reflects the macrocosm. The Divine exhale fills all of Creation and then returns in a cosmic inhale. This return is immediate, almost simultaneous, so as to allow finite reality to remain in existence and not become overwhelmed by the infinite: exhaling and inhaling, running and returning, 'reaching and not reaching' — such is the cycle of all life.

Every moment the world is being breathed into existence, and the world receives this flow and gathers it inward, and every other moment, as it were, the world is inhaled back into the Divine, Supernal Breath. In each moment the world is receiving and letting go of Chayus.

AN EXHALE BELOW ALLOWS FOR A SUPERNAL INHALE BEFORE THE SUPERNAL EXHALE

The blowing of the Shofar initiates and inspires this creative, cosmic exhale. There is a beautiful image recorded in *Sefer haKanah* (*Sod Tekias Shofar*), an early Kabbalistic text that some attribute to the First Century sage Rebbe Nechunya Ben Hakanah. The inspired author of *Sefer haKanah* speaks how the voice of the Shofar awakens an arousal Above. To loosely quote him: "Just like the breath of a person inhaling and exhaling whose inhale is the cause of his following exhale...so it is with the Blessed One. There is no arousal to continue to create, no movement from Above to below, until there is first a movement from below to Above (an exhale on the part of the world), and then there is a return of life from Above to below (an exhale on the part of the Blessed One)." The ultimate exhale from below is the blowing of the Shofar.

Our Shofar-blowing below, our exhale, becomes the 'oxygen' or 'inspiration' for the inhale Above, and this inhale in turn allows for a new Divine exhale, which blows new life and *Shefa* / flow of blessings and abundance into the world.

FOUR STAGES OF CREATION

Toras haSod / the inner teaching of the Torah articulates the revealed account of *Bereishis* / Genesis in much greater detail, including the above description of the cosmic creative process. Prior to that process there is a *Tzimtzum* / an internal constriction, allowing the possibility for 'others' to exist. Then there is an inner 'movement' within the Mind of Hashem — a paradoxical desire to create within the context of Divine Unity. This becomes an undifferentiated 'breath of life', as in, "He blew into his nostrils" (*Bereishis*, 2:7). This breath of life constitutes the level of *Neshamah* / higher rational soul of humanity. That is followed by the 'wind within the (Divine) mouth' (*Tehilim*, 33:6), which is what gives birth to Divine Speech, as in, "He spoke and it came to be." These are meta-physical vibrations which create physical expressions of energy and eventually matter.

'Breath', 'wind', and 'speech', are three layers of Creation, each one nestled within the other. And even before 'breath', as mentioned above, there is 'movement', a desire and idea to create or express stirring within the Mind of the Creator. This idea becomes externalized, first as breath within the 'lungs' or *Penimiyus* / inner depths of the Creator. Then the idea becomes more externalized as a free-flowing wind within the 'mouth' of the Creator. Finally, the world appears as an external Creation, virtually separate from the Creator, as the World of Speech.

These four Stages of Creation correspond to the Four Inner Worlds and the four letters of the Name of Hashem: Yud (thought/desire/movement), Hei (breath), Vav (wind), and Hei (speech):

Four Stages of Divine Creation	Four Inner Worlds	Four Letters of the Name
Inner movement, thought or desire, 'within the Mind'	*Atzilus* / Emanation within Unity	Yud (ʼ)
Breath, 'within the Lungs'	*Beriah* / Subtle Creation	Hei (ה)
Wind, 'within the Mouth'	*Yetzirah* / Pre-Manifest Formation	Vav (ו)
Speech, 'outside the Mouth'	*Asiyah* / Materialization	Hei (ה)

This process is continuous and perpetual. At every moment there is a cosmic exhale of Divine Light into the world, creating, forming, animating and sustaining Creation anew. The desire to create — the Yud — becomes the Supernal exhale, the Hei, which then becomes the Supernal wind, the Vav, which becomes the Supernal speech, the Final Hei, and this gives rise to physical vibration, energy, and finally matter. But on Rosh Hashanah there is also an added dimension. There is a manifestation of this process in the renewal of a much larger cycle of creation — the great Divine exhale of the coming year.

THE OUTBREATH OF THE NESHAMAH

The four letters of the Name of Hashem and the Four Inner Worlds are also reflected in the four levels of soul within each of us. The Yud corresponds to our *Chayah* / transcendent life force, which is our will and desire. The Hei is our *Neshamah* /

higher intellect, our rational soul. The Vav is our *Ruach* / wind, our emotional self. The final Hei is our *Nefesh* / functional, physical consciousness.

Neshamah comes from the word *Neshimah* / breath. This refers to the Divine breath, as when the Creator "blew into his nostrils the breath of life," and man became a being capable of rational consciousness and abstract thought.

Our Nefesh, and even on some level our Ruach, can be affected by our negative behavior, however, our Neshamah is eternally pure. It may seem to leave us at times, but it can never be soiled (*Nefesh haChayim*, 1).

When we blow the Shofar, first we have the 'idea' to breathe; this is the stirring of our Chayah, our will and intention. This impulse then flows to our Neshamah and, we give forth a *Neshimah* / breath, and we blow into the Shofar. This produces a pure 'wind', a *Ruach*, which eventually vibrates into the world as a 'voice' in the physical world of Nefesh. In a manner of speaking, this process gives Hashem the 'idea' to reciprocate the same pattern from Above, as our Shofar-blowing becomes the 'oxygen' or 'inspiration' for the Divine cosmic exhale which fills and enlivens our world.

THE SHOFAR MIRRORS THE SUPERNAL EXHALE

On a deep level, the root of all Creation is the Yud-Hei-Vav-Hei, the Ineffable Name of Hashem. Another way to refer to this name is *HaVaYaH* (a permutation or rearranging of the four letters). *Havayah* literally means *Haviyah* / bringing being into being. Hashem is Ultimate Being-ness, which is the source and stuff of all being. Since all being, all of Creation, is rooted in the Name Havayah, the blowing of the Shofar mirrors the movement through these four letters, and embodies the quality of this Name.

In truth, every time we open our mouths to speak we are subtly articulating the Four Letters of the Name of Hashem, and the Four Worlds to which these letters correspond. The 'Sheivet Mussar', Rebbe Eliyahu haKohen of Smyrna (c. 1659–1729), writes in the name of his teacher that when a person has a will to speak, immediately there is a movement of the 'speech' within his heart and mind. This is the letter Yud, the world of Atzilus, the world of thought within. When the 'speech' of the mind reaches the chest and becomes breath, it is like the letter Hei, the world of Beriah. When it reaches the mouth, filling the mouth with 'wind', it is the letter Vav, the world of Yetzirah. And finally, when the 'speech' of the mind, breath of the lungs, and wind of the mouth comes out of the mouth in speech, it is the letter Hei, the world of Asiyah. Therefore, every time a person speaks, he is creating the Name of Hashem (*Sheivet Mussar*, Chap. 43).

- Yud is the 'thought' within the mind.

- Hei is the breath, the origin of speech.

- Vav is the *Kol* / sound which travels from the lungs through the windpipe, a Vav-shaped line.

- The Final Hei is the actual speech that uses the five potentials of the mouth to form words.

This expression and embodiment of the four Letter Name of Hashem is most pronounced when exhaling, and particularly when blowing the Shofar.

The Shaloh haKadosh (Rebbe Yeshaya haLevi Horowitz) writes (on *Meseches Rosh Hashanah*, p. 169), that the Yud is the small opening of the Shofar, the mouthpiece (and the opening of a person's mouth) where the actual blowing begins. It is the space from which everything emerges. In fact, placing one's mouth directly on the Shofar is an integral part of the actual Shofar blowing (according to the Arizal, *Peh* / mouth is 85, which is the Name *Sa'g* / 63 — connected with Binah — plus the 22 letters of the Aleph Beis = 85: *Pri Eitz Chayim*, Sha'ar haShofar, 1. Blowing the Shofar sweetens the Din in the place of Binah, and this is the deeper reason that the mouth must touch the Shofar).

Placing one's mouth directly on the Shofar is essential. The Mishnah (*Rosh Hashanah*, 27b) teaches that ציפהו זהב במקום הנחת פה פסול / "If the Shofar is plated with gold at the place where one puts his mouth, it is unfit." This is because of the laws of חציצה / barrier (as the Ritva, ad loc., explains). In other words, if there is a foreign object separating the mouth from direct contact with the Shofar, the blowing is invalid. There is a *Chidush* / novel teaching from the Ramban, which rules that besides a חציצה / barrier, there cannot be any separation at all between the blower's mouth and the Shofar (the Ritva, *ibid*, writes the same, but it seems that for him it is a Din in חציצה). For example, one may not place the Shofar an inch from his mouth and blow forcefully across the gap into the Shofar (although there is no barrier or obstruction, there is an actual separation between the mouth and the Shofar: See *Magid Mishnah*, Rambam, Hilchos Shofar, 1:6. Tur, *Orach Chayim*, and *Shulchan Aruch*, 586:19. Yet, the Rambam rules, שופר הגזול שתקע בו יצא שאין המצוה אלא בשמיעת הקול אף על פי שלא נגע בו ולא הגביהו השומע יצא. Thus, according to the Rambam, even without touching the Shofar whatsoever, one fulfills his obligation: *Hilchos Shofar*, 1:3, so long as there is no obstruction, such as gold), rather his lips must press against the Shofar. The Ritva (*ibid*) offers an allusion to this idea in the verse, אל חכך שופר / "To your palate, a Shofar" (*Hoshea*, 8:1. See also, *Mishna Berurah*, ibid).

Again, the mouth touching the small opening of the Shofar is the Yud. In the physical procedure of actually blowing, the first Hei is the inhale, the subtle sound of the *Hevel* / breath (*hhh* sound) that enters into the body. The Vav is the *Kol* / the voice or 'unarticulated' vibrations within the tube (Vav) of the Shofar. This voice is composed of the three basic elements of Creation: wind, water (or vapor) and fire (heat). Finally, the lower Hei is the exhale (*haa* sound) emanating through the larger opening of the Shofar, creating the projection of sound into the world. This sound is distinct from the unarticulated vibration inside the Shofar, which is the Vav.

In order to perform this Kavanah, first pause and mindfully clarify the following intentions. Then,

1. Place your mouth on the opening of the Shofar, silently forming the letter Yud.

2. Take a long inhale through your nostrils — listen to the nearly silent letter Hei inside your body.

3. Exhale sensing the gentle wind and unarticulated vibration within the channel of the Shofar — the vibratory letter Vav.*

4. Be *Shome'a Shofar* / listen to the louder sound, almost like a human voice, projecting out of the Shofar along with the breath — the Final Hei.

As such, who is really blowing the Shofar? It is the Creator, Hashem Himself, who is blowing; *Hashem b'Kol Shofar* / 'Hashem is *in* the sound of the Shofar' (Free interpretation of *Tehilim*, 47:6).

There is a wonderful Medrash (*Sifri*, Beha'alosecha, Piska 19) that says, "...And Shofar is the sound of freedom...But do we not know who blows? Says the verse, *Hashem Elokim baShofar Yis'kah* / "Hashem, G-d, with a Shofar will blow" (Zecharyah, 9:14). In other words, Hashem Elokim, the Creator of all life, is blowing the Shofar *within* our blowing. At that moment we are the embodiment of the Name of Hashem, כי חלק ה' עמו /

---

* Although the exhale (*hhh* sound) comes before the Vav, there is a tangible vibrating 'silence' that ripples and reverberates following a sound, almost like an echo, and this too can be viewed as the final Hei after the Vav.

(literally) "for the Nation is a part of Hashem" (*Devarim*, 32:9). Indeed, when we blow, the Neshimah of our Neshamah blows; the part of us that is one with Hashem and embodies the Four Letters is being expressed within the Shofar. Hashem's breath is blowing through us.

Elokim is connected with the natural, created, often predictable world. Elokim creates the Heavens and the earth. Yet, the deeper source of Creation is the Yud-Hei-Vav-Hei. These four letters spell Yud-*Hoveh* — 'Yud of the *Hoveh* / being, present tense. The prefix 'Yud' renders the word into a continuous act (Rashi, *Iyov*, 1:5. *Tanya*, Sha'ar Yichud v'Emunah, 4), so Yud-*Hoveh* means the ever-continuous act of 'becoming', or creation.

Through the dimension of *Elokim*, the world 'was' created (*Bereishis Bara Elokim* / "In the beginning, Elokim created," past tense). However, through the dimension of *Hashem* (*Yud-Hoveh*) the world is continuously 'being' created. This continuous creativity is the *Hischadshus* / renewal of our world and our lives.

THE COSMIC INHALE

Every year, on the eve of Rosh Hashanah, the cosmos is overtaken by a state of slumber. During this time a Divine inhale and moment of 'breath-retention' occurs, at which point the Creator's will to create, is *Nistalek* / 'rises up and is elevated within Itself'. The will to create a world then retracts back into its Source — returning to its Essence as if the Creator were holding His breath, contracting His Light (Rav Shem Tov ibn

Shem Tov, *Sefer haEmunos*, Sha'ar 4). This is the act of *Tzimtzum* / contraction through which the world was darkened, and then from this darkness the world was revealed, crafted and carved. As the Light of the past year is inhaled into its Source Above, every created phenomenon, event and experience is withdrawn within. Only afterward, with the blowing of the Shofar, the cosmic exhale, is the great void re-filled with life, and Divine plenty and vitality.

This cosmic slumber is in a way analogous to our own sleep; when our souls are drawn upwards into the higher worlds, while our body remains down here in this world, dormant and seemingly lifeless (*Medrash Rabbah*, Bereishis, 14:9). Blowing the Shofar below, on the morning of Rosh Hashanah, awakens the Divine will and desire to continue to create and to blow a new year into existence and fill the world with life and blessing. The will to be King again is rekindled within the slumbering King. In other words, HaKadosh Baruch Hu's desire to become King of this world is aroused through our blowing of the Shofar; our coronation thus bestows conviction upon Hashem as King. Mirroring this Divine awakening, as it were, the Shofar also serves as our spiritual alarm clock, awakening us and beckoning our soul to return back to the world, re-filling our bodies with its light, aliveness, purpose and determination.

THE GAME OF LIFE

A question can be asked: 'Why is a cosmic inhale, retention and slumber necessary before the new year? Why should there be a withdrawal and ascent of Hashem's desire and will to create? Also, why does Hashem's Presence only 'descend' and assume Kingship of the world when we blow the Shofar?'

The truth is that this Divine withdrawal and retention of Light is a benevolent subterfuge in order to awaken humanity's desire to seek HaKadosh Baruch Hu. Only by seeking and unifying with Hashem can we become co-creators and participators in the ongoing process of perfecting Creation. First, however, we need to reveal to the Creator, through our actions, that we desire and deserve new life. Only then, will the Creator's desire to 'descend' and continue creating, sustaining, enlivening and ruling Creation be aroused.

Our *Isarusa d'leTata* / arousal from below, our effort to seek Hashem, awakens an *Isarusa d'leEila* / arousal from Above within Hashem to find us. By revealing a purpose and reason for the world to exist, we stimulate, so-to-speak, the Creator's desire to continue recreating it.

FILLING THE EMPTY SPACE
WITH DIVINE LIGHT & SOUND

At the beginning of every new year we blow the Shofar and arouse a new, fresh Divine desire to animate Creation and continue to nourish it with passion and purpose. This is the *Hischadshus* / renewal that happens on Rosh Hashanah.

The very act of blowing the Shofar is life-giving. Essentially what we are doing when we blow the Shofar is taking an inanimate, hollowed-out horn and blowing life into it — bringing life to the lifeless — resurrecting the 'dry bones' of our old year which has 'passed away' and giving life to a new and unique coming year.

The difference between a regular animal horn and a Shofar is that a Shofar is hollowed out, emptied of its old substance and patterns. The word *Shofar* itself means 'hollow', as in *Shoferes / hollow pipe* (See *Pri Eitz Chayim*, Sha'ar haShofar, 3).

When we blow it, the hollow Shofar is literally filled with lifebreath and sound. This filling of the Shofar mirrors Hashem's filling of the macrocosmic void with light, life and renewed Divine flow.

The cosmic 'inhale' or Tzimtzum forms a *Makom Chalal / empty*, hollow space, and then afterward the Infinite Light fills that empty space with a Divine will and desire to create. Ever since that initial Creative act on the part of Hashem, we too are asked to be co-creators and to initiate the process — to awaken, so to speak, the Divine desire from its Heavenly slumber, to resuscitate the Supernal 'breath-retention'.

The blowing of the Shofar effectively begins the stimulation of the Supernal exhale. The Shofar is a hollow, empty instrument, and when we blow into the Shofar, filling it with passionate intentions of living our lives with purpose, we are mimicking the Divine creative process. We are blowing G-dliness, purpose and meaning through the empty space of the Shofar into the empty space of the world, thereby filling it with inspiration and intention.

This act causes the Divine will to fill the emptiness of the world and gives us the potential to recreate ourselves anew with a new breath of Life, revealing a unique Light that has never descended and filled this world before.

BLOWING LIFE INTO AN INANIMATE OBJECT

As discussed, the act of blowing the Shofar is an act of 'giving life'. We take an inanimate, empty horn and 'animate' it with a breath of life.

When something is alive, it means that the Divine lifeforce is integrating and activating a particular composite of four primordial elements: fire, wind, water and earth; or alternatively, hot, moist, cold and dry. The element of earth is essentially included within the three primary elements of fire, wind and water (*Pardes Rimonim*, Sha'ar 9:3. 'Earth' is the element hidden within the other three: Maharal, *Netzach Yisrael*, 57). Breath is mostly associated with the element of fire. The letters of הבל / *Hevel* / breath can be rearranged to spell להב / *Lehav* / flame (*Tikkunei Zohar*, Tikkun 21.p. 49b. *Siddur Maharid*, p. 15a). On the other hand, an exhale releases into the atmosphere the elements of wind and water, in the moist vapor of the breath. It also releases 'fire' in the heat of the breath, and thus an exhale includes all three elements (*Zohar* 2, 238b. *Zohar* 1, 114a. *Metzudas Dovid, Ta'amei haMitzvos*, Mitzvah 112).

The Shofar itself is of the inanimate, lifeless, dry element of earth or 'dust', and when we fill it with the fire, wind and water of our breath, we are giving life to a dead object. The lifeless horn is suddenly vibrating with vitality and an expressive voice. This enlivening breath from below initiates the Supernal blowing in of a new year, calling forth an influx of new *Chayos* / life force, and a *Hischadshus haBeriah* / renewal of Creation.

When we blow the Shofar, we are thus participating in bringing down Hashem's Infinite light into this finite world. We are filling — with our lifebreath and intention — the *Chalal* / emptiness and 'hollowness' of this world with a new Divine light and blessing. We thus become, in effect, co-creators of the world and midwives of a new reality that is being born from Above.

Chapter Eight

THE SOUND THAT CENTERS US:
Shofar and Tikkun haBris

NOT COINCIDENTALLY, IN THE WEEK BEFORE ROSH HASHANAH, WE READ IN THE TORAH, "You are all standing *this day* before Hashem…" (*Devarim*, 29:9). "This day," the Alter Rebbe teaches, refers to the essential and first day of the year, Rosh Hashanah (*Likutei Torah*, Nitzavim). The Torah continues, "…that you may enter the *Bris* / covenant of Hashem" (29:11). This illustrates the fact that there is an intrinsic connection between Rosh Hashanah, the Shofar, the idea of a Bris as a "covenant," and perhaps even with a *Bris* as "circumcision."

In one of the many *Piyutim* / hymns of our Rosh Hashanah liturgy, we recite, "We blow the 'one' Shofar like the 'one' Bris on our bodies." And at the end of the passages of *Zichronos* / rememberings we conclude, "Blessed are You, Hashem who remembers the *Bris* / covenant." What is the connection between this "covenant," circumcision, and the Shofar? For starters, there is a clear parallel between the ברית המעור / *Bris haMa'or* / circumcision and the ברית הלשון / *Bris haLashon* / covenant of the tongue (*Sefer Yetzirah*, 1:3, *Pirush haGra*. The Gemara also connects the tongue with a type of Bris: *Moed Katan*, 18a). Since we blow the Shofar with our mouth, it is also pertinent for us to further explore that connection.

The Taz writes (*Orach Chayim*, 584:2) that he heard about certain illustrious sages who, if they were the Mohel on Rosh Hashanah, would not wash their mouths and they would blow the Shofar with traces of the blood of the Milah in their mouths, to commingle these two Mitzvos as one (שמעתי שהגאון הרב מהר"ר פייוויש מקראקא ז"ל היה מל בר"ה ולא קנח פיו אחר המילה אלא בפה המלוכלך בדם מילה תקע בשופר לערב מצות מילה בשופר Although generally, the Mohel needs to wash his mouth before reciting a blessing, Rama, *Shulchan Aruch*, Yoreh De'ah 265:1, וכשהמוהל מברך ברכה זו רוחץ תחלה ידיו ופיו כדי שיברך בנקיות. Shofar is a more primal form of Tefilah, as explored). This custom clearly links Milah with Shofar in a very visceral, even primal way.

Circumcision is performed on the body part associated with the Sefirah of *Yesod* / foundation, connection, and as the Baal Shem Tov teaches, pleasure. The primary *Tikkun* / rectification for unbalanced Yesod / masculine bodily expression, is to give birth to 'wanted' or desired children. In a healthy and holy relationship, the male's active giving of life-force is fully received by the female, and a 'child', literally or figuratively, is conceived and created. This balanced and mature unity engenders a Tikkun of Yesod. Rosh Hashanah is the 'Sixth Day of Creation' and is a cosmic embodiment and expression of the sixth Sefirah (when counting from Chesed-Malchus), the Sefirah of Yesod. And, as bringing children to this world is so intimately connected with the Tikkun of Yesod, Sarah, Rochel and Chanah, who were all barren, conceived on Rosh Hashanah (*Rosh Hashanah*, 11a). The names Sarah, Rochel and Chanah form the acronym *SaRaCH*, the name of the woman who gently informed Yaakov that his beloved son Yoseph was still alive and well in Egypt. Yoseph is the Torah character most connected with the Sephira of Yesod, particularly its rectification.

Yesod's connection to Rosh Hashanah is clearly understood, but how does Yesod and the idea of the Bris connect to Shofar?

As the Arizal teaches (see, *Pri Tzadik al-haTorah*, Rosh Hashanah), the Shofar facilitates a *Tikkun* / correction of the *Midah* / attribute of Yesod. This Tikkun includes all of the manifestations of Yesod including focus, giving, intimacy, and sensual or procreative expression.

The profound Chassidic teacher, Rebbe Yaakov Yitzchak Rabinovitch, known as the *Yid haKadosh* / the Holy Jew, says that the word *Shofar* is an acronym of the words שרש פרה ראש ולענה / *Shoresh Poreh Rosh veLa'anah* / "a root sprouting poison and wormwood" (*Devarim*, 29:17). The Targum Unkelos on these words writes that this phrase refers to *Hirhurin* / thoughts of sin (גבר מהרהר חטאין). *Hirhur*, in general, refers to thoughts of illicit physical intimacy (הרהורי עבירה - תאות נשים: Rashi, *Yuma*, 29a), creating a blemish in the *Bris* / capacity for focussed intimacy and loving connection in relation to others, the world and the Divine.

Similarly, the word *Tekiah* comes from the word *Teka*, which can mean, in the language of Chazal, 'physical intimacy' (*Yevamos*, 54a). Indeed, according to the Yid haKadosh's son, Rebbe Yerachmiel, the most important *Kavanah* / intention we should have in blowing the Shofar is to break through our blemished Yesod and bring it to correction and alignment.

The root of the word 'to blow', *Toka*, is Tav-Kuf, which is numerically 500 (Tav/400, Kuf/100). The number 500 is connected with *Zivug* / coupling and *Yichud* / unity, as many early Mekubalim write. The Torah's command to Adam and Chavah, פרו ורבו / "be fertile and increase" (*Bereishis*, 1:28), is numerically 500. The Yichud between a male, having 248 body parts, and a female, with 252 body parts (*Bechoros*, 45a), is 500. When there is a perfect, harmonious, loving, mutual, mindful and holy Yichud of body and soul, there is the possibility of drawing down healthy, aligned and focused 'children', literally and metaphorically.

WHAT IS YESOD?

Let's gradually unpack this idea to more deeply understand what it is trying to make us aware of. Cosmically, Yesod is a masculine Sefirah, and it is the 'space' through which all the Sefiros Above it (such as Chesed or Gevurah, Chochmah or Binah) are expressed into the lower, outer worlds. In this image, our physical world is *Malchus* / the receiver, and Yesod funnels all the above Divine attributes, as it were, and channels them into our world.

Microcosmically, we assume the qualities of 'Yesod' when we are interacting with the world and influencing or giving to it. For example, whenever we are speaking to someone, we are the 'masculine' expressor, and the person receiving our speech is 'Malchus', the feminine receiver.

Conversely, when we are receiving from the world or from others, we are in the mode of Malchus, receiving from a manifestation of Yesod. When something emotionally touches or stimulates you, it is Yesod affecting your Malchus. Yesod is the point of contact in every gift, encounter, impression and influence, as we interact with our surroundings.

In general, there is a giver and receiver in every event and moment of relationship. In any situation the giver or influencer is Yesod, the masculine, and the receiver of influence is Malchus, the feminine.

On a deeper level, "Male *and* female He created them," and thus within each individual person there are dimensions of both masculine and feminine, Yesod and Malchus. When your thoughts or feelings arouse you to act, this is Yesod actively flowing into your Malchus. When you listen receptively to your inner wisdom and put it into practice, this is your attribute of Malchus receiving from your attribute of Yesod.

A perfect or 'rectified' flow of Yesod within you is achieved when you are in total alignment within yourself. There is a clear, uninterrupted channel flowing from your thoughts to your feelings, and then into your actions. There is no felt dichotomy, tension or blockage inhibiting this flow within you. Your Yesod is irrigating your Malchus, your power to act, in a way that causes it to flourish and flower with good deeds. These good deeds, in turn, act as yet another Yesod, nourishing the recipient of the good deeds, the Malchus outside of yourself, as well as the Malchus within yourself, cultivating a positive self-image through the pleasure of giving.

A person who is actualizing their Yesod in a rectified manner outside of himself is bringing his intimate and procreative expressions into perfect alignment; everything is occurring in the appropriate time, with the appropriate person, with a sense of honor and consent. Unrectified expressions of Yesod involve 'waste' and selfishness; perhaps there is no Malchus or 'vessel' to receive that expression of intimacy (as in 'wasted seed'), or perhaps the vessel is not appropriate, as in intimacy outside the sacred covenant of marriage.

While all of this usually refers to literal physical intimacy with another, it also applies to any realm of relating and communicating with others, and even in one's speech and thoughts, as Yesod is the archetypal point of contact between communicator and receiver, on any level. For instance, in the realm of conversation, perfect Yesod manifests when there is a proper connection between the speaker and listener; one speaks with meaningfulness and mindfulness, and the other fully receives the implications and effects of their words.

Imperfect or blemished Yesod occurs when there is a misalignment between the giver or speaker, and the receiver or listener. When one's Yesod is out of alignment they are prone to say and do things that are inappropriate, meaningless, or even harmful to the recipient. One may say something impulsively, or they may say something that is generally appropriate, but at the wrong time or without sensitivity or in the wrong tone. Furthermore, one may speak without regard for the receiver, or without an appropriate receiver whatsoever. Thus, one's capacity for caring and intelligent communication is 'wasted', further eroding the potential alignment between givers and receivers. This is a blemish in the *Bris Sif'sayim* / covenant of the lips. The 'energy' of the body that is connected with speech and expression is thereby 'wasted'.

Even within oneself, if you are constantly wandering in daydreams, getting lost in foreign or 'alienating' thoughts, or if your mind is out of sync with your body, your Yesod is out of alignment and you are wasting its potency.

Bris literally refers to the circumcision of the flesh, but the meaning extends to the covenant or 'circumcision' of the lips and heart. In a 'circumcised vessel', the expression or intended influence is focussed in a truly beneficial direction. Just as physical intimacy means being with the right person at the right time in the right way, 'intimacy' in words means saying the right thing at the right time in the right way.

A Tikkun for Yesod in any kind of interpersonal relationship or encounter is to be totally present with the other person when they are in communication with you. The mitzvah, "You shall love your neighbor as yourself," is followed by "Do not plant your field with two kinds of seed. Do not wear clothing woven of two kinds of material" (*Vayikra*, 19:18-19). The Mitzvah to love is followed by the prohibitions of Shatnez and Kilayim, which are both about mixing elements inappropriately. Inwardly, this means that to love someone is to be present with them, and not to energetically 'mix' anything or anyone else into the relationship. When you are communicating with one person, don't think about someone or something else. Be fully present, listen to them without mentally 'multitasking'. This is the greatest gift of love you can give.

Of course, this is of vital importance when being physically intimate with one's spouse as well; nothing else, and certainly no one else, G-d forbid, should be on your mind during the moments of intimacy (*Nedarim*, 20b). You must be totally present with your partner, on all levels of being.

In fact, a defect in the Bris is the root of all heresy, all ideas about there being a separation between Creation and Creator, or worse (*Heichal haBerachah*, Devarim, p. 125). A misguided outer expression of one's procreative instinct creates separation within oneself, a separation between one's sense of self and HaKadosh Baruch Hu, and certainly a tangible separation between one's expression and the receiver of such expression. This physical act of misdirected energy manifests as a loss of focus or energy in one's thoughts and words as well.

Why do people find themselves scattered and unfocused, lacking perfect *Yesod* and alignment in their actions and outer expressions? Most likely, they are scattered in their inner expressions — their inner thoughts and imagery, resulting in an unfocused mind — and this causes actions and behaviors to be disoriented and disorienting as well.

Meaningless chatter, for example, or misdirected expression in the world of speech, is rooted in unfocused or 'random' thinking. The speech is a symptom, not the disease itself. If you have no control over your actions or words, it is because you have no control of your thoughts.

Most people want to believe that they choose their thoughts, when in truth, their thoughts 'choose' them. Sadly, most people's thoughts merely occur to them, or bubble up from their subconscious mind. When a person takes a stroll and sees a beautiful home, the thought of the home occupies their mind. Then a siren sounds and their thoughts turn from the home to the siren and the noise and what it may mean. Whatever is placed in front of them automatically fills their mind. This is what the Chassidic Rebbes called having "horse thoughts." More commonly, such thoughts are called *Machshavos Zaros* / foreign thoughts.

When one opens their mouth, the place from where their words emanate, they are meant to focus their speech by means of the covenant of the mouth. And that is bound with the Bris of the *Guf* / body, the place of the procreative organ. Yesod is the center column, the place of centering and alignment. The mouth is the center of the upper part of the body, and the procreative organ is the center of the lower part of the body. Both are linked to the middle of the brain between the right and left hemispheres, the place that balances creativity and comprehension.

The Rokeach, in his commentary to *Sefer Yetzirah* (Mishnah 1), writes that there are five fingers on each hand, and together there are ten, reflecting the entire gamut of the ten Sefiros. The toes have the same pattern. The vertical midpoint between the hands above and the toes below is the Bris, the procreative organ, which, when focused, can create a *Yichud* / unity between the upper and lower expressions of the Sefiros.

Additionally, there is a lateral middle point of the upper level of the Yichud, which is the mouth ('between' the hands). And there is a lateral middle point of the lower level Yichud, which is the Bris ('between' the feet).

Creating a Tikkun of the Bris is the fundamental way to repair and rebalance one's Yesod and its power to unify.

YOSEPH EMBODIES RECTIFIED YESOD

Yoseph was let out of jail on Rosh Hashanah (*Rosh Hashanah*, 11a) and the sound of the Shofar represents freedom and redemption (*Maharsha*, ibid). Yoseph is the embodiment of the attribute of Yesod, and as such he brings correction and balance to all the other Sefiros, all the other sons of Yaakov, and even saves the great world power, Egypt, from famine. Yoseph is our guide in balancing, refining, and embodying rectified Yesod.

While there was certainly internal strife between the sons of Yaakov, and that strife was mostly in relationship to Yoseph, it was in the end Yoseph who was able to bring a Tikkun to the entire family. Yoseph was the one who was sold into slavery by his brothers, and yet, he was the same brother who was able to bring the whole family back together at the end of their father Yaakov's life.

Yaakov had two 'eldest' sons, Reuven, his first son from his wife Leah, and Yoseph, his first son from his wife Rochel. Initially, Yaakov had desired to marry Rochel, and he had worked many years to gain her hand in marriage. On the wedding night, Lavan, Rochel's father, gave his other daughter, Leah, in marriage to Yaakov instead, and Yaakov did not know this until the next morning. Our sages tell us that Yaakov was intuitively suspicious of Lavan and he therefore created signals and taught them to Rochel, so she could prove, when the time came, that it was really her he was marrying. But when Rochel realized her father had replaced her with Leah, Rochel sensed the tremendous embarrassment that Leah would feel if Yaakov were to find out, and so she secretly taught Leah the signals.

Reuven was conceived that night, as Yaakov called him "my strength and my initial vigor" (*Bereishis*, 49:3). Says Rashi, "initial vigor" means his first drop of semen, for he had never even experienced a nocturnal emission before his wedding night (*Yevamos*, 76a). All of this means that on the night that Yaakov conceived Reuven, he thought he was with Rochel, but was in fact with Leah (Arizal, *Sefer HaLikutim*, Matos. *Megaleh Amukos*, Matos, Derush 4). This misdirected focus and intention represents a very subtle (although impactful on the level of the Avos haKedoshim) blemish in Yesod.

Yoseph, on the other hand, was conceived with totally focused Yesod, as Yaakov was with Rochel in transparent awareness and intention. The fruit of such a conception is totally balanced Yesod. Yoseph was always in the right place at the right time, and all his experiences led to his destiny of being a ruler in Egypt and sustaining his family, along with the entire ancient world, in a time of famine.

Reuven, on the other hand, had a lot of good intentions, such as saving Yoseph from the pit and making sure his mother Leah took precedence among Yaakov's wives after Rochel had passed on. Yet, he was seemingly always just slightly off the mark (*Medrash Talpiyos*, Yaakov, p. 756).

For instance, Reuven was slightly late when he came to save Yoseph. When he hears the other brothers plot to kill Yoseph, he says, "Let us not deal him a deadly blow. Do not shed blood! Cast him into this pit, which is in the desert, but do not lay a hand upon him." Reuven said this in order to save Yoseph from their hands and return him to his father. Then, when Reuven had left his brothers for a little while, they sold Yoseph as a slave. "And Reuven returned to the pit, and behold, Yoseph was not in the pit, so he rent his garments" (*Bereishis*, 37:18-29). His true intention was to save his little brother, but his well-meaning words bore no fruit.

Additionally, his actions were a little off the mark when he moved his father's bed into his mother's tent. Yaakov had two primary wives, Leah, Reuven's mother, and Rochel, Yoseph's mother, plus two handmaids, Zilpah, Leah's handmaid, and Bilhah, Rochel's handmaid. When Rochel passed away, the Torah says, "And it came to pass... that Reuven went and lay with Bilhah, his father's concubine" (*Bereishis*, 35:22). What actually happened was that Reuven was trying to protect his mother's honor (*Shabbos*, 55b. Rashi, ad loc.). When Rochel was alive, Yaakov kept his bed in Rochel's tent. When Rochel passed away, Yaakov moved his bed into the tent of Bilhah, Rochel's handmaid. When Reuven saw this, he said, "If my mother's sister was a rival to my mother, should her handmaid (now also) be a rival to my mother?"

Reuven understood that Yaakov loved Rochel, and all along wanted to marry her, even before he actually married his mother, Leah. So, if Yaakov wanted to place his bed in the tent of Rochel, it made sense. But, surely Rochel's handmaid held a lower position in the household than his mother Leah, and so Reuven moved his father's bed from Bilhah's tent and placed it in the tent of his own mother, Leah, to guard her honor.

His intentions were noble and honorable, yet, the Torah describes the event as a terrible sin, stating quizzically that "Reuven went and lay with Bilhah," although of course he did not, G-d forbid, actually lay with her (*Shabbos*, ibid. Note, Rambam, *Hilchos Sotah*, 3:2. Although see *Kesef Mishnah*, ad loc.). Why does the Torah then describe this event in the most misleading and defamatory of ways? Essentially, the Torah is trying to convey the message that Reuven's meddling in his father's private life, by moving his bed from one tent to the other without his consent, was upsetting to the delicate balance in his father's household. It was perhaps such a corrosive erosion of his father's authority in his own home, that it caused Reuven to be considered as if he had (G-d forbid) committed a cardinal sin with Bilhah.

Yoseph's life, by contrast, is always 'on the mark'; he is always in the right place at the right time. He is conceived in perfect Yesod, where the male and female, the giver and receiver are in perfect unity on every level. Thus, Yoseph embodies the perfected attribute of Yesod. His human attribute of Yesod is transparent to the Divine attribute of Yesod.

Yesod resides in the place in the body where the Bris is performed, the place that generates new life. Every drop of a person's *Koach* / vigor and life is transmitted in the act of coupling, and because of this, the act potentially creates a new life, a new full human being, a new world. To make a Tikkun of the Bris, a Tikkun of Yesod, is to become like the Creator, the Source of Life. To make this Tikkun is to bring one's vigor, life-force and all their desires into total focus, directing this transmission of creative force in the right place (Olam), in the right time (Shanah), in the right mode of consciousness (Nefesh) — and in the embrace of the proper person, the one Divinely ordained and prepared to receive that creative force.

CENTERING ONESELF THROUGH THE SHOFAR

There are three major points of Yesod along the centerline of our body: a) the area between the right and left hemispheres of the brain, which is the headquarters of *Daas* / consciousness or mind, b) the center of the outside of the head, the mouth, the locus of speech, and c) the procreative organ in the middle of the lower body, the locus of creation of new life. These three points are deeply interlinked. When we lack Tikkun of Yesod in one, we will lack it in all three.

Without centeredness in our procreative life, we cannot have centeredness in our mind and our speech. Without mental centeredness and focus, one experiences scattered, mindless chatter and "horse thoughts." When the mind rapidly swings from one subject to another, bouncing around like a kernel of popcorn as it is being popped, this causes a lack of focus or integrity in speech. A mindless tumbling of words from one's mouth is a symptom of a lack of 'unity' in the mind. And if there is little focus or control in one's words, there is likely a proportionate dispersion of physical procreative energy as well.

Verbal mindlessness is when people say something, but then catch themselves a minute later, ask: "Did I just really say that"? In such a state, people say things, but don't mean them. This lack of focus on the verbal level is connected with a lack of focus in the mind; one cannot think through a complex thought, make a methodical analysis of a concept, or even make well-considered plans in their life. Such a person is often confused, and sometimes even unaware of what their thoughts are really saying. Their "horse thoughts" manifest as meaningless speech, spoken with no intention or purpose.

However, since the three centerpoints mentioned above are interlinked, we can begin to make a Tikkun and center ourselves starting from either the upper point or the lower point. For instance, one can begin with the lower Bris, taking compassionate control of their physical energies, and by doing so, gain more control over their words, and ultimately their thoughts and state of consciousness. On the other hand, one can begin with their thoughts, gaining control of the mind, and consciously choosing its tone and direction. Once control of the mind has been achieved, mastery of one's speech and physical actions will surely follow. This is the mode of Tikkun accomplished by the blowing of the Shofar.

Most people think that they cannot control their thoughts;

this may be true on some level and at some moments of pressure or weakness in their life. But the truth is, even if one's mind is wandering all over with no coherence at all, if suddenly they step on a nail, there will be absolutely nothing on their mind besides the piercing pain. For at least five to thirty seconds they would be totally present and focused on the intense sensation. Although the pain is an outside 'object' taking control of their inner thoughts, the mind nonetheless gains a particular focus for an extended amount of time. And in fact, there will likely be no mental distraction until they have reached a doctor, the wound has been cleaned and dressed, and the pain has subsided.

Imagine walking down the street and hearing a loud car's horn behind you. Again, for a moment or two, your mind is completely focused on that noise. It centers you in the immediate present. The Shofar is such a centering sound, it forces you to focus, first simply on the sound, and then on yourself as you, like a tuning fork, begin to resonate and vibrate along with that piercing cry. If you imbue this experience of audio immersion with Kavanah, the sound not only centers you in the moment, it helps you center yourself for the entire year to follow. The sound of the Shofar is thus the unified source from which all the diverse experiences and attainments in the coming year will flow.

SHOFAR & TIKKUN YESOD

The Baal Shem Tov teaches (*Meor Einayim*, Beshalach) on the verses "תעו במדבר / *Ta'u baMidbar* / they wandered in the wilderness...ה' / *Vayitz'aku el-Hashem* / then they cried out to Hashem..." (*Tehilim*, 107:4-6). The word *Midbar* also comes from the word *Dibbur* / word, speech. This Pasuk is therefore speaking of someone who has wandered and strayed in their Dibbur. In their *Tefilos* / prayers they lacked focus, and they were not able to put themselves fully into the words. Their antidote for this lack of focus is to "cry out to Hashem," to scream without words, just a simple cry to Hashem. This cry comes from our essence, our pre-verbal 'Tree of Life' state, as explored earlier.

Any time our words lack focus, coherence or meaning, whether in prayer or communicating with others, we are as if "wandering in a desert." In such a mindless state, the simple act of screaming out to HaKadosh Baruch Hu orients and focusses es us. The Shofar is the inward and outward cry of someone who desperately desires to return Home. He might not even know where 'home' is, or how he should go about getting there, only that his current aimlessness hurts him at his core. He feels so much *Merirus* / bitterness that he is unable to verbally articulate his yearnings, so in great anguish, he lets out a cry. This vulnerable vibration leaves him totally centered and alert, sensitized to the immensity and potential of the moment.

Blowing the Shofar is like crying out *OY!* when you step on a nail and snap into sharp focus. When you hear the sound of the Shofar, your mind is not wandering into the future or reminiscing about the past; you are totally focused in the now. This refocusing of the mind causes a Tikkun to Yesod on all levels, bringing your whole being into unified alignment

FIXING 'JUDGMENT'

According to a deeper understanding, *Machshavos Zaros* / foreign thoughts come from *Kilkul haMishpat* / destruction of judgment, meaning, and discernment (*Likutei Moharan* 1, 2:5). When there is a misalignment in one's practice and perception of 'law and order', when theory is not lived out in actuality, this is a sign that there is a misalignment on the level of the mind. Proper judgment creates mental alignment and focussed attention. Rosh Hashanah is 'the Day of *proper* Judgment', and the redemptive judgment that comes to us from Above is a mirror reflection of our faithful judgment below (as discussed earlier regarding the 'books' that are opened on Rosh Hashanah). When we have a wholesome, balanced focus and judgment below, it awakens a wholesome positive judgment from Above.

If our mind is sleepy and unfocussed, we cannot have proper judgment; our priorities will not reflect reality, our vision will be cloudy. The startling cry of the Shofar wakes us up, opens our capacity to see things as they truly are, and strengthens our capacity for accurate 'judgment'.

SHOFAR AND RECTIFYING COMMUNICATION

Shofar awakens us to Teshuvah, a return to and realignment with the wholeness of life, a Tikkun of Yesod. Breath is the source of life. When we breathe in, we are enlivened; when we breathe out in speech we can project ourselves outwards in a way that can enliven others or not. Our words can bring *Tikkun* / wholeness or *Tohu* / chaos to others: "Life and death are in the domain of the tongue" (*Mishlei*, 18:21).

We are constantly breathing out and projecting ourselves toward others. The question is, what type of breath are we communicating? Look closely at the ways you communicate in different circumstances and relationships. Does your breath fall within one of these three basic categories?

1. *Breath of the soul:* this is a fully rectified mode of communication that is imbued with our true self and our highest values.

2. *Breath of the mind:* this is communication that is articulate, coherent and rational, though not necessarily aligned with our soul.

3. *Breath of the instinctual self:* this mode of communication is based on our survival instincts; fight, flight or immobilization. When aggression, fear and dissociation are guiding our communication, our real values and our coherence are clouded or confused.

The sounds of the Shofar correspond to these three forms of communication, and offer a Tikkun and healing for each:

1. *Tekiah:* this unified, long breath conveys the integrity of

Yesod and the confident power of the soul. This sound communicates to us the possibility of Tikkun for having strayed from our higher values in life.

2. *Shevarim*: three coherent, concise sounds, conveying clarity. This sound communicates the possibility of Tikkun for our loss of Da'as, focus and intellectual clarity.

3. *Teru'ah*: nine short, fragmented notes, conveying a deeper lack of wholeness. This sound communicates to us the possibility of Tikkun for our chaos-producing speech based in anger, fear or immobilizing spiritual slumber.

As you listen to the sounds of the Shofar, consider the ways you have been communicating. Reflect on how you have conveyed either Tikkun or Tohu to others. Allow the Tekiah, Shevarim and Teru'ah to initiate you into the higher wholeness of the *Bris Sif'sayim* / covenant of holy speech, and to communicate and share that wholeness with others.

THE MOTHER'S CRY

As explored above, the root of the sound of the Shofar is the cry of Sisra's mother. A mother's cry for her child is purely and completely focused. There is nothing else on her mind when a mother is urgently concerned for her child's safety. This is the root of the sounds of the Shofar, a pure, focused cry of concern and yearning for connection. In fact, according to the Aruch, the 100 sounds of the Shofar we blow on Rosh Hashanah correspond to her 100 cries (*Tosefos*, Rosh Hashanah, 33b).

Similarly, in the narrative of Sarah in the Medrash (*Pirkei d'Rebbe Eliezer*, 32) mentioned above, Sarah's cries also correspond to the sounds of the Shofar. Her cries for her son were expressed with such focus and intensity, that her soul became absorbed to the point at which it departed. 'Total sound' equals total presence and unity; it cuts away and negates all other sounds and all other thoughts.

When you blow the Shofar, all of your *Koach* / energy is expressed and absorbed in the sound. When the congregation hears the Shofar it is as if they are actually blowing it, and their energy is likewise absorbed and expressed in the blowing. This immersive experience is so powerful that we only need to blow the Shofar on a Yom Tov for its effects and lessons to permeate the rest of our year, inspiring and empowering us to create a proper Tikkun for all of our self-expressions throughout the entire coming year.

When there is such a complete focussing and alignment of consciousness and sensation, such as with the blowing of the Shofar, an alignment of speech and action will eventually follow. Indeed, the entire coming year of our lives will be born through the 'birth canal' of the Shofar and we will have a year of rectified Yesod; all our thoughts will be focused, all our words will be properly directed, and all our physical energy will thus be given over to the proper recipient, in the proper time and appropriate place.

SHOFAR, THE SOUND OF REDEMPTION

The Rambam writes (*Hilchos Shofar*, 3:1), "How many Shofar blasts is a person required to hear on Rosh Hashanah? Nine. (This figure is derived as follows:) The Torah mentions the word תרועה (sounding the Shofar) three times in association with Rosh Hashanah and the Yovel. Every תרועה must be preceded and followed by a (single) long blast. According to the oral tradition, we learned that — whether on Rosh Hashanah or on Yom Kippur of the Yovel — all the soundings of the Shofar of the seventh month are a single entity."

This parallel drawn between the Shofar of Rosh Hashanah and that of the Yovel is not merely to teach that we need to blow nine sounds on Rosh Hashanah. Rather, as the Rambam writes, "The Shofar used for the Yovel and Rosh Hashanah are the same in all matters" (Rambam, *Hilchos Shemitah v'Yovel*, 10:11). Moreover, just as the Yovel Shofar symbolizes an ushering in of socio-economic freedom, the Shofar of Rosh Hashanah ushers in freedom from sin, worry and uncertainty, as explored.

This is what happens in the Yovel year: "From Rosh Hashanah until Yom Kippur, servants would not be released back to their homes, nor would they be subjugated to their masters... Instead, the servants would eat, drink, and rejoice, with crowns on their heads. When Yom Kippur arrived and the Shofar sounded in the court, then the servants were released to their homes and the fields returned to their owners" (Rambam, *Hilchos Shemitah v'Yovel*, 10:14).

Considering the above it would make sense that the sound of the Shofar on Rosh Hashanah is also announcing a type of redemption and a level of freedom. Indeed, our sages say, "One who sees a Shofar in a dream should aspire to expect redemption" (הרואה שופר בחלום ישכים ויאמר והיה ביום ההוא יתקע בשופר גדול קודם שיקדמנו פסוק אחר Berachos, 56b). The Maharal writes, "When the Torah speaks about a Shofar it is always connected with some type of redemption, or (a situation in which) HaKadosh Baruch Hu saves Klal Yisrael" (*Chidushei Agados*, Rosh Hashanah, 11b).

What exactly is the connection between the Shofar and redemption? The blowing of the Shofar creates, as mentioned, a return to center. This can even be understood literally, as Klal Yisrael in the Desert would gather together in one place at the sound of the Shofar. Inwardly, too, a 'gathering' is created by the blast of the Shofar.

Simply put: Centering is redemption. When someone returns to their proper condition and to the truth of their existence, they are "redeemed." Years back, the Shofar sound was sounded to mark the point when an indentured servant could return to their original state of freedom. Freedom is at the center of everyone's reality. An indentured servant is one who has left their center and lost their way. For instance, a person who had stolen and was unable to repay, might qualify to become an indentured servant, a "slave." After working for some time, gradually rebalancing the scales of justice, the sound of the Shofar would complete their Tikkun and bring them back into their center and core.

Our collective exile is divided into four historical exiles: the Persian, Babylonian, Greek and Roman exiles. Without getting into all the details of what these four exiles represent (see the book *Eight Lights* for more), one correlation is the four directions of east, west, north and south; tangents moving away from our center. Redemption is to return from these misdirected tangents back to the center, the place of unity where we come from and ultimately belong. The Shofar, as such, initiates an internal and literal return to alignment and Home.

The center of a square represents the internal essence of who we are. The four sides are externalities; elements of identity that are external to who we really are at our core. When a person is living on the edges, in the externalities and superficialities of life, this is exile, because he is not true to himself. Furthermore, these externalities become influences upon his very mode of living. Instead of living as a free person, moving from his center outwards, being the influencer of his life and making choices based on his internal reality, he becomes like a slave, continuously being influenced by external forces, with no real center to ground him. He is controlled by his thoughts, impressions and automatic reactions to external stimuli. His voice is not his, and his reality is not his own. He forgets who he really is and makes a 'graven image' of himself to replace his real dynamic self.

Just as an individual can lose his center in this way, so can an entire people, and even the whole world, *Rachmana Litz'lan /* may the Compassionate One rescue and redeem us.

The sound of the Shofar is the sound of freedom and the sound that brings freedom. It has the power to return us to the center and core of our existence and identity, to who we really are in the deepest depths. The Shofar can return us home to our deepest selves. And it can and will bring us all Home to the Land of Israel with the coming of Moshiach. As the Navi Yeshayahu proclaims, והיה ביום ההוא יתקע בשופר גדול ובאו האבדים בארץ אשור והנדחים בארץ מצרים והשתחוו לה' בהר הקדש בירושלם / "And on that day, a Great Shofar shall be sounded; and those who strayed in the land of Assyria and the expelled who are in the land of Egypt shall come and worship Hashem on the holy mount, in Jerusalem." May we merit to experience this ingathering and recentering speedily, in our days.

Chapter Nine
FOUR PARABLES OF THE SHOFAR:
Alarm, Cry, Remembrance & Master Key

THE MAIN MITZVAH OF SHOFAR IS *SHEMIAH* / HEARING THE SHOFAR AS OPPOSED TO *TEKIAH* / BLOWING IT. In the words of the Rambam, "There is a positive Mitzvah לשמוע / to hear the sound of the Shofar on Rosh Hashanah" (*Hilchos Shofar*, 1:1). Proof of this principle is also found in the wording of the blessing. Before we blow the Shofar we recite a blessing: *Baruch Atah…* / "You are the Source of all Blessings… and have commanded us *Lishmo'a Kol Shofar* / to hear the sound of the Shofar."

This is the *Nusach* / liturgical form as recorded in the *Shulchan Aruch* / Code of Jewish Law (*Orach Chayim*, 585:2, as the ruling of the Tur, *ibid*, 585. This is also the Nusach from the Geonim: *Otzar ha-Geonim*, Rosh Hashanah, 101-104').

---

*According to the Rambam, clearly the Mitzvah is to 'hear' the sound of the Shofar (*Hilchos Shofar*, 1:1-3. Ibid, 2:1. In *Shu't Pe'er haDor*, Siman 51, the Rambam writes, שהמצוה אינה בתקיעה אלא בשמיעה, ואין התקיעה אלא מעין הכשר מצוה וכעשיית הסוכה. This is also the final ruling in *Shulchan Aruch*, and Tur, *ibid*). There are some Geonim and Rishonim (such as Rav Achai Gaon, *She'iltos*, 171, the *Semag*, Positive Mitzvah 42, Rabbeinu Tam, *Rosh Hashanah*, Rosh, 4:10, and *Yire'eim*, Siman 117) who say that the Mitzvah is to 'blow' the Shofar (and not to the 'hear' the Shofar). Thus their Nusach is ...*Al Tekias Shofar* / "to blow the Shofar": see Rosh, *Rosh Hashanah*, 4:10. *Shu't Yeshuas Yaakov*, Siman 585. This seems also to be the opinion of the Zohar as well: "This Mitzvah is to *blow* the Shofar" (*Zohar* 3, 98b). Now, since "hearing is like responding" (not just passively but actively), thus everyone who hears the Shofar fulfills the obligation to 'blow' it, as listening on this level is like blowing. Although see *Avnei Nezer*, Orach Chayim, 431:3, where he argues that this principle of "hearing is like responding" only works with speech, not with Shofar, which is 'sound'. Active listening and reinterpretation on the part of the listener — participation on the part of the listener — primarily occurs with spoken words, and not so much with undefined sound. Yet, as the Mordechai writes clearly, even with regard to the sound of the Shofar, the principle of "hearing is like responding" does apply: Mordechai, *Rosh Hashanah* 4, Siman 721. *Sha'agas Aryeh* (Siman 6) brings proof to say that the Mitzvah is *also* to blow; the Mitzvah is both blowing and hearing.

Even though according to Rashi, the Rambam, the Tur and the *Shulchan Aruch*, the Mitzvah is to "hear the Shofar," still, one cannot fulfill the Mitzvah by hearing the Shofar blown by a child, for example (*Mishnah Rosh Hashanah*, 29a), since the Mitzvah is to hear the sound from the 'Shofar-blowing of a Mitzvah': *Minchas Chinuch*, Mitzvah 405. And, although according to Semag and Rabbeinu Tam, the Mitzvah is to 'blow' the Shofar, still, if a person blowing the Shofar does not himself hear the direct sound of the Shofar, but rather only the rebound and echo, he himself does not fulfill the obligation of 'blowing' the Shofar: *Mishnah Rosh Hashanah*, 27b. As the Alter Rebbe explains, this refers to the person in a pit as well, not just those outside the pit: *Shulchan Aruch haRav*, Orach Chayim, Siman 587:1). The blower needs to blow a sound that he can at least potentially hear himself as well.

Inwardly, this means that our main *Avodah* / work is to truly 'hear' the call of the Shofar. And to truly 'hear' a call is to respond to it.

While a parallel is drawn between the sound of the Shofar of the Yovel year, and the sound of the Shofar on Rosh Hashanah, they are still distinct. On Rosh Hashanah, as we have established above, the *Ikar* / main Mitzvah is to 'hear' the sound of the Shofar, "There is a positive Mitzvah לשמוע / 'to hear' the sound of the Shofar on Rosh Hashanah" (*Hilchos Shofar*, 1:1), whereas, in the Yovel year, "It is a positive commandment לתקוע / 'to sound' the Shofar on the Tenth of Tishrei in the Yovel year" (Rambam, *Hilchos Shemitah v'Yovel*, 10:10). The sound of the Shofar in Yovel is a blast that ushers in a new world of freedom and returning home; what is of utmost importance is the actual blowing, making the sound that marks the end and beginning of the 50 year Yovel cycle. Regarding the Shofar on Rosh Hashanah, however, the main objective is to awaken within us some type of movement and desire to change, as such it must be 'heard' and internalized. We need to truly listen to the sound for it to arouse within us emotions powerful enough to propel us along a new path of transformation.

THE FOUR PARABLES

Our sages have provided us with a myriad of symbols and stories to illustrate the function of the Shofar, and a matrix of metaphors to explain its deeper significance. The following four basic parables have been selected because they help to paradigmatically illuminate and activate the Four Worlds of Body, Spirit (Heart), Mind and Soul. Towards this end, the sound of the Shofar is likened to:

1) an alarm, waking up the **body**,

2) a child calling out to his parents, awakening love in the **spirit**,

3) a reminder of our past, and the covenant we entered with HaKadosh Baruch Hu, awakening an attentive presence in the **mind**,

4) a simple cry that opens all the doors of Heaven; a transcendental cry, beyond speech and language, and beyond the Tree of Knowledge — arousing the **soul**.

These four categories are also related to the four types of sound that are blown on Rosh Hashanah: the *Tekiah* / long blast, the *Shevarim* / the broken sounds, *Teru'ah* / short quick blasts in succession, and the *Shevarim-Teru'ah* / a unification of the above two sounds. Our obligation is to listen to all of these sounds on Rosh Hashanah.

SHOFAR METAPHOR	SOUND	SOUL LEVEL	WORLD	FACULTY	LETTER IN THE NAME OF HASHEM / PHASE OF 'BLOWING'
Alarm	Teru'ah	Nefesh / *Body*	Asiyah	Action	Lower Hei / *exhale*
Call of a child to its parent	Shevarim	Ruach / *Spirit*	Yetzirah	Emotions	Vav / *inhale*
Reminder of the past	Tekiah	Neshamah / *Mind*	Beriah	Thought	Higher Hei / *exhale*
Cry that opens the gates of Heaven	Shevarim-Teru'ah	Chayah / *Soul*	Atzilus	Transcendence	Yud / *inhale*

FIRST PARABLE:
BODY/NEFESH/ASIYAH/TERU'AH:

The metaphor of an alarm that spiritually awakens and motivates us is related to the Dubna Maggid's parable of the villager and the fire alarm sirens (told in full in Chapter 2). In short, a villager visiting the city once observed that a sounding of sirens would summon a host of firemen who would put out fires in town without any help from the surrounding residents of the town. He excitedly brought sirens back to his small village, assuring everyone that rousing everyone in town to bring water-buckets to put out any fires was now unnecessary. The next time there was a fire, the villagers sat back and waited for the nonexistent firemen to arrive, and the village soon burned down.

An alarm itself is not what saves us — it is what we do in response. The sound of the Shofar is vital for our awakening, but it is only a call to action. We must accompany it with much effort and inner work. The sound alerts us to the fact that there is a fire burning in our 'home', whether it is an attachment to negative temptations, fears, or other damaging 'external' influences. We alone have the power, with the waters of Torah, to put out our own inner fires, sever harmful attachments, and restore balance and integrity to our life.

The Teru'ah sound is nine very quick blasts in short succession, much like an alarm urgently warning us to take action. It grabs our attention and centers us, and it awakens an initial *Hirhur* / arousal for Teshuvah, but the process of actual Teshuvah is up to us.

SECOND PARABLE:
HEART / RUACH / YETZIRAH / SHEVARIM

A parable from the Holy Baal Shem Tov (*Keser Shem Tov*, Hosofos, 108. Rebbe Maharash, *Hemshech v'Kacha* 5637, p. 70) reveals that the Shofar is a primal sound that arouses HaKadosh Baruch Hu's infinite and intrinsic love for us:

Once there was a king who had an only son who he loved dearly. The child was wise, ambitious, and excelled in all his studies. His father was very proud of him. As his son grew, the king decided that the best thing for the child's growth, although terribly painful for himself and the child, would be to send him away to a distant land, so that he could master different fields of knowledge and experience other cultures. The king entrusted his beloved son with a small fortune of gold and silver to sustain his studies and explorations, and reluctantly and with tears sent him off.

Sadly, however, within only a few years of being on his own, the prince had irresponsibly squandered all of the money and was left totally destitute. Distraught and living in a foreign land where no one had ever heard of his father, the king, the prince resolved that it was time for him to journey back home to the palace. When, on foot, he finally arrived at the gate of the courtyard of the palace, he looked like a dusty vagabond. Dazed and malnourished, he had even forgotten his native language, which was the language of the guards.

Using sign language, he tried to communicate to the guards that he was the lost prince. Even if they understood, no one believed him, and they ignored his gestures. Soon, they were sharply ordering him to leave the premises.

In utter despair he began wailing and crying loudly. His cries echoed through the chambers of the palace and reached the chamber of the king. Hearing the cry, the king froze in recognition — the voice of his beloved child! In haste, the king ran outside to the gates of the courtyard. In front of the stunned guards, the king embraced his long lost child and brought him home.

The 'king' is the King of kings, the Master of the Universe. We are Hashem's children, princes and princesses. The King sends our souls down into this world, to a 'distant land', seemingly very far from the Royal Palace. Our souls are entrusted with a purpose; to learn and experience, while never forgetting where we come from and who we truly are. It may happen that because of the apparently vast separation, we forget our purpose and who we are. We can even forget our native, spiritual language, the light of Torah. When we finally want to change our lives and return to our true home, we find ourselves lost, with no means of connecting or articulating this need.

Finally, with no other option, we pick up a ram's horn and blow a raw sound, crying out to Hashem with all our feelings. This is a sound of brokenness, of letting go, of coming home, as if to say, 'Hashem, my Father in Heaven, have compassion on me, set me free, bring me home!' Indeed, HaKadosh Baruch Hu hears our Shofar blast and suddenly 'remembers' His long-lost princes and princesses. Hashem rushes out from the 'palace' to embrace us and bring us back to our true home, helping us to heal and redirect our lives. The cry of the Shofar arouses, as it were, Hashem's 'emotions' of love for us.

Shofar is connected with a path of trickery, as it were. It is not a conventional path or modality of communication. In the metaphor of the Baal Shem Tov, it is the breakdown of inarticulate crying when words fail. It is the cry of someone who has become aware that he has lost his way and yearns to return Home. It is the cry of someone who is desperately seeking a more tangibly spiritual existence; one who knows what he is missing but does not have the language to express it. This is the cry of the prince who knows that right behind the door, so close yet so far, is his Father the King, but he cannot speak to the guards. As all else has failed, he becomes so overwhelmed that all he can do is scream and cry.

Deep within us, the place from which this primal cry emanates is not normally revealed. It is certainly not our normal way of connecting or communicating, and it only authentically arises when there is no other method available.

For example, perhaps you are trying to speak sensibly to your child or another person, and no matter what logic you use, nothing is being heard, there may in such a situation arise an inner urge to scream or shout. Now, *actually* screaming or becoming angry at someone is probably reactive behavior and is damaging. The raw *urge* to scream, however, can come up due to a complete failure of language and logic. In the context of the Shofar, this urge can be compared to our non-reactive realization of being fundamentally powerless as a limited individual. We are completely and utterly dependent upon the King of All Reality; all we can do is blow our prayers through a ram's horn.

The *Zohar* (Emor) links the blowing of the Shofar to the episode in the Torah in which Rivkah suggests to Yaakov that he should dress up like Esav to receive the blessings from Yitzchak. Yitzchak seems to want to give the blessings to

Esav, but Rivkah thinks Yitzchak should give the blessings to Yaakov, and so she conceives a plan to dress Yaakov in hairy garments and trick Yitzchak into blessing Yaakov. The Shofar is connected with precisely this kind of subterfuge or trickery — going beyond all conventional routes to accomplish its goal.

Yitzchak embodies and represents *Din* / strict judgment. To receive the blessings Yaakov needed to deceive and bypass the normal course of Din. This, the *Zohar* says, is the function of the Shofar. It bypasses the normal paths of communication, and also the judgments that naturally result from negative action. It is like the heartfelt cry of a young, beloved child; even if he has been misbehaving, when he is deeply frustrated and surrenders in sobs, his parents drop any disciplinary consequences for the misbehavior and rush to help him.

When we have strayed from the path of our Father, the King, perhaps transgressed the laws of the Torah, which is the 'Mind' of the King, the cry of the Shofar bypasses all the guards and reaches the depths of the King's Heart.

Regarding the primal sound of the Shofar, the *Yerushalmi* teaches (*Ta'anis*, 2:1), "Why do we blow using the horn of an animal? It is to say (to Hashem): 'Relate to us as if we are bellowing like animals before You.'" This is a raw, visceral, existential, and immediate cry. We sound like a trapped and humbled animal; our spiritual survival instincts are activated as we desperately reach out to our Creator for life. (The Gemara calls blowing the Shofar a *Chochmah* / wisdom *Rosh Hashanah*, 29b, as one needs wisdom to be humble and be able to cry out like an 'animal'. אדם ובהמה תושיע ה' / "Man ואמר רב יהודה אמר רב אלו בני אדם שהן ערומין בדעת ומשימין עצמן כבהמה and animal You preserve, Hashem, and Rav Yehuda says that Rav says: These are people who are clever in terms of their intellect, like people, and despite their intelligence they comport themselves humbly and self-effacingly, like an animal": *Chulin*, 5b.)

An inverted Shofar, whose natural wide end was narrowed and whose natural narrow end was widened is invalid; we need to blow the Shofar in its natural state, in the exact same form that it had when it was removed from the animal (*Rosh Hashanah*, 27b). We are not sounding our own human 'voice' or ingenuity through the horn of an animal, rather we put our lips to an animal's body part and make a primal sound. In a way, we become the animal itself, as if we have no more articulate human language and all we can do is howl.

Before we blow the Shofar we chant loudly: אשרי העם יודעי תרועה ה' באור־פניך יהלכון / "Fortunate are those who *know* Teru'ah, Hashem, they walk in the light of Your countenance forever" (*Tehilim*, 89:16). There are some people who "know" what the Shofar is all about, and there are some people who simply lift themselves up with the sound of the Teru'ah, transcend all limitations and break all *Kelipah* / inner concealments. Indeed, "fortunate are they" all. Yet we need to remember the second part of the verse: "...they walk in the light of Your countenance." To 'walk in' the ways of Hashem means, "Just as He is compassionate so shall you be compassionate." 'Walking in the light of Hashem' means to feel sympathy for another person's struggles and hurt. We cry out, maybe not for our own pain in particular, but for the pain of Klal Yisrael and the whole world. We may know all the mystical secrets of Shofar, but the deepest secret is to know that the cry of the Shofar is not just our cry, or for our own pain, but a cosmic cry for all creation. It is a cry from the heart of all beings calling us to walk in the Light of Hashem's countenance and rectify all of our brokenness.

As mentioned, we blow 100 blasts of the Shofar throughout the day, which parallel the 100 cries of Sisrah's mother when she was anxiously waiting for her beloved son to return from battle (See above, Chapter 4). On a deep level, our Shofar sounds are sounds of compassion, bringing *Tikkun* / rectification and healing to Sisra's mother herself, and all that she may represent as other, mother, enemy, ally. Our cries, our yearnings, our dreams, are not only for ourselves but for the people we love, the people around us, and the world at large. Our deepest desire is that we should all have a year of blessings, and that this should be the year of the Shofar Gadol, announcing Redemption for all.

Everything happens by Divine orchestration, and we always need to ask: 'What is the message in this for me?' 'How am I related to the events happening around me?' We should never say, 'It simply happened.' Nothing simply happens.

Sisra was an arch enemy of our people, and in fact, he was killed running away from battle, a battle he was waging against Klal Yisrael. However, regarding our part, our collective responsibility, we need to think deeply: perhaps the reason an enemy waged war against us in the first place was because of a spiritual misalignment within ourselves.

To extend this idea further, Sisrah's death was also our responsibility, because if we would have been perfectly aligned, there would have been no war, and if there was no war, there would be no death in battle. Although his death would have occurred anyway, this narrative would not have happened without our part in it, and his mother would probably not have cried like she did.

On Rosh Hashanah we are therefore creating a Tikkun for the tears that we caused a mother to cry for her child. She was a non-Jewish mother, and in fact the mother of an archenemy of our people, yet she was a mother nonetheless, and like all mothers, she was created to love her child unconditionally. As Hashem is compassionate, so must we be compassionate.

Through the blowing of the Shofar we cry out to HaKadosh Baruch Hu, saying, 'Your love for us is infinitely greater than any natural, parental love. You feel our pain and compassionately hear our cries of the Shofar with love!'

This parable is connected with the *Shevarim* / broken sound, the sound of crying, the sound of a child at the entrance to his father's palace, the sound of a mother at the window anxiously awaiting her child's return. The cry of the Shofar is saying, 'HaKadosh Baruch Hu, please bring us back Home to Your palace; bless us and Your entire world with a good year.'

THIRD PARABLE:
MIND / NESHAMAH / BERIAH / THE TEKIAH BLAST

The Shofar is an instrument of remembrance, as illustrated by a parable by the legendary Rebbe Levi Yitzchak of Berditchev (*Kedushas Levi*, Derush l'Rosh Hashanah. Rebbe Maharash, *Hemshech v'Kacha 5637*, p. 70):

There was once a king who was hunting in the forest, and lost his way. While hunting, the king did not dress in his royal garments, and so, when he found his way out of the forest he came to a small village where no one recognized him or was willing to take him in for the night. Only one villager saw and believed that he might in fact be the king. In any event, this man accepted upon himself the commitment to be kind to a lost stranger even if he might not be the king. The villager took the stranger in, fed him, dressed him in the best clothing he could find, and escorted him to the king's palace. Upon reaching the palace, the king rewarded him handsomely, and elevated him to the rank of a minister.

Years later, the villager, now a minister, committed an offence which was viewed as treason, and he was sentenced to death. Before being executed, the king allowed him one last request. "I request," said the condemned minister, "that I be allowed to wear the clothes I wore the day I met the king and escorted him back to his palace, and that the king do the same — wear the clothes he wore on that day."

An odd request it was! Nevertheless, the king complied and donned his hunting attire, and ordered that the minister's old villager clothing be brought. Both dressed as on the day they met, the king viscerally remembered the great kindness this villager did to him, and how the villager believed that he was the king despite the cold refusal shown by everyone else — and called off the execution.

Before the Torah was given, before monotheism was revealed to the world at large, says the Medrash, HaKadosh Baruch Hu offered the Torah to the nations of the world, and they all refused it. Only the Nation of Israel believed in the Torah and willingly accepted upon themselves the Torah and the commitment to fulfill the Mitzvos.

Like the minister in the parable, some of us have strayed from our inner path, let go of the King's ways and perhaps even committed 'treason' on some miniscule level. At the Day of Judgment, Rosh Hashanah, we turn to the Master of the Universe and say, 'Let us get dressed in the "clothes" we wore on the day we met: we will blow the Shofar, just as on the day at Mount Sinai when we received Your Torah accompanied by the sound of the Shofar. Hearing the sound of the Shofar, the King 'remembers the kindness' we did by accepting the Torah, immediately nullifies all negative decrees, and allows us to draw down a year of life and blessing for ourselves and our loved ones.

The cry of the Shofar is a reminder of our initial commitment to Hashem and Hashem to us. This is the Tekiah sound, the sound of a minister reminding the king of his kindness and loving service. It is a blast of spiritual confidence.

Shofar is the 'secret language' or 'secret code' that lovers share between themselves. It is our special way to reach out and communicate with our Beloved in Heaven and tell Hashem that we want to be close. Hashem lovingly reached out to us and revealed the Torah with the sounds of the Shofar. Now, in turn, we reach out to Hashem and reawaken His love with the sounds of the Shofar.

These sounds on Rosh Hashanah also remind HaKadosh Baruch Hu of how we lovingly blew the Shofar every day in Elul while Moshe was on the Mountain accepting the Second Luchos / Tablets of the Torah, after shattering the first. We blew these sounds to mark the days, so that we would not repeat the mistake we made when we thought Moshe was late and fell into worshiping the Golden Calf. HaKadosh Baruch Hu is 'moved' by this memory of our commitment.

Imagine a king and queen who love each other very deeply. One day, the king needs to travel to a distant land. The king continuously sends love letters to his beloved queen, but in order to prevent the couriers from intercepting their personal messages, they use a special code language that they have created, calling each other by secret names and terms of affection, and using certain allusions and symbols that only they understand. Anyone can 'read' the letters, but no one knows what they mean except the queen and king.

In the same way, we reach out to Hashem on Rosh Hashanah with the sounds of the Shofar, with its long and short notes, its arrangement within the prayer service, its subtle allusions to events in our lives and relationships, and its concealed expressions of passionate emotion. Our secret language ensures that no accuser, no Satan, whether within or without, objective or subjective, can intercept or interpret our messages and expressions of longing and love.

FOURTH PARABLE:
SOUL / CHAYAH / ATZLIUS / THE SHEVARIM-TERU'AH SOUND

One year, some time before Rosh Hashanah, the Baal Shem Tov summoned his student Reb Ze'ev Volf and instructed him to study the Kabbalistic intentions in preparation for blowing the Shofar. Realizing this tremendous responsibility, Reb Ze'ev dedicated every waking hour to delving into the deeper intentions and mystical Divine names connected with the Shofar blowing. In order to remember everything he was learning, he wrote notes for himself and kept them in his Machzor / prayer book. On the morning of Rosh Hashanah, as Reb Ze'ev was walking to the Shul, his Machzor opened slightly, and without him noticing, his notes slipped out. When the time came to blow the Shofar, Reb Ze'ev opened the Machzor and to his disbelief the notes were nowhere to be found. Overcome with uncertainty, he began trembling and weeping. But the time to blow the Shofar had come and he was forced to proceed. With a broken heart, he picked up the Shofar, gasped out the blessings and managed through his tears to blow the required sounds. After Davening / the prayers, the Baal Shem Tov came over to his student, collapsed in his chair in a corner, and complimented him for the deepest Shofar blowing he had ever heard. He explained: "In the place of the King there are many chambers, and each door has its own distinct key. The deeper Kabbalistic intentions are the keys to the rooms. There is, however, a master key that opens all doors — a broken heart."

Sounding the Shofar conveys the soulful wails of a broken heart. The sound of the Shofar itself is the master key, or an ax, that will open all the doors to Heaven — the door of Compassion, the door of Kindness, the door of Patience. The simple, humble, preverbal cry of helplessness is the Kavanah that includes and unites all other intentions. Its simplicity is connected with the Tree of Life. The Tree of Knowledge is the paradigm of duality and multiplicity, and in this state of consciousness, we need multiple spiritual keys for multiple functions. But when we are completely simple, as in blowing Shofar just because we must blow the Shofar, we are in the paradigm of the Tree of Life, of all-inclusive Unity, and this is the highest intention.

Inwardly, this is the cry of someone who has lost his way and his footing, overcome with uncertainty, he knows he must change his course and return Home. As in the second parable, not only is he unable to articulate his yearning, he does not even know where Home is. He does not know where to turn. He has forgotten everything. He knows that he does not know, but he does not know *what* he does not know.

He is overwhelmed with existential angst, having lost his 'notes', his 'manual' for living, and does not recall anything except that he is a prince and that he does have a former home. Intuitively, he senses he is very close to the King; perhaps the King is just on the other side of the door. He just does not know the way in, and so he experiences desperate emptiness and confusion.

This desperation fuels the deepest cry of the Shofar. It produces a cry of pain, like the cries of Klal Israel enslaved in Egypt: "And they groaned…and Hashem heard their groan…" (*Shemos*, 2:23-24). It was a wordless groan from the pain of exile, as the Ohr haChayim writes, yet Hashem heard their groan *as a prayer*, and responded. From their side it was not a prayer, just a sheer groan of pain, but like a prayer it awoke Hashem's compassion and recognition of His People. Hashem heard the articulate prayer and implicit need within their inarticulate groan.

What is the difference between this cry and the cry illustrated in the second Mashal, the prince who had forgotten the language of his father the King? Each Shofar blast needs to be preceded and followed by a Tekia, a sound of confidence and triumph. A desperate cry that is sandwiched by confidence and triumph is already sweetened; the joy surrounding it lifts the helplessness to a higher level, and the feeling of exile is inter-included with redemption. Reb Ze'ev Volf had done the spiritual work before the Shofar blowing. His compassionate spiritual master, the Baal Shem Tov, was standing with him supportively throughout his difficult experience, and he was warmly congratulated afterwards.

This is the most transformative kind of 'desperate cry'; it naturally leads to a response of complete Teshuvah because it is suffused with trust. It is clear that one's yearning cry immediately brings about salvation and the opening of all the doors and chambers of every blessing.

To blow the Shofar on Rosh Hashanah takes technical work; we need to know how to use the instrument, the exact lengths and patterns of the sounds, and perhaps even the inner intentions. But once these guidelines and skills are in place, the most important element is channeling our own cry through the Shofar. It takes inner work to produce a transformative Shofar cry, one that will move all who hear its sound, transporting one from a state of 'distance' to a state of sensing 'closeness' to HaKadosh Baruch Hu.

Our sages tell us (*Rosh Hashanah*, 27b) that if someone somehow placed a small Shofar within a larger Shofar and blew them together, if the sound of the inner Shofar was heard, then *Yatzah* / he has fulfilled his obligation. But if only the sound of the outer Shofar was heard, then *Lo Yatzah* / he has not fulfilled his obligation.

On a deeper level, this Halachah teaches us that any time we perform the Mitzvah of blowing the Shofar, if only the 'outer', external dimension of the Shofar blowing was heard, than *Lo*

Yatza — literally, "he has not gone out of his situation." Yes, he blew the Shofar according to the laws. But the deeper movement "out of" his past, and into a better present and future, has not been accomplished. Only when the "inner" sound, the inner cry is heard, then indeed *Yatzah* / "he has left," he has gone out of his previous situation and left his internal exile.

This is the important part of the parable; not only does the Shofar need to produce a cry, but the cry needs to be "heard." The King is behind the wall, Hashem is behind the 'screen', and, as the second parable teaches, He needs to hear, and recognize the cry so that He will rush out and open the gate. As in this parable, we too need to offer a cry of existential angst, from the abyss of desperation, in which one has no more ego-based resources and is about to give up. This is the ax or the master key that opens Heavens.

When our ego is so destabilized that we lose all habitual perceptions, stories and concepts about where Hashem is, when we do not even know where to look to find refuge in the world of self, we can only cry out to HaKadosh Baruch Hu with a broken heart, like dust calling out to the stars. And this single cry spontaneously opens all doors and we find ourselves at Home, embraced by our beloved Master, the King of the Universe.

This parable corresponds with the all-inclusive, perfectly simple Divine Essence, and includes all the other parables, levels and types of sounds — thus it corresponds to both the Shevarim and the Teru'ah.

Chapter Ten

THE 'SITTING' & 'STANDING' SHOFAR SOUNDS: Blowing Apart & Unifying

WHEN THE TORAH SPEAKS OF ROSH HASHANAH, THE FIRST DAY OF THE SEVENTH MONTH, IT SIMPLY SAYS, "This shall be to you a day of *Teru'ah.*" The sages (*Rosh Hashanah,* 33b) understand this to mean that it should be a day of sounding the Shofar. Therefore, as another Gemara says, we sound the Shofar simply because רחמנא אמר תקעו / *Rachmana Amar Tiku* / "The Merciful One says to sound it" (*Rosh Hashanah,* 16a). Ultimately, we do not need graspable reasons for Mitzvos for they are rooted in the absolute simplicity of Hashem's Unity, and reasons suggest something outside itself.

Nevertheless, we are thinking beings, and we are created to seek meaning. Therefore, we may explore, and have for millenia explored, ethical, philosophical and mystical reasons for the Mitzvos. The great lover of reason, the Rambam, writes that we sound the Shofar in order to awaken Teshuvah within ourselves, as explained in detail, earlier. The sages and mystics offer many more reasons for every detail of the Mitzvah of sounding the Shofar. We will now explore an idea about the 'sitting' and 'standing' Shofar services, which will help us understand and feel the sounding of the Shofar with new depth.

SOUND REASONING

There are two sets of Shofar sounds that we blow on Rosh Hashanah. The first set, called *Tekios Meyushav* / sitting blasts, is performed before the Musaf service, and the second set, *Tekios Me'umad* / standing blasts, is performed during the Musaf service (*Ran*, on the Rif, Rosh Hashanah, 3a. The Baal HaMaor understands that Mesyushav means the Shofar that is blown during the (repetition of the) Amidah, *Baal HaMaor*, Ibid, 12a). We will come back to discuss the subtle spiritual differences between these two, but first let us note that by blowing the first set, which consists of thirty Shofar blasts, we fulfill the Mitzvah of Shofar. The question is: Why should we proceed to blow a second set, the Tekios Me'umad? The Gemara says the reason for this second set is לערבב השטן / *l'Arbev es ha-Satan* / "to confuse the Satan."*

---

* *Rosh Hashanah*, 16b. Therefore, the main Shofar service is the *Meyushav*, and the *Me'umad* service is "to confuse": Meiri, *ad loc*. Rif, end of *Rosh Hashanah*. Ravyah, *Rosh Hashanah*, Siman, 529. Baal haItur, *Shofar*, p. 101a. Rambam, *Hilchos Shofar*, 3:12. See also Tosefos, *Rosh Hashanah*, 33a. See, however, the Rosh and Ran (*ad loc.*), which understand this the opposite

But what does this mean? What is Satan, and how does Satan become confused by our blowing another set of Shofar blasts?

CONFUSING SATAN

Rabbeinu Shlomo Yitzchaki, the great 11th Century commentator otherwise known as 'Rashi', gives a simple explanation of why the Satan is confused. Rashi writes that when the Satan sees that we honor and love the Mitzvos so much that we take it upon ourselves to do an extra set of Shofar blasts, he is dumbfounded and cannot prosecute humans for their mistakes (שלא ישטין כשישמע ישראל מחבבין את המצות מסתתמין דבריו).

---

way; that the *Ikar* / main Shofar blowing is the *Me'umad,* that is, the Shofar that is blown together with the *Malchiyos, Zichronos* and *Shofaros* in Musaf, and the earlier *Meyushav* Shofar is only blown in order to confuse the Satan. This is also the opinion of the Tur, and Mechaber, *Orach Chayim,* Siman 585; see also Tosefos, *Pesachim,* 115a, where Tosefos rules differently than the Tosefos in *Rosh Hashanah.* Perhaps Tosefos — if in fact it is the same author of The Tosefos, as there are hundreds of authors within that body of writing — maintains that the Ikar Mitzvah in its fullness, with Malchiyos, Zichronos and Shofaros, is the 'standing' Shofar blowing, yet, one still fulfills the basic obligation with the first set, the 'sitting' Shofar blowing. The Rif speaks of blowing a set of four, three and three sounds in total during the three parts of the Amidah, and not a total of nine sounds in each part of the prayers, the Malchiyos, Zichronos and Shofaros (although these nine are technically counted as 10 in any case). The Ramban (*Rosh Hashanah,* 11a) suggests that these are sounds to awaken the heart in a time of prayer and judgment, much like the sounds of Shofar on fast days. Thus, writes the Ritva (*Rosh Hashanah,* 31), these sounds are not part of the Mitzvah of Shofar on Rosh Hashanah, and are rather two separate types of Shofar sound.

Rashi's grandchildren, the authors of the *Tosefos*, write that the second set of blasts is associated with "the sound of the Great Shofar." The Great Shofar, according to the prophecy, is a mystical sound that will mark the beginning of the cosmic Redemption.* When this time comes, "Death will be swallowed up"; all separation and evil, and the Satan itself, will vanish. Therefore, when the Satan hears our second round of Shofar blasts on Rosh Hashanah, he becomes agitated and cannot focus on our prosecution.

This explains why the Satan is confused. But another question is, what exactly is the Satan? The 'Ran', Rabbeinu Nisim of Gerona (1320–1380) writes that the Satan is none other than the adversary that dwells within our own lower selves — the inclination to oppose goodness and truth. "The Satan is the *Yetzer haRa*" (*Bava Basra,* 16a), the inclination to egoism, which, when unchecked, can eventually lead to destructive self-centered imbalance.

---

* There are different types of sounds blown throughout the Shofar services. Some are staccato and others are extended, unbroken sounds. The Torah tells us to make a *Teru'ah* on Rosh Hashanah, which etymologically suggests making broken sounds, or sounds that break obstacles. Yet with regard to the Great Shofar of the future Redemption, it says והיה ביום ההוא יתקע בשופר גדול / "On that day the Great Shofar will be *Taka*," alluding to the unbroken, drawn out sound called *Tekiah.* This is a sound of strength and confidence, rather than brokenness. *Tekiah* comes from the word *Teka,* which can also mean 'physical intimacy' (*Yevamos* 54a). Therefore, it is a sound that gathers and unites, as opposed to one that breaks apart and melts.

Rebbe Pinchas of Koritz, a disciple of the Baal Shem Tov, asks, "How can the Satan be confused every single year with the same trick?" And he answers, "It is because every year, every day, and every hour and minute, there is a 'new' Satan." In every moment we have new challenges and 'adversaries'. According to the Ran's understanding of Satan, we blow the extra sounds to confuse, quiet and silent this inner adversary.

The *Teru'ah* / Shofar blast literally means 'breaking', from the word *Re'u'a* / broken. The sound of the Shofar is also said to be *Mispashet* / spreading out, breaking down all barriers in its way. The Navi Amos (3:6) says, "Could the Shofar be blown in the city, and the nation not tremble?" The Shofar was sometimes sounded to alert the public of an ensuing battle. "My heart stirs within me; I cannot be silent, for you, my soul, have heard the sound of the Shofar, the תרועת מלחמה / alarm of war" (*Yirmiyahu*, 4:19). This sound of the Shofar inspires alarm and fear, breaking people's complacent state of mind and preparing them for war. War is not merely an external phenomenon, for there are also internal struggles and enemies. Furthermore, a soldier who is worthy to do battle with an external enemy is someone who has first battled his internal enemy and 'fears' sin, or is in active pursuit of Teshuvah (*Sotah*, 44a). This could be another reason that the Rambam writes that the Shofar awakens Teshuvah. The sound 'spreads out' into the ego, as it were, causing the inner adversary to tremble and break down, readying the soldier to have success in his spiritual battle.

THE ACT OF SITTING VERSUS STANDING

The sounds of the first set of Shofar blasts are called 'sitting sounds' because we are technically allowed to sit while listening to them, even though today most people stand while listening to both the 'standing' and the 'sitting' Shofar sounds (צריך לתקוע מעומד / "The blower should stand": *Shulchan Aruch*, Orach Chayim, 585, as the Tur writes, like when reciting *Sefiras haOmer*). Allegorically, however, the term 'sitting sounds' can mean that the sounds themselves 'sit us down'. When a person sits down, the straight line of his standing body is broken into angles. Part of the line then extends horizontally, breaking the space around the line and expanding into it. This is an illustration of how the sounds of the first set expand into the inner space of the ego and disrupt the inner Satan.

The sounds of the second set are 'standing sounds', because we are standing in the Amidah prayer when they are blown. As a person stands, he no longer expands into horizontal space as in sitting, but he straightens the 'line' of his body, bringing the space around him closer, and lifting his energy upward. This confuses the Satan, for after the person has been broken and sent away, suddenly he is integrated and uplifted.

The root of the word לערבב / *l'arbev*, is *Iruv*, from the word to mix in, to include and it is also related to the word meaning ערב / *Arev* / sweet. As we include our neutralized inner adversary into our whole being, we sweeten it or elevate its nature. This is called *Hamtakas haDin*, the sweetening of the judgment.

THE RECITATIONS BEFORE AND AFTER BLOWING

FIRST SET / SITTING SHOFAR SOUNDS:

Before we sound the first set of Shofar blasts, we recite selected verses from *Tehilim* / Psalms that prepare us to meditate deeply on the sound of the Shofar. In the first selection, Chapter 47, the Name *Elokim* appears seven times. *Elokim* represents Divine constriction or concealment. By reciting this name seven times, we begin to break through the seven veils that conceal Reality. We then recite the verse (*Tehilim*, 118:4), מן־המצר קראתי קה עָנָנִי במרחב קה / "From a place of constriction I call upon Hashem; answer me from a place of expansion." Again, we are focusing upon overcoming adversarial energies, moving from a state of inner constriction to a state of expansive consciousness. Next, we recite six verses. The first letters of these verses (the acrostic) spell out *Kra Satan* / 'rip apart the Satan'. Finally, we repeat a verse from Tehilim, 47: *Ala Elokim b'Teru'ah* / "Elokim is elevated with a Teru'ah." When the Shofar is blown, the Name Elokim itself will be elevated to a more expansive level, dissolving all spiritual opposition, as discussed. (Note that Teru'ah is numerically 681, which is the same as the words קטרוג השטן / Kitrug HaSatan, with the Kolel/the word itself).

Shofar is spelled Shin-Vav-Pei-Reish. Numerically, *Shin* is 300. *Pei-Vav*, 86 and *Reish*, 200. All three of these numbers are intricately connected with the Name Elokim, the power of judgment and constriction.

The numeric value of the letters that spell the Name *Elokim* is 86:

Aleph (1), Lamed (30), Hei (5), Yud (10), Mem (40) = 86.

When counting the full value of each of these same 5 letters, the total is 300:

The word *Aleph* is spelled Aleph (1), Lamed (30), Pei (80) = 111.

The word *Lamed* is spelled Lamed (30), Mem (40), Dalet (4) = 74.

The word *Hei* is spelled Hei (5), Yud (10) = 15.

The word *Yud* is spelled Yud (10), Vav (6), Dalet (4) = 20.

The word *Mem* is spelled Mem (40), Mem (40) = 80

111+74+15+20+80=300.

The numeric value of these five letters, when cumulatively counted, is 200:

Aleph = 1.

Aleph, Lamed = 31.

Aleph, Lamed, Hei = 36.

Aleph, Lamed, Hei, Yud = 46.

Aleph, Lamed, Hei, Yud, Mem = 86.

1+31+36+46+86=200.

The word *Shofar* itself thus implies constriction, and the blowing of the Shofar symbolizes a blowing open of all constriction.

When we take a Shofar in our hands and blow 'through' the Name *Elokim* with the proper *Kavanah* / intention, we are opening all gates, widening all paths, blowing asunder all barriers.

In fact, the word *Rosh Hashanah* is numerically 861, the same numeric value as the Name *Elokim* (86) times ten (10+86=860), with 1 for the word itself, totaling 861. This is the pinnacle or full manifestation of the Name Elokim.

SECOND SET / STANDING SHOFAR SOUNDS

In the second set of Shofar blasts, the verses we recite begin with the words *Lo Hibit Aven b'Yaakov* / "Do not see any fault in Jacob." The word *Yaakov* is related to the word *Ekev* / heel. This verse therefore suggests that now, with the second Shofar blasts, we need not focus on or fight with any obstruction within our heel, our lower self, for the negativity of the Satan has already been neutralized. Now, we are able to taste the fruit of the Future Redemption. The Arizal teaches that the "sitting Shofar" is the sound of "this world" but the "standing Shofar" is the sound of "the World to Come." These are the sounds of Redemption.

During this part of the Davening, we also recite verses urging Divine Reality to "reign over the entire world," verses affirming

Hashem's remembrance of love for us, and verses describing how Hashem was revealed to us on Mount Sinai. Other verses speak of the Great Shofar that will announce the coming Redemption. Along with this cosmic renewal and realignment, we will leave the exiles of history behind us and be gathered back together again, as it says: "…They will come from Ashur and from Egypt." Each of these verses suggests a theme of bringing separate parts together, rather than spreading out and splintering apart. Unification is the secret of sweetening.

THE UNIFICATION

The word *Shofar* is spelled שופר / Shin-Vav-Pei-Reish. We can split this word up and analyze it in order to derive deeper spiritual meanings than what are apparent on the surface of its semantic significations.

Pei and Reish together (פר / *Par*) have a numerical value of 280. The number 280 is also the sum of the *MaN-Tze-PaCh*, the five letters of the Hebrew alphabet that change shape when they appear at the end of a word (*Mem* / 40, *Nun* / 50, *Tzadik* / 90, *Pei* / 80 and *Chaf* / 20), as explored earlier in greater detail. Because these shapes appear only at the ends of words, the *MaN-Tze-PaCh* letters are considered limiting letters; thus they represent the five Gevuros or *Dinim*, the five basic forces of constriction and concealment in the universe.

שו / *Shin* and *Vav*, the other two letters of the word *Shofar*, together spell the word *Shav* / equal. Thus, שו-פר / *Shav-Par*, the שופר / *Shofar*, unifies and equalizes the constrictive *Gevuros* and their expansive opposites, in such a way that the forces of judgment throughout the world are sweetened.

When this sweetening is accomplished, then the Divine will of the Merciful One will reign over all the earth and we will hear the triumphant cry of the Shofar haGadol. May we merit to experience this inwardly and outwardly on Rosh Hashanah, and immediately, right now.

Chapter Eleven

THE STANDING SHOFAR SOUNDS:
The Verses on Kingship, Remembrance
& the Sound of the Shofar

A S DISCUSSED ABOVE, THERE ARE TWO SETS OF SHO-
FAR SOUNDS THAT WE BLOW ON ROSH HASHANAH.
The first set is called *Tekios Meyushav* / sitting blasts,
and the second set is called *Tekios Me'umad* / standing blasts.
The Tekios Meyushav are the thirty sounds of the Shofar that
are blown following Shacharis, the morning prayers, and following the reading of the Torah. They are called 'sitting blasts'
because, theoretically, one may sit down while hearing these
sounds of the Shofar. The custom of many is to blow the standing blasts both during the silent Amidah and during the repe-

tition of the Amidah. The Amidah is said standing and *Amidah* means standing, thus the term 'standing blasts'.

The 'sitting blasts' of the Shofar are not part of the 'prayers', per se. In fact, centuries ago the Shofar was blown right away in the morning, at the first available time, and only later in history was it placed in the middle of *Davening* / prayers, after Shacharis (See *Rosh Hashanah*, 32b). The standing blasts of the Shofar, on the other hand, are part of the prayers, placed within the Musaf Amidah, itself.

Outside of Davening, the Tekios Meyushav are blown 'as the Mitzvah in itself'. First we blow the Shofar this way, and then later there is also an idea of the Shofar as the 'sound of prayer'. When we blow the Shofar during the Amidah, the Shofar sounds are considered *part* of the Tefilah. In general, just as we Daven with words, sometimes we Daven with the sounds of the Shofar. We find this in times of hardship and days of fasting: "It is a positive Torah commandment *to cry out and to sound trumpets* in the event of any difficulty that arises... On these fast days we cry out in prayer and offer supplications... In the Beis haMikdash, we sounded both the trumpets and the Shofar" (Rambam, *Hilchos Ta'aniyos*, 1:1-4. *Mishnah Ta'anis*, 15a). In this way, the sound of the Shofar becomes a form of prayer, a means of Tefilah.

The Brisker Rav, writes that the sound of the Shofar has two *Dinim* / two principal laws: one is the Mitzvah of blowing the Shofar on its own, and the other is blowing the Shofar as a form of Tefilah. Normally, we Daven, pray, with our mouth, as the Beis haLevi, the Brisker Rav's grandfather writes (*Sh'ut Beis haLevi*, 2, Derush 15. *Reshimos haTalmidim*, HaGriz, *Tehilim*, 81:4, Ha'aros, 170), while on Rosh Hashanah we also Daven from the depths of our being through the instrument of the Shofar (Ibid, Ba'alascha, p. 396. This type of Davening, with a Shofar, is unique to Klal Yisrael. Ibid, Balak, 427).

We Daven, cry out, and seek to connect with HaKadosh Baruch Hu, through the raw sounds of the Shofar.

MALCHIYOS, ZICHRONOS, SHOFAROS

During the Amidah on Rosh Hashanah we recite ten verses from Tanach that speak about Hashem being the Master of the Universe, then we recite ten verses that speak of Hashem's Remembrance of us, and finally ten verses about the Shofar itself. Interspersed throughout these three sets of ten verses, we blow the Shofar.

In the words of our sages, "Hashem said, 'Recite before Me *Malchiyos*' / scriptural verses that speak of Divine Kingship, *Zichronos* / verses that speak of Divine Remembering, and *Shofaros* / verses that speak of the Shofar. (Recite) Malchiyos so that you will proclaim Me King, Zichronos, so that your remembrance, for good, may come before Me. *U-baMeh* / and through what? The Shofar" (אמר הקב"ה אמרו לפני בר"ה מלכיות זכרונות ושופרות מלכיות כדי שתמליכוני עליכם זכרונות כדי שיבא לפני זכרוניכם לטובה ובמה בשופר: *Rosh Hashanah*, 34b).

There are two aspects to this teaching: first, that we must re-cite these verses, אמרו לפני בר"ה מלכיות זכרונות ושופרות / "Recite before Me, Malchiyos, Zichronos and Shofaros," and second, that we must conclude them in a particular way: by blowing the Shofar, ובמה בשופר / "And through what? The Shofar."

When we conclude reciting the Torah verses regarding Hashem's kingship (Malchiyos) we say, "Assume kingship over the entire world," and we blow the Shofar. When we con-clude the scriptural verses regarding Hashem's remembrance (Zichronos), we say, "Remember us for goodness," and we blow the Shofar. And when we conclude the verses regarding the Shofar (Shofaros) we say, "Blow the great Shofar and redeem us," and we conclude by blowing the Shofar.

It seems our sages spoke simply and clearly when they began to reveal the Mitzvah of reciting these verses: "Recite before Me Malchiyos, Zichronos, Shofaros…" What is the reason for the additional statement, ובמה בשופר? / "And through what? The Shofar." Why did they need to ask "and through what," and why did they answer "The Shofar"?

"Recite before Me" suggests more than just a recital of vers-es, rather, it is a reciting *in front* of Me — meaning a type of prayer. So the question is, what kind of *Tefilah* / prayer is a collage of Torah verses about (for example) the Torah being given with the sound of a Shofar? This is not, seemingly, a form of 'prayer' at all, but a sampling of scriptural sources. As such, the question needs to be asked, "and through what" — by what means does this recital of verses become a 'prayer'? How do these words of Malchiyos, Zichronos and Shofaros come לפני / leFanai / before Me? It must be through the Shofar (See *Sefas Emes*, 5648-49). The Shofar transforms these texts into Tefilah, as the blowing of the Shofar is itself a cry of Tefilah.

In this way, the Shofar blowing at the conclusion of each set of verses, recited within the context of the Amidah, creates a unity between pure sound and articulate speech. The Shofar becomes the instrument through which our words of Malchiyos, Zichronos and Shofaros are unified and elevated in the Presence of the King.

On Rosh Hashanah there is a Mitzvah from the Torah to blow the Shofar, and there is a Mitzvah of the sages to recite these three groups of ten verses. The fact that the former is a Torah law, while the latter is a Rabbinic Mitzvah, is clearly indicated in an illustrative case in Gemara: in one city the people only know how to blow the Shofar and in another city they only know how to recite these passages. The ruling is that a person should travel to the city where they can blow, as blowing Shofar is the Torah based Mitzvah (*Rosh Hashanah*, 34b). Yet, it also appears, from other sources, that the actual reading and reciting of the passages is also a Mitzvah from the Torah, in the words of Rebbe Akiva: רחמנא / "*Rachmana* / 'the all Merciful One' said we should remember" (אמר לו ר"ע אם אינו תוקע למלכיות) :למה הוא מזכיר למה הוא מזכיר רחמנא אמר אידכר *Rosh Hashanah*, 32a. Note Rashi, *Vayikra*, 23:24: זכרון תרועה זכרון פסוקי זכרונות ופסוקי שופרות). *Rachmana* is generally an allusion to the law of the Torah (although it can also refer to the sages, see Ran, *ad loc.*). This is because, by blowing the Shofar at the conclusion of each group of ten, these recited passages become 'unified' and one with the Torah Mitzvah of actually blowing Shofar. The Shofar thus completes the passages, and the passages are elevated through the Shofar.

Since we blow thirty 'sitting blasts' after the Torah reading, another thirty 'standing blasts' during the Silent Amidah, another thirty in the repetition, and finally at the end of Musaf another ten, the total amount of Shofar blasts comes to 100 (*Tosefos*, Rosh Hashanah, 33b). These correspond to the Ten Utterances of Creation, which themselves contain ten levels. Our sages teach (*Rosh Hashanah*, 32a), that we recite ten verses of Malchiyos, of Zichronos and of Shofaros, corresponding to the Ten Utterances of Creation and the *Eser haDibros* / Ten 'Words' or Commandments. Each set of ten verses also corresponds to the ten Sefiros (*Metzudas Dovid*, Mitzvah 112), and as each of the ten Sefiros are inter-included within all ten Sefiros, there are actually a total of 100 Sefiros, echoed in the 100 sounds of the Shofar.

As we read the ten verses of Malchiyos, we should have the Kavanah that we are right now coronating Hashem as King and Master of the universe. While reciting the ten verses of Zichronos, we should have in mind that all our thoughts, words and deeds are recorded, Hashem remembers every instant of our life, and that our life truly matters to HaKadosh Baruch Hu. When reciting the verses of Shofaros, we should recall all the wondrous events that occurred with the blowing of the Shofar, and yearn, Daven and anticipate hearing the sound of the Great Shofar at the conclusion of history and end of all exiles.

Over time, the recitation of Malchiyos, Zichronos and Shofaros became the central event of the Rosh Hashanah Davening. This is particularly curious because each of these three groups present us with a different issue.

QUESTIONS ON MALCHIYOS, ZICHRONOS AND SHOFAROS

That we human beings can anoint HaKadosh Baruch Hu as Master and King of the Universe is peculiar. A human being might have the right to nominate another human being as his ruler or master if he so desires; they are of the same type. But what power and right do we have as fleeting, finite creations to anoint the Eternal Creator of the Universe as its King?

The idea of Hashem 'remembering' us is also quite puzzling. The reason we human beings remember is that the events of our past are continuously updated and imprinted within our present or we would forget them. We are particularly vulnerable to forgetting because we operate in a time-based reality, in which the past is generally not felt or seen in the present. And in this realm of linear time, the past is only recalled if it is 'imported' and made to be felt in the present. But Hashem, the Infinite One, the Creator of time, is beyond time, and so is not susceptible to any memory loss. For the timeless Creator of time there is no past, as there is no future, hence there is no possibility of forgetting. What then does it mean that Hashem 'remembers'?

Additionally, the idea that us reciting verses about and blowing the Shofar, could actually 'awaken' Hashem, is also odd. Sleepiness, distraction or a limited scope of will, knowledge or focus, are completely irrelevant to the Omniscient, Omnipotent One.

Finally, what is the relationship between the sound of the Shofar and the events that occurred when the Shofar was sounded at other times, such as the giving of the Torah at Mount Sinai?

MALCHIYOS AND THE DESIRE TO BE KING

Rosh Hashanah celebrates a renewal of the Divine desire to create, sustain and give life to physical reality, and to rule over this kingdom. In truth, the essence of Hashem is beyond the 'role' of Kingship and even of being a Creator. Yet, there was a Divine desire to create 'others' within a finite physical world, and to be their Master and King. Furthermore, Hashem chose to become King through a specific process. There needed to be a created being that assumed an inner sense of separation from the Creator, so that through the exercise of its free will, this being would recognize Hashem's Presence and Reign throughout the entire universe. As humans, this is what we have been created for — to crown the King of All Creation. It did not *have* to be this way, that the crowning of the Infinite Creator as King would require the free will choice of a mere finite creation. Certainly, the Infinite One, defying all finite logic, could theoretically create a world of separation, as well as otherness, without actually creating finitude; but Hashem *desired* it this way.

On Rosh Hashanah our Avodah is to arouse in HaKadosh Baruch Hu a new desire to rule and nourish all of existence, and to sustain His servants with goodness and blessings. To arouse and satisfy the Divine desire, we crown Hashem as our Master and King. This is the idea of Malchiyos. Perhaps, it is not that the world would cease to exist without our Shofar blowing, rather, there would be no Divine desire to continue giving it existence.

Our finite activities as limited created beings cannot logically influence the Infinite Creator of everything. Nonetheless, it is the inscrutable desire of Hashem that it should be so — that a mere 'effect' should determine the inner will of the Original Cause.

In summary, Malchiyos activates our awareness of and alignment with Hashem as the Creator and Master of the Universe. This is a revelation of the 'Infinite One' as related specifically to the finite world of form, and thus we finite beings are empowered to participate in it.

ZICHRONOS AND THE DESIRE

TO REMEMBER CREATION

To remember is to select an event of the past and to bring into consciousness a residue of its impression in the present. Zichronos is similar to Malchiyos in that human beings are given the radical responsibility of 'influencing' the Creator's relationship to Creation. In this method, however, we seek to stimulate HaKadosh Baruch Hu's memories of our righteous ancestors in a way that moves Hashem emotionally, so-to-speak. When Hashem remembers their 'unlimited' deeds, He overlooks our limitations.

HaKadosh Baruch Hu chooses to be influenced, as it were, by being reminded of His love for our Ancestors, and of how He established intimate covenants with them. Reminding Hashem of these times 'causes' Him to respond to us in the present with a compassion that is far beyond what we have 'earned' ourselves. Even though human actions, by definition, are finite, we seek the arousal of Divine compassion on a level that is 'infinite' — far beyond anything we can do or say. The Infinitely Compassionate One thus looks past our faults, transcends our limitations and imbues our lives with blessing and radiance for the sake of our righteous Ancestors.

In summary, Zichronos activates Hashem's revelation as the Transcendent One. Hashem is detached and beyond finite actions and events, yet is still 'connected' through memory of Creation and the created beings who have reflected His Infinity and established bonds of eternal love. We are empowered in this way to draw the Transcendent Compassion of HaKadosh Baruch Hu into our lives, into the world, and into the coming year.

SHOFAROS AND THE DESIRE TO REVEAL ESSENCE

On the deepest level, the ultimate revelation is of the Essence of HaKadosh Baruch Hu, and this is accomplished through the Shofar. The sound of the Shofar expresses the essence of sound beyond anything that can be linguistically expressed — it is a sound beyond language, the deepest of prayers. We sound the Shofar to connect to the Essence of Hashem, beyond words.

The Shofar is a physical object, and one that is totally separated from its life force. Not only has it been separated from the head of the animal, but it was the part of the animal's body that was most coarse and lifeless, its skull. While the Transcendent dimension of *Elokus* / Divinity is infinitely removed from this level of inanimate physicality, the Divine Essence is one with all levels of existence, and is revealed vividly in this most physical of levels. Nothing is ever outside the Omnipresent, Omniscient One, we only need to recognize this.

Our verbal Tefilos are channeled through the mouth, lungs, mind and heart of a living being — us. To reveal HaKadosh Baruch Hu within even the silent, inanimate, material world, we channel our Tefilos through a dead, separated extension of an animal. In so doing, we recognize that our physical bodies, even down to our 'inanimate' toenails, are one with Hashem's Essence.

When the Torah was revealed at Mount Sinai with the sound of a Shofar, the world experienced an eternal moment of infinite oneness with HaKadosh Baruch Hu. Similarly, the Complete Redemption will be activated with the sound of the Shofar when Hashem is revealed as one in Essence with all beings including even the lowest physical realms of existence.

On Rosh Hashanah we Daven that the new revelation of the coming year should emanate from the Essence of Hashem. The power to awaken these levels within creation comes from the Torah. The Torah and Hashem are one — the Torah is the Creator's deepest wisdom and will that is revealed and entrusted to us. By reciting verses of Torah, we 'touch' the Essence of Hashem and through the Torah's power we inspire a revelation of the deepest order. By blowing the Shofar at the culmination of these verses, we demonstrate their essential meaning in a raw and visceral way. In this moment, the Divine becomes tangible in our lives and experience, similar to the synaesthetic theophany at Mt. Sinai.

In summary, Shofaros activates a revelation of Divine Essence, just as a physical Shofar is an expression of this ultimate reality. We are thereby empowered to bring the recognition of Essence into our year, and with it the potential for Complete Redemption.

On all levels, Creation has ten dimensions, corresponding to the ten Sefiros, the ten spheres or channels of Divine Light with which the Infinite creates every year and animates every moment. Each of the three groups of verses, Malchiyos,

Zichronos and Shofaros, contains ten verses from Tanach, the idea being that through our Tefilos we are drawing down blessings into all worlds and all realities, and receiving the seeds of everything we need, physically and spiritually. It is then up to us to cultivate those seeds in the coming year, allowing our infinite blessings to blossom in this world for the good of all.

Prayer Verses	Divine Desire Stimulated	Mode of Revelation
Verses of Malchiyos	To be King over Creation	Revealing Divine Imminence through our finite agency
Verses of Zichronos	To have Compassion on Creation	Revealing Divine Transcendence by looking beyond our finite nature
Verses of Shofaros	To dwell within Creation, to be One with Creation, to redeem Creation	Revealing Essence

THE INNER MEANING OF MALCHIYOS, ZICHRONOS & SHOFAROS

Whatever we do below awakens a similar response Above. 'Hashem is our shadow,' as it were (*Tehilim*, 121:5. *Keser Shem Tov*, Hosafos, 60. *Shaloh*, Sha'ar haGadol, 22a). In order to awaken Malchus Above, in such a way that Hashem is revealed in this world, we need to reveal that Hashem is King in our own personal life. Certainly, it would mean nothing to call on HaKadosh Baruch Hu to be King over everyone but ourselves.

To live with the awareness that Hashem is King of our own life, we need to deeply recognize that everything we experience is orchestrated and guided by the Hand of Hashem, and that everything is *Echad* / One. Our *Moach* / mind needs to be *Shalit* / in control of our heart, as explained earlier. In this way, when we know the Presence of Hashem in all places, at all times, and in all our states and levels of mind, then all our struggles, temptations, and the forces that would lead us astray, simply dissolve back into oneness. Admittedly, this is a difficult level of awareness to maintain. Which is why we need to actively 'remember' it, as in *Zichronos*.

ZICHRONOS

Remembrance is an integral part of Rosh Hashanah, so much so that in the liturgy Rosh Hashanah is actually called *Yom haZikaron* / the Day of Remembrance (As Rashi writes in *Eiruvin*, 40a, we call Rosh Hashanah *Yom haZikaron* because the Torah itself uses the word *Zikaron* with regards to Rosh Hashanah: את יום הזכרון הזה דרחמנא קרייה זכרון דכתיב זכרון תרועה. See also Tosefos, *ibid*). Inwardly, the act of Zichronos is to remember who we really are. We remember our collective history all the way back to the story of the *Mabul* / the Flood of the generation of Noach. This is our life, our story.

Essentially, there are two options in dealing with life's challenges: either the situation is controlling us and we just deal with it, or we are Above the problem and able to control it. Without remembering who you really are, you are below, or underneath, your problems, constantly fighting with yourself. But if you remember who you really are, you will be able to rise above your problems, in a position to see them clearly and transform them.

Part of us struggles with imperfection, lack and deficiency, and part of us is always 'perfect'. We have an inner 'struggler' and an inner 'perfect one'. Faced with a challenge or temptation, we can either strive to overcome it directly, or we can envision ourselves standing above the challenge as a master over it.

Deep down, you really are this master, this perfect one. And this is the idea of 'remembering'. When we remember who we really are, then, "When we remember Hashem, Hashem remembers us," as it were (*Resisei Layla*, 35. *Likutei Amarim*, 13).

When we wake up to who we truly are and then remember Hashem, Hashem 'wakes up' to us, and reveals to us more and more clarity in our mission and purpose. Often it is difficult to wake up and rise to our potential perfection and mastery, and to remember Hashem's Presence. We have resistances and our focus has been diluted through our struggles. This is why we need the sound of the Shofar.

SHOFAROS

The Shofar sound is the cry that breaks down all barriers, limitations, constrictions and resistances. It's piercing sound brought down the walls of *Yericho* / Jericho and set slaves free on the day of Yovel. The blast of the Shofar is the 'shout' that destroys all concealments and reveals who you are at your primal core. With sudden force, we find ourselves standing humbly in our own perfection, free, above our struggles, beholding Hashem's Presence in the sound of the Shofar at Matan Torah, at Yericho, at the Yovel, immersed in the brilliant glory of the Final Redemption.

In this moment, we truly understand the words that we sing or shout with fervor throughout Rosh Hashanah: *Hashem Melech, Hashem Malach, Hashem Yimloch l'Olam Vaed!* / "Hashem *is* King (Malchiyos), Hashem *was* King (Zichronos), and Hashem *will be* King forever and ever (Shofaros)!"

Chapter Twelve
THE DEEPER REASON WHY WE DO NOT BLOW THE SHOFAR ON SHABBOS:
Three Levels of Non-Being

R EGARDING THE PERFORMANCE OF THE MITZVAH OF SHOFAR ON ROSH HASHANAH, THERE ARE THREE BASIC SCENARIOS: 1) When Rosh Hashanah is during the week, there is a Mitzvah to blow the Shofar on Rosh Hashanah. 2) When a day of Rosh Hashanah falls on Shabbos, we do not blow Shofar on that day, rather we 'remember' the Shofar without blowing it. 3) In the Beis haMikdash (and in a place where the High Court convened), when a day of Rosh Hashanah fell on Shabbos, the Shofar was blown even though it was Shabbos. These three scenarios correspond to three levels of spiritual attainment, and these will be discussed at the end of this chapter. First, we need to build a context for that insight to take shape.

As mentioned, today, when Rosh Hashanah falls on Shabbos, the Shofar is not blown. In the Torah itself there are two verses that speak of the *Teru'ah* / blowing of the Shofar on Rosh Hashanah; one says *Yom Teru'ah* / "a day of Teru'ah" (*Bamidbar*, 29:1), and the other verse says *Zichron Teru'ah* / "a remembrance of Teru'ah" (*Vayikra*, 23:24). According to the *Yerushalmi* / Jerusalem Talmud, *Yom Teru'ah* refers to Rosh Hashanah falling on a weekday, when we actually blow the Shofar, while *Zichron Teru'ah* refers to Rosh Hashanah falling on Shabbos, when we merely 'recall' the blowing of the Shofar (*Yerushalmi, Rosh Hashanah*, 4:1. The Rokeach, *Hilchos Rosh Hashanah*, 201, quotes this in the name of the *Pesikta*. The *Bavli* rules this out: *Rosh Hashanah*, 29b). With this in mind, perhaps it is a 'Torah Law' (or at least this allusion in the Torah) that guides us to blow the Shofar on a weekday and not blow it on a Shabbos.

A more widely known reason that we do not blow the Shofar on Shabbos comes from the *Gezeiras Rabba* / decree of the Fourth Century sage, Rabba. From this decree, the guidance to refrain from blowing Shofar on Shabbos is not Torah rooted as above, rather, it is a Rabbinic decree (*Rosh Hashanah*, 29b). Rabba reasons that an unlearned person, not knowing how to blow the Shofar, might go outside and carry the Shofar to a more learned person[*] so the latter can teach him how to blow it (שמא

---

[*] This is the simple reading of the גזירה / Gezeira of Rabba, the worry that an unlearned person will go to the more learned person, so the other can blow the Shofar or teach him how to blow. Speaking about the reason we do not read the Megilah on Shabbos, says the Gemara, Rabba said: "Everyone is obligated to read or hear the Megilah, yet not everyone is proficient in reading the Megilah. (Therefore, the Sages issued a rabbinic decree that

יטלנו בידו וילך אצל הבקי ללמוד, Or the more learned one will actually blow the unlearned one's Shofar for him, as the Rambam writes, שמא יטלנו בידו ויוליכנו למי שיתקע לו: *Hilchos Shofar*, 2:6), and thus violate the Shabbos prohibition against carrying objects from one domain to another

---

the Megilah is not read on Shabbos), lest one take (the Megilah) in his hand and go to an expert to learn, and will carry it four cubits in the public domain and thereby desecrate Shabbos. והיינו טעמא דשופר והיינו טעמא דלולב / "This is also the reason for Shofar and the reason for Lulav." Yet, regarding Megilah on Shabbos, Rav Yoseph adds, another reason why we do not read the Megilah on Shabbos is מפני שעיניהן של עניים נשואות במקרא מגילה / "because the eyes of the poor are focused on the reading of the Megilah" (*Megilah*, 4b). In other words, when the Megilah is read many people are gathered and it is a good time to collect gifts for the poor; now, if the Megilah would be read on Shabbos, people would not be able to give money, as it is Shabbos, and the poor would lose out. The question is, why does Rav Yoseph need another reason; why isn't the reason of Rabba sufficient, as Tosefos, *ad loc.*, explores. And clearly Rav Yoseph would agree with Rabba regarding Shofar and Lulav, that the reason we do not blow a Shofar or shake a Lulav on Shabbos is because someone may carry it in a public domain? The Pnei Yehoshua, offers a novel interpretation: the Gezeira of Rabba is referring to a learned or at least semi-learned person, who knows that there is the opinion of Rebbe Eliezer that holds that not only does a time bound Mitzvah (such as Milah or Korban Pesach) push aside Shabbos (and we are allowed to perform a Bris Milah and offer a Korban Pesach on Shabbos), but even מכשיריהן / the preparations, such as carrying the Mohel's knife etc., also pushes aside Shabbos — and thus he thinks this would apply as well to carrying the Shofar and the Lulav in a public domain on Shabbos. With the Megilah he would not make this mistake, as reading the Megilah is a Mitzvah of the sages. Thus, Rav Yoseph offers another reason — לולי דבריהם היה נראה לי לפרש בענין אחר דדוקא בשופר ולולב חייש ר״י לשמא יעבירנו משום דאפילו יודע שהוא שבת ושהמלאכה אסורה אפ״ה אתי למיטעי ולומר דמצות שופר ולולב דוחין שבת דהא לקושטא דמלתא לרבי אליעזר דמילה שופר ולולב וכל מכשיריהן דוחין שבת משא״כ הכא במגילה הכל יודעין שאינה אלא מדרבנן הכל יודעין שאינה דוחה שבת ותו ליכא למיחש למידי מש״ה איצטריך לטעמא אחרינא: *Pnei Yehoshua,* Megilah, 4b.

(meaning carrying more than four cubits in a public domain). Therefore, in order to protect the sanctity of Shabbos against a possible violation, Rabba forbids the blowing of the Shofar on Rosh Hashanah when it coincides with Shabbos (and perhaps this careful guarding of Shabbos itself, despite that fact that blowing the Shofar is beneficial to us, stands as a merit equal to the Shofar-blowing. In this way, it is perhaps similar to a spiritual *Akeidah* / 'binding': *Meshech Chochmah*, Vayikra, 23:24).

The act of blowing the Shofar itself is not prohibited on Shabbos, as it is a *Chochmah* / wisdom and not a *Melacha* / work (*Rosh Hashanah*, 29b. Yet, it is prohibited by the Sages: Rashi, *Shabbos*, 114b. Tosefos, *Shabbos*, 3b), and on Shabbos only 'work' is prohibited. Rather, the issue is the *Chashash* / worry that Shabbos will be violated by someone carrying the Shofar in a public domain.

Now, even with a Rabbinic decree against blowing the Shofar on Shabbos, which means there is no longer a *Chiyuv* / obligation to blow it, if someone *does* blow it, he can still be seen as fulfilling a Mitzvah (as Rebbe Akiva Eger writes, גדול שתוקע בשבת מקיים מצות ש ופר דזמנו גם בשבת אלא דעבר על שבות דשבת. דו"ח מערכה ח' ד"ה והנה המג"א, וחי' רעק"א פסחים סט,א. וראה שו"ת מהרש"ג או"ח סימן ל"ו, וע' פמ"ג או"ח סימן תרל"ד). From a deeper perspective, however, there is no longer any Mitzvah to blow the Shofar on that day.*

---

* See *Chelkas Yoav*, Keva d'Kashisei, Question 99. *Kuntres Divrei Sifri*, Koveitz Shi'urim, 2. The decree of the sages may 'uproot' a Mitzvah of the Torah, so long as it is not clearly stated to the contrary, דאין כח ביד חכמים לאסור דבר שפירשה התורה בפירוש להיתר: *Taz*, Yoreh De'ah, 117:1. Although see *Likutei Sichos*, 3, Tzav, note 4, regarding the opinion of the Alter Rebbe. שבמקום שגזרו חז"ל על דבר מסים שלא לעשותו, אם יבוא אדם ויעשהו, לא זו בלבד שעבר על גזירת חכמים, אלא גם לא יצא ידי דאורייתא: Tosefos, *Sukkah*, 3a. See, however, Ran on *Sukkah*, 28a and on *Pesachim*, 116a.

If, because of the worry that an uneducated person may come to carry a Shofar on Shabbos, the sages uprooted the Torah's Mitzvah to blow the Shofar, and there is no longer any Mitzvah to blow the Shofar on Shabbos, the question is blatant and obvious: how can this most important Mitzvah be set aside because of a worry about an unintentional violation by a simple Jew? (Rebbe Rashab, *Hemshech Samach Vav*, beginning*)

---

* It seems like the opinion of the Alter Rebbe is that the גזירה is added to the issue of עובדין דחול. This is what the Alter Rebbe writes: יו"ט של ר"ה שחל להיות בשבת אין תוקעין בשופר אע"פ שהתקיעה בשופר אינה מלאכה ואינה אסורה בשבת ויו"ט אלא מד"ס משום עובדין דחול, ולמה אין דוחין איסור קל כזה מפני מ"ע של תורה כמו שדוחין אותה בכל יו"ט של ר"ה הואיל ואין בו שבות גמור. לפי שהכל חייבין בתקיעת שופר ואין הכל בקיאין בתקיעת שופר, גזירה שמא יטלנו בידו וילך. אצל הבקי ללמוד ויעבירנו ד' אמות ברשות הרבים. שו"ע אדמו"ר הזקן הלכות ראש השנה סי' תקפ"ח סעי' ד' See also מחצית השקל, סי' תקפ"ח ס"ק ד'. דבאמת כן כונת הש"ס במ"ש שמא יעבירנו ר"ל גם גזירת שמא יעבירנו איכא נוסף על שמא יתקן על שיר כלי שבותים אבל משום חד שבות לא היו מעמידים דבריהם.

According to the Rambam, it seems clear that the *Gezeira* of Rabba, the Rabbinic decree, cannot push aside the Mitzvah of the Torah to blow the Shofar, as it does not push aside the Mitzvah of the Torah of Lulav — ולמה לא גזרו גזרה זו ביום טוב הראשון מפני שהוא מצוה מן התורה ואפלו בגבולין: *Hilchos Lulav*, 7:14. Although with regards to Shofar, it does seem that the Gezeira of Rabba pushes aside the blowing of the Shofar — יום טוב של ראש השנה שחל להיות בשבת אין תוקעין בשופר בכל מקום. אף על פי שהתקיעה משום שבות היא ומן הדין היה שתוקעין יבוא עשה של תורה וידחה שבות של דבריהם. ולמה אין תוקעין גזרה שמא יטלנו בידו ויוליכנו למי שיתקע לו ויעבירנו ארבע אמות ברשות הרבים. או יוציאו מרשות לרשות ויבוא לידי אסור סקילה: *Hilchos Shofar*, 2:6. This is because Rosh Hashanah is the first day of the month, and during the period when we sanctified the new months by witnesses, it was possible that it was not yet known when the day of Rosh Hashanah is in actuality, and we keep both days because of ספיקא דיומא / uncertainty of the day, thus blowing that day is not Min haTorah, a law of the Torah, rather, just a Rabbinic law. See Tosefos, and Ran, *Sukkah*, 43a. In fact, it seems that even during the times of the first Beis haMikdash, in all of Eretz Yisrael Rosh Hashanah was practiced as two days. *Harchev Davar*, Vayikra, 25:9, 1.

Should all of Klal Yisrael negate the lofty Mitzvah and spiritual experience of the Shofar just because a rare individual might, in his innocent desire to learn to blow it, mistakenly carry one to his mentor's house? (Besides, it is merely a case of טעה בדבר מצווה / "he made a mistake in performing a Mitzvah" and performed another Mitzvah, if the educated person blows for him, and in this case, he is פטור: *Shabbos*, 137a). Surely there are many other potential mistakes in Shabbos observance that an uninformed person could make, which we do not treat with such extraordinary concern. Even more troubling is the fact that Shofar is the *Mitzvas ha-Yom* / central Mitzvah of the day, and the only Mitzvah indigenous to Rosh Hashanah, and the Torah's very definition of this Yom Tov. One might rightly ask, what is Rosh Hashanah without the Shofar?

On a spiritual level, Shabbos represents the silent 'Shofar'. Shabbos is the deepest, innermost stratum of our reality; thus we do not blow the Shofar on Shabbos because Shabbos itself is already the deepest 'cry' to Hashem possible. Shabbos can be understood as a cry to HaKadosh Baruch Hu that is completely absorbed in a state of *Bitul* / nullification of separateness, in which there is no outward expression whatsoever (Tzemach Tzedek, *Derech Mitzvosecha*). There are times in life when we may be moved inwardly, and tears and a cry well up within our depths, but are not released. Although this silent, inner cry has no voice or expression, it is nonetheless deafening to the one experiencing it, and it is certainly heard by the Hearer of all cries.

Yet, this cannot be 'the' inner reason that we don't blow the

Shofar, since on Shabbos we are generally guided to refrain from crying or crying out, even inwardly. So perhaps the silence is not due to an unexpressed cry deep within, but rather we do not blow the Shofar on 'Shabbos Rosh Hashanah' because we are *beyond* crying, above crying. We are also above needing an instrument to achieve whatever we may need to achieve on this day. Shabbos is the answer to the cry of the Shofar, the teleology of all Teshuvah.

From a deeper point of view, the fact that we are directed to not blow the Shofar on Shabbos indicates that the sages intuitively understood that we do not *need* to blow the Shofar on Shabbos, and what is achieved on a normal Rosh Hashanah day with the Shofar is accomplished on Shabbos *without* blowing. In this way, Rabba's reason not to blow, even if it doesn't seem to be a strong reason, is sufficient. If Rabba understands that on Shabbos we do not really need the Shofar, he is also aware that even his seemingly minor consideration can push it off.

The notion that Shabbos itself achieves the function of the Shofar without the actual blowing is hinted at in the Torah, as the *Yerushalmi*, quoted above, learns. In the Torah one verse says, "A day of *Teru'ah* / blowing (the Shofar)," and another verse says "A *remembrance* of Teru'ah." This reveals that there is an act of blowing, and there is an act of 'remembering the blowing'. In some years, there is a Mitzvah to actually blow the Shofar on both days of Rosh Hashanah. In other years, when Rosh Hashanah falls out on Shabbos, there is a Mitzvah to blow the Shofar on one day, and 'remember' the blowing on the other. What occurs spiritually on the weekday Yom Tov through the blowing of the Shofar, occurs spiritually and naturally on Shabbos Yom Tov *on its own*, precisely through the Shofar not being blown.

In this way, there seems to be a type of non-physical 'Shofar' present on Shabbos Rosh Hashanah. The verse mentioning *Yom Teru'ah* / "Day of Sounding the Shofar" appears in the "Parsha of *Musafin*" in the portion of Pinchas, where the Torah describes all the *Musafim* / extra offerings that need to be offered during all the *Yamim Tovim* / holidays.* The verse describing Rosh Hashanah as *Zichron Teru'ah* / "Remembrance of Sounding the Shofar" appears in the "Parsha of *Moadim*," in the portion of Emor, where the Torah speaks about what the Yamim Tovim are. This is very peculiar, since the Torah is describing what every Yom Tov of the year is and what it represents, and the Torah simply calls Rosh Hashanah *Zichron Teru'ah*, seemingly suggesting that when we do *Zichron Teru'ah* we are fulfilling the Yom Tov on Rosh Hashanah in its truest form.**

---

* Indeed, because the Torah calls Rosh Hashanah *Yom Teru'ah* in the Parsha of Musafin, according to many Rishonim, the *Ikar* / main blowing of the Shofar is the *Tekios Meumad* / standing blasts that are blown during Musaf.

** In the name of Rebbe Akiva Eger, there is a wonderful explanation of why the Torah calls Rosh Hashanah *Zichron Teru'ah* in the portion of Moadim, the main text describing what every Yom Tov is all about. This, Rebbe Akiva says, is because on the year that Klal Yisrael left Egypt, Rosh Hashanah was actually on Shabbos (since Klal Yisrael left Egypt on Thursday (*Shabbos*, 87b) and the third day of Pesach was on Shabbos, which is always

During a weekday, says Rebbe Levi Yitzchak of Berditchev, when we blow the Shofar, it is possible that it will not be performed one hundred percent correctly, or that our ego will become involved in it or get in the way of its potential impact. On Shabbos, however, our desire is to blow the Shofar, yet we do not blow it because of the decree of our sages, and, "If a person intended to perform a Mitzvah but was prevented from doing so, because of an unpreventable circumstance, the Torah considers it as if he *had* done the Mitzvah (*Berachos*, 6a). When the Torah considers our refraining from blowing the Shofar as if we had blown it, certainly this is the most perfect Shofar blowing possible, ideal in every detail. On Shabbos we thus have the perfect Shofar-blowing, precisely because we do not blow it, rather HaKadosh Baruch Hu, the Torah is blowing for us, so-to-speak.*

---

the same day of the week as the coming Rosh Hashanah (a hint to this is that the third letter of the Aleph Beis, the letter Gimel, and the third to the last letter, Reish correspond to each other, and Reish stands for Rosh Hashanah). Therefore, the Torah tells Klal Yisrael, "It (Rosh Hashanah in general) is a *Yom Zichron Teru'ah*, as the first Rosh Hashanah celebrated by Klal Yisrael as a nation was on Shabbos.

* The *Shulchan Aruch* rules that on Erev Rosh Hashanah we do not blow the Shofar: Orach Chayim, 581:3. This is done, להפסיק בין תקיעות דרשות לתקיעות דחובה / to differentiate between the blowing in Elul, which is a custom, and the blowing on Rosh Hashanah, which is a Mitzvah. Even when the first day of Rosh Hashanah is Shabbos, as the *Mishnah Berurah*, (ibid), Sha'ar haTziyon 35, explains, דכיון שאומרים זכרון תרועה, הוי כמו תקיעה. In other words, there *is* a level of 'blowing' on Shabbos.

Let us take a moment to understand what this means. As explored earlier, there is a dual purpose for the sounding of the Shofar, a) to break all the *Din* / constriction or concealment, and b) to arouse on High a renewed desire for Kingship. On Shabbos we do not blow the Shofar, as on Shabbos there is no Din. Additionally, on Shabbos the Divine desire for Kingship is already awakened from Above 'on its own'; we do not need to do anything below to create this revelation. As such, ultimately, there is no reason that the Shofar should be blown on Shabbos, we are already there.

The theme of Rosh Hashanah suggests that the awakening of Hashem's desire to be King comes from us, below; it arises as a result of our actions, and in particular as a result of our blowing of the Shofar. On Shabbos, however, the day of 'being, not doing', this Divine 'awakening' comes about as a result of our *inaction* — in particular, our refraining from the blowing of the Shofar.

Keep in mind that in order for Shabbos to truly nullify all Din, we need to actively keep Shabbos and enter the state of Shabbos fully, resting in deed, speech, emotion, thought and consciousness. Only by keeping Shabbos fully can we achieve what the Shofar achieves during the weekday Yom Tov.[*]

---

[*] Although there is an argument among the *Amoraim* / the sages of the Gemara, regarding whether there is a positive Mitzvah to rest on Yom Tov, and it is only Rav Ashi who holds that on Yom Tov there is a positive Mitzvah to rest (רב אשי אמר: "שבתון" דיום טוב – עשה הוא, ואין עשה דוחה לא תעשה ועשה. Shabbos, 24b. Pesachim, 84a), but most Amoraim do not hold that there is a positive Mitzvah to rest on Yom Tov. Regarding Rosh Hashanah, as the

And therefore, an individual person who does blow the Shofar on Shabbos is essentially demonstrating that he is not keeping Shabbos fully — otherwise, he would not *need* to blow the Shofar. This, says the Chasam Sofer (*D'rashos*, Chaf Zayin Elul), is the reason why members of the High Court in Yerushalayim blew the Shofar on Shabbos. They were blowing on behalf of the entire congregation of Israel, even for those who had not kept Shabbos in the fullest way, who thus needed to hear the Shofar.

Let us go a little deeper.

Netziv points out, since the Pasuk says יהיה לכם שבתון / on the first day of the month, you shall observe complete rest (*Vayikra*, 23:24), which is not simply שבתון / rest, but the Torah is saying, you shall observe rest, suggesting that it is a positive Mitzvah to rest on Rosh Hashanah. In the words of the *HaAmek Davar*, יהיה לכם שבתון. מכאן למדו חז"ל בשבת דכ"ד ובכ"מ דיו"ט עשה אע"ג דבגמ' הביאו שבתון עשה מכ"מ עיקר ההוכחה מדכתיב בר"ה יהיה לכם שבתון בלשון צווי. ומכאן למדנו בכל מועדי ה' דכתיב שבתון. ונראה דאע"ג דרב אשי הוא שאמר דיו"ט הוי עשה ול"ת ואמוראי קמאי פליגי ע"ז מכל מקום בר"ה הכל מודים. כי סתמא דגמרא הוא במסכת ראש השנה דף ל"ב ב' ובזה מיושב קו' הטורי אבן על ש: שיטת ר"ת יע"ש: *HaAmek Davar*, Vayikra, 23:24. In other words, Chazal can say (according to all opinions), regarding violating Shabbos to procure a Shabbos: מ"ט שופר עשה הוא ויו"ט עשה ולא תעשה ואין עשה דוחה את לא תעשה ועשה / "What is the reason that one may not perform a prohibited labor on Rosh Hashanah to fulfill the positive Mitzvah of sounding the shofar? The Gemara answers: Sounding the Shofar is a positive Mitzvah, but performing prohibited labor on a Yom Tov violates both the positive Mitzvah to rest and the prohibition against performing prohibited labor, and a positive Mitzvah does not override both a prohibition and a positive Mitzvah" (*Rosh Hashanah*, 32b). Even though, normally, regarding other Yamim Tovim this is only the opinion of Rav Ashi, with regards to Rosh Hashanah this is everyone's opinion.

To review, there are three scenarios for the blowing the Shofar on Rosh Hashanah: 1) When Rosh Hashanah falls on a weekday, the Shofar is blown, 2) when Rosh Hashanah falls on Shabbos, the Shofar is not blown, and 3) in the Beis haMikdash, when Rosh Hashanah fell on Shabbos, the Shofar was blown. These three situations parallel three levels of spiritual attainment, namely three kinds of ego-transparency or 'nullification' of the separate 'I'. I once merited to hear the Rebbe explain this teaching (now printed in *Sefer Hasichos* 5749, pp. 704-710), and what follows is an extrapolation of his holy words.

The three levels of transparency of the self are: 1) *Bitul haYesh* / humbling the ego, 2) *Bitul b'Metziyus* / total nullification of ego, and 3) *b'Chol Levav'cha* / with all your heart(s)

Level One	Weekday Rosh Hashanah; *the Shofar is blown*	*Bitul haYesh*
Level Two	Shabbos Rosh Hashanah; *the Shofar is not blown*	*Bitul b'Metziyus*
Level Three	Shabbos Rosh Hashanah in the Beis haMikdash; *the Shofar is blown*	*B'Chol Levav'cha*

1) ROSH HASHANAH ON A WEEKDAY,
Shofar Is Blown — Level One, Bitul haYesh

To awaken a renewed Divine desire for kingship, we need to demonstrate surrender and *Bitul* / self-nullification to the Will of the King. The Shofar expresses this, evoking in the blower and listeners thoughts of Teshuvah, a posture of humility, and inspiration to perform the inner 'coronation' of Hashem over one's own life. Such is the service of Rosh Hashanah on a weekday Yom Tov. We express a measure of surrender through the vehicle of the Shofar, and to do this we must act: we must blow the Shofar.

Since any action requires a person who acts, there is necessarily some degree of 'self' or 'I' being expressed in performing such an obligation. In blowing the Shofar there is the 'I' of the blower, yet it is humbled. In the same way, there is selfhood in the listener, but it too is humbled by the sound of the Shofar.

This is the level of *Bitul haYesh*, humbling the ego. One's petty, egoic, 'small i' still exists, yet one is actively humbling it and guiding it to serve HaKadosh Baruch Hu. There is thus effort exerted in minimizing the ego, in both blowing the Shofar, and in focussing on its sound.

However, this is all still from a paradigm of separation and 'weekday' or mundane life, which requires active overcoming or transformation. Yet through the Shofar, any tendencies to self-indulgence or negativity one may have, are made to 'prostrate' themselves before the King, allowing the seeds of loving virtue and positivity to flourish.

2) ROSH HASHANAH ON SHABBOS —
Level Two: Bitul b'Metziyus

Shabbos is of a higher order than the weekday; on it we reach the level of complete self-nullification called *Menuchah /*

rest. In Menuchah there is no need for any activity whatsoever, not even the act of humbling oneself. By intentionally refraining from blowing the Shofar, by not doing anything — by resting from selfhood — we demonstrate a much deeper state, in which the illusion of separateness between us and our Creator dissolves.

Bitul b'Metziyus / total nullification of the ego, is achieved when we function transparently, without any ego whatsoever. Our small 'i' ceases to exist as an independent entity. It is a paradigm of 'only You', as 'I do not exist,' so to speak. There is no selfishness or negativity to minimize; all is already in harmonious service of the King, for the kingdom is nothing but an extension of the King's own Being. Shabbos itself effortlessly accomplishes the intended effect of the Shofar. This is the state of transcendent Shabbos rest, available when Rosh Hashanah occurs on Shabbos.

3) ROSH HASHANAH ON SHABBOS IN THE BEIS HAMIKDASH —
Level Three: B'Chol Levav'cha

In the Beis haMikdash the Shofar was blown on Shabbos, even though Shabbos supersedes the need for Shofar blowing. And this is actually the deepest, most essential form of Shofar blowing: Rebbe Eliezer of Worms writes that the first letters of the words שופר בחדש תקעו / *Tiku BaChodesh Shofar* / "Blow, on the new month, the Shofar" (*Tehilim*, 81:4), spell the word שבת / *Shabbos* (*Sefer Rokeach*, Hilchos Rosh Hashanah, 210).

In the Beis haMikdash, the transparency of the ego was so penetrating and pervasive that it included everything, and there was no separateness at all, not even a separation between 'action' and 'rest'. Everything in existence simply expressed Hashem's will, whatever that would be.

On Shabbos outside of the Beis haMikdash, we must rest and not act; we do not blow the Shofar. But even then, our 'in-activity' is to some extent an expression of an independent self; just as the 'I' acts in certain situations, it refrains from acting in other situations. Even if it is completely effortless, there is still an 'I' choosing to refrain and rest.

To act is to express oneself, but so is refraining from acting — there is an expression of self in the choice to transcend self.

In the Beis haMikdash, we were able to access a level that transcends all aspects of separate selfhood. We reached a state in which acting or not acting made no difference, since there was no separate i to express or nullify. If Hashem's desire was for the Shofar to be blown, so it must be. This is a blowing from the Unitive reality of Essence.

B'Chol Levav'cha means 'with all your hearts', including and integrating both your ego-self and your transcendent, selfless Self. Here your 'small i' still exists, but it becomes utterly transparent to your 'transcendent I'. It is 'you' who blows the Shofar, yet you are but an expression of the Ultimate Divine I.

May we merit to blow the Shofar once again even on Shabbos, speedily in our days.

Chapter Thirteen
THE ORIGINAL SOUND

HE SHOFAR BLOWING IS THE 'FIRST BREATH' OF THE
YEAR, AND EVEN DEEPER, IT IS THE FIRST PRIMOR-
DIAL SOUND, THE ORIGINAL VIBRATION UPON WHICH
ALL SOUND AND ALL CREATION ARE FOUNDED. It should, therefore, at least theoretically, be performed at the earliest opportunity. (Especially since the Shofar causes a mitigation of Din, and Divine
Din is during the first 3 hours (or second 3 hours) of the day Hashem judges:
Avodah Zarah, 3b and 4b. In fact, because of this the Magen Avraham [582]
rules that we do not wish someone "You shall be inscribed for a good year"
after the third hour of Rosh Hashanah. However, in practice, we blow after
the sixth hour of the day, as Rashi explains, below).

Rosh Hashanah is a renewal of life, the beginning of a new reality, in which an unprecedented Divine flow descends into the world. A new light, one that has never before been revealed in this world, comes into view. The blowing of the Shofar is the channel through which the new breath of life enters and awakens the world, and so it should seemingly be performed immediately upon awakening in the morning.

Yet, we blow Shofar in the middle of Davening, after Shacharis and the reading of the Torah, and before beginning the Musaf service. The question is why?

Our sages explain that we do not blow the Shofar on Rosh Hashanah during the morning prayers, rather later on, because of "a decree of the (Gentile) rulers" (*Rosh Hashanah*, 32b). Rashi elaborates that there had been a decree that did not allow Klal Yisrael to blow the Shofar. The authorities kept a close watch for the first six hours of the day until Shacharis was completed, and so the Rabbis moved Shofar to the Musaf service, and this way the Shofar blowing was postponed till the afternoon.

The 16th Century Polish rabbi, Rebbe Mordechai ben Avraham Jaffe ('the Levush'), writes that centuries before, they would indeed blow the Shofar in the morning. But once the surrounding gentiles heard the sounds of the Shofar and assumed that it was a battle cry — a call to arms — they would respond by entering the Shul/synagogue and killing those who were assembled. It was then that the decision was made to blow the Shofar during the later prayers, so that the people in the neighborhood could see the Jews were gathered to Daven and that the blowing of the Shofar was part of their Tefilos (*Yerushalmi*, see Tosefos, *Rosh Hashanah*, 32b: שדמו האויבים שנתאספו לתקוע תרועת מלחמה ועמדו עליהם והרגום ולכך. תקנו תקיעות וברכות במוסף דכי חזו דקרו בקריאת שמע ומתפללין וקורין בתורה וחוזרין ומתפללין ותוקעין אמרי בנימוסייהו אינון עסקין כלי בחוקיהם ובתורתם. According to the *Yerushalmi* [*Rosh Hashanah*, 4:8], however, since in the Torah the Mitzvah to blow the Shofar is placed within the laws of the *Musafim* / the extra offerings that were offered on every Yom Tov, thus, the correct place to blow the Shofar is within the Musaf service, and not in the morning. The Rokeach [*Hilchos Rosh Hashanah*, 201] writes that we blow the Shofar later on during the day so that we should be saturated with Mitzvos. Indeed, the Medrash writes that we blow the Shofar in Musaf, once we are already filled with Mitzvos, and thus receive favorable judgment. למה אין ישראל תוקעים מן התפילה ראשונה אלא בתפילת המוספים כדי שבשעה שהם עומדים בדין יהיו מצויין מליאי מצות הרבה ויזכו בדין *Pesikta Rabasi*, Parsha 40).

Essentially, if the Shofar should be blown first thing in the morning, it is only due to a technical reason that we do not, and as such, "If a person intended to perform a Mitzvah but was prevented from doing so because of an unpreventable circumstance, the Torah considers as if he had done the Mitzvah" (*Berachos*, 6a). It is then as if we did blow first thing in the morning, mimicking the first 'exhale' of Hashem in His desire to continue creating and sustaining the world — and the first breath of the new year is the sound of the Shofar.

Through the power of our free choice and the power of our *Neshamah* / spiritual 'breath', we become the medium through which the Divine breath, the new vitality of the New Year, flows into Creation.

On the day of our collective birthday, the day that says 'we matter', we also use our faculty of choice to arouse once again a desire on High to continue to create and sustain Creation. We 'invite' the Creator to become our King, as opposed to a forceful dictator. All of this subtle but powerful Avodah is funneled and felt through the sound of the Shofar, as it says, "Recite before Me (verses of) kingship, so that *you* shall crown Me king over you... And how? With the Shofar" (*Rosh Hashanah*, 16a).

THE RENEWED DESIRE TO CREATE

For there to be a Divine King there need to be subjects who freely desire the King. By blowing the Shofar on Rosh Hashanah we arouse a new desire Above to create, nourish, and rule over all existence with revealed goodness and blessings. Our Shofar blowing on Rosh Hashanah merges, so to speak, with the first primordial 'sound' of the Divine creative process, ushering in a new phase of creation.

The world is created through *Asarah Ma'amaros* / Ten Utterances. The first Ma'amar, the First Utterance and vibration, the first movement from Oneness to Duality, is the sound pattern *Be-rei-shis* / "In the beginning" (*Rosh Hashanah*, 32a. This is the 'hidden utterance': *Maharsha*, ad loc.). The word *Bereishis* contains the letters that, when sequenced differently, comprise the words *Bara Tayish* / "created a goat" (*Tikkunei Zohar*). Both a ram's horn and a goat's horn can be used as a Shofar ("All horns are Kosher, except of a cow": *Mishnah Rosh Hashanah*, 3:2) — although the preference is for that of a ram (מצותו בשל איל וכפוף ובדיעבד כל השופרות כשרים:

Shulchan Aruch, Orach Chayim, 586:1. Although see Rambam, *Hilchos Shofar*, 1:1 — וכל השופרות פסולין חוץ מקרן הכבש).

בראשית ברא / *Bereishis Bara* / "In the beginning created," writes the Rokeach (*Sefer Rokeach*, Hilchos Rosh Hashanah, 200) numerically equals 1,116 — the same value as the words בראש השנה נברא / *b'Rosh Hashanah Nivra* / on Rosh Hashanah it was created.

Our Shofar blowing is the Hidden Utterance, *Bereishis*, the vibration that creates the world anew. The sound of the Shofar is the vibrational foundation of Creation, the Divine expression of love and of the Creator's desire to create us. HaKadosh Baruch Hu created human beings as the final, culminating event of the Six Days of Creation, yet even before the First Day, in the hiddenness of Bereishis, before time, the Creator was already 'dreaming' of us and 'hearing' the distant echoes of our Shofar blasts, awakening the Divine and initiating Creation.

Chapter Fourteen

FROM BACK-TO-BACK TO FACE-TO-FACE: The Shofar and What It Means to Be a Human Being

ROSH HASHANAH IS THE TIME WE CELEBRATE THE COLLECTIVE BIRTHDAY OF THE HUMAN BEING ON THE SIXTH DAY OF CREATION. Yet we also celebrate Rosh Hashanah as the reawakening of the Divine desire to create and sustain Creation through continual recreation. The question is obvious: why do we celebrate the creation of the universe on the day that human beings were created, rather than on the day the world was created, the First Day of Creation — the 25th of Elul?

Really, on a more fundamental level, the question is, *what is Rosh Hashanah*? What are we celebrating? And how does this connect to the essential Mitzvah of the day, the blowing of the Shofar?

In order to answer these questions, let us first 'decode' the basic ideas of Rosh Hashanah in the deeper teachings of Torah, and specifically in the teachings of the holy Arizal. Once we have a good working grasp of the 'terms' of these teachings we will delve deeper to perceive the *Ohr* / Light that is being revealed in them.

'Before' the first Rosh Hashanah, that is, in the world as it existed before the creation of Adam, ZA / *Zeir Anpin* / the Small Face — the Six Emotive Sefiros represented by the Sefirah of Tiferes (also referred to as *Kudsha Brich Hu*) — was unified with Malchus, in a manner of *Achor b'Achor* / back-to-back. Due to this 'impersonal' relationship, the *Hashpa'ah* / flow of Divine life-force from ZA to Malchus was channeled in a way of *Achorayim* / behind the back, so to speak. This implies that the flow does come and is given to the receiver, but it is done so with very little desire, much like a person who reluctantly throws a coin over his shoulder toward a person asking for alms. While the poor man does receive the coin, it is clear that the giver is annoyed with him and is only giving because he feels like he 'has to' give. This is called Hashpa'ah from the *Achorayim* (*Tanya*, Chapter 22. Ramchal, *K'lach Pischei Chochmah*, 76).

Like the English expression 'to turn your back on someone', to be in an *Achorayim* position with someone means the other person might be present but you are not present for them. It is like someone deliberately facing away from a person even as they continue to talk to them. There is even more disconnect when both parties are facing away from the other *Achor b'Achor* / back to back' energy is circulated and exchanged, but with very little sense of connection or care.

Before the creation of a human being possessed of free-choice, the world received Divine nourishment in a way of *Achor b'Achor*. At some point there was a new Divine desire for a genuine relationship, *Panim-el-Panim* / face-to-face. In order for both parties to shift their relationship from back-to-back to face-to-face, there needed to be a transitional state of *Tardeimah* / falling asleep. This means Tiferes, ZA, needed to lose its *Mochin* / mind or consciousness, and fall temporarily into a 'sleeping' state. When Tiferes has no Mochin, it loses its *Chayus* / life-force and vitality, and thus inevitably separates from Malchus.

Tiferes is the 'masculine' Sefirah and Malchus the 'feminine'. When Tiferes loses its Mochin and Chayus, and falls asleep, there is no longer a *Yichud* / connection or unification between Z'A and Malchus. When there is no *Da'as* / mind, intention, or Mochin, there is no possibility for unity (אין קישוי אלא לדעת / there is no connectivity except through Da'as). It is important to note that what the Arizal calls *Mochin*, the Baal Shem Tov calls *Chayus*, and they represent the same idea.

This separation between Tiferes or ZA and Malchus is called the *Nesirah* / cosmic severing — and it is by definition a time of great *Din* / judgment, harshness and separation. The Arizal explains that the main reason that Rosh Hashanah is a time of Din is because of this great Nesirah. It is also described as a separation between *Kudsha Brich Hu* / the Holy One Blessed be He and His *Shechinah* / Indwelling Presence. This represents an interruption of the downflow of life to us, Klal Yisrael and humanity in general. In this separation there is the possibility for יניקה לחיצונים / a *Yenikah* / absorbing or 'suckling' of Divine lifeforce by negative 'outside' forces, and Malchus is 'exposed' as it were, with no protection.

When Malchus and Tiferes are back-to-back, there is very little possibility for Yenikah from negative forces. Since their 'backs' are 'touching', there is no place for the *Sitra Achra* to receive energy, and receiving energy from the place of the 'face' is difficult. (Even though there is a minor possibility for the Yenikah to Chitzonim, as their backs are touching, still the entire Hashpa'ah is only from Achorayim, thus it is a state of *Katnus* / smallness.)

When the Mochin of Tiferes is lost, the intelligence, Shefa, and Chayus, from the higher Sefiros (Chochmah-Binah-Da'as) depart, much like when a person goes to sleep and his Mochin departs. In this non-active state of the masculine Sefirah, it cannot unify with Malchus (this can be thought of in anatomical terms in masculine-feminine relations). At this point, Malchus has only Dinim, as there is no flow of blessing coming its way. Although it stays 'alive' through receiving

Mochin from beyond ZA, this separation in fact allows for the building up of the *Partzuf* / persona of Malchus as an 'independent' reality, so that eventually it can stand Panim-el-Panim, in its own right, facing ZA as an equal.

All of the above is what happened on the first Rosh Hashanah; this is therefore the backstory of the creation of the human being. As a cosmic pattern, this also continues to be expressed through the world's continual creation. Every year, in fact, on Rosh Hashanah, there is a renewal of the entire Creation. Then, following each Rosh Hashanah, there is a continuing renewal of Creation, every day, every hour, and every moment; a near-simultaneous returning to the *Tardemah* / slumber of *Ayin* / non-existence and an immediate re-emerging into the wakefulness of *Yesh* / existence. Within the cycle of a day, the time of sleep is a miniature form of the supernal slumber, described above.

So what is the purpose of the Shofar in this process? Essentially, the Shofar is our Divine instrument to draw down new Gadlus, new Mochin, and thus new Chayus, from Chochmah, Binah and Da'as into Tiferes. Through this renewed influx of flow, Tiferes is resuscitated and enlivened and can now reunite with Malchus, but this time in a manner of Panim-el-Panim. In this way, when a new flow of animating force enters into Tiferes from the Mochin of *Aba* / Father / Chochmah and *Ima* / Mother / Binah (and thus Da'as), Tiferes 'wakes up' from the Tardeimah, and 'desires' to become a *Mashpia* / giver again, and to reconnect with Malchus. Drawing Mochin through Tiferes and all the way down into Malchus, allows the fully receptive Malchus to give the Chayus over to physical reality. The Shofar is the medium which initiates and inspires this process.

Let us keep in mind that the actual Mochin of Aba and Ima are always active, and there is a *Zivug Temidi* / constant state of unity between them. This perpetual union is what gives birth to Tiferes or ZA, which in turn generates a flow of Mochin and life force for Malchus. Thus, there is an aspect of the world which constantly exists, whether we do Mitzvos and blow the Shofar, or not. The difference between whether we do or do not blow the Shofar is whether this unity between Malchus and Tiferes remains merely Achor b'Achor, which is not only a Zivug Temidi, but also a *Zivug Chitzoni* / superficial unification, or whether it achieves the status of *Panim el Panim*, also referred to as a *Zivug Penimi* / inner unification.

Rosh Hashanah and the blowing of the Shofar (and all Mitzvos in general) create a deeper Mochin in ZA, so there can be such a Panim-el-Panim connection, resulting in a Zivug Penimi. In other words: our actions and intentions, particularly our performance of Mitzvos, have the power to transform the quality of existence, and to deepen the connection between Creator and creation. This is a fundamental *Yesod* / principle in the teachings of the Arizal.

The three sounds of the Shofar that draw down higher Mochin into Malchus, vivifying all of Creation with a year of life and blessings, correspond to the Avos, the Sefiros of ZA, and the Mochin as such:

Shofar	Avos	Sefirah of ZA	Roots in Mochin
Tekiah	Avraham	Chesed *(right side)*	Chochmah *(right side)*
Shevarim	Yitzchak	Gevurah *(left side)*	Bina *(left side)*
Teru'ah	Yaakov	Tiferes *(central column)*	Da'as *(central column)*

Similarly, the three sets of verses that we recite, Malchiyos, Zichronos and Shofaros, and the blowing of the Shofar that we perform after each set, also correspond to Avraham, Yitzchak and Yaakov.

Malchiyos is connected with Avraham, who revealed Hashem's Presence and kingship in this world. In the words of the Rambam (*Hilchos Avodah Zarah*, 1:3):

ובן ארבעים שנה הכיר אברהם את בוראו. כיון שהכיר וידע התחיל להשיב תשובות על בני אור כשדים ולערוך דין עמהם ולומר שאין זו דרך האמת שאתם הולכים בה ושבר הצלמים והתחיל להודיע לעם שאין ראוי לעבד אלא לאלוה העולם ולו ראוי להשתחוות... והתחיל לעמד ולקרא בקול גדול לכל העולם ולהודיעם שיש שם אלוה אחד לכל העולם ולו ראוי לעבד / "And when Avraham was forty years old he recognized his Creator. After he came to this comprehension and knowledge he started to confute the sons of Ur of the Chaldeans, and to organize disputations with them, cautioning them, saying: 'This is not the true path that you are following,' and he destroyed their images, and commenced preaching to the people warning them that it is not right to worship any save the G-d

of the universe, and unto Him alone it is right to bow down....
There he stood up anew and called out in a great voice to the
whole world, to let them know that there is One G-d for the
whole universe, and unto Him it is proper to render service."

Yitzchak, 'whose ashes are a remembrance forever', is connected with *Zichronos* / remembrances.

Yaakov is connected to *Shofaros*, as Chazal use a word that
has the same root as *Shofar*, when speaking of Yaakov: שופריה
דיעקב אבינו מעין שופריה דאדם הראשון / "The beauty of Yaakov
our forefather is a semblance of the beauty (*Shufra*) of Adam"
(*Bava Basra*, 58a).

With the blowing of these three sounds within the three
sets of 'the Standing Shofar', we are drawing down into the
world Chesed (Avraham — rooted in Chochmah), Gevurah
(Yitzchak — rooted in Binah), and Yaakov (Tiferes, rooted in
Da'as). And once ZA, meaning 'Kudsha Brich Hu' or Hashem,
is in an 'active' mode and has Mochin, He comes into a state of
Panim / direct relationship with Malchus, which is His bride,
Klal Yisrael. The Shofar also makes sure that our Panim is facing the Panim of Kudshah Brich Hu, and that we, Malchus,
are therefore Panim-el-Panim with Hashem, and in a conscious relationship with the Source of our life and blessings.

Regarding Matan Torah it says, פנים בפנים דבר ה' עמכם / *Panim-el-Panim Diber Hashem Imachem*, "Hashem spoke to you
face to face" (*Devarim*, 5:4). This was a time of ישקני מנשיקות פיהו
/ "Kiss me with the kisses of Your mouth" (*Shir haShirim*, 1:2),

the peak and *Tachlis* / purpose of Creation, a full revelation of HaKadosh Baruch Hu's intended conscious, covenantal relationship with Klal Yisrael. This Panim-el-Panim relationship continues when we do the will of the Creator, illustrated by the fact that when Klal Yisrael were in alignment with Hashem's will, the Keruvim on the *Aron haBris* / Ark of the Covenant turned "face-to-face" (*Bava Basra*, 99a). Or as the *Zohar* (*Zohar Chadash*, 1, 79a) teaches, "When Yisrael were of one heart with Hashem, then we were in a posture of *Panim-el-Panim Diber Hashem*; when we were not, we were on the level of *Achorayim* (Achor b'Achor)."

Whereas Creation, on its own, is sustained continuously through a mere Achor b'Achor dynamic, through our acceptance of the Torah and blowing the Shofar on Rosh Hashanah, we ensure that the Chayus that flows into this world is coming through a Panim-el-Panim dynamic, with love.

As the parts reflect the whole, this cosmic dynamic applies to our own lives as well. After the Nesirah, the Shofar draws down Mochin into Tiferes, so that Tiferes is 'awakened' and ready to be Mashpia, face-to-face — and we too (the micro-Malchus, the other 'face' in the face-to-face relationship) need to become 'awakened' through the sounds of the Shofar. We too need to be enlivened with the new Mochin and Chayus that are flowing into the world on Rosh Hashanah.

In blowing the Shofar, heat and vapor emanate along with our breath. Heat is the element of fire, vapor is the element of water, and the breath itself is the element of wind — also termed 'air'. Water is a manifestation of Chesed (rooted in Chochmah). Fire is a manifestation of Gevurah (rooted in Binah), and wind is a manifestation of Tiferes (rooted in Da'as). As we blow these three primal elements into the Shofar, we are also blowing these three emotional Sefiros, and their three roots within Mochin, into Malchus.

Our blowing of the Shofar, as the Zohar writes, awakens not only our own 'Shofar', which is our 'Malchus', it also awakens the Shofar Above, which is the Divine 'breath' of Binah (and Chochmah and Da'as) as it flows into Tiferes. In other words, our Shofar blowing below draws down into our Malchus the Chesed, Gevurah and Tiferes from Above, by stimulating their roots in supernal Chochmah-Binah-Da'as to be *Mashpia* / bestowing life force through the 'Divine Shofar' of Tiferes.

This double act of Shofar (drawing Tiferes into Malchus below and stimulating the Mochin to be Mashpia into Tiferes Above) is alluded to in the Medrash (*Sifri*, Beha'alosecha, Piska 19): "The Shofar is the sound of freedom... But we do not know who blows. Says the verse, 'Hashem Elokim with a Shofar will blow'" (*Zecharyah*, 9:14). In other words, Hashem, the Creator of all life, is blowing the Shofar from Above *through* our Shofar blowing, and we are drawing His life-giving breath into our lifebreath as we blow the Shofar. As mentioned earlier, the Shofar is a spiritual *Kaneh* / pipe through which we draw down Eternal Light from Above.

❹
Chesed, Gevurah
and Tiferes
are drawn
down
into Malchus
and into our breath
and our
Shofar blasts

←

❸
Chochmah, Binah
and Da'as are awak-
ened and flow down
into Chesed, Ge-
vurah and Tiferes
(which correspond
with our fire, water
and wind)

↓

↑

❶
We, the representative
of Malchus, blow the
shofar, below

→

❷
Our fire, water
and wind
'rise' Above

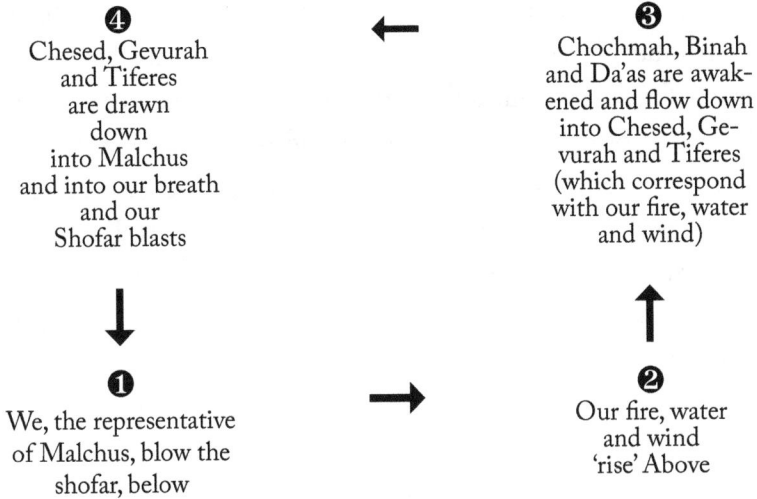

All of this means that we draw down 'new Mochin' into the actual Shofar that we hold in our hands on Rosh Hashanah, and then broadcast it out into the world, invigorating and transforming the quality of Creation. The three basic sounds that we blow also evoke this influx: Chochmah and Chesed are drawn down through the Tekiah, Binah and Gevurah are drawn down through the Shevarim, and Da'as and Tiferes are drawn down through the Teru'ah (and Shevarim). Then, when these Shofar sounds cycle back above, they stimulate the Mochin to flow down into ZA (Tiferes) again, so that it can become 'awakened' in order to connect intimately with Malchus — our world, thereby giving birth to blessings and new life. This cosmic circuit repeats with each set of Shofar sounds, intensifying until every atom of space-time-consciousness is overwhelmingly saturated with vitality and blessing.

In a more detailed view of this process, the full structure of the Shofar blowing is nine sounds (or ten sounds if the Shevarim-Teru'ah is counted as two). To review, we need to blow three Teru'os and every Teru'ah sound must have a Tekiah before and after. Since we do not know what the Teru'ah is, we blow a plain Teru'ah, a Shevarim and a Shevarim-Teru'ah, totaling nine sounds. These sounds correspond to the nine Sefiros, which are drawn down into Malchus with the Shofar blowing:

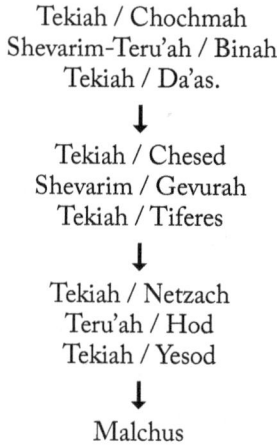

Tekiah / Chochmah
Shevarim-Teru'ah / Binah
Tekiah / Da'as.

↓

Tekiah / Chesed
Shevarim / Gevurah
Tekiah / Tiferes

↓

Tekiah / Netzach
Teru'ah / Hod
Tekiah / Yesod

↓

Malchus

A full order of Shofar blasts is 30 sounds (three sets of ten, each with their Shevarim-Teru'ah counted as two sounds). This structure corresponds to the fact that we draw down Mochin from the highest realm of Atzilus into the three lower worlds, Beriah, Yetzirah and Asiyah.

These three worlds, in turn, correspond to the ideas of 1) *Rosh* / 'beginning' or *Penimi* / internal dimension, 2) *Toch* / 'middle' or intermediary dimension, and 3) *Sof* / 'end' or *Chitzoni* / external dimension. In the human body there are also three such levels, each with ten 'Sefiros'. When we blow the Shofar, we draw Mochin down into every dimension of our life, even into the lowest of the ten levels of our physical body.

Nefesh Elokis / Divine soul — our "internal" dimension, with its ten levels

Nefesh Behamis / animal soul — our "intermediary" dimension (subconscious mind), with its ten qualities

Guf / body — the "end" or lowest dimension, with its ten parts (the body itself is a map of the Ten Sefiros).

This is the basic outline and *K'li* / vessel of the Arizal's vision and explanation for the process that is initiated with the blowing of the Shofar. Now we need to delve more deeply into its *Ohr* / light and corresponding *Avodah* / practical inner work, so that we can experience it ourselves.

THE OHR AND AVODAH OF SHOFAR BLOWING

To better understand the structure that the Arizal revealed in a more 'inspirational' and practical way, we first need to examine the hints of that structure within the Torah itself. More specifically, we need to take a deeper look at the narrative of the creation of the human being in a way that relates to the deeper mysteries of Rosh Hashanah, the birthday of mankind. The creation of Adam and Chavah is a master template that unites the Kabbalistic structures above with our own personal Avodah. This way, from the microcosm (the creation of the human being) we can better understand the macrocosm (the abstract, cosmic teaching of the Arizal) — and from the abstract teaching we can more easily derive practical advice for our Avodah and daily life. Ultimately all of the teachings of the Torah are one — it is, as the sages say, *Toras Achas* / a single, unified, integral Divine teaching (Inyan Echad. Tosefta, *Sanherdrin*, 7:5).

There are two ways the Torah describes the creation of the original man and woman. In Chapter One of *Bereishis*, the Torah relates how Adam and Chavah were created with one body, half male and half female: "And Elokim created man in His image; in the image of Elokim He created him; male and female He created them" (*Bereishis*, 1:27). This means that the male and female dimensions of the human being were created as one body with two 'faces' or sides, which were back-to-back (דו פרצופין נבראו : *Eiruvin*, 18a-b. *Berachos*, 61a. *Medrash Rabbah*, Bereishis, 8:1). This is a depiction of the Arizal's teaching of being Achor b'Achor.

In Chapter Two of Bereishis, there is a seemingly contradictory story. Hashem says, "It is not good that man is alone; I shall make him a helpmate opposite him" (2:18). Was not Chavah already created? And was she not with him and he with her? What does it mean that the man was "alone"?

"...So Hashem Elokim cast a deep sleep upon the man, and while he slept, He took one of his ribs (or 'sides' — namely the feminine side) and closed up the flesh at that spot. And Hashem Elokim fashioned the side that He had taken from the man into a woman; and He brought her to the man." Here, it appears that Chavah was created from Adam — yet in Chapter One, they were already referred to as "them," with the understanding that Adam and Chavah were integral parts of a single being.

In Chapter One, Adam-Chavah are created as one being by *Elokim* — the Divine Power that creates nature and vests Itself in nature. In this scenario, Adam-Chavah are natural 'parts' of each other, and parts of their surrounding environment, almost like an unselfconscious animal, or a single plant with two opposite-facing blossoms.

In Chapter Two there is a completely different story of their creation, almost as if the first story had not happened. "And *Hashem*-Elokim formed man of dust from the ground, and He breathed into his nostrils the soul of life, and man became a living soul" (2:7). In this scenario, Adam and Chavah are created as fully 'human', with the ability to speak and communicate. Thus, at the outset, they are invested with 'soul', something that sets them apart from their natural environment; as their souls come from the Divine "breath," this part of them is otherworldly, and as such not part of Creation or nature as we know it. Furthermore, the Name *Hashem*, the Transcendent dimension of Divinity, is mentioned in this version of creation, not only the Name *Elokim,* as in Chapter One:

"And *Elokim* said, 'Let us make man in Our image, after Our likeness, and they shall rule over the fish of the sea and over the fowl of the heaven and over the animals and over all the earth and over all the creeping things that creep upon the earth.' And *Elokim* created man in His image; in the image of *Elokim* He created him; male and female He created them" (1:26-27).

In Chapter Two, it is "*Hashem Elokim*" who blows into Adam's nostrils a breath of life. The Name Hashem, sometimes called 'the Tetragrammaton', is made up of four Hebrew letters: Yud, Hei, Vav, and Hei. These four letters can be rearranged and permuted to spell the words *Hayah* / was, *Hoveh* / is, *Yihyeh* / will be. They can also be read as *Yud-HoVeH. Hoveh* / 'is' means the present, and the Yud transforms that word into a 'continuous act' (Rashi, *Iyov,* 1:5. *Tanya,* Sha'ar Yichud v'haEmunah, 4). In this way, *Yud-HoVeH* means 'Eternally Present '. This is the attribute of the breath transmitted from the *Penimiyus* / 'inside' of Hashem to the Penimiyus of the human being, allowing us to be consciously present in the 'now', and to 'begin again' at any moment, for it is always eternally now, no matter what time it is.

"In (with) the beginning, Elokim created" (1:1). Elokim "created" the world, in the *past tense.* Yet Hashem is the Creator in the *present tense* (*Kedushas Levi,* Bereishis). Conscious presence is only available in the world of *Sheim Hashem* / the Name

Hashem. Free choice and Teshuvah are also only possible in the world of *Sheim Hashem*. If we have deviated from who we are and what we are meant to be doing in this world, we can return to presence and begin again, because our beginning as humans was the breath of the Eternally Present One.

In the world of *Elokim*, everything is absolute and linear. Animals and plants do not wield free choice. They are created in the mode of cause and effect.

What does it mean to be human? Originally, Adam and Chavah were created as one, *Achor b'Achor*. They were attached or merged with each other, but did not encounter each other as complete beings unto themselves. Wherever one moved, the other moved as well. Theirs was always a 'one-sided discussion' or relationship. It was, in the above language of the Arizal, a *Zivug Temidi* / constant connection, and a *Zivug Chitzoni* / superficial relationship, as there was no real genuine encounter with the 'other', in all of their uniqueness.

This state mirrors Creation as a whole, which was created and nourished from *Sheim Elokim* / the Name Elokim. *Elokim* refers to the attribute of Judgment, and the speech of a judge is a one sided conversation. The Divine Judge sets the rules of Creation, and all of Creation does exactly as told in that world of judgment and order. A lion hunts to eat, and an elephant grazes. At all times nature performs the will and patterns set forth by its Creator.

In terms of a back-to-back relationship, it is the *Mashpia*, the 'active' male, that moves and the *Mekabel*, the 'passive' female, follows him: "The male walks first" (*Berachos*, 61a). This is perhaps why the singular being of Adam-Chavah is sometimes termed "him" in the Torah. In terms of our relationship with HaKadosh Baruch Hu in the world of Sheim Elokim, He is the Mashpia and we are the Mekabel; we just move as He wants. In this stage of development, we are not yet full human beings with free choice; like an animal or plant, we cannot fall or stray from our path, and neither can we do Teshuvah, change our ways, or even consciously choose to get close to HaKadosh Baruch Hu. We simply are what we already are, there is no becoming, only being.

In an Achor b'Achor relationship with Hashem, as it were, we are like lions who automatically hunt zebra, and like the tree who automatically blossoms with the spring rains. Everything within us functions exactly as it was created. Nothing deviates from its original intention and there are no arguments — there is no possibility for a lion to choose to take a vacation from hunting.

There is also no *Cheishek* / yearning for something more, and correspondingly, there is no *Ya'eir Hashem Panav Eilecha* / "Hashem will illuminate His Face for you" in this paradigm. The Light of the Divine Face cannot be appreciated because the *Hashpa'ah* / giving of it is in a *Bechinah* / paradigm of *Achorayim* / facing away. There is no 'free will', on either side of this relationship, as it were. And there is no 'romantic' yearning of opposites being attracted to each other, as there are no opposites or others.

This is why Hashem (not Elokim) says, "It is not good that Adam is alone; I shall make him a helpmate opposite him" (2:18).

On the level of 'nature', Adam is not alone, as Chavah is physically with him. And Chavah is not alone, as Adam is physically with her. However, as they become more fully human they realize that they are in fact spiritually, mentally and emotionally alone. The nature of a human being is to be in a conscious, face-to-face relationship with another, and hence as they grew into their full humanity, they observed this inner lack within themselves. In their initial state of creation (Elokim), there is not yet an 'other' or 'helpmate' that is 'opposite' them. As they receive the Divine Breath of Life (from Hashem), they suddenly yearn to meet and truly encounter each other.

Creation in general mirrors this dynamic of human relationship with one another and with their Creator. Until the end of Chapter One, there is only one voice and one choice; that of the Creator. On the other hand, the Creator's intention in Creating the universe was to create an 'other' who could have a relationship with Hashem, and be a co-partner in creating and perfecting the world. This 'other' comes into being through the Name and Breath of Hashem.

As such, Hashem puts Adam (who, at this junction, is both

male and female) to sleep, and creates a *Nesirah* / separation, 'sawing' the one person into two. "And in the seventh hour Eve becomes his wife" (*Sanhedrin*, 38b). She becomes his *Kenegdo*, literally someone who is "against him" or facing him. Like a surgery in which the patient is 'put under', this sleep state was needed for the parting to be accomplished.

Once the first *Yichud* / unity, the Zivug Tamidi, is broken and there are two separate people, then there can be a higher level of Yichud: one that is consciously chosen. One becomes two in order to become One. "Therefore a man shall leave his father and mother, and cleave to his wife, and become as one flesh." This command and prediction "therefore man...as one flesh" is for both men and women (*Sanhedrin*, 57b).

'Leaving one's father and mother and cleaving to one's soul-mate' is another depiction of moving from a Yichud Chitzoni to a Yichud Penimi. The type of longing one has for his or her fiancée is not like one's love for their parents. If one grew up with their parents, there were probably times when the connection was taken for granted or even tested. In a mature parental relationship, the love is natural and calm. Until some point in life one might in fact feel as if they are a mere extension of their parents. It is a Zivug Temidi, much like Adam and Chavah before the Nesirah, but it is not a genuine, face-to-face encounter. Although through adolescence, a child gradually becomes their own individual, and the individuation process is hopefully completed when a person is able to "leave" their parents and join with an 'other', an 'opposite', a partner in a deep face-to-face relationship. Now they can work toward developing and maintaining a relationship that is *Panim-el-Panim* / face-to-face. They can truly encounter each other, and see the *Ohr* / light of the other's face.

As Adam-Chavah have only one body in their initial stage of creation, it means that *ZA*, the masculine aspect of the Sefiros, and 'Malchus' or *Nukva* / the feminine, are Achor b'Achor. Although they are outwardly one, there is an inner *Gevul* / boundary between them, keeping them isolated and truly "alone." At some point, Hashem sees that it is no longer good for a human being to be 'alone' as a constantly unified self; such an unconscious state of identification has served a temporary purpose, but now they each need to rise to their own potential through free choice.

Adam/ZA needs to awaken to something outside of himself, and be invigorated with the Mochin that will cause him to desire reunification on a more mature level. In order to achieve this deeper and higher unity, he must work to refine or evolve his unconscious patterns and hidden boundary issues, and heal from his current sense of separation and isolation.

Chavah/Nukva had needed to separate from her passive dependency on ZA and develop as an individual of her own. She would not be able to rise to her potential if she remained a mere extension, or in the image of our sages, like "Adam's tail," his appendage. Now that she is separate and on her own, she can grow by being a "help against him," a conscious partner with power of her own, who uses her power to benefit the 'other'. The clear cut roles of who leads and who follows in such a relationship have now become more complex and interdependent, requiring ever greater presence, sensitivity, and respect from and for each partner. She can thus only help him develop emotionally, mentally and spiritually by being face-to-face with him, where he can recognize who she really is:

"Then the man said, 'This one, at last, is bone of my bones and flesh of my flesh...'" (2:23)! This recognition of the reality of the 'other' is a new infusion of *Mochin* / consciousness into Adam, who is ZA. Now he is 'awake' and 'enlivened' and is able to unite with Chavah/Malchus on a much higher level, and together they can give birth to a new family and a new era. Through their separation and reunion they have experienced a 'redemption' of sorts.

FINITE BEING IS REVEALED FOLLOWING THE TZIMTZUM OF INFINITY

Beyond the process of human individuation and maturation, this process of moving from Achor b'Achor, into a state of Nesirah, and then finally to Panim-el-Panim, is a reflection of the cosmic event of creation as well. Before the Tzimtzum, the contraction of the Infinite Light, only Infinity was revealed, and the *Koach haGevul* / power of finite boundaries was included (but unexpressed) within the Ein Sof, the Infinite, as if in a state of Achor b'Achor. In other words, there was a Koach haGevul within the Creator, but before the Tzimtzum of the

Infinite Light, this finite Light of Gevul was completely subsumed and overwhelmed within the Infinite Light — like a child being subsumed in the wills and desires of their parents, with no separate, revealed will of their own.

The Nesirah is the Tzimtzum, the separation between the *Koach haGevul* / power of limitation and *Koach haBilti Gevul* / power of being without limit. This allows for the creation of a revealed *Ohr haGevul* / light of limitation and eventually for creation itself. In this way, the possibility for a "face-to-face relationship with HaKadosh Baruch Hu" would be present within creation, as this was the original desire that initiated the creative process in the first place.

THE NESIRAH AND ADAM
NOT WAITING UNTIL SHABBOS

Before the Nesirah — as the Arizal explains (*Sha'ar haKavanos*, Inyan Rosh Hashanah, Derush Aleph), Nukva, Malchus, was not a full Partzuf. At that time, Nukva only had 'one point'; was only one-dimensional, as it were, and not yet 'her' own 'person'. In order for Nukva to become a full *Partzuf* / structure, Nukva needs to separate from her Achor b'Achor dynamic with ZA, and become an independent Partzuf; this is achieved by completing the process begun through the Nesirah.

Before the Nesirah Nukva needed to be Achor b'Achor because she could not expose her back, her level of Achorayim. This is because the Yenikah for Chitzoniyim is from the back side; spiritual danger lurks in what is 'behind' one's attention, the place of the subconscious mind and the 'unexpected'. As Kelipah can take hold in the Achorayim, Nukva derives (and provides) security by remaining fused with ZA.

Once Adam-Chavah Davened for the grass to grow (*Chulin*, 60b), they had the *Kelim* / vessels or capacity to ensure that there would be no 'unexpected' leeching or siphoning of their spiritual energy and awareness by the Chitzonim. They were more protected from the danger of exposing their hidden side to the elements. Their yearning for self-expression and true relationship grew until finally it came time for the Nesirah. Adam/Chavah was put to sleep and Chavah separated from him, creating the possibility for a Panim-el-Panim relationship. In the process, they each become a full Partzuf, an independent being, with free choice, who each desires to be connected with the other.

In the next Chapter of the Torah, only a couple verses later, Adam and Chavah use their nascent free choice to eat from the Tree of Da'as, lowering themselves into the world of the duality of good and evil, light and dark. In the language of the Arizal, "One sin led to the next," and Adam ended up being intimate with Chavah on Friday afternoon, a weekday, before Shabbos, a day of unity, which would have been the more appropriate time for them to be together. This act created even more harsh judgment. This Friday, the same day they were created, was and is the First Day of Rosh Hashanah, which is characterized by *Dina Kasha* / harsh judgment.

Adam and Chavah were not patient enough to wait for the right time to have intimate relations. If they had waited, their Zivug would have been on Shabbos, the Second Day of Rosh Hashanah, which is characterized by *Dina Rafia* / weak judgment. Because they did not wait, they and the world remained in a condition of Nesirah for 21 days, and their first proper Zivug finally happened on the holy day of Shemini Atzeres. As a result, ever since then, we too must follow the same process and wait for our full unification and Yichud with Hashem until Shemini Atzeres, rather than the second day of Rosh Hashanah.

Yom Kippur and Sukkos are therefore stages of preparation for this Zivug. Yom Kippur represents the stage called שמאלו תחת ראשי / "Your left hand is under my head." Sukkos represents the stage called וימינו תחבקני / "Your right hand embraces me"(*Shir haShirim*, 8:3. *Sha'ar haKavanos*, Derushei Chag haSukos, Derush 4). This embrace is a hug, manifest in the walls/arms of the Sukkah that enfolds us within it. Hoshanah Rabbah is the stage of *Neshikin* / kisses. These 'kisses' are manifest in the Aravos, which are shaped like lips (*Medrash Rabbah*, Vayikra, 30:14), and when we slap the Aravos on the ground it is like them "kissing" the earth, and it also causes the "lips" of the Aravos to "kiss" each other with great passion and friction. Shemini Atzeres, the culmination of the holy days, is the day of the Zivug (as the *Zohar* (1, 64b) tells us, we are בלחודוי עם מלכא / "alone with the King").

On Rosh Hashanah we celebrate our birthday, the day Hashem says to us, 'Today I have created you, and I did so because I would love to have a Panim-el-Panim relationship with you. I want to look at you and to really *see* you, to know you; and I want you to really know Me.' Kudsha Brich Hu yearns for a Yichud Penimi with us. Because of our act of impatience on the day we were created, we are not yet ready for such a Yichud for another 21 days, on Shemini Atzeres. We must refine and prepare ourselves for such a holy and profound unification.

On Rosh Hashanah it is revealed that Hashem desires to have a face-to-face relationship with Creation, and for this reason, Hashem created the human being, and specifically the man of Chapter Two. This version of the human is not only created b'Tzelem Elokim, like the human in Chapter One, he is also endowed with a Neshamah from Hashem, Who "blew into his nostrils a breath of life." Certainly, Adam-Chavah were already alive in Chapter One; what does it mean then that they only received a breath of life in Chapter Two? "He who blows, blows from his essence" (*Zohar.* See Tanya, 2). As breath originates from the deepest recesses within the blower, Adam-Chavah were filled with the 'Essence' of Hashem within them. Our body is formed *b'Tzelem Elokim*, but our soul is created *b'Etzem Hashem*.

On Rosh Hashanah, *ZA / Zeir Anpin*, a term for *Kudsha Brich Hu /* the Holy Blessed One, wants to have a Panim-el-Panim relationship with us, Malchus. Such an authentic, honest relationship requires a partner who has a sense of independence, a being with the ability to freely choose. Because of this, Tiferes, which is also connected with the Name of Hashem (each of the Names of Hashem are connected with different Sefiros, and the Name Hashem is connected with Tiferes), 'goes to sleep'. This allows us, the *Nukva* / feminine, Malchus, to 'detach' and become a full Partzuf, an independent entity. Through this separation, there is a grave risk of *Yenikah* / parasitic diversion of life force into *Chitzonim* / superficialities, such as atheism, heresy, egomania, or harmful addictions, etc. All of these are risks and byproducts of the potential for free choice. Kudsha Brich Hu of course knows all of this, but feels the Nesirah is worth it, *Keviyachol* / as it were, since there is now a possibility for a real face-to-face encounter, a Zivug Penimi.

In fact, it is not enough to be endowed with a Tzelem Elokim, an image of the Divine Ruler of the world of nature, physicality and multiplicity. The Name *Elo-him* can be read as *E-l* / power over, *Heim* / them, the many. But then, *VaYipach Hashem* / "Hashem blew into him" a higher life, a state of independence and self-sovereignty. We are from that moment no longer a mere natural, physical being, another member of the animal world, a mindless being who only follows their instincts and inbred tendencies. We now have a Neshamah, a Divine soul. We now have the ability to be a 'creator' of our life, to be like The Creator (as it were) — with "infinite" abilities, including, most importantly, the ability to overcome our innate and instinctive nature, and to go beyond our defined self. We are now a fitting 'soulmate' for Kudsha Brich Hu, as it were.

Now that the night of Rosh Hashanah has passed, and we are an independent being imbued with freewill, the way we connect with HaKadosh Baruch Hu is by expressing our deepest yearning and desire to be face-to-face. The cry of the Shofar gives voice to this sweet and sorrowful longing of the soul.

On an interpersonal level, sadly, there can be situations in which a person is living with the potential for face-to-face connection, and yet, they still feel the deepest loneliness and disconnection. For instance, sometimes couples live in the same physical space, share many viewpoints, preferences and experiences, yet they both live in a state of devastating loneliness. Beyond all the superficial "connections" they may share with their partner, they still long for a deeper, more authentic relationship; for all they really want is for the other to look at them and truly *see* them for who they really are.

You may be a very 'obedient' spouse, taking out the garbage when asked, shopping, cooking, earning a reasonable salary and even pampering your partner ; in fact, you may be an 'attractive' life partner in many ways, but if you never take the time to become fully present and receptive with your spouse, if you never see or deeply hear them, he or she will forever feel alone.

A Panim-el-Panim relationship is the best gift we can give to one another — both to a human 'other', and to our Creator. In a human-Divine paradigm, when we are 'back-to-back' with Hashem, both parties feel estranged and inaccessible. When we are face-to-face, there is tangible closeness for both partners. Hashem 'yearns' to have a genuine relationship with us, where we 'see' Hashem, (as if), as *Elokim Chayim* / the Living G-d; vivid, passionate, real and personal.

Again, to turn from back-to-back to face-to-face, there first needs to be a desire for *Teshuvah* / turning around. But this desire necessitates a 'falling asleep', followed by a 'separation'. Imagine two people who are as if attached to each other 'back-to-back' (metaphorically of course), who now wish to encounter each other face-to-face. To achieve this transformation and maturation, they first need to forget, or 'fall asleep to', what they think they know about each other. They need to let go of *how* they 'know' each other, because they really do not *know* each other. There is no Mochin; no real awareness or understanding of the other. Nor is there any Chayus; no presence, vitality, passion or depth of love. As painful or counter-intuitive as it might seem, to create a healthy and genuine relationship, they must first *move away* from each other so that they can subsequently turn around to face each other.

The night of Rosh Hashanah is the night of the Supernal slumber, the cosmic 'sleep' that allows for the necessary next stage of separation, the Nesirah. On our microcosmic level, our old self is no longer, but our new self has still not yet begun. To progress, there first needs to be an even further movement away, and here is where the primordial wound lies. Think about the painful years of post-childhood, the age of adolescence. It can be a painful time both for the parents and for the children, as they are moving 'away' from each other, often without a clear sense of direction, compelled by a blind desire deep within. G-d willing, after letting go of each other, they can, in time, return to each other and form a mature and genuine, face-to-face relationship.

SPIRAL STAIRCASE

The Alter Rebbe once said *(Sefer haMa'amarim*, Tav / Kuf / Samach / Hei)* that what the Arizal taught in Eitz Chayim, the Baal Shem Tov was able to put into a *Mashal* / metaphor. The metaphor of the Baal Shem in the present discussion (see *Ohr haTorah* [Magid], Ekev), is a spiral staircase (*Shevindel* / spiral, *Trep* / steps. "A winding staircase, and that is called in our language... *Shevindel Steing*": Rashi, *Melachim* 1, 6:8), in which every landing and every step seems to move away from the goal. We want to climb to the next floor, but we keep moving at an angle that seems to point toward a door or window. Only faith in the process of climbing allows us not to give up or turn back. With persistence, we eventually find ourselves at the top. We seemed to move away only to actually come closer and climb higher.

The Alter Rebbe offers a parable for this feeling of separation and the corresponding desire for an authentic relationship. A father decides to test the love and wisdom of his child. He hides himself, in order to entice the child to actively seek and find him (*Likutei Torah*, Devarim, 82a). This is the purpose of the Nesirah, the turning around and 'finding' each other, the moving away which paradoxically allows us to get closer.

Another example is brought by the Rebbe Rashab (*Sefer ha-Ma'amarim*, Tav/Reish/Ayin/Zayin, p. 9) from the Medrash (*Medrash Rabbah*, Shir haShirim, 2:2). There was once a king who had an only child, a daughter, whom he loved dearly. The king really wanted to know her loyalty and what she really thinks of him, so he told his servant to sneak up on her and surprise her. When he did so, she began to scream, "Father, father, save me!" Our King in Heaven wants to hear what is really in our hearts, our deepest cries and yearnings, and upon Whom we really depend. He wants us to reach out to Him, and say, 'Hashem, only You can save me,' 'Hashem help me.' The hiding or the seeming peril is but a ruse to draw out this yearning cry of the child to his or her Parent. This is the deep longing that is aroused through the process of Nesirah.

The Night of Rosh Hashanah is the night of 'sleep' and Nesirah. Then, in the morning, we 'cry out' with the Shofar, the cry of the pain of Teshuvah, which arouses the strength within us to attain a face-to-face orientation. In this 'hiding' of the first night of Rosh Hashanah, we recognize that it is our Father Who is hiding, and we too pine to be reunited with Him, to see and be seen in the Light of His Face.

In the act of blowing the Shofar two things are occurring (as explored earlier, the Shofar has both the element of humility or Teshuvah, and the element of confidence or empowerment). On one level there is an expression of humble Teshuvah. This is the crying, moaning of the Shofar, expressing a climactic desire to return, to turn around to see Hashem, as it were . On another level, the Shofar blowing is already an enactment of an actual face-to-face encounter in which we are the ones 'empowering' the Master of the Universe as King. In this second paradigm, the Nesirah happens at night. Then in the morning, when we blow the new year into existence, we are acknowledging our Panim-el-Panim relationship with the Creator. We are thus already acting within a paradigm of Panim-el-Panim; we are facing the King, and blowing the horn to proclaim His Sovereignty.

This cry from below arouses the Shofar Above, drawing new Mochin (Chochmah, Binah and Da'as) into Tiferes, activating and enabling it to unify with Malchus, who is now a full *Partzuf* / 'face', ready to both receive and respond.

In terms of our personal Avodah, what actually creates the Panim-el-Panim reality is the cry of pain itself, the regret of the actions and mindsets that caused the separation, or made it necessary. This awakens our higher consciousness and motivates us to make Teshuvah, to 'turn around' toward HaKadosh Baruch Hu and to seek a face-to-face relationship with Him, a real partnership and collaboration.

HASHEM AS MELECH

On Rosh Hashanah, Hashem is crowned as a *Melech* / king, not merely a *Moshel* / ruler. A Moshel is a forced, top-down dictatorship, a one way relationship: "The ruler says, and the mountain is uprooted." This means, whatever the Ruler says will be or should be. Hashem, however, wants to be a Melech in the context of "There is no king without subjects." Conscious subjects empower a king and make him 'real'. A Melech is elected by the subjects by their own uncoerced choosing. This is ultimately what Hashem wants and desires from us.

We are trusted to release our grip and, on our own volition, to leave the confines of the Achor b'Achor relationship experienced by all animals, plants, and every other being created with the Name Elokim. We are empowered to choose to enter a deeper, face-to-face relationship with our Creator, to lovingly make Hashem our King and the King of the Universe.

While the desire to connect with Hashem may become strong, and the yearning to become One with Him may become difficult to bear, we also need to ensure that the Zivug happens in the correct time: "I adjure you... do not awaken or arouse Love until it is desirable" (*Shir haShirim*, 2:7, 3:5). We need to be patient and ensure that Malchus is prepared, meaning that our *Keilim* / vessels are strong enough to maintain their integrity in the midst of un-unification with the Transcendence of ZA. This is an important issue on a 'cosmic' level, and also on a personal level, with regard to our own Malchus.

In the more down-to-earth context of a couple, if one spouse is not strong enough in personality or self-confidence, they may be swallowed or overwhelmed by the other. They may 'break' and be consumed within the overbearing presence of the other. The Panim el-Panim relationship may then collapse in a way that is difficult to rebuild.

Waiting until the right time is the inner idea of *Binyan haMalchus* / building up Malchus. When Malchus is built up and strengthened, when she is able to assert her own personality and free choice, then she can withstand the Zivug, and there can be a healthy, sustainable, and fruitful unity. Conversely, when Tiferes is refined, he can be sensitive to the needs of the other, and proactively create space for Malchus, rather than unconsciously eclipsing Malchus all the time. This is a relational application of the cosmic function of Tzimtzum.

Aseres Yemei Teshuvah / the Ten Days of Teshuvah are ten days from the beginning of Rosh Hashanah through the end of Yom Kippur. These are ten days of Binyan haMalchus. Since Malchus, the K'li, has within it ten dimensions, these ten days correspond to the ten Sefiros, starting on Rosh Hashanah with Malchus of Malchus, and concluding on Yom Kippur, with Keser of Malchus.

On Rosh Hashanah we are like a person who knows someone else our entire life or many years, and then one day we realize that they are our Bashert, the person we should marry. The first step is coming before the other and humbly confessing, "I don't know why I was so blind, you were here all along, I just did not realize it, I did not recognize you." The other says, "I actually love you too, but first you need to face the fact that you ignored me and even embarrassed me many times over the years. Give me some time; if you can consistently act in a way that builds my trust, then we can move forward." On Rosh Hashanah we turn to Hashem and proclaim, "It is You Whom

I have been seeking all my life, I'm sorry I have been so blind, I didn't even look at You!" Hashem says, "Of course, I love you too, but we need to wait a little while; if you really want to have this genuine and face-to-face relationship, get rid of your negative baggage, open your eyes, and show Me that you are capable and committed to a mature love."

Throughout the Aseres Yemei Teshuvah we build up our ability to demonstrate our sincere love for Hashem.* Once the day of Yom Kippur is complete, Hashem gives us a big hug in the form of the Sukkah, and finally on Shemini Atzeres we consummate the relationship in a healthy, balanced way.

Today, we live in a postlapsarian world. We expect instant gratification in everything, including even our spiritual service. We are therefore liable to try and experience Zivug even on Rosh Hashanah, even though it is certainly too early. Yet, the process of Binyan Malchus will only be complete after passing through the purifying process of Yom Kippur, Sukkos, Hoshanah Rabbah and Shemini Atzeres. If we are too impatient to go through the refining process and perform all the prayers and Mitzvos, if we just want to jump to the gratification at the end of the journey, we will not have developed our vessels, and

---

* Also, between the end of Rosh Hashanah and the beginning of Yom Kippur there are seven days. Each of these days, says the Arizal, corresponds to another day of the week of the past year. Our service on the Sunday between Rosh Hashanah and Yom Kippur has the power to make up for all the Sundays of the past year, and so on.

the unification will not be sustained nor will it produce the fruit of a true Panim-el-Panim relationship.

WHY IS ROSH HASHANAH CELEBRATED ON HUMANITY'S BIRTHDAY?

Up until the arrival of the human being, all of Creation was in a state of Achor b'Achor; the lion, the tree, the sun, all move and function exactly as Hashem, their Creator wants them to. The human being, however, has an unprecedented power: free choice, the ability to step back, to see the big picture and to 'edit' the arc of his life. This power allowed the human being to move away from the Creator, in order to encounter the Creator more consciously, Panim-el-Panim. And this was the very intention of Creation. The nature of the Creator is to bestow goodness, and in order to truly bestow goodness, there must be someone to face Him, to 'see' Him, and to appreciatively receive that goodness. Without a recipient, there can be no gift.

On a deeper level, the ultimate goodness Hashem bestowed upon us is the ability to become like the Source of that goodness, meaning, to be like the Creator, as it were. This is what it means to be created and vested with a soul, to have the power to freely choose, and in this case, to freely choose to be in a collaborative relationship with the Source of all Goodness.

The Creator is like a host who wants only to serve His guests. However, there is no pleasure for such a host in serving guests who are ungrateful or unaware of what they are receiving. Thus the gift we can 'give' to the Creator is not merely to receive goodness from Him in a back-to-back relationship, but to 'give back' to the Creator by turning around to face Him, to give thanks and to join Him in serving others. The greatest goodness in life is to be like the Source of Goodness.

To live fully in a Panin-el-Panim relationship means that we take responsibility for our own life and co-create it. We therefore do not just receive Divine goodness as the "effect" of this relationship, but we become the cause and the source, the creator, as it were, of the goodness in our life by choosing to 'Face Hashem', as it were. In this way, we too become hosts, serving the guests of all creation.

TO BECOME 'LIKE THE CREATOR'

Rosh Hashanah is established on our birthday because this is the first day that an element of creation had the ability to take full responsibility for its choices, to master life and not be mastered *by* life as in a mode of Achor b'Achor. This is the first day of creation in which there was the possibility for a Panin-el-Panim relationship, the Creator's desire in creating the world.

Rosh Hashanah was not established on the day the rest of the world was created, because then the world was in a state of Achor b'Achor, a 'natural' state devoid of free choice. Creation was lacking until it had a representative with the volition to turn and to face our Creator.

To enter a Panim-el-Panim relationship with the Creator is to become *like* the Creator. When we are not just passively receiving Divine goodness, but actively exercising our will to connect and to 'give' to the Creator through gratitude and Avodah, we too become a cause, a source, a 'creator', as it were.

THE 'HEAD' OF THE YEAR

As discussed earlier, *Rosh* Hashanah is the 'head' of the year, not merely its beginning. The head is the seat of the 'brain', representing the faculty of free choice. The word *Hashanah* is 360 in numerical value, representing the full 360 degree circumference of the circle of life, including cyclical time, and the seasons of the natural world. On Rosh Hashanah *we* are potentially the Rosh, carrying the human capacity for free choice. *We* are meant to be the 'head' of *Shanah* / natural time, the cycles of our life, and the circumference of nature. We need to be the head, the truly human consciousness that stands above the year and everything it will bring, and continually acknowledge the Source of all Blessings on behalf of the rest of Creation.

We need to lift our "heads" above the endless, inevitable circle of natural or 'animal' life, the world of the first creation of Adam-Chavah, in which the human being was still indistinguishable from the rest of nature. As explained earlier, the Adam-Chavah of Chapter One of Bereishis is connected with the Divine Name Elokim, as they were created by Elokim, in the Tzelem of Elokim. Elokim is 86 in numerical value (Aleph/1, Lamed/30, Hei/5, Yud/10, Mem/40 = 86), which is the numerical value of the world *haTeva* / 'the natural'.

Only in Chapter Two of Bereishis is the Name Hashem introduced in the Torah, when Adam-Chavah receives a 'breath of life', a 'living soul', a higher level of consciousness that transcends 'nature' through its attribute of free choice. As it says: ויפח באפיו נשמת חיים ויהי האדם לנפש חיה / "He blew into his nostrils the breath of life, and man became a living being" (Bereishis, 2:7). Says Rashi, שנתוסף בה דיעה ודבור / "To him was granted (Da'as, the capacity of) understanding and speech," the capacity to choose.

Ten times Elokim (86) equals 860. The word Rosh (as in 'poor', without the letter Aleph; Rosh with an Aleph means 'head': See Sanhedrin, 70a) in numerical value is 500 (Reish/200, Shin/300), Hashanah is 360 (Hei/5, Shin/300, Nun/50, Hei/5 = 360), and 500+360=860. This means that Rosh Hashanah, without the Aleph in Rosh, is 860 — representing the fullness of the natural world. When the Aleph, the soul of Adam-Chavah, is introduced to the world, and they lift their Rosh / head, the value of 861 comes alive. The Aleph (1) means the 'One', Hashem, that which transcends the multiplicity and 'poverty' of nature. Our presence in the world breaks the limited, natural circle of life and raises all of the world back toward the Creator in an infinite spiral.

THE AWESOMENESS OF PANIM-EL-PANIM

As the Baal Shem Tov teaches, "...A person shall always be in a joyous state and he shall think and believe (sense) with complete faith (clarity) that the Shechinah (Divine Immanence) is always with him and protecting him — and that he is looking at the Creator and the Creator is looking at him" (*Tzava'as haRivash*, p. 18a. *Baal Shem Tov al haTorah*, Eikev, 38).

Panim-el-Panim is the sense of being seen, observed and protected, and that all of your life is being recorded. This sensation is another word for *Kabbalas Ol Malchus Shamayim* / "accepting upon oneself the yoke of Heaven," accepting Hashem as the Melech. Such awareness and acceptance is the main theme of Rosh Hashanah, this sense that your life is lived in the presence of an Omnipresent, All-Powerful Observer, charging you with a sense of urgency, alertness, and importance. In the powerful words of the *Tanya*, "And indeed, Hashem is standing over him, and the whole earth is full of His glory, and He searches his mind and heart to see that he is serving Him as is fitting" (*Tanya*, 41).

This consciousness of being *seen* motivates us to live a deeper, higher, holier, and more meaningful life. If we truly know this, not conceptually but experientially, then in a sense we have no other choice; we are awakened, alert, and ready to accept Hashem as our King. This consciousness empowers us to sense that every detail of our life has tremendous value. We have a mission and purpose, as well as a partner.

Ultimately, we are soldiers with marching orders to make this world a better, holier place. We are entrusted to be the conduit of the revelation and recognition of the Creator and to be a co-creator with the Master of the Universe. It is almost overwhelming to recognize the majesty of the human being, the magnitude of our abilities and calling.

If you ponder this idea deeply, you will, in fact, be awestruck, and this is the sensation that we are meant to feel on Rosh Hashanah, the day of judgment and our collective birthday. This is the 'awe' in the Days of Awe. In the words of Rabbeinu Yonah, on these days, "A person shall tremble and be in awe from the dread of judgment" (*Sefer haYirah*, towards the end). It is not the more shallow 'fear of being judged' that makes these days the Days of Awe, rather it is the urgency and the awesome responsibility that HaKadosh Baruch Hu's judgment inspires: 'This little "me" can alter and impact all of reality? How can I live with this awareness and honor this responsibility, and not be overwhelmed?'

Yet, the truth is, every day we are being judged, and even every moment. It is always Rosh Hashanah, on some level. Every moment we are being born and reborn again. And every moment we are being entrusted with this awesome mission.

A birthday is the day when Hashem says "I (choose to) need you." Every day we wake up is thus like our birthday, and every moment we are alive Hashem is saying "I really need you to complete My Creation with your free choice." The whole world and all things together are saying, "Without you, life would be different."

All of history has led up to this present moment, and all of the past is waiting for us to make the right choices right here and now, and to consciously further Hashem's Presence in the world. We are given the Divine ability to choose, and so every moment is infinitely precious.

Just thinking about this awakens us to the *Ol Malchus Shamayim*, our sense of vast responsibility in and to the present moment.

THE QUESTIONS OF ROSH HASHANAH

This is the day of our judgment and the birthday of our humanity. And so, the big question is, can we justify our existence.

We need to look deeply into ourselves and see if we can honestly answer this question, 'Why do I exist? Why am I here?' Before Hashem created us, He asked us if we wanted to be created, and we said yes. Today, on Rosh Hashanah, we need to be able to answer a resounding affirmative once again.

Are we living up to our purpose? Are we doing our part in our Panim-el-Panim relationship, are we vulnerably and confidently facing our Creator? Are we living in relationship with others according to our deepest intentions and highest values? This is the awesomeness of Rosh Hashanah, the recognition that we must 'crown' Hashem as Master of the Universe.

Why am I? This is the question of Rosh Hashanah, and the responsibility to justify our own existence. Everything is being judged in relation to its potential. Is another year of life justified? Am I fulfilling my mission? Is the existence of the world justifiable before its Creator?

Who am I? Stripping away all conditions and influences, who am I really? This is the question of Yom Kippur. We come to the realization that what we truly are is the result of a constant encounter with the Other, the Creator.

On Rosh Hashanah we awaken to our inner calling as a human being endowed with a Divine spark, a participant in creation, not merely an extension of the natural world, but an independent being with our own voice and choice. This is overwhelmingly daunting, yet utterly inspiring.

Hashem wants us, believes in us, and paradoxically 'needs' us as a partner: are we ready, are we willing?

Chapter Fifteen

THE REDEMPTION OF SISERA:
Submission, Separation and Sweetening
Greater Light Revealed Through the Darkness

וראיתי אני שיש יתרון לחכמה מן־הסכלות כיתרון האור מן־החשך

"And I saw that wisdom has an advantage over folly, as the
advantage of light over darkness"
(*Koheles*, 2:13).

T HE SIMPLE MEANING OF THE WORDS "THE ADVANTAGE
OF LIGHT OVER DARKNESS," IS THE RECOGNITION OF
THE VALUE OF LIGHT IN CONTRAST TO DARKNESS.
For example, after a person feels pain for some time and then
it disappears, he may value the absence of pain more than ever
before. The deeper meaning of this verse is revealed in the
word מן, which usually means 'from' not 'over': 'I have seen...the
advantage of light מן־החשך / *from* [i.e., within and through]
the darkness.'

This implies not merely that light is better than darkness, nor that one appreciates light more when contrasted with darkness, rather that there is a greater light that comes *from* darkness itself.

Such dialectical teachings, referred to as the *Toras haHipuch* / Torah of Opposites, are explored by the Maharal at great length. He begins his *Sefer Netzach Yisrael* in this way: "A good thing is really known by its opposite...from the color black we can know what is white" (*Netzach Yisrael*, 1. *Be'er haGolah*, 5). Later, the Alter Rebbe's student Reb Aharon haLevi of Strashelye also explored these principles in depth.

Geulah / redemption comes from *Galus* / exile, explains the Maharal. Not only is a redemption the end of an exile, but the redemption itself is only reached *through* the exile.

GREAT IS A SIN FOR A HIGHER PURPOSE

Our sages tell us, גדולה עבירה לשמה ממצוה שלא לשמה / "A sin performed with good intentions is greater than a good deed performed without good intentions" (*Nazir*, 23b. *Horayos*, 10b). From whom do the sages learn this? From Yael and Sisera. Regarding Yael, it says, תבורך מנשים יעל... מנשים באהל תבורך / מאן נשים שבאהל שרה רבקה רחל ולאה / "Blessed above all other women shall Yael be... above 'women in the tent' she shall be blessed" (*Shoftim*, 5:24). "Who are these 'women in the tent'? They are Sarah, Rivkah, Rochel, and Leah" (*Nazir*, ibid).

Sisera features prominently on Rosh Hashanah, as we know what a Teru'ah should sound like from the anxious cries of his mother, as explored earlier.

But who was Sisera himself? He was the powerful army general of a regime that was the archenemy of Klal Yisrael during the times of the prophetess Devorah. Sisera was the chieftain of the army of Yavin, the king of Canaan. He was young and extraordinarily powerful and seemingly 'beyond this world'. He struck terror even in the animals of the field (*Yalkut Shimoni*, 247. *Gevuras Hashem*, Hakdamah, 3).

Devorah said to the Jewish general, Barak, "Rise, for this is the day which Hashem has given Sisera into your hand... And Barak went down from Mount Tabor, with ten thousand men after him. And Hashem confused Sisera and all the chariots and all of the camp with the edge of the sword before Barak; and Sisera alighted from his chariot, and fled on foot...And Yael went out to meet Sisera and said to him, 'Turn in, my lord, turn in to me; fear not.' And he turned with her into the tent, and she covered him with a garment. And he said to her, 'Give me now a little water to drink, for I am thirsty.'"And she opened the flask of milk and gave him to drink, and covered him. And Yael...took the tent-pin, and placed the hammer in her hand, and came to him stealthily, and thrust the pin into his temple, and it pierced through into the ground. And he was in a deep sleep and weary, and he died" (*Shoftim*, 4:14-21).

For Yael to be able to kill Sisera, besides giving him milk to drink, making him sleepy and unaware (*Shavuos*, 23a. Rambam, *Hilchos Bi'as Mikdash*, 1:2), she actually had relations with him, and in fact, she committed adultery with him seven times (שבע בעילות בעל אותו רשע באותה שעה). Although she committed these sins, her only intention was to weaken and exhaust Sisera so that she could safely kill him. And this is the reason why she is blessed beyond even the blessedness of Sarah, Rivkah, Rochel and Leah, the holy matriarchs of Klal Yisrael. This is the idea of "redemption through sin"; through an encounter with darkness it is sometimes possible to attain an even greater light than one could attain without encountering darkness.

When is it proper to apply this principle, that of גדולה עבירה לשמה / *Gedolah Aveirah Lishmah* / "Great is a sin for a (higher) purpose"? In *Nefesh haChayim*, Rav Chayim Volozhin (*Nefesh HaChayim*, 7, Miluim) writes that this approach was only valid before Matan Torah. But this is a little troubling, as the story with Yael occurred many years after Matan Torah, and Yael was also Jewish at that time, so she was liable to receive the Torah's consequences for these sins (*Yalkut Shimoni*, Yehoshua, 1, Remez 9).

The Nefesh haChayim also brings down (in the notes), that the principle of *Aveirah Lishmah* took hold only if it was for *Hatzalas Klal Yisrael* / rescuing the entire Community of Israel — not just for rescuing the *Yachid* / individual. The story of Yael was indeed for the entire Klal Yisrael, and therefore it was allowed (ועשתה עבירה לשמה כדי להציל את ישראל: *Tosefos*, Kesuvos, 3b.

See also Rav Elchanan, *Kovetz haOros*, Siman 48. *Shu't Shevus Yaakov, 2,* Siman 117. *Shu't Maharik*, Siman 167. This is the opinion of the Meiri in *Sanhedrin*).

According to the Ramchal, Rav Moshe Chayim Luzato (*Kinos Hashem Tz'vaos*), Gedolah Aveirah Lishmah is only with regards to issues of *Ishus* / marriage and *Zenus* / forbidden relationships, and nowhere else. (Indeed, the Gemara in Nazir mentions only cases of Ishus. Interestingly, on the verse, "And Rochel stole her father's household idols" (*Bereishis*, 31:19), Rashi seemingly quotes the Medrash Rabbah, writing, להפריש את אביה מע"ז נתכונה / "Her intention was to wean her father from idol-worship." Yet, the terminology in the Medrash Rabbah was (*Bereishis*, 74:5) is והיא לא נתכוונה אלא לשם שמים / "And her intention was only for the Sake of Heaven" — Rashi changes the wording, apparently because he does not wish to write that theft can be לשם שמים. Note, however, the language of *Tanchuma*, Vayetze, 12: כדי לעקור עבודה זרה מבית אביה נתכונה.)

A student of the Baal Shem Tov, the Toldos Yaakov Yoseph, writes (*Parshas Ki Tetze*) that this principle can only function if the individual performing the sin has absolutely no pleasure from the sin, and he or she is in fact disgusted by the act. Then and only then does the principle of גדולה עבירה לשמה / *Gedolah Aveirah Lishmah* have any validity.

Either way, in the story of Yael, all of the above was true. It was for the sake of Klal Yisrael, it was an *Ishus* issue, and she had no interest or desire to be physically intimate with him.[*]

---

[*] Additionally, with regards to women in a prohibited relationship, there is a principle of *Isha Karka Olam* / "A woman is 'mere land', i.e. she is passive and not an active participant": Tosefos, *Sanhedrin*, 74b. The Rambam holds

THE COSMIC PROCESS OF LIGHT REVEALED THROUGH DARKNESS

Yael and Sisera are therefore important for understanding this idea of 'redemption through sin' — and how higher light can be revealed specifically through darkness. To better decipher this dynamic and its relationship with Rosh Hashanah and Yom Kippur, let us explore the cosmic process of creation.

At first there is only the Infinite Light and the Oneness of Hashem (this entire temporal and spatial metaphor is not to be taken literally, and Oneness is eternally unchanged). There is only One. Then, in order to 'make space' for an 'other' to exist, there was a *Tzimtzum* / cosmic contraction and withdrawal, a setting aside of the Infinite Light, which allowed for the *Chalal* / empty space to emerge. This is the place of void, of darkness and emptiness. Once the space is emptied, there is then a *Chazar veHe'ir* / a return of the light which fills and illuminates creation. This process of emptying, returning and re-filling is all for achieving a greater purpose and attaining a level that could not have been reached without it.

Again, first there is only the Infinite Light, a state of infinity, perfection and unified being. Then, a 'lack of perfection' is introduced, as a result of the Tzimtzum. Once the Light returns it creates the context for a different kind of perfection: perfection in a state of 'becoming', creating the conditions for a deeper revelation of Infinite Light. Whereas before the Tzimt-

---

differently: *Hilchos Yesodei haTorah*, 5:5; see *Chidushei Rebbe Chayim al ha-Rambam*, ad loc.

zum the Infinite Light *excludes* finitude, after the Tzimtzum the Infinite Light is revealed *within* finitude. This is an integral dimension that is deeper than 'Infinity', as Infinity and finitude are paradoxically coexisting without canceling each other out. Being and becoming, perfection and 'imperfection', are mysteriously conjoined as one in a revelation of Unified Light within a place of duality and separation.

THREE STAGES, THREE SOUNDS OF THE SHOFAR

These three cosmic stages (emptying, returning, re-filling) mirror the three most basic sounds of the Shofar: the Tekiah, the Teru'ah (Shevarim) and the Tekiah that follows. Tekiah is the sound of Infinity 'prior to' or beyond the Tzimtzum; a unified, whole sound, that is one and complete. This is the perfect sound before 'brokenness' exists. Teru'ah is the sound post-Tzimtzum, the state of brokenness and separation. This, at least on the surface, is the sound of life in our world. The Tekiah after the Teru'ah is the wholeness that comes after the brokenness, the *Yichud* / Oneness after the *Pirud* / separation — the deeper level of Yichud. It is the place of our work of Tikkun in this world: taking all the fragmentation, separation and brokenness of creation, and bringing it all into a state of Yichud.

Now let us go back to Rosh Hashanah, and understand how it activates the process of redemption, namely the revelation of light from within darkness.

SUBMISSION, SEPARATION, AND SWEETENING

In general, as the Baal Shem Tov revealed, every redemptive process unfolds in three stages: הכנעה / *Hachna'ah* / submission, הבדלה / *Havdalah* / separation, and המתקה / *Hamtakah* / sweetening. In terms of Teshuvah and the period of the high holidays, these three stages can be mapped out to the days of Elul, Rosh Hashanah and Yom Kippur, the forty days of transformation.

Elul is a time of *Hachna'ah*, the humbling stage of 'submission' and acceptance. This is the process of looking honestly at your life up until and including this present moment, fully acknowledging all past and current mistakes and shortcomings, and humbly accepting them as your own doing. It is a time of soul searching and evaluation, of submitting to *what is*.

At this stage, a person needs to take full responsibility for their life and claim their past as their own; only then can the second stage of *Havdalah* / severance begin.

We cannot 'forget' that which we do not remember. There first needs to be Hachna'ah, a remembrance and acceptance of the past, a submission to what we have done and who we have become. This is our work in Elul.

Only when we acknowledge the darkness that we have created and accept responsibility for all of it, can we ascertain a complete and accurate 'diagnosis'. Only then can we effectively apply the 'treatment' of *Havdalah* / severance, separating from all that is toxic to our soul or even just undesirable and contrary to our desired direction in life.

ROSH HASHANAH IS HAVDALAH

Rosh Hashanah is the "Day of Judgment," meaning 'of *alignment*'. When we cleanly break off or cut away all negativity from our consciousness, we become internally unified and singularly focused on our purpose, mission and destiny. This Havdalah is accomplished through the sound of the Shofar, which both orientates us in the moment and cuts away all other (distracting) noise.

Similarly, if a person is suffering from *Machshavos Zaros* in Davening he should clap his hands (*Likutei Eitzos*, Tefilah, p. 157. See also *Likutei Moharan*, 1:46. See also *Noam Elimelech*, Parshas Shemini, and *Degel Machaneh Ephrayim*, Parshas Noach). The sound focuses his scattered thoughts and energies. Sound can pull our wandering minds back to center.

Additionally, if one were to fall down the steps, Chas v'Shalom, in the first 'Oy' he is fully present; all of him is there in that immediate moment of shock and sensation. Immersed in a kind of silence before all words and analysis, there are no thoughts or even feelings discernable except the pain. Perhaps a moment or two later, when the mind wakes up again, one's rationalizations and judgments begin to circumscribe the event, 'It was not such a bad fall,' or 'That was a terrible fall,' 'It is the builders' fault,' 'Now how am I going to do the shopping'.

As we have discussed at length, the Torah does not explain what the sound of the Teru'ah is, all it says is, "It shall be a day of Teru'ah...." Our sages learn that the sound of Teru'ah is derived from the mother of Sisera (*Rosh Hashanah*, 33b).

In fact, according to the *Aruch*, all of the 100 sounds of the Shofar correspond to the 100 sounds that the mother of Sisera cried (Tosefos, *Rosh Hashanah*, 33b). "The mother of Sisera looked out the window and cried through the lattice, 'Why is his chariot so long in coming? Why do the hoofbeats of his chariots tarry?'"(*Shoftim*, 5:28) A mother's cry for her child is a complete sound; she is totally present and one with her cry. Like someone who has just fallen down the steps, there are no other thoughts that enter the mother's mind when she is crying, for nothing exists outside her pain. The essential sound of this cry cuts away and negates all other sounds. This is the second stage in the process of Teshuvah: to exclusively focus on the good, and to cut and 'blast' away all the negativity in our life and consciousness. Thus, on Rosh Hashanah we go to perform *Tashlich* (see Appendix 3) and "throw away our sins," as the Pasuk says in *Michah* (7:19), "And *Tashlich* / cast into the depths of the sea all of their sins."

In Elul we claim our whole selves, including our entire past, so that when Rosh Hashanah comes along we can become totally 'aligned' with and focused on the good; in order to do this we perform a Havdalah from everything 'negative' in our lives. We cast all our sins into the sea, as it were, "to a place where they will no longer be remembered, nor counted, nor ever brought to mind." This is why on Rosh Hashanah we are all like Tzadikim and there is no mention in our Davening of penitence or regret for negative actions. There is also no Tachanun on Rosh Hashanah (*Magen Avraham*, Orach Chayim, 584:2). This is the step of Havdalah, the spiritual 'surgery' that follows the 'diagnosis' described in Elul.

On Rosh Hashanah, beyond the fact that we do not say *Al Cheit* / 'For we have sinned,' there is in fact not any mention of sin whatsoever. We even go so far as to refrain from eating nuts, אגוז / *Egoz* (nut, singular). This is because אגוז is numerically 17, and while the word חטא / sin is actually 18, we can subtract the Aleph, leaving חט, which is phonetically equal to *Cheit* / 'sin' (*Shulchan Aruch*, Orach Chayim, 583:2, Rama: אגוז בגימטריא חט). In other words: On Rosh Hashanah we are so *Muvdal* / separated from the idea of sin, we do not even eat an item that has a numerical value of a word that only *sounds* like the word for sin.

On a deeper level, Havdalah means that we define ourselves by 'who we are', rather than 'what we do' or have done. On Rosh Hashanah we confirm that we are ultimately beyond sin; this 'perfection' is who we are, and although we may have done 'imperfect' things in the past, that is not ultimately who we are. Therefore, we 'separate' ourselves from our past actions to the point that they no longer even come to mind.

And then comes step three: Yom Kippur.

After having fully inhabited the stage of Havdalah, we progress to the full *Hamtakah* / sweetening, the full reclamation and integration of the light from within all the past darkness. This is the hidden elevation in the original descent. It is spiritual 'recycling' so to speak, as in the end result of composting, in which all the energy stored in the waste now returns to vitalize the blooming of a new, beautiful flower.

This is the Teshuvah of Yom Kippur, when we circle back and revisit our negative past, recite Tachanun, mention our 'sins' and confess *Al Cheit*. But, now there is a great sweetening and integration, in which even "intentional sins become merits" (*Yuma*, 86b).

All of your past together creates your present. There is a way of looking at every past mistake and failure as a merit, as it got you to the place that you are now; it is the waste that has become compost, which is fueling the blossoming of your Teshuvah today. On Yom Kippur, in the moments of deep Teshuvah and high aspiration, it is precisely 'who you were' that is becoming 'who you are'. Your mistakes are becoming Mitzvos.

This is the wonderful paradoxical nature of Yom Kippur, when we push beyond our physical limits and transcend our normal human needs, demonstrating to ourselves that we can do what is necessary to attain greatness. Yet, coupled with this elation is an acute and profound sense of humility, an unfiltered awareness of our failures. It is simultaneously a 'high' and a 'low' state, a beautiful blend of self-confidence, rooted in the recognition that we are special, exalted beings with something distinct to contribute to life, and humility, rooted in the recognition that perhaps we have not yet made this contribution.

Yom Kippur peels away all the layers, revealing our paradoxical essence. We are like pure angels, and yet we are like dust and ashes. We are frail, fallible human beings, and yet we are Hashem's beloved. The more that full-spectrum reality becomes revealed, the more elated we become, until we realize we are the *Yechidah* / unified essential soul that both transcends and includes all soul levels and bodily experiences.

Recall the teaching *Gedolah Aveirah Lishmah* / "great is a sin for a (higher) purpose," in the above exploration of Yael's encounter with Sisera. The 'light' and higher purpose was revealed precisely through the darkness of 'sin' (although in that context, her acts were to save all of Klal Yisrael, and she had no personal pleasure or gain, therefore it was not 'sinful' in the normal sense). The advantage of light is revealed precisely through darkness.

THE LIGHT OF REBBE AKIVA BEGINS IN THE DEPTH OF DARKNESS

Our sages tell us, "Among the descendants of Sisera there were those who studied Torah in Yerushalayim" (מבני בניו של סיסרא למדו תורה בירושלים. *Sanhedrin*, 96b). In the version of Rabbeinu Nisan Gaon it continues: "And who was that? Rebbe Akiva" (*Berachos*, 27b).

Rebbe Akiva, the great light of Klal Yisrael, is a descendant of an infamous enemy of Klal Yisrael (*Pesach Einayim, Sanhedrin,* ibid. *Asarah Ma'amaros,* Ma'amar Chikur Din, 5:10-11).

Yael and Sisera were intimate seven times, and on the third time, she became pregnant with a child who would become a grandparent of the great luminary, Rebbe Akiva: "The spark of Rebbe Akiva was brought down to the world that night" (*Ibid. Megaleh Amukos,* 88, Va'eschanan).

Mahara miFano, an Italian Kabbalist, writes that from the unholy union between Yael and Sisera eventually Rebbe Akiva was born, whom the Master of the Universe placed in his generation (the period of the destruction of the Second Beis haMikdash and the beginning of the current exile) to protect the entire world and the Torah that it should not, G-d forbid, be forgotten (*Ibid,* Ma'amar Chikur Din, 5:11. See also *Pri Tzadik,* Rosh Hashanah).

Rebbe Yitzchak ben Moshe of Vienna, an early *Rishon / Medieval Rabbi* (13th Century), was unsure whether the name *Akiva* should be spelled with a Hei at the end as in עקיבה, or with an Aleph, as in עקיבא (in the *Bavli,* Akiva is spelled with an Aleph, and in the *Yerushalmi* with a Hei, related to how vowels are used in Hebrew and Aramaic). One night, as he was pondering this issue he had a dream, and in the dream he saw the verse אור זרע לצדיק ולישרי לב שמחה / *Ohr Zaru'a laTzadik ul'Yishrei Lev Simchah* / "Light is sown for the righteous, and for the upright of heart, gladness" (*Tehilim,* 97:11). The last letters of the words of this Pasuk spell out the name *R. Akiva* with a Hei, and he thus knew that Hei was the appropriate ending, and this prompted him to entitle his major work *Ohr Zarua* (*Seder haDoros*).

Rebbe Akiva is the אור זרוע לצדיק / *Ohr Zarua laTzadik*. There is a deeper teaching that suggests that Rebbe Akiva at first spelled his name ending with the letter Aleph, and only later in life, when he had reached a higher level, was it spelled with the letter Hei, as in the verse of *Ohr Zarua* (*Likutei haGra*, Pirush Be'er Yitzchak (Rav Yitzchak Chaver), Erech, *Ohr Zarua laTzadik*). This means that at some stage, Rebbe Akiva 'becomes' the Ohr Zarua, the great luminary of Torah, embodying the *Ohr haGanuz* / Hidden Light of the First Day of Creation that had been set aside or 'sown' for the righteous of the future (*Chagigah*, 12a).

Rebbe Akiva is the embodiment of Torah she-b'al-Peh — the Ohr haGanuz hidden throughout the Torah, and especially in the Torah she-b'al-Peh (*Degel Machaneh Ephraim*, Bereishis. *Yosher Divrei Emes*, 3. See also, *Nefesh HaChayim*, end of Sha'ar 1, Haga'ah. Note, *Zohar* 1, p, 264a. *Tanchumah*, Noach), and he is the Ohr Zarua for all future generations.

Rebbe Akiva becomes the ultimate 'redeemed soul'. A poor, uneducated shepherd boy, a child of converts, becomes the greatest Talmudic sage and embodiment of the Oral Torah, in which "the law always follows the opinion of Rebbe Akiva." This holiest of people came from the unholiest of unions, that of Yael and Sisera (Thus, it was specifically Rebbe Akiva who was able to declare, שכל הכתובים קדש, ושיר השירים קדש קדשים / "All the writings are holy, but Shir HaShirim (which is seemingly about mere romantic and lower love) is holy of holies": *Yadayim*, 3:5).

"Through the window the mother of Sisera looked forth" (*Shoftim*, 5:28). "The mother" refers to the holy Shechinah, the 'Mother of the World' who was "looking forth" to make sure that the holy spark within Sisera — the seed of the great Rebbe Akiva, would not be lost. In fact She was also making sure that Sisera was not completely lost, as the light of Rebbe Akiva was 'hidden' within him and it needed to be brought out, eventually birthing this holy spark.

Torah she-b'al-Peh / Oral Torah is referred to as 'the Torah of Rebbe Akiva'. He is the Nefesh, the soul of the Torah she-b'al-Peh, and it is named after him in the same way that the *Torah she-b'Kesav* / the Written Torah is named after Moshe: '*Toras Moshe*' (*Asarah Ma'amaros*, ibid). Moshe was born into the priestly *Sheivet* / tribe of Levi, whole and circumcised, and as he was born the entire home became filled with light. Thus he embodies the Torah she-b'Kesav, the immediately revealed light. Whereas the great Rebbe Akiva was born in a lowly state, lived for years as an uneducated person, and only later on in life did he become the greatest of sages. Thus Rebbe Akiva embodies Torah she-b'al-Peh, the light that emerges from darkness. Our sages tell us that Yael's beauty is connected with her voice (יעל בקולה: *Megilah*, 15a). The Oral Torah, the Torah of the 'voice', is connected to Yael and revealed by her descendant, Rebbe Akiva.

In the depth of the 'sin' of Yael's intimacy with Sisera, the seed of Rebbe Akiva was planted in the soil of darkness, to later be revealed and released into the world in a great flowering of light.

100 CRIES OF BIRTH, 100 CRIES OF SISERA'S MOTHER, 100 BLASTS OF THE SHOFAR

A mother cries out 100 cries during childbirth (Medrash, *Vayikra Rabbah*, 27:7). The first 99 cries are pre-birth during labor, and with the one-hundredth cry the child comes out of the womb, and the mother knows she is going to live (*Tanchumah*, Tazria, 4. *Meshech Chochmah* Emor).

Sisera's mother's cry, which she let out while Sisera was cohabiting with Yael, represent the release of the sparks of Kedushah that lay deeply hidden within the body of Sisera, and their transmission into Yael (*Resisei Laylah*, 46). The cries of the mother, mirroring the cries of the Shechinah, release the soul of Rebbe Akiva from Sisera into Yael. These cries are like a startling wordless Tefilah that accomplished the *Zarua* of the *Ohr*, the sowing of the Hidden Light in Yael, which would become the *Tzadik*, Rebbe Akiva.

These cries, in our own lives, are the 100 blasts of the Shofar on Rosh Hashanah, birthing us as the Tzadik we could be and revealing the light that can come from our own darkness.

YOM KIPPUR: The Hamtakah & Revealing of the Light of Torah she-b'al-Peh / Rebbe Akiva

Rebbe Akiva, the light of Torah she-b'al-Peh, the light that comes from within and through the darkness, is revealed on a seed level on Rosh Hashanah, but it only becomes fully revealed on Yom Kippur. Yom Kippur thus unleashes the power of Teshuvah; facilitating redemption through darkness, and *Hamtakah* / sweetening all judgments.

In the Torah's narrative, first the people sin with the Golden Calf, then Moshe pleads with Hashem for forty days — and then another 40 days — and finally on Yom Kippur, a day of atonement is given. This seems to be a redemption 'after' sin, a light shining after a time of darkness.

On Yom Kippur we were given the *Luchos Shniyos* / second Tablets, which Moshe had carved himself; signifying the idea of Torah she-b'al-Peh. If we had only received the first Luchos we would only have Torah she-b'Kesav, and *Sefer Yehoshua* (*Nedarim*, 22b). There would have been only *Ohr Yashar* / direct light; the 'first Tekia', without the 'Shevarim' and the 'second Tekia'. The *Cheit haEgel* / sin of the Golden Calf, brought about the *Sheviras haLuchos* / breaking of the First Luchos. It was also the cause of the Teshuvah of Klal Yisrael, leading to the revelation of a greater light: the Oral Torah. The master key of Teshuvah, the Thirteen Attributes of Mercy revealed through Moshe, are inwardly aligned with the Thirteen Principles of Torah she-b'al-Peh — enumerated by Rebbe Yishmael.

Torah she-b'al-Peh consists of answers that are revealed through questions and uncertainties — representing a light that emerges from within darkness. "The people who walked in darkness saw a great light" (*Yeshayahu*, 9:1). This passage refers to the Oral Torah. Questions are darkness, and the "great" light is the resolution (*Tanchumah*, Noach, 3), the 'second Tekia'.

Our sages tell us that the verse במחשכים הושיבני כמתי עולם / "He placed me in darkness, like those long dead" (*Eichah* 3:6), refers specifically to the Talmud of *Bavel* / Babylon (*Sanhedrin*, 24a. The sages of Bavel are connected with 'darkness': *Zevachim*, 60b. Ritva, *Yuma*, 57a, and the light that comes from darkness). It is a type of learning where wisdom and clarity, light and resolution, are attained by means of toiling in questioning, debate, and being persistently present with 'not-knowing'.

This is a "great" light specifically because it is revealed through resolving doubts and difficulties. It is "the advantage of light from darkness," for darkness allows us to perceive a light that is deeper than pure, 'unbroken' light. And this is the ultimate redemption of Sisera himself; he becomes the progenitor of the great revealer of Torah she-b'al-Peh.

Tishrei is spelled Tav, Shin, Reish..., the last three letters of the Aleph-Beis in reverse order. The acronym of the sounds of the Shofar, *Tashrak*, is the same: Tav, Shin, Reish, Kuf. Both the Month of Tishrei and the sounds of the Shofar embody a reverse or backward flowing light; light that passes through darkness in order to reveal a more complete illumination that is much greater and sweeter than the original light itself.

'Lower Teshuvah' merely renders intentional *Aveiros* / transgressions as 'unintentional' acts. This is the work of *Hachna'ah* / submission, the work of Elul. 'Higher Teshuvah', the work of Tishrei, transforms liabilities into assets, intentional sins into virtues.

From Rosh Hashanah, with the 100 blasts, we are empowered to move on to Yom Kippur, to revisit our past and redeem all of it, to retrieve the sparks from within the darkness to convert them into even greater light.

Appropriately, the culmination of Rebbe Akiva's life, the day of his passing, was on Yom Kippur (*Ben Yehoyadah*, Berachos, 61b).

Tragically, at the end of Rebbe Akiva's life he was put into prison for teaching Torah in public. The Gemara (*Berachos*, ibid) relates: "When they took Rebbe Akiva out to be executed, it was time for the recitation of Shema. And they were raking his flesh with iron combs, and he was reciting Shema; accepting upon himself the yoke of Heaven. His students said to him: Our teacher, even now? (as you suffer, you recite Shema)? He said to them: All my days I have been troubled by the verse: With all your soul, meaning: Even if Hashem takes your soul. I said to myself: When will the opportunity be afforded me to fulfill this verse? Now that it has been afforded to me, shall I not fulfill it? היה מאריך באחד עד שיצתה נשמתו באחד / He prolonged his uttering of the word Echad / אחד / One, until his soul left his body as he uttered his final word Echad / אחד / One. A voice descended from heaven and said: Happy are you, Rebbe Akiva, that your soul left your body (as you uttered) Echad / אחד / One." At the culmination of the first day of creation the Torah says; ויהי־ערב ויהי־בקר יום אחד / "And it was evening and it was morning, day Echad / One" (*Bereishis*, 1:5). The sages ask; Why call it 'day one', and not the 'first day', which would be the normative way to list something in an ordinal series? Indeed, the Torah enumerates the rest of the days of creation as the 'second day', the 'third day', and so on. Says, the Medrash; Yom Echad / day One refers to Yom Kippur (יום אחד, שנתן לו הקדוש ברוך הוא, ואיזה זה, יום הכפורים. *Medrash Rabbah*, Bereishis, 2:3). Yom Kippur is the Echad, the day of One, of ultimate Unity, the day that sweetens and transforms all darkness and negativity into light. אחד / Echad is the level Rebbe Akiva attained at the moment his soul soared from this world on Yom Kippur, he left this world in a state of אחד on the day of אחד.

In conclusion, the final Mishnah in *Yuma*, the laws of Yom Kippur, ends, "Rebbe Akiva said, 'How fortunate are you, Israel: before Whom are you purified, and Who purifies you? It is your Father in Heaven,' as it is stated: 'And I will sprinkle purifying water upon you, and you shall be purified' (*Yechezkel*, 36:25). And it says: 'The ritual bath of Israel is Hashem' (*Yirmiyahu*, 17:13). 'Just as a ritual bath purifies the impure, so too, the Holy One, Blessed be He, purifies Israel'" (*Yuma*, 85b).

The Nefesh of Rebbe Akiva, the light of the Oral Torah, which is deeply seeded within the darkness of Sisera and within the darkness of the acts of Yael, shines forth with the power of redemption from exile. Rebbe Akiva confirms that we have the power to be purified, elevated, illuminated, and totally redeemed, even now, in the midst of our own darkness. So may it be, soon and in our days.

Appendix

Essay One
THE SYMBOLIC FOODS
OF ROSH HASHANAH

T HERE ARE VARIOUS CUSTOMS FOR EATING ASSORTED
FRUITS AS SIGNS OR *SIMANIM* / SYMBOLS OR OMENS FOR
GOOD THINGS TO COME IN THE NEW YEAR. "'Now that
you have said an omen is significant,' says Abaya, 'a person
should habituate himself למיכל / to eat at the beginning of
the year קרא / *Kara* / gourds, רוביא / *Rubya* / fenugreek (a type
of herb), כרתי / *Karti* / leeks, סילקא / *Silka* / beets, and תמרי /
Tamrei / dates'" (*Kerisus*, 6a. In another version, Abaya says, למיחזי / to
'see' the omens: *Horayos*, 12a. Yet other versions say, "One should *bring* these
items to the table": Ran, on the Rif, *Rosh Hashanah*, 12b, or to "hold" in your
hand; in some older versions of Gemara, in *Horayos* and *Kerisus* it is written
the same way).

The symbolism of these particular foods is either that they ripen quickly (*Rashi*, Horayos, דהני גדלי לעגל טפי משאר ירקות), and as such represent increased merit, or they are sweet tasting and as such signify a sweet new year. In this way, the Simanim are symbolic, and the mere act of eating them with intention and prayer, facilitates a manifestation in our lives of what they symbolize.

Other commentators write that the significance of these foods is in their name. For example, the word *Rubya* is related to the Hebrew word *Rov* meaning 'a lot' or 'increase', as in, 'Our merits should increase.' The word *Karti* is related to the Hebrew word *Kares* / cut off, so that when we eat it we can hold the intention that all of our external and internal enemies should be cut off. In this way, the Simanim are more semantic than symbolic.

Yet, clearly, there is nothing inherent in, for example, a Rubya that suggests an "increase in merits." And even, semantically, the word *Rubya* / "increase" does not necessarily suggest an increase in merits, it could just as easily mean an increase in demerits, as the Shaloh points out (*Siddur Shaloh*, Minhagei Leil Rosh Hashanah). Rather, when we eat a fruit that has a name that suggests 'increase', or looks a certain way or tastes sweet, this is meant to inspire us to pray that our merits increase and that we have a sweet year. These items stimulate us to set beneficial goals and resolutions for the coming year (*Me'iri*, Horayos, 12a).

Many people have a custom on Rosh Hashanah to eat the above five foods and recite a short prayer before eating them. The following are traditional examples of numerous symbolic foods eaten at the beginning of the new year.

קרא / KARA / GOURDS:

Before eating gourds, one says, "May it be Your will, Ado-noi our G-d, and the G-d of our ancestors, that the decree of our sentence be torn apart; and may our merits be proclaimed before You."

רוביא / RUBYA / FENUGREEK:

Before the eating of fenugreek, one says, "May it be Your will, Ado-noi our G-d, and the G-d of our ancestors, that our merits increase."

כרתי / KARTI / LEEKS:

Before eating leeks, one says, "May it be You will, Ado-noi our G-d, and the G-d of our ancestors, that our enemies be decimated."

סילקא / SILKA / BEETS:

Before eating beets, one says, "May it be Your will, Ado-noi our G-d, and the G-d of our ancestors, that our adversaries be removed."

TAMREI / DATES:

Before eating dates, one says, "May it be Your will, Ado-noi our G-d, and the G-d of our ancestors, that our adversaries be consumed."

POMEGRANATE:

There are others that also eat pomegranate, and they say before they eat, "May it be Your will, Ado-noi our G-d, and the G-d of our ancestors, that our merits increase as (the seeds of) a pomegranate."

HEAD OF A SHEEP OR FISH:

There is a general custom to eat fish on Rosh Hashanah, and some eat specifically from the head of a sheep or fish. When eating the head of a sheep (or fish) they say before they eat, "May it be Your will, Ado-noi our G-d, and the G-d of our ancestors, that we be as a head and not as a tail."

FISH:

When eating fish (not necessarily the head), there are those who say before they eat, "May it be Your will, Ado-noi our G-d, and the G-d of our ancestors, that we be fruitful and multiply like fish."

Over the centuries, Jews from all over the world have developed indigenous customs of foods to eat on Rosh Hashanah related to their particular meanings in those countries. For example, in Yiddish carrots are called *Meren*, which also means 'increase', so many Jews who spoke Yiddish would eat carrots on Rosh Hashanah with the same intention as for eating fenugreek, namely, the idea that our merits shall increase.

THE NATURE OF AN OMEN

How does this work? What is an omen? How can simply eating a food that tastes sweet or whose name means 'increase' have the effect of sweetening our year or helping us increase in merits?

The world of prayer and blessings is a spiritual universe, and it is not *necessarily* related to the physical domain. It is possible for a person to pray and be 'answered' only on a spiritual plane; for example, when someone prays for healing, attributes of Divine healing are released into a 'higher' realm of existence, where it remains removed from the person who prayed. Sometimes this will allow other people who need healing to more easily tap into that healing potential, while the person who prayed is not actually healed. By eating a symbolic food with a corresponding intention and short prayer, we seek to connect the spiritual realm with the physical realm, making certain that the Divine blessing does not remain in a higher realm, unconnected with the specifics of our intention and prayer. The physical act of eating cements a merger of Divine blessing with our embodied existence.

This practice is consistent with the explanation offered by the Ramban with regards to prophecy (*Bereishis*, 12:6). Often, we find the prophet physically 'acting out' his prophecy. This is because in order for a prophecy to become 'real' and manifest in this world, it may need an action that mirrors the prophecy as a vessel to receive it. For example, the prophet Yirmiyahu asks Seraiah to throw a scroll into the river, and somehow that casting and drowning of the scroll will facilitate the prophecy of the downfall of Babylon (*Yirmiyahu*, 51:63). Similarly, to receive the blessing of a 'sweet year' we eat 'sweet foods', and so on.

Rosh Hashanah is especially conducive to merging spiritual blessings and material vessels, since on Rosh Hashanah our prayers for our physical needs are in fact deeply spiritual. We ask that we be judged favorably with regards to all our physical wants and desires, but not for egoic purposes, nor for those of mere bodily survival. From deep within, we ask for abundant physical resources so that we may employ them in our Divine service.

Our physical blessings are not actually for the sake of physical gain, rather they are tools that assist us in our mission here on earth. In a certain way, physical things are mere signs or symbols for us. And so, when we eat the symbolic foods on Rosh Hashanah, we demonstrate the symbolic value of all our physicality, which provides assistance in our journey of actualizing our soul potential and creating a dwelling place for the Creator here in the world below.

THE SWEETENING OF ALL JUDGMENT

Din / judgment is the force of division, constriction, concealment and separation. When we blow a simple Tekiah sound on the Shofar, we are blowing a sound of *Chesed* / kindness, flow and expansiveness into the New Year. Through the constriction of the narrow tube of the Shofar flows the vibration of life, animation and expansiveness for the coming year.

Language, too, is the world of Din, of judgment and constriction, as it is generally connected with the left side of the brain, and the work of focussing, distinguishing, separating, contextualizing and deciphering the disparate elements of the world of duality. These qualities are related to the Tree of *Da'as* / Knowing of distinctions. The sound of the Shofar is a simple sound like an indistinct cry, a sound that is beyond language. By blowing the Shofar we thereby sweeten all the Din, constrictions and limitations, and draw down from the Tree of Life, the sweet inner world beyond all duality.

This is another reason that we eat the *Simanim* / signs on Rosh Hashanah. The idea of a Siman is that it is "above the idea itself," gesturing toward an idea, whether by taste or name. When a person is speaking (language, Din), and cannot express in words the full extent of what he means, he will resort to a gesture of the hands, head, eyebrows, and so forth. The 'gesture' is a Siman, a 'symbol' that is conveying an idea that is beyond speech. On Rosh Hashanah we eat Simanim, expressing ideas that are above language, these are symbolic spiritual 'gestures' connected with the Tree of Life, the Source of all Blessings. In this way we can draw down blessings beyond all Din and constrictions of duality, ordinary causality and limitation. *

---

* Many have the custom to eat the Simanim on both nights of Rosh Ha-

shanah, as the Ya'avetz brings down in his Siddur. Yet, the prevailing Chassidic and Chabad customs are to eat them only on the first night. The *Bnei Yissaschar* (Tishrei, Ma'amar 2, 11) brings down that the first day of Rosh Hashanah is connected with Leah and the second to Rochel — as explored earlier in great depth. Rochel gave away her *Simanim* / signs to Leah on the night Yaakov was with Leah, thinking he was with Rochel. As Rochel was left with no Simanim, we therefore do not eat any Simanim on the second night. The languaging of the Gemara is (*Horayos*, 12a): אמר אביי השתא דאמרת סימנא מילתא היא [לעולם] יהא רגיל למיחזי בריש שתא / "Abaye said, 'Now that you said that an omen is a significant matter, a person should always be accustomed to *seeing* these on בריש שתא / the beginning of the year." This suggests only the first night, the beginning of the year.

Essay Two
APPLES & HONEY

FAMOUSLY, AT THE OUTSET OF THE ROSH HASHANAH MEAL, we have a custom to take a sweet apple and dip it in honey, doubling the physical experience of sweetness and symbolically ensuring a sweet year. This is also a reference to what Kabbalah calls the *Chakal Tapuchim Kadishin /* Sacred Apple Orchard, which represents the Shechinah's presence within the souls of Israel (who are also similar to an apple tree, *Shabbos,* 88a) during our exile.

On Rosh Hashanah there are specific judgments delivered with regard to our physical life and material welfare, especially on the first day. In the Torah, Yaakov receives the blessings for material abundance from his father Yitzchak on Rosh Hashanah (*Zohar* 3, 99b. Other sources say it was on Pesach, *Medrash Rabbah,*

Shemos, 15:11). When Yitzchak senses Yaakov's presence he declares, "Behold, the fragrance of my son is like the fragrance of a field" (Bereishis, 27:27), and this was the pleasant fragrance of a field of apple trees (Rashi, ad loc. *Ta'anis*, 29b). This is yet another reason (*Biur haGra*, Shulchan Aruch, Orach Chayim, 583) why we eat apples on Rosh Hashanah; we are reminded of this auspicious blessing, and as the children of Yaakov, we too are the inheritors of this blessing.

Honey, writes Rabbeinu Yonah, is by nature powerful: whatever is placed in it becomes sweet like the honey itself (*Berachos*, 35. Rosh, *ad loc*. And honey can transform a non-Kosher object that falls therein to become Kosher: Rabbeinu Yonah. See Tur, *Orach Chayim*, 216, although see *Magen Avraham*, ad loc.). Therefore, by dipping an apple in honey, we are requesting that our entire life should have the sweet quality of honey, able to sweeten any judgment that we encounter in our lives.

As we dip the apple, we ask for a good and sweet year. 'Good' refers to openly revealed and obvious goodness, pure Chesed. 'Sweet' means that all types of Din, negativity and harsh judgment should be positively transformed, just as whatever is placed in honey becomes sweet like the honey itself.

'Good' is also an evaluation or judgment that we make; only we can declare what we see or experience as good. Taste, too, involves active participation; assessing a taste as sweet requires eating and the application of a subjective rubric. We actively ask for the year to be good and tasteful on all levels — and we in effect affirm and declare it to be so, by 'acting it out' and immediately eating the apple and honey.

Essay Three
THE TASHLICH SERVICE:
Blending Chesed with Din

O VER THE CENTURIES, A CUSTOM DEVELOPED TO WALK OUT TO A BODY OF WATER ON ROSH HASHANAH AND RECITE CERTAIN PASSAGES AND PRAYERS. This custom is called *Tashlich*. Perhaps the reason for the custom is (Maharil, Hilchos Rosh Hashanah, 9) to evoke the merit of Avraham, who, on the way to the *Akeidah* / binding of Yitzchak, walked through a body of water and was not deterred (*Yalkut Shimoni*, Vayera 99). Some offer a reason that since the day of Rosh Hashanah was the day that Yoseph was released from prison, thus it was also the night of the dreams of Pharaoh (*Rosh Hashanah*, 11a). His dream was of the Nile river, and so many centuries later, we now walk to a river on Rosh Hashanah.

"Now all the people gathered as one to the square that was before the 'water gate', and they said to Ezra the scholar to bring the scroll of the Law of Moshe… And Ezra the priest brought the Law before the congregation, both men and women, and all who could hear with understanding, on the first day of the seventh month" (*Nechemyah*, 8:1-2). In these verses we have an allusion of people gathering near a body of water on Rosh Hashanah, "the first day of the seventh month," in the beginning of the times of the Second Beis haMikdash.

ROSH HASHANAH, A TIME OF DIN / JUDGMENT

At a time of *Din* / Divine judgment, we must attempt to do all we can to bring into manifestation an element of *Chesed* / loving-kindness.

In a world of absolute Din, every cause has immediate effects and the result of our actions is seen right away. The world of Din is a relentless universe which most of us find intolerable; there is no room for human error in such a mode of existence, everything is absolute, clear and objective. So we must try, as much as we can, to sweeten the judgment and to mix into it aspects of Chesed.

Therefore, besides our Tefilos / prayers, which are meant to draw down blessings of goodness and kindness from Above, we also need to make sure that loving-kindness does not remain in the upper realms above, but permeates our reality below.

Our Tefilos, originating within us below, travel upwards, so to speak, and pierce one level after the next until they reach the Source Above. When prayers are effective, they arouse a new

Divine will; then the answer gradually travels downward until it reaches our world below.

Between the most finite of realities — a human being lodged in a time-space continuum, and the most infinite reality, the ultimate transcendence of the Creator — there exist realms within realms, entire structures within structures. Prayers 'move' through these structures, journeying upward and inward, while the responses to prayers travel downward and outward.

Every meaningful Tefilah is answered, although sometimes the answer remains elusive from our vantage point. At times, the effects of our prayers are felt not by us, but within realms of existence beyond this world. Our Tefilos may even have cosmic effects, and spiritually alter the creative roots of existence, but these effects may not be seen or felt in our daily lives.

Here is where Tashlich comes into play (*Orach Chayim*, 583:2, Rama). Tashlich involves going to a body of flowing, natural water that contains fish, reciting a prayer and, at its conclusion, taking hold of the *Tzitzis* / fringes of our four-cornered garment and shaking them. Ideally, this body of water should be located outside the city boundaries (*Magen Avraham*, 583:5), and there we would symbolically "cast away our sins." We call this practice 'Tashlich' based on the verse in The Book of Michah (7:19): "...And cast (*Tashlich*) into the depths of the sea all of their sins." What does this signify?

We walk to a 'living' body of water, a source of life, because 'life' is the idea of *Chesed* / giving. Fish also hint at Chesed — their eyes remain open at all times, and openness is a key element of giving. We then recite Scriptural verses (by merely 'reciting them', with focus and intention (Maharal, *Be'er haGolah*, Be'er 4) they draw down Divine mercy: Chida, *Chomses Onecha*, Tehilim, 50. *Bnei Yissaschar*, Elul, Ma'amar 2:4) that correspond to the Thirteen Divine Attributes of Compassion, to invoke the Ultimate Source of Kindness and arouse a Divine desire to shower us with blessings from Above (the Thirteen Attributes from the Torah draw down physical blessings, and the Thirteen Attributes from *Sefer Michah* draw down spiritual blessings: Alter Rebbe, *Siddur Im Dach*, Sha'ar Elul).

By doing something tangible and physical, we ensure that these blessings manifest in our day-to-day life here on earth below, so as not to remain inaccessible in the ethereal world Above.

WHY WATER?

Until water is introduced into a vessel, it does not have form; it is mere 'potential'. Water is also a symbol for Chesed. As Rosh Hashanah begins — the 'head' of the year that contains the entire year in potential — we go out to a body of water representing Chesed (*Siddur*, Alter Rebbe), and recite a Tefilah asking that the year should attain its potential for kindness and revealed blessings.*

---

* A body of living water represents Shefa, a Divine flow of life and blessings (*Moreh Nevuchim*, 2:12. See *Berachos*, 56b. As the Rogatchover writes "כתב הרמב"ם במורה דמקור השפעה נקרא גדר מים חיים": *Michtevei Torah*, 75). Pharaoh dreams of standing on the river, symbolic of the years of plenty and blessings.

WHY SHAKE THE TZITZIS?

At our core, we are all noble and transcendent beings, souls enclothed within bodies. Our souls are linked up with their Infinite Source, and this part of us — our authentic self — cannot be tarnished or affected by our negative actions, words, thoughts or feelings, for they are not really expressions of who we are in essence. These negativities are appendages to our real character — they are like clothes that we might wear, which can be shed with a mere conscious act of will.

And so we take the corners of our most prominent garment — the four-cornered fringed garment that is, according to Torah law, our true clothing — and we shake its fringes. Symbolically, we are shaking off our external negativities, ridding ourselves of anything that might bring harsh judgment, and 'throwing' it into the water to be cleansed in the flow of purity.

Essentially we are throwing our negativities in the water to be washed, rather than to discard them all together. Nothing in life is altogether negative; every action we do contains sparks of holiness, subtle aspects of our vital energy. Eventually, the purpose of our *Avodah* / spiritual work is to reclaim these energies, which previously hindered our growth, and to use them to return to our pure essence.

Yoseph was released from prison on Rosh Hashanah (*Rosh Hashanah,* 11a), thus it was also the night of the dreams of Pharaoh. Writes the Rogatchover, since omens are significant, certainly on Rosh Hashanah (*Kerisus,* 6a), we therefore go to a body of water on Rosh Hashanah: *Tzafnas Paneach,* Torah, Miketz. Besides the above reason, water represents humility (*Elef L'Magen,* l'Mateh Ephrayim, 598:5), and evokes an awareness of Hashem's Malchus within creation. Rama, *Toras HaOlah,* 3:56. See also, *Shaloh HaKadosh,* Rosh Hashanah, Ner Mitzvah, 23.

Essay 4
BLOWING, HEARING OR BOTH?
Sounds of the Shofar Recreated by the Listener*

CAPACITY TO RECEIVE

In the laws of physical harm and damages, if G-d forbid, someone injures another person, and breaks his leg for example, then he gives him the value of his leg as compensation for damage (and also, for example, compensation for loss of livelihood). But if he injures another person's ear, and the person becomes deaf, then the law is חירשו נותן לו דמי כולו / "If one deafened another, he gives him his entire value as compensation for damage" (*Baba Kamah*, 85b).

---

*Transcribed from a Shiur by Rav Pinson given at The IYYUN Kolel, in honor of the Shemiah learning, 25th of Elul, 2018

It seems that deafening a person is even more severe than even blinding him (although סומא חשיב כמת: *Nedarim*, 64b), and this suggests the truth that to be human and interact fully with others, we need to communicate, especially through speaking and hearing. Robbing a person of their potential to hear is robbing them of the fullness of their humanity.

For this reason, many of the Rishonim write that the sense of hearing is the most refined of all the senses, even more *Dak /* refined and *Nechbad /* honored than seeing. This is the opinion of the Ramban (*Emunah u-Bitachon*, 18), Rabbeinu Yonah (*Sha'arei Teshuvah*, Sha'ar 2:12), Rabbeinu Bachya (*Kad Kemach*, Z'nus haLev v'haAyin, 7. *Rabbeinu Bachya*, Shemos, 3:7), the Rikanti (*Bereishis*, 29:32), and Chassid, Rebbe Yoseph Yavetz (on *Avos*, 6:2).

The *Chush /* sense of *Shemi'a /* hearing, is the most refined and delicate of the senses. Indeed, in the words of the Maharal שהאדם נעשה כלי רק על ידי השמיעה... ואין האדם בעל הקבלה רק על ידי האוזן / "A human being becomes a 'vessel (to receive)' through hearing... and one becomes a vessel to receive only through the ears" (*Chidushei Agados*, Kidushin, 22a).

WHAT DOES IT MEAN TO 'HEAR'?

In general, *Shmi'a* can mean three things: *Shmi'as haOzen /* physical hearing of the ears, *Da'as /* intellectual understanding, and *l'Kabel /* to receive or accept something and bring it into your heart in order to understand it (*Teshuvos haRashba* 5, Siman 55. *Tzeida laDerech*, 1, 1:33. It can also mean 'calling out', or 'gathering': *Shmuel* I, 15:4, Rashi and Radak, *ad loc.*).

ולא שמעו אל־משה מקצר רוח / "They did not listen to Moshe because of shortness of breath" (*Shemos*, 6:9). Regarding this verse, Rashi asks what does it mean that they "did not listen"? It means לא קבלו תנחומין / "They did not accept the words of comfort (that Moshe was offering)." In other words, to listen, to hear, means to receive and accept (ושמיעה זו לשון קבלה: *Mizrachi*, ad loc.).

Another example is שמע בני מוסר אביך / "*Shema* / Hear, my child, the tradition of your ancestors" (*Mishlei*, 1:8). Here, too, 'hear' means to 'receive' (קבל מוסר מאביך: *Metzudas Dovid*). And as the Mittler Rebbe writes, the idea of listening means to accept, assimilate, and understand: *Havanah v'Hasagah* / understanding and comprehension (*Ner Mitzvah v'Torah Ohr*).

To listen is to be fully human, and to truly listen means to fully receive. In fact, physiologically the ears are instruments that are 'open to receive'. In the words of the Maharal (*Be'er haGolah*, 3), "You can open or close your eyes and your mouth, but your ears are always open. If the doctors or scientists will give you a natural, biological explanation, do not favor this interpretation, rather know that the sense of hearing is a capacity to receive, and the ear is open to receive at all times" (אמנם מה שלא היה כסוי לאוזן בעצמו, כמו שהוא לעינים ולפה. אם יאמרו לך הרופאים או בעלי טבע דברים טבעים לזה, אל תאבה להם ואל תשמע להם, כי רופאי אליל המה, לא ידעו בחכמת היצירה והבריאה כלום. אבל דבר זה הוא, מפני שהאוזן הוא משמש הקבלה בלבד, כמו שהתבאר למעלה. ושלימות הקבלה בעצמה שיהיה פתוח לקבל). The ear is meant to listen and be a *Kli l'Kabel* / vessel to receive, absorb, and to interpret information subjectively, at any time.

TO BLOW OR TO HEAR THE SHOFAR?

To better understand the nature and value of hearing, let's explore the Mitzvah of Shofar, a Mitzvah deeply connected to the world of hearing.

There is a great debate regarding the Mitzvah of Shofar: is the Mitzvah to blow or to hear the sound of the Shofar? And by extension, what is the proper *Nusach* / wording of the Beracha, the blessing we recite before we blow the Shofar?

Among the Geonim and early Rishonim the question was whether the *Ikar Mitzvah* / the main aspect of the Mitzvah is to 'blow' the Shofar (Rav Achai Gaon, *She'iltos Rav Achai Gaon*, 171. Rav Yehudai Gaon. *Semag*, Mitzvah 42. Rabbeinu Tam on *Rosh Hashanah*. Rosh, *Rosh Hashanah*, 4:10, as the *Korban Nesanel* explains. Yire'eim, Siman 117. *Shu't Yeshuas Yaakov*, Siman 585. This seems also the opinion of the *Zohar* as well: "This Mitzvah is to blow the Shofar": *Zohar* 3, 98b), or is the main part of the Mitzvah to 'hear' the Shofar, which is the opinion of Rav Hai Gaon, Rav Amram Gaon, Rav Saadia Gaon, Rashi (*Pardes*) and the Rambam (*Hilchos Shofar*, 1:1-3. *Ibid*, 2:1). The latter is the way the *Shulchan Aruch* rules (*Orach Chayim*, 585:2, as the ruling of the Tur, *ibid*, 585).

This debate also extends itself in terms of the liturgy of the *Berachah* / blessing before we blow the Shofar. If the main part of the Mitzvah is the blowing, then we should bless על תקיעת שופר / *Al Tekias Shofar* / "...to blow the Shofar" (*Ibid*, and the Rosh, *Rosh Hashanah*, 4:10, in the name of Rabbeinu Tam). If the main part of the Mitzvah is the hearing, the receiving of the sound, the blessing should be לשמוע קול שופר / *Lishmoa Kol Shofar* / to hear the sound of the Shofar (In *Shu't Pe'er haDor*, Siman 51, the Rambam writes, שהמצוה אינה בתקיעה אלא בשמיעה, ואין התקיעה אלא מעין הכשר מצוה וכעשיית הסוכה. See also, *Avnei Nezer*, Orach Chayim, 431). The latter is indeed the way we actually practice.

Even though you cannot hear the Shofar if you do not blow it, the main aspect of the Mitzvah is to hear the Shofar. In other words: we blow in order to hear. Similarly, the Mitzvah of Sukkah is to sit in the Sukkah, not to make a Sukkah; it is only that you can't sit in a Sukkah if you do not build it first. In this way, blowing the Shofar and making a Sukkah are each called a *Hechsher Mitzvah* / preparation for a Mitzvah.

By contrast, regarding the Mitzvah of Shofar on Yovel, the Rambam writes clearly that the Mitzvah is to blow the Shofar, whereas on Rosh Hashanah it is to hear the Shofar. On Rosh Hashanah, as the Rambam writes, the Ikar Mitzvah is to 'hear' the sound of the Shofar: "There is a positive Mitzvah לשמוע / 'to hear' the sound of the Shofar on Rosh Hashanah" (*Hilchos Shofar*, 1:1), whereas, in the Yovel year, "It is a positive commandment לתקוע / 'to sound' the Shofar on the Tenth of Tishrei in the Yovel year" (Rambam, *Hilchos Shemitah v'Yovel*, 10:10).

What we need to understand is why this distinction; why on Rosh Hashanah is the Mitzvah to hear, whereas on Yovel the Mitzvah is to blow?

In the simple reading of the Torah, where the Torah says,

"A Yom Teru'ah it shall be for you," it seems to suggest that the Ikar is the blowing of the Shofar. Similarly, whereas the verse in Tehilim, תקעו בחדש שופר בכסה ליום חגנו / "Blow Shofar on the new moon, on the full moon for our feast day" (*Tehilim*, 81:4), also seems to tell us that the Mitzvah is to blow, where do Rashi, Rambam and the others deduce that the Mitzvah is to hear the Shofar rather than to blow it?

THE MITZVAH INCLUDES BOTH;
the Debate is Regarding the Main Point

It must be understood that although the argument seeks to determine what is the main point of the Mitzvah, according to both opinions, certainly we need to blow *and* hear the Shofar (*Sha'agas Aryeh*, Siman 6. *Minchas Chinuch*, Mitzvah 405). Therefore, the Alter Rebbe rules, ולמה אין מברכין לתקוע בשופר לפי שהתקיעה אינה עיקר המצוה אלא שמיעת קול שופר הוא עיקר המצוה... ומכל מקום אם עבר או טעה לתקוע בשופר ובירך או על תקיעת שופר יצא / "Why do we not recite a blessing to 'blow the Shofar?' Because the blowing is not the *Ikar* / main aspect of the Mitzvah, rather, hearing the sound of the Shofar is the Ikar... Nevertheless, if one makes a mistake and recites the blessing as '...to blow the Shofar' or '...regarding the Mitzvah of blowing the Shofar', he has fulfilled his obligation" (*Shulchan Aruch*, Orach Chayim, 585:4).

Although the Mitzvah according to Rashi, the Rambam, the Tur and the Shulchan Aruch, is to hear the Shofar, still one cannot fulfill the Mitzvah by hearing the Shofar blown by a child, for example, who is exempt from the Mitzvah of Shofar

(Mishnah, *Rosh Hashanah*, 29a). This is because while the Mitzvah is to hear the Shofar, the sound that is being heard needs to be produced from a Shofar that is blown as a Mitzvah. In other words, although the Ikar is the hearing, still, the aspect of blowing is integral.

Similarly, although according to Semag and Rabbeinu Tam, who maintain that the Ikar Mitzvah is to 'blow' the Shofar, still, if a person blowing the Shofar does not himself hear the direct sound of the Shofar, but rather only the echo, he does not fulfill the obligation of 'blowing' the Shofar, even though he himself blew the Shofar. The Mishnah (*Rosh Hashanah*, 27b) says, התוקע לתוך הבור או לתוך הדות או לתוך הפיטס אם קול שופר שמע יצא ואם קול הברה שמע לא יצא / "If one sounds a Shofar into a pit, or into a cistern, or into a large jug, if he clearly heard the sound of the Shofar, he has fulfilled his obligation; but if he heard the sound of an echo, he has not fulfilled his obligation."* Regarding this Mishnah, Rav Huna explains, לא שנו אלא לאותן העומדים על שפת הבור אבל אותן העומדין בבור יצאו / "They taught this only with respect to those standing at the edge of the pit, i.e., on the outside, as they would hear only the echo coming from the pit. But those standing in the pit itself have fulfilled their obligation, since they initially hear the sound of the Shofar." The assumption is that those standing in the pit, certainly heard the sound of the Shofar and those standing outside the pit, certainly heard the sound of the echo (As Rashi writes, שהן קול השופר לעולם שמעו / "The sound of the Shofar they forever hear." Or in the language of the Alter Rebbe, אבל התוקע עצמו וכן אותם העומדים עמו בבור יצאו שבודאי קול שופר שמעו: *Orach Chayim*, 587:2. Although the Ritva writes, ‏(אבל העומדין בבור סתמן יצאו שלעולם שומעין קול שופר מן הסתם).

What happens if the blower in the pit is uncertain if he heard the actual sound of the Shofar or the echo, for example? If its a very large pit, then he does not fulfill his obligation (‏אם ברור להם ששמעו קול שופר יצאו ואם לאו לא יצאו: *Ibid.* See also Rambam, *Hilchos Shofar*, 1:8), as he would have mainly heard his own echo. In this case, if the Mitzvah were only 'to blow', the blower would have fulfilled his obligation, despite the fact that he did not hear the actual Kol Shofar, but only an echo. This is proof that we need both blowing and hearing. For the Mitzvah to occur it needs a blower and a listener, and while the debate is which is the most important, all agree that both are integral, as we will understand more deeply a little further on. In fact, any auditory communication occurs through the joint effort of the communicator and listener. [*]

שומע כעונה / HEARING IS LIKE RESPONDING

According to the opinion that the Ikar of the Mitzvah of Shofar is the blowing, how would one fulfill his obligation by simply listening to another person blowing the Shofar? However, as the Mitzvah is to hear the sound of the Shofar, by listening to someone else blow it one can perform the Mitzvah. If the Mitzvah was only to blow Shofar, how could one person blow it for others? The answer is the principle of שומע כעונה /

---

[*] He is blowing in a pit because it is a time of religious persecution: Ritva, *ibid*, 27b, ‏שעת שמד היה.

"hearing is like responding."* In this sense, hearing is like an act; it is as if you yourself actually blew the Shofar. Thus, anyone who 'hears' the Shofar fulfills the obligation to 'blow' it; "Listening is like blowing" (As the Mordechai writes, וכי היכי דהשומע כעונה ה"נ שומע כתוקע: Mordechai, *Rosh Hashanah* 4, Siman 721).

It is not just that the blower of the Shofar is the *Shaliach* / messenger of the listeners. One is not able to nominate a Shaliach to perform a Mitzvah that is obligated on "the body." For example, one cannot nominate a Shaliach to put on Tefillin for you. But with regards to hearing the Shofar there is a principle of שומע כעונה / "hearing is like responding," and thus, it is as if you, the listener, have physically blown the Shofar.

---

* The source of the principle of שומע כעונה is from Pesukim in Tanach, as the Gemara says "אתמר נמי אמר רבי שמעון בן פזי אמר רבי יהושע בן לוי משום בר קפרא מנין לשומע כעונה דכתיב / It was also stated that Rebbe Shimon ben Pazi said that Rebbei Yehoshua ben Levi said in the name of Bar Kapara: From where is it derived this principle of שומע כעונה? As it is written..." *Sukkah*, 38b. Yet, it seems to also be derived from common sense, in a larger gathering of people, one person may speak on behalf of all. As such the Gemara (Ibid) says, "בעו מיניה מרבי חייא בר אבא שמע ולא ענה מהו ענה אמר להו חכימיא וספריא ורישי עמא ודרשיא אמרו שמע ולא ענה יצא / the Sages raised a dilemma before Rebbe Chiya bar Abba: If one heard a passage recited and did not recite it himself, what is the law? (Did he fulfill his obligation or not?). He said to the sages, and the schoolteachers, and the heads of the nation, and the homiletic interpreters: One who heard a passage recited and did not recite it himself fulfilled his obligation." In other words, Rebbe Chiya is saying, every school teacher and public orator knows that שומע כעונה. Everyone who speaks in public knows that one person speaks and speaks on behalf of all. In this way, this Halachah is common sense, as every school teacher and public speaker will affirm.

There are two ways to understand the principle of שומע באוזן (*Chazon Ish*, Orach Chayim, Siman 29): either it means that the listener fulfills his obligation by merely listening, or it means that the mouth of the blower is like the mouth of the listener (שפיו כפיהם: *Shulchan Aruch*, Alter Rebbe, Orach Chayim, 213:6).

Specifically, what needs to be explored is 'why' there is such a principle with regards to blowing Shofar— and what is its relationship to issues of *Dibbur* / speech, as well. Why, for example, is there no Mitzvah performed if I nominate you to put Tefillin on your arm for my sake, as if your arm is like my arm? What is unique about speech or making a sound and listening to it, that creates this possibility of 'your mouth is like my mouth,' to the extent that the *Mekabel* / the receiver, the listener, can be considered the *Mashpia* / giver, and the hearer of the Shofar is like the blower?

שומע כעונה APPLIES ONLY TO 'SPEECH', NOT TO 'TYPES' OF SPEECH

The Avnei Nezer (*Orach Chayim*, 431:3) argues that the principle of "Hearing is like responding" only applies to *Dibbur* / speech, and *not* to the sound of Shofar, which is an unarticulated *Kol* / sound.

Another scenario can help deepen our understanding: on Purim, the prevailing custom is that the names of the ten sons of Haman are read by each individual who has been listening to the Megilah. Here, the listeners do not rely on the reader to fulfill their obligation (Although, see *Chayei Adam*, Kelal 151:21).

The Rogatchover suggests that the reason is as follows. If the Mitzvah of reciting the names of the ten sons of Haman in one breath (*Megilah*, 16b) was just a Mitzvah of 'speaking', one could fulfill his obligation using the principle of שומע כעונה. However, since there is a *particular way* the names need to be recited — namely, reciting them in one breath — the principle of שומע כעונה does not apply.

Similarly, the Beis haLevi (end of Bereishis) writes that Kohanim cannot nominate another Kohen as a Shaliach to recite the blessing of Kohanim for him. Since there is a particular way in which the blessing has to be recited, for example, it needs to be recited with a loud voice, as one person calling to another (*Sotah*, 38a), thus, the principle of שומע כעונה is not effective (Although, see *Chazon Ish*, Orach Chayim, Siman 29, 3, who argues with the Beis HaLevi. The Netziv has a slightly different understanding of the Beis HaLevi, indeed, שומע כעונה creates as if the words spoken are said loudly, yet, the words of the listener are not heard. *Emek Beracha*, Nesias KaPayim, Siman 5).

All the above examples are suggesting that if it is plain Dibbur then the principle of שומע כעונה applies, but when its a specific type of Dibbur, or a Kol, then this principle does not apply. Why? What is the difference?

MOUTH TO THE SHOFAR

The Gemara (*Rosh Hashanah*, 27a) teaches that ציפהו זהב במקום

הנחת פה פסול / "If the Shofar is plated with gold at the place where one puts his mouth, it is unfit." This is because of the laws of חציצה / barrier (as the Ritva, *ad loc.*, explains). In other words, since there is a foreign object separating the mouth from the Shofar, the blowing is invalid as he is blowing the gold not the Shofar. There is a major *Chidush* / novel teaching from the Ramban, which is actually the ruling of the *Shulchan Aruch*, based on this Gemara (Ramban, *Derashos l'Rosh Hashanah*), and that is that besides the issue of a חציצה / barrier, there also cannot be any הפסק / separation at all between the blower's mouth and the Shofar, whatsoever. For example, one may not place the Shofar an inch from his mouth and blow forcefully across the gap into the Shofar, even if there is no barrier or obstruction. Since there is a separation between the mouth and the Shofar, one does not fulfill the obligation of Shofar when it is blown in this fashion (*Magid Mishnah*, Rambam, *Hilchos Shofar*, 1:6. *Tur*, Orach Chayim, and *Shulchan Aruch*, 586:19. Although the Rambam rules that שופר הגזול שתקע בו יצא המצוה אלא בשמיעת הקול אף על פי שלא נגע בו ולא הגביהו השומע יצא / "Even without touching the Shofar whatsoever, one fulfills his obligation" (*Hilchos Shofar*, 1:3), so long as there is no obstruction, such as gold. Note that the Ritva, *Rosh Hashanah*, 27b, writes the same as the Ramban, but for the Ritva, it is a Din in חציצה).

In other words, the blower's lips must be pressed against the Shofar. An allusion to the idea that the lips need to be touching the Shofar is found is the verse, אל חכך שופר / "To your palate, a Shofar" (*Hoshea*, 8:1) — but still the question is *why* does the mouth need to touch the Shofar?

In the Gemara the ruling is, "If the Shofar is plated with gold at the place where one puts his mouth, it is unfit," and this is the source of the Ramban's Chidush, although by the case of gold there is a חציצה / barrier and in the case of blowing from a distance there is no חציצה / barrier, rather only a הפסק / separation. The Avnei Nezer (Teshuvah, in the beginning of Chelkas Yaakov) explains that the Ramban deduced his Chidush from the law of the Gemara about plating the mouthpiece with gold. There is another principle that says כל לנאותו אינו חוצץ / "Any addition whose purpose is to beautify does not create a חציצה / barrier" (Sukkah, 37a). As such, says the Avnei Nezer, in the ruling of the Gemara that putting gold on the mouthpiece renders the Shofar invalid, it cannot be because of the חציצה / barrier, since the gold is placed for the purpose of beautification and "Any addition for the purpose of beautification does not create a barrier." Why then is the Shofar unfit? It must be because of a הפסק / separation, as there is a separation between the mouth and the Shofar, and this is the ruling of the Ramban. As such, the law is clear that the mouth of the person must actually touch the Shofar when being blown.*

---

*The Kozoglover Gaon asks where is the source of this Chidush of the Ramban? And writes that it is from the language of the Torah. Since the Torah says תקעו /you shall blow, this means בגופו ולא בכוחו / with his body and not his power, thus, one must have the mouth touching the Shofar, as if it would be removed from the Shofar it would be his power, but not his body. Siach HaSadeh, Sha'ar Brachos 4, Siman 4. In a note, (14, ad loc) he adds that he has become aware of an interpretation of his Rebbe, the Avnei Nezer, (Siman 435, 7) and that his Chidush is consistent with the Chidush of his Rebbe, that it is because of חציצה.

According to the holy Arizal, as explored earlier in great depth, the sounds of the Shofar create a *Hamtakos HaDin* / "sweetening of judgment," as all of the symbolism of the Shofar demonstrates. Din, as also explained, is ultimately sweetened by and through its 'source' which is Binah. *Peh* / mouth in numerical value is 85. And Peh is connected to the Divine Name of Hashem, *SaG* / 63,* as adding the 22 letters of the Aleph Beis = 85 (*Pri Eitz Chayim*, Sha'ar haShofar, 1).

MOUTH SPECIFICALLY

To fully decipher and appreciate this association, and perhaps the inner reason why the Shofar needs to be connected to the mouth, we will continue to explore the mouth-Shofar relationship.

It is now clear that the Shofar is intricately connected with the mouth. It is not merely a coincidence that the only controlled orifice of the body that can produce breath is the mouth. It is not that we need to blow Shofar with our mouth, but if, theoretically, one could blow Shofar with his nose, that too would be permitted. Rather, we *must* blow with our mouths. The mouth, which is the place of speech and communication, is precisely the place from which the sound of the Shofar is meant to emit.

---

* The Shofar itself is also connected with the Name *SaG* / 63, the Name of Hashem (Yud-Hei-Vav-Hei) as spelled out to equal 63. This Name represents the world of Binah, the root of all Din. Yud/10, Vav/6, Dalet/4 = 20. Hei/5, Yud/10 = 15. Vav/6, Aleph/1, Vav/6, Hei/5, Yud/10 = 15. In total is *SaG* / 63.

In the laws of Chalitzah,* the Rambam explains how it is done and writes that the man puts on the shoe with high straps: והיא יושבת ופושטת ידה בפני בית דין ומתרת רצועות המנעל מעל רגלו וחולצת המנעל ומשלכת אותו לארץ / "And she sits down, stretches out her hand in front of the court, unties the straps of the shoe from his foot, takes off the shoe and throws it upon the ground" (Rambam, *Hilchos Yibum v'Chalitzah*, 4:6).

In other words, the widow needs to untie the straps of his shoes with her hands, and her hands are so essential that she first must stretch out her hand in front of the court to demonstrate that she is going to perform the action with her hands. And yet, in a case where she, G-d forbid, has no hands, חולצת לכתחלה ואפלו בשניה שלא נאמר וחלצה בידה / "She can untie his shoe even with her teeth, as the Pasuk never says, 'And she should untie with her hands'" (*Ibid*, 4:18). It seems this principle should be the same for the Mitzvah of Shofar; nowhere does the Torah explicitly state that one must blow the Shofar with his mouth. Yet, *Peh* / mouth is essential to the Shofar, so much so that his mouth cannot even be detached from the Shofar when blowing.

---

* If a man passes on and does not have any children, the brother of the man who died is permitted and even encouraged to marry the widow. This is called *Yibum*. However, if they do not wish to marry and go through with the marriage, they are required to perform Chalitzah (today this is the way the rule is followed). The process involves the widow making a declaration, removing the shoe of her brother-in-law, and spitting on the floor. Through Chalitzah, the brother, and any of his brothers as well, are released from the obligation of marrying the woman, and the widow is free to marry whomever she desires, except a Kohen.

Still, the question remains: why is this so?

A LEFTY IN THE BEIS HAMIKDASH AND TEFILLIN

איטר בין ביד בין ברגל פסול / "One whose left side is dominant, whether his left hand or his left foot, is disqualified from performing service in the Beis haMikdash" (*Bechoros*, 45b. *Menachos*, 6a). Says Rashi, איטר ביד פסול דכתי' וטבל אצבעו כל מקום שנא' אצבע וכהן אינו אלא ימין / a left-handed person is disqualified from serving in the Beis haMikdash since when the *Pasuk* / verse says with regards to a Kohen "his finger," this means of his right hand (*Bechoros*, ibid, from *Zevachim*, 22a). As such, the reason a lefty is disqualified from serving in the Beis haMikdash is that he 'does not really have' a right hand.*

---

* והא לית ליה ימין: Ramban, *Yevamos*, 104a. The Rambam writes it is because a lefty is a *Baal Mum* / one who has a 'blemish': *Hilchos Bi'as haMikdash*, 8:11. On Yom Kippur, however, the Avodah of Ketores was Kosher using the left hand (מאי שנא שמאל דאשכחן לה הכשירא ביום הכפורים: *Menachos*, 6b). This is because Yom Kippur is the highest level of Teshuvah and the transformation of sins into merit and 'the other side' into Kedushah. This is especially true of the Avodas haKetores, which included 11 (symbolizing the side of Kelipah) ingredients, and included the *Chelbanah*, the foul-odored galbanum spice. Thus, כל תענית שאין בה מפושעי ישראל אינה תענית שהרי חלבנה ריחה רע ומנאה הכתוב עם סממני קטרת / "Any fast that does not include the participation of some of the sinners of Israel is not a fast, as the smell of galbanum is foul and yet the verse lists it with the ingredients of the incense" *Kerisus*, 6b. The elevation of even פושעי ישראל /the sinners of Israel is thus a 'left hand' Avodah. Similarly, "טרף בקלפי, והעלה שני גורלות / The Cohen Gadol would mix the lots in the lottery receptacle used to hold them and draw the two lots from it, one in each hand" *Yuma*, 39a. If indeed, the drawing of the lottery is an Avodah (see *Ibid*, 39b), this too is an Avodah (like the Ketores) that is permitted with the left hand. (וכשרה עבודה זו בשמאל כמו הוצאת כף ומחתה בכ"ג דיה"כ. *Tosefos Yeshanim*, ad loc). Perhaps because this too is an Avodah of elevating the 'dark' side, the Azazel, as a Karbon Chatas. The

Now, if the reason a left-handed person is *Pasul* / disqualified from serving in the Beis haMikdash is that 'he has no right hand', then the obvious questions are: a) he does have a 'right hand', as his left hand is considered his right hand, and b) why is there a difference in principle between the Avodah in the Beis haMikdash and the Mitzvah of Tefillin? Chazal tell us that we need to put the Tefillin on our left arm because it is our weaker arm, but if he has no right arm, then he has no 'left' or 'weaker' arm either, yet he should put Tefillin on his only arm. Why is there no obstacle to such a person putting on Tefillin, while there is an obstacle to a left-handed person serving in the Beis haMikdash? (*Chazon Ish*, Bechoros, Siman 26. See also, *Avnei Nezer*, Yoreh De'ah, Siman 32).

The obvious answer is that Tefillin is not connected to the left arm per se, rather, we need to put Tefillin on our weaker arm, and there is no difference if the weaker arm is the left or the right arm. Whereas the Avodah needs to be performed specifically with the right hand, and as such, when one cannot serve with his right hand — only his left — he is disqualified from serving in the Beis haMikdash.

Pasuk says "ומאת עדת בני ישראל יקח שני־שעירי עזים לחטאת" (*Vayikra*, 16:5), simply, this means that even the goat that is sent to the Azazel is also a Chatas. The Brisker Rav questions if in fact the goat sent to the Azazel has a Din / law of a Karbon Chatas. *Chidushei HaGriz*, Zevachim, 113b. See also, *Meiri*, Yuma, 62b. Although, see, *Even Ezra, Ramban*, Vayikra, 16:5 המשתלח איננו קרבן.

This analogy seems more aligned with the issue of the mouth and the Shofar. It is not merely a coincidence that the mouth is the most powerful 'Shofar-blower' of the body, rather there is an intrinsic connection between the mouth, the place of speech and communication, and the Shofar.

SIGHT VS. HEARING

There are a few major distinctions between the sense of sight and hearing. For one, sight is connected to the tangible world, whereas hearing is connected to the inner world. The eye perceives physical things, whereas the ear perceives what is beyond the physical and immediate reality.

What's more, seeing proceeds from the *K'lal* / general to the *P'rat* / detail, whereas hearing is from details to the general. In seeing, we receive the entire image in one shot (See *Rosh Hashanah*, 18a). We thus first get a glimpse of the entire image and then gradually break it down or decipher it piece by piece, from the K'lal to the P'rat. In hearing, we receive information gradually through bits of data, first a letter, then a word, then a sentence until we get the full picture. Hearing is bringing together separate letters and words into a cohesive sentence. It operates by moving from the *P'ratim* / details to the K'lal bit by bit until a full sentence is 'received'.

To put it simply, when you see something, you first get a glance of the entire picture, and then you zoom in and notice all the details of the picture. Hearing functions in the opposite manner. You hear speech detail by detail, word by word, until you finally arrive at a sentence or a full idea.

There is another great distinction between hearing and seeing, and that is seeing is objective and hearing is subjective. When you see something there is still some 'separation' between you and what you see. There is a necessary level of detachment — or so it seems — between the observer and the observed. Hearing, on the other hand, is internal and intimate. In the language of the Chasidic teachers, hearing "enters *into* the ear."

When you see something, if you are able to strip your inner narrative and prism from what you are seeing, then the seeing is purely an 'outside' experience, you see something outside of you, and the thing seen remains detached and objective from the seer. Therefore, it is possible to see "without pleasure or deriving any benefit" (עין שלא רצתה לזון וליהנות מדבר שאינו שלו. *Zevachim*, 118b), whereas hearing is an inward process and a subjective experience by definition.

The subjective nature of hearing is connected with its process of building and moving from P'rat to K'lal, because as we are hearing we are actively participating in constructing bits of information into a cohesive idea. Hearing is thus a proactive activity. Truly hearing something demands participation, interpretation, and construction.

This is why in terms of listening to the Shofar there is a very deep level of שומע כעונה / "hearing is like responding," since an action *is* being taken by the listener, it is not a mere passive activity. A person cannot put on Tefillin for another, as my arm is my arm and your arm is your arm, but in listening there is the possibility that your mouth is my mouth and the *Mekabel* / receiver or listener, can be in effect the *Mashpia* / giver, the speaker or blower.

Listening is therefore a joint activity; there is a *Shituf* / partnership, a mutual dependency in the act of speaking or blowing and listening (ויוצא ידי חובה בשיתוף השמיעה והדיבור של חברו: *Chazon Ish*, Orach Chayim, 29).

THE OPINION OF THE AVNEI NEZER

Active listening and participation on the part of the listener is more clearly expressed and prevalent when it comes to actual speech than in relation to a simple *Kol* / sound, such as that of the Shofar.

This helps us better understand the opinion of the Avnei Nezer, who argues that the principle of "hearing is like responding" only applies with Dibbur, not with the Kol of Shofar. With Dibbur there is more of an interplay, a mutually dependent partnership between the speaker and the listener, whereas with Kol, it is more about the act of the Mashpia, the projector of the sound, who is not so much in dialogue with the receiver of the sound.

Kol is connected with the world of Unity and rooted in silence, whereas Dibbur is connected with the world of duality:

מן השמים השמיעך את קלו / "From Heaven you heard His *Kol*" (*Devarim*, 4:36). Kol is thus associated with Heaven and Dibbur is associated with earth, the physical, finite world (*Pirush haGra*, Shir haShirim, 2:6. *Ohr haTorah*, Devarim 4, p. 1934. *Besha'ah Shehikdimu* 5672, p. 497).

In the teachings of the Arizal, Kol has no distinct parts, and is by nature 'one'. It also corresponds to *Sheim Havayah* / the Name Hashem (Yud-Hei-Vav-Hei), the Infinite Transcendent Name of Hashem. Dibbur, which is composed of many distinctions and separations, vowels and consonants, syllables and modifications in tone, corresponds to *Sheim Elokim*, the Divine present in the world of plurality, the many. Sheim Havayah is the Mashpia, and Sheim Elokim is the M'kabel.

Kol is the world of the Mashpia alone, whereas Dibbur is connected to the Mekabel, the world of the receiver and interpreter of speech.

EVEN KOL IS A JOINT EFFORT

Putting aside the Avnei Nezer for a moment, even in the world of Kol we actually say שומע כעונה / "hearing is like responding," and as the Mordechai writes, וכי היכי דהשומע כעונה ה"נ שומע כתוקע / "Just like hearing is like responding, similarly, hearing (the *Kol* / sound of the Shofar) is like blowing." Even in the world of pure sound there is a strong presence of the Mekabel, and an interpretation, a transformation of the sound when it is heard.

Principally, we say תרי קלי לא משתמעי / "Two sounds cannot simultaneously be heard" (*Rosh Hashanah*, 27a). Yet, in the Beis ha-Mikdash "there were two trumpets, one on each of the sides of the person sounding the Shofar" (*ibid*, 26b). Asks the Gemara, 'Don't we say "Two sounds cannot simultaneously be heard?"' And the Gemara answers, 'If one hears two sounds produced by two (or three) different people, in a case where "it is dear to him" to hear this sound, then we say, כיון דחביב יהיב דעת / "Since the sounding of the Shofar is dear to the listener, he directs his attention to the matter and discerns between the two sounds."'

What does it help that the sound is dear to him or not, if "two sounds cannot simultaneously be heard?" The logic is seemingly that the sound of the Shofar and the sound of the trumpets intermingle with each other, and when the receiver receives the sound there is only one merged sound. But then how does it help if the sound of the Shofar is "dear to him"?

We therefore are compelled to assert, that although the two sounds mingle and become one sound in the ether, as a sound wave before it hits the ear of the listener, the listener has the capacity to unmingle, separate and discern the sounds, and pay exclusive attention to the sound of the Shofar, as that sound that is 'dear to him'. In this way, he can creatively produce, as it were, a new sound as he is listening. In other words, even with the 'preverbal' Kol Shofar, there can be a subjective 'reinterpretation', and the Mekabel becomes a Mashpia (This is perhaps related to what the Ritva writes — אבל גבי שופר והצוצרות דה״ל תרי קלא מתרי גברי ואין צריך לשמוע אלא אחד מהן דהיינו קול השופר שהוא מצות היום שפיר משתמעי

Ritva on *Rosh Ha-* :לכוין בקול השופר שהוא צריך ולשומעו מבין קולות החצוצרות
shanah, 27a).

This is the power of listening: a unity is created between the
outside and inside, the speaker and listener, the objective and
subjective. The power to absorb but also co-create in the process of listening is such that there is a re-creation of the sound
in the subjective experience of the listener, and the listener in
effect becomes the 'speaker' or a 'Shofar blower'.

THE WAY THE SOUND OF THE SHOFAR IS RECEIVED

This can help us better understand a) the prevailing opinion
that holds that the Mitzvah is to 'hear' the sound of the Shofar, and b) how and why the *Rishonim* / Early Commentators
actually offer reasons for the Shofar. The Torah simply says, "A
Yom Teru'ah it shall be to you," a day of sounding the Teru'ah,
and in the words of *Tehilim*, the passage says, תקעו בחדש שופר
/ "Blow (the Shofar) on the new moon" (*Tehilim*, 81:4). Similarly,
our sages use the phrase רחמנא אמר תקעו / "The Merciful One
says to sound it" (*Rosh Hashanah*, 16a). These all suggest that a) the
Mitzvah is the blowing and b) that it is a Mitzvah without any
revealed reason, certainly without a reason of awakening and
arousing within the listener a desire for Teshuvah and inner
transformation.

If in fact there would be a reason for the Mitzvah, then
would it not be connected with the blowing and not with the
hearing? If it is about the blowing, then perhaps the reason the
Rasag offers, the 'coronation of the King', is more resonant.

How can we understand the Rambam's reason, that the reason for Shofar is to wake us up?

The answer is that blowing, like speaking, entails two participants; it is a joint endeavour between the giver and receiver, and it cannot be performed without the existence of a listener, a recipient. Since blowing/speaking entails also listening, from the perspective of the listener the impression these sounds of the Shofar have upon him is that they arouse him to awaken — thus the Rambam's 'reason' for Shofar. Appropriately, according to the Rambam, the Mitzvah is to hear the sounds of the Shofar.

Indeed, the main objective from the vantage point of the one performing the Mitzvah, the 'Mekabel' of the Mitzvah (our perspective) is to awaken and arouse some form of movement and desire for change. When this is aroused, it demonstrates that the sounds of the Shofar have been truly 'heard' and internalized.

With this in mind we can better understand the Chidush of the Ramban that the Shofar must be touching the mouth when blown. The *Peh* / mouth is the place of expression and communication, the place where the 22 letters of the Aleph Beis (as explained earlier in a teaching of the Arizal) and all its derivative sounds, emanate from the speaker to the receiver. The mouth is the place that reveals the inside to the outside. It is the place of the interplay between the internal and the external, between the place of the speaker/blower and the recipient/receiver.

Our Peh is the place where the subjective is expressed and becomes objective, and then the ear is the place where that objective utterance is heard and it again becomes subjective.

As such, the Mitzvah of Shofar to blow *and* to hear — in fact blowing and hearing are considered part of a single gesture of communication — needs to be directly performed by the mouth, the seat of all communication.

MITZVAH OF ROSH HASHANAH IS A MITZVAH WITH THE MOUTH; OUR HUMANITY

Our *Peh* is not only the seat of communication, it is actually the point where our humanity is most manifest. When in Chapter 2 of Bereishis, where it speaks about man becoming fully human, as explored earlier, the Torah says ויפח באפיו נשמת חיים ויהי האדם לנפש חיה / "And He below into his nostrils a breath of life, and man became a living being" (*Bereishis*, 2:7). What does it mean that he became a living being? It means he became fully human and the power of speech and communication was gifted to him (*Unkelos*, ad loc.). The being becomes fully human with the introduction of his capacity for expression and communication, dialogue and conversation.

To be human is to express, to open our inner world to another and to truly listen to another, to truly receive another person's world and to hold space for their story.

Most appropriately, the Mitzvah of Rosh Hashanah, the day we celebrate the fullness of our humanity, is a Mitzvah that involves the mouth, as well as the ear. The Mitzvah of Shofar thus includes and combines both faculties of expression and reception.

TO KNOW THE TERU'AH

Yom Teru'ah suggests that we need to blow the Shofar, and blowing Shofar, like speech, creates a union between the blower and the listener. The Mitzvah of Shofar thus requires not only blowing it, but hearing it, processing it, and 'subjectively' understanding it as a call to Teshuvah

Truly hearing and internalizing the sounds of the Shofar, awakens us to return to a genuine *Panim-el-Panim* / face-to-face relationship with HaKadosh Baruch Hu. As such, on the day we celebrate being human — a speaking, understanding, and thus a choosing creation,[*] who can exist in a face-to-face relationship with the Creator of All Life — the main Mitzvos of the day are to *speak* words of Tefilah (especially, Malchiyos, Zichronos and Shofaros), and to blow the Shofar with *Da'as* — to be a יודעי תרועה / a 'knower of Teru'ah'. And אשרי העם יודעי תרועה / *Ashrei ha-Am Yodei Teru'ah* / "Fortunate is the one who

---

[*] On the Pasuk ויפח באפיו נשמת חיים ויהי האדם לנפש חיה / "...And He blew into his nostrils a breath of life, and he became a living being" (*Bereishis*, 2:7), Rashi writes, אף בהמה וחיה נקראו נפש חיה, אך זו של אדם חיה שבכולן שנתוסף בו דעה ודבור / "Also cattle and beasts are called נפש חיה / 'living being', but the נפש / soul of man is the most highly developed of all of them, because to him was granted *understanding and speech*. Our humanity is defined by our דעה ודבור / *Da'as* / understanding and *Dibbur* / speech. As such, on the day we celebrate our humanity we speak and blow Shofar, and do so with Da'as.

knows Teru'ah" (*Tehilim* 89:15). Indeed, fortunate is the one who knows even a modicum of the endless mysteries and holy secrets of the Shofar.

Other Books by Rav Pinson

RECLAIMING THE SELF
The Way of Teshuvah

Teshuvah is one of the great gifts of life. It speaks of a hope for a better today and empowers us to choose a brighter tomorrow. But what exactly is Teshuvah? How does it work? How can we undo our past and how do we deal with guilt? And what is healthy regret without eroding our self-esteem? In this fascinating and empowering book, the path for genuine transformation and a way to include all of our past in the powerful moment of the now, is explored and demonstrated.

THE MYSTERY OF KADDISH
Understanding the Mourner's Kaddish

The Mystery of Kaddish is an in-depth exploration into the Mourner's Prayer. Throughout Jewish history, there have been many rites and rituals associated with loss and mourning, yet none have prevailed quite like the Mourner's Kaddish Prayer, which has become the definitive ritual of mourning. The book explores the source of this prayer and deconstructs the meaning to better understand the grieving process and how the Kaddish prayer supports and uplifts the bereaved through their own personal journey to healing.

UPSHERNISH: The First Haircut
Exploring the Laws, Customs & Meanings
of a Boy's First Haircut

What is the meaning of Upsherin, the traditional celebration of a boy's first haircut at the age of three? Why is a boy's hair allowed to grow freely for his first three years? What is the deeper import of hair in all its lengths and varieties? What is the meaning of hair coverings? Includes a guide to conducting an Upsherin ceremony.

———

A BOND FOR ETERNITY
Understanding the Bris Milah

What is the Bris Milah – the covenant of circumcision? What does it represent, symbolize and signify? This book provides an in depth and sensitive review of this fundamental Mitzvah. In this little masterpiece of wisdom – profound yet accessible —the deeper meaning of this essential rite of passage and its eternal link to the Jewish people, is revealed and explored.

———

REINCARNATION AND JUDAISM
The Journey of the Soul

A fascinating analysis of the concept of Gilgul / Reincarnation. Dipping into the fountain of ancient wisdom and modern understanding, this book addresses and answers such basic questions as: What is reincarnation? Why does it occur? And how does it affect us personally?

———

INNER RHYTHMS
The Kabbalah of MUSIC

Exploring the inner dimension of sound and music, and particularly, how music permeates all aspects of life. The topics range from Deveikus/

Unity and Yichudim/Unifications, to the more personal issues, such as Simcha/Happiness and Marirus/ sadness.

MEDITATION AND JUDAISM
Exploring the Jewish Meditative Paths

A comprehensive work encompassing the entire spectrum of Jewish thought, from the sages of the Talmud and the early Kabbalists to the modern philosophers and Chassidic masters. This book is both a scholarly, in-depth study of meditative practices, and a practical, easy to follow guide for any person interested in meditating the Jewish way.

TOWARD THE INFINITE

A book focusing exclusively on the Chassidic approach to meditation known as Hisbonenus. Encompassing the entire meditative experience, it takes the reader on a comprehensive and engaging journey through this unique practice. The book explores the various states of consciousness that a person encounters in the course of the meditation, beginning at a level of extreme self-awareness and concluding with a state of total non-awareness.

THIRTY – TWO GATES OF WISDOM
into the Heart of Kabbalah & Chassidus

What is Kabbalah? And what are the differences between the theoretical, meditative, magical and personal Kabbalistic teachings? What are the four paths of interpreting the teachings of the ARIzal? What did Chassidus teach? These are some of the fundamental issues expanded upon in this text. And then, more specifically, why are there so many names of G-d and what do they represent? What are the key concepts of these deeper teachings?

The book explores the grand narrative of the great chain of reality, how there was and is a movement from the Infinite Oneness of Hashem to a world of (apparent) duality and multiplicity.

THE PURIM READER

The Holiday of Purim Explored

With a Persian name, a masquerade dress code and a woman as the heroine, Purim is certainly unusual amongst the Jewish holidays. Most people are very familiar with the costumes, Megilah and revelry, but are mystified by their significance. This book offers a glimpse into the hidden world of Purim, uncovering these mysteries and offering a deeper understanding of this unique holiday.

EIGHT LIGHTS

8 Meditations for Chanukah

What is the meaning and message of Chanukah? What is the spiritual significance of the Lights of the Menorah? What are the Lights telling us? What is the deeper dimension of the Dreidel? Rav Pinson, with his trademark deep learning and spiritual sensitivity guides us through eight meditations relating to the Lights of the Menorah, the eight days of Chanukah, and a fascinating exploration of the symbolism and structure of the Dreidel. Includes a detailed how-to guide for lighting the Chanukah Menorah.

THE IYYUN HAGADAH
An Introduction to the Haggadah

In this beautifully written introduction to Passover and the Haggadah, we are guided through the major themes of Passover and the Seder night. This slim text, addresses the important questions, such as: What is the big deal of Chametz? What are we trying to achieve through conducting a Seder? What's with all that stuff on the Seder Plate? And most important-ly, how is this all related to freedom?

PASSPORT TO KABBALAH
A Journey of Inner Transformation

Life is a journey full of ups and downs, inside-outs, and unexpected de-tours. There are times when we think we know exactly where we want to be headed, and other times when we are so lost we don't even know where we are. This slim book provides readers with a passport of sorts to help them through any obstacles along their path of self-refinement, reflection, and self-transformation.

THE FOUR SPECIES
The Symbolism of the Lulav & Esrog

The Four Species have inspired countless commentaries and traditions and intrigued scholars and mystics alike. In this little masterpiece of wis-dom both profound and practical - the deep symbolic roots and nature of the Four Species are explored. The Na'anuim, or ritual of the Lulav move-ment, is meticulously detailed and Kavanos,, are offered for use with the practice. Includes an illustrated guide to the Lulav Movements.

THE BOOK OF LIFE AFTER LIFE

What is a soul? What happens to us after we physically die?

What is consciousness, and can it survive without a physical brain?

Can we remember our past lives?

Do near-death experiences prove immortality?

What is Gan Eden? Resurrection?

Exploring the possibility of surviving death, the near-death experience and a glimpse into what awaits us after this life.

(This book is an updated and expanded version of the book; Jewish Wisdom of the Afterlife)

THE GARDEN OF PARADOX:

The Essence of Non - Dual Kabbalah

This book is a Primer on the Essential Philosophy of Kabbalah presented as a series of 3 conversations, revealing the mysteries of Creator, Creation and Consciousness. With three representational students, embodying respectively, the philosopher, the activist and the mystic, the book, tackles the larger questions of life. Who is G-d? Who am I? Why do I exist? What is my purpose in this life? Written in clear and concise prose, the text, gently guides the reader towards making sense of life's paradoxes and living meaningfully.

BREATHING & QUIETING THE MIND

Achieving a sense of self-mastery and inner freedom demands that we gain a measure of hegemony over our thoughts. We learn to choose out thoughts so that we are not at the mercy of whatever belches up to the mind. Through quieting the mind and conscious breathing we can slow the onrush of anxious, scattered thinking and come to a deeper awareness of the interconnectedness of all of life.

Source texts are included in translation, with how-to-guides for the various practices.

VISUALIZATION AND IMAGERY:
Harnessing the Power of our Mind's Eye

We assume that what we see with our eyes is absolute. Yet, beyond our ability to choose what we see, we have the ability to choose how we see. This directly translates into how we experience life. In a world saturated with visual imagery, our senses are continuously assaulted with Kelipa/empty/fantasy imagery that we would not necessarily choose. These images can negatively affect our relationship with ourselves, with the world around us, and with the Divine. This volume seeks to show us how we can alter that which we observe through harnessing the power of our mind's eye, the inner sanctum of our imagination. We thus create a new way to see and experience the world. This book teaches us how to utilize visualization and imagery as a way to develop our spiritual sensitivity and higher intuition, and ultimately achieve Deveikus/Unity with Hashem.

SOUND AND VIBRATION:
Tuning into the Echoes of Creation

Through our perception of sound and vibration we internalize the world around us. What we hear, and how we process that hearing, has a profound impact on how we experience life. What we hear can empower us or harm us. A defining human capacity is to harness the power sound -- through speech, dialogue, and song, and through listening to others. Hearing is primary dimension of our existence. In fact, as a fetus our ears were the first fully operating sensory organs to develop.

This book will guide you in methods of utilizing the power of sound and vibration to heal and maintain mental, emotional and spiritual health, to fine-tune your Midos and even to guide you into deeper levels of Deveikus / conscious unity with Hashem. The vibratory patterns of the Aleph-Beis are particularly useful portals into our deeper conscious selves. Through chanting and deep listening, we can use the letters and sounds to shift our very mindset, to induce us into a state of presence and spiritual elevation.

THE POWER OF CHOICE:
A Practical Guide to Conscious Living

It is the essential premise of this book that we hold the key to unlock many of the gates that seem closed to us and keep us from living our fullest life. That key we all hold is the power to choose. The Power of Choice is the primary tool that we have at our disposal to impact the world and effect change within our own lives. We often give up this power to outside forces such as the market, media, politicians or peer pressure; or to internal forces that often function beyond our conscious control such as ego, anger, lust, greed or jealousy. Making conscious, compassionate and creative decisions is the cornerstone of living a mature and meaningful life.

MYSTIC TALES FROM THE EMEK HAMELECH

Mystic Tales of the Emek HaMelech, is a wondrous and inspiring collection of stories culled from the Emek HaMelech. Emek HaMelech, from which these stories have been taken, (as well as its author) is a bit of a mystery. But like all good mysteries, it is one worth investigating. In this spirit the present volume is being offered to the general public in the merit and memory of its saintly author, as well as in the hopes of introducing a vital voice of deeper Torah teaching and tradition to a contemporary English speaking audience

---

INNER WORLDS OF JEWISH PRAYER
A Guide to Develop and Deepen the Prayer Experience

While much attention has been paid to the poetry, history, theology and contextual meaning of the prayers, the intention of this work is to provide a guide to finding meaning and effecting transformation through the prayer experience itself.

Explore: *What happens when we pray? *How do we enter the mindstate of prayer? *Learning to incorporate the body into the prayers. *Discover techniques to enhance and deepen prayer and make it a transformative experience.

This empowering and inspiring text, demonstrates how through proper mindset, preparation and dedication, the experience of prayer can be deeply transformative and ultimately, life-altering.

WRAPPED IN MAJESTY
Tefillin - Exploring the Mystery

Tefillin, the black boxes and leather straps that are worn during prayer, are curiously powerful and mysterious. Within the inky black boxes lie untold secrets. In this profound, passionate and thought-provoking text, the multi-dimensional perspectives of Tefillin are explored and revealed. Magically weaving together all levels of Torah including the Peshat (literal observation), to Remez (allegorical), to Derush, (homiletic), to Sod (hidden) into one beautiful tapestry. Inspirational and instructive, Wrapped in Majesty: Tefillin, will make putting on the Tefillin more meaningful and inspiring.

SECRETS OF THE MIKVAH:
Waters of Transformation

A Mikvah is a pool of water used for the purpose of ritual immersion; a place where one moves from a state of Tumah; impurity, blockage and death— to a place of Teharah; purity, fluidity and life.

In SECRETS OF THE MIKVAH, Rav Pinson delves into the transformative powers of the Mikvah with his trademark all-encompassing perspective that ranges from the literal, Pshat observation and Halachic implications of the texts, to the allegorical, the philosophical, and finally, to the deep secrets of the Mikvah as revealed by Kabbalah and Chassidus.

This insightful and inspirational text demonstrates how immersion in a Mikvah can be a transformative and life-altering practice, and includes various Kavanos—deep intentions—for all people, through various stages of life, that empower and enrich the immersion experience.

THE MYSTERY OF SHABBOS
Shabbat Rediscovered

Delving into the transformative power of Shabbos. With an all-encompassing perspective that ranges from the literal, Pshat observation and Halachic implications of the texts, to the allegorical, the philosophical, and finally, to the deeper secrets as revealed by Kabbalah and Chassidus, creating an elegant tapestry of thought and experience. THE MYSTERY OF SHABBOS is a profound meditation on the meaning of Shabbos and demonstrates the physical, emotional, mental and spiritual possibilities available and given to us with the gift of Shabbos. Studying and contemplating this inspired text on the depths of Shabbos will unveil a redemptive light in your experience of the Seventh Day -- and by extension, every day of your life.

THE SPIRAL OF TIME:
A 12 Part Series on the Months of the Year

VOL 1: THE SPIRAL OF TIME:
Unraveling the Yearly Cycle

Many centuries ago, the Sages of Israel were the foremost authority in the fields of both astronomical calculation and astrological wisdom, including the deeper interpretations of the cycles and seasons. Over time, this wisdom became hidden within the esoteric teachings of the Torah, and as a result was known only to students and scholars of the deepest depths of the tradition. More recently, the great teachers, from R.Yitzchak Luria (the Arizal) to the Baal Shem Tov, taught that as the world approaches the Era of Redemption, it is a Mitzvah / spiritual obligation to broadly reveal this wisdom.

"The Spiral of Time" is volume 1 is a series of 12 books, and serves as an introductory book to the basic concepts and nature of the Hebrew calendar and explores the special day of Rosh Chodesh.

VOL 2: THE MONTH OF NISAN:
Miraculous Awakenings from Above

The month of NISAN is the first month of the lunar cycle of the year, a month that brings in the spring and a month of redemption. Spring represents a time of plenty, abundance, sunshine, hope, and possibility. Redemption, on whatever level, feels palpable and accessible. In spring, the world is redeemed from the cold winter, the flower is redeemed from the tree, the grass from the earth, and we too feel that redemption is possible. A whole complex of ideas, including newness, redemption, going out of Egypt, and being freed from slavery, is intricately bound with the idea of Aviv / spring and the powerful month of Nisan.

VOL 3: THE MONTH OF IYYAR:
EVOLVING THE SELF
& The Holiday of LAG B'OMER

The month of IYYAR is the second month of the spring, a month that connects the Redemption from Egypt in Nissan with the Revelation of Torah in Sivan. The Chai/ Eighteenth day of the Month is the day we celebrate the Rashbi (Rabbi Shimon Bar Yochai) and the revealing of the hidden aspects of the Torah. This is the 'Holiday' of Lag b'Omer. The book explores the unique quality of this special month, a month that has a Mitz-vah of counting the Omer every day. In addition, the book explores the roots and significance of the mystical 'holiday' of Lag b'Omer. Including the customs & Practices of Lag b'Omer, such as, bonfires, bows & arrows, parades, Upsherin, and more.

VOL 4: THE MONTH OF SIVAN:
The Art of Receiving: Shavuos and Matan Torah

Sivan is the third month of the lunar cycle. One is a singularity. Two is division. Three is harmony, a unity that synthesizes individuality and multiplicity, Heaven and Earth, Spirituality and Physicality. During this month we celebrate Shavuos and the giving of the Torah, the ultimate expression of the unity of the Above and Below and we aspire to connect with the Keser/Crown of Torah that Transcends and yet includes all Worlds. Learning how to truly receive Higher wisdom in our Lower faculties is the mental, emotional, and spiritual exercise of the month.

VOL 5: THE MONTHS OF TAMUZ AND AV:
Embracing Brokenness –
17th of Tamuz, Tisha B'Av, & Tu B'Av

Each month and season of the year, radiates with distinct Divine qualities and unique opportunities for growth and Tikkun.

The summer month of Tamuz and Av contain the longest and hottest days of the year. The raised temperature is indicative of a corresponding spiritual heat, a time of harsher judgement and potential destruction, such as the destructions of the first and second Beis HaMikdash, which began on the 17th of Tamuz and culminated on the 9th and 10th of Av.

A few days later, on Tu b'Av, the darkness is transformed and reveals the greatest light and possibility for new life. During these summer months of Tamuz and Av we embrace our brokenness so that we can heal and transform darkness into light.

VOL 6: THE MONTH OF ELUL:
Days of Introspection and Transformation

Each month of the year radiates with a distinct quality and provides unique opportunities for growth and personal transformation. Elul, as the final month of the spring/summer season is connected to endings. Elul gives us the strength to be able to finish strong, to end well. Elul also serves as a month of preparation for the New Year/Rosh Hashanah.

We inhale our past year, ending with wisdom and then we also gain the wisdom to begin anew and exhale a positive year into being. The mental, emotional, and spiritual objective of this month is introspection and the reclaiming of our inner purity and wholeness.

VOL 7: THE MONTH OF TISHREI:
A Time of Rebirth & Upward Movement

Each month of the year radiates with distinct Divine qualities and unique opportunities for growth and spiritual illumination. As Tishrei begins the new yearly cycle, it is an appropriate month to introspect, reflect and resolve to move forward and preserve moving forward into the more inward months of the winter. This month creates the space to unburden ourselves from our negativities, and enter a more sacred, grounded sacred space. In Tishrei we are given the gift of forgiveness and then the ability to truly regain our space and inner joy.

VOL 8: THE MONTH OF CHESHVAN:

Navigating Transitions, Elevating the Fall

Directly on the heels of the inspiring and holiday-filled month of Tishrei, Cheshvan is a month that is quiet and devoid of holidays. In the month of Cheshvan we use the stored up energies of the previous months to self-generate our inspiration and creativity and provide ourselves with the strength to rise up after a fall. In Cheshvan we are entering into a stormier, wetter and colder season. It is a month of transition. The mental, emotional and spiritual objective of this month is to weather the transitions, learn to self-generate and stand tall. And if we do fall, we use the quality of this month to get back up and do so with more conviction, strength, wisdom and clarity.

VOL 9: THE MONTH OF KISLEV:

Rekindling Hope, Dreams and Trust

Kislev is the final month of the fall. Throughout this month, daylight progressively shortens, and the temperatures drop. Towards the end of the month, at the darkest hour, the winter solstice arrives and we begin the celebration of Chanukah. We commemorate the miracle of a small jug of oil that burned for eight nights, and as we celebrate, daylight expands. In the month of Kislev-despite the darkness, or perhaps because of it-we have the ability to tap into the Ohr HaGanuz, the hidden light of hope that rekindles our dreams and aspirations.

VOL 10: THE MONTH OF TEVES:
Refining Relationships, Elevating the Body

The quality of Teves is generally harsh—much like its counterpart Tamuz in the summer, thus the tendency for many is to hunker down, retract, curl up and wait for the month to pass by, only to reemerge when the harshness has dissipated. Think for a moment about the 'easier' months of the year, which, like gentle waves in the ocean, carry us where we want to go. We can ride these energies easily and they can propel us forward effortlessly, we just need to go with the overall flow, so to speak. The harsher months, on the other hand, can be compared to the more powerful waves that emanate from the belly of the ocean, which come forcefully crashing down and can easily drown a person before they even realize what has happened. However, those who want to utilize the momentum of the powerful energy that is available during such times can, with caution and creativity, harness these intense waves and ride them higher and farther than other, more gentle circumstances may allow. However, harnessing the power of Tohu, the raw energy of the body, does in fact need to be approached with great care and attention.

VOL 11: THE MONTH OF SHEVAT: ELEVATING EATING
& The Holiday of Tu b'Shevat

Each month of the year radiates with a distinct Divine energy and thus unique opportunities for growth, *Tikkun* and illumination. According to the deeper teachings of the Torah, all of these distinct qualities, opportunities and natural phenomena correspond to a certain data set. That is, the nature of each month is elucidated by a specific letter of the Aleph Beis, a tribe, verse, human sense, and so forth. The month of Shevat is particularly connected to food and our relationship to bodily intake. During this month we celebrate Tu b'Shevat, the New Year of the Tree, and aspire to create a proper and physically/emotionally/spiritually healthy relationship with food.

VOL 12: THE MONTH OF ADAR:
Transformation Through Laughter & Holy Doubt

Each month of the year radiates with distinct Divine qualities and unique opportunities for growth and spiritual illumination. As Adar concludes the monthly cycle of the year, as well as the solar phenomena of the winter, it is an appropriate month to think about our essential identity, before moving out to meet the world come spring. This month we strive to create a healthy relationship with holy humor, unbounded joy, and a general sense of lightness of being. Through the work of Adar we transform negative, crippling doubt and uncertainties into radical wonderment and openness.

ILLUMINATED SOUND:
The Baal Shem Tov on Prayer

In the year 1698 a great light was revealed to the world with the descent of the holy soul of the Baal Shem Tov. In time, the Baal Shem Tov became one of the most important and influential teachers of Torah in all of history, and the founder of Chassidus.

Amongst the vast repository of profound and revolutionary teachings of the holy Baal Shem Tov, the teachings on the path of Tefilah / Prayer are the most elaborate. The teachings of the Baal Shem Tov on Tefilah include some of his most innovative expressions, or Chidushim. Tefilah is the essential and central tenet from which all other teachings flow.

In this masterful and practical text, Rav Pinson revives the awe-inspiring and transformational teachings of the Baal Shem Tov, and illuminates his unique path to Tefilah.

www.ingramcontent.com/pod-product-compliance
Lightning Source LLC
Chambersburg PA
CBHW060411100426
42812CB00038B/3493/J